"Oh, Get o  "

C000193165

An inspir ... g
tramps around Great Britain

Colin Snook

r

To my family,
Jenny and Bill

[handwritten inscription: To Mick Best Wishes Colin Snook 1.12.12]

Cover design © Geo Parkin.
Back cover photograph: Mike Parry.
Title page photograph: Relaxing at Llanbadrig Winery, Anglesey.

Published by Pomegranate Press,
Dolphin House, 51 St Nicholas Lane, Lewes, Sussex BN7 2JZ
pomegranatepress@aol.com
www.pomegranate-press.co.uk

ISBN: 978–1–907242–35–9

British Library Cataloguing-in-Publication Data.
A catalogue record for this book is available from the British Library

Printed and bound by 4Edge, 7a Eldon Way, Hockley, Essex SS5 4AD

Contents

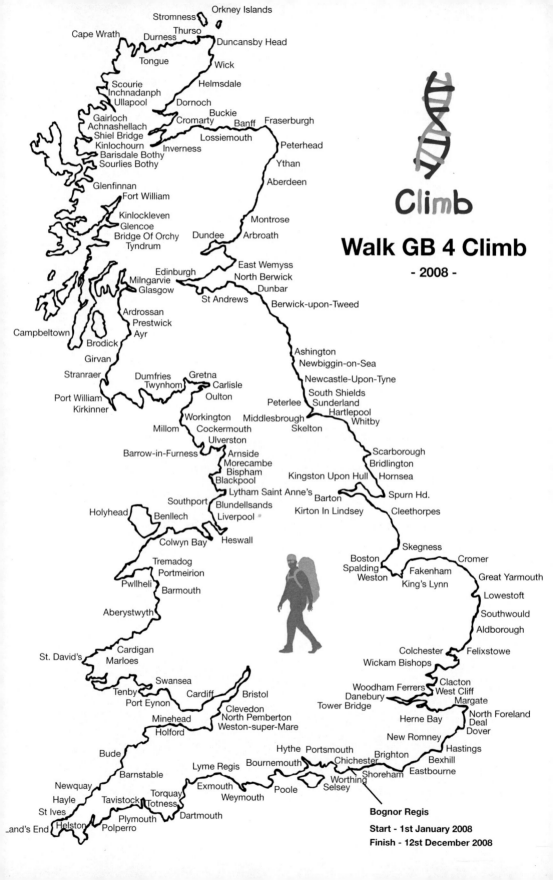

Foreword

by Jonathan Pearce, BBC football commentator

12th December 2008 was a cold December afternoon. There was a raw-boned wind at Bognor Regis on the south coast as I went to meet the remarkable 72-year-old Colin Snook. It was the end of his gruelling 347-day 4,000-mile trek around Great Britain raising funds for CLIMB, a charity which supports families suffering from metabolic disorders. Some of those affected families had been involved in the epic slog too, giving Colin a bed for the night during his adventure. It was heart-stirring for everybody concerned.

CLIMB had told me that Colin was a big football fan. In over thirty years commentating on football I have always enjoyed chatting to fans about the 'beautiful game', but this was to be a special meeting. My family has suffered dreadfully through a metabolic disorder. I lost my eight-month-old niece Lily to a mitochondrial disease in April 2008, at the same time as Colin was undertaking his walk. I understand personally the sense of confusion, hurt, loss and utter devastation it causes. Like so many suffering families, we felt completely alone. Suddenly we realised just how little is known about the condition and what scant funding is available for research into effective treatments and a cure – so we set up a family charity, The Lily Foundation, in Lily's memory to fund research and support families who suffer from mitochondrial diseases and other metabolic disorders.

Raising awareness of these diseases is crucial to finding a cure. Colin spent a year of his life walking to raise the profile of an unknown group of metabolic disorders, and he raised £30,000 doing so. He is a rare and incredibly brave man.

It was an honour to meet you, Colin, and I look forward to reading about your journey is this book.

Jonathan Pearce
BBC football commentator, and
chairman of The Lily Foundation
www.thelilyfoundation.org.uk

WALK

GB 4

CLIMB

2008

Preface

There are many ways to define why one is suddenly faced with a life-changing experience. It can be destiny, fate, providence or even luck, call it what you will. I am convinced it was two chance encounters that produced the true events behind this book.

The first came about in 1995 when I was solo walking in the remote Knoydart peninsula of Scotland, regarded as the last wilderness on mainland Britain. Early one morning in summer I chanced upon a couple just arising from their tent close by Lock Nevis who informed me they were engaged on a walk around Great Britain. They had abandoned their professional careers for a year to walk the periphery of the land in order to raise money for the provision of a hospice at Tunbridge Wells. (The incident is outlined later in the Knoydart chapter.) Suffice to say it lit the fuse of an idea that I, too, could take up the same challenge and fulfil a long held aspiration. As with so many of my ideas I shelved it. Perhaps deep down I was relying on fate to show its hand – and it did!

The second occurred several years later. Once again by chance, I visited the bedside of a teenager under care in a respite centre. Suffering from an inherited neurodegenerative metabolic disorder since infancy, the young person was now in the latter stages of life.

Later at home the same day I became struck down with sorrow and sobbed uncontrollably. I couldn't come to terms with the randomness and unfairness of it all.

Looking back, it's true to say that this second encounter had a profound effect on me. I am not a religious person and shun piety, but I have no qualms describing this experience as my 'light on the road to Damascus'.

These encounters occurred seven hundred miles and many years apart, but time and distance have little bearing on such dramatic experiences. Like a chemical reaction, the compounding of the idea's aims was immediate. Walking ambition and supporting a noble cause came together and I had to start planning my journey of a lifetime. The die was cast: I just had to go!

My resolve was announced with certain caveats. I would be walking around Great Britain but not necessarily around the entire coastline, as my journey had to be completed within a year. To avoid a Scottish winter I would begin my journey on the south coast in January.

This was to be a sponsorship effort in association with the charity CLIMB – that is, Children Living with Inherited Metabolic Diseases, based at Crewe – and it was given the project title 'WALK GB 4 CLIMB.'

I have to admit that the project was put together in a bit of a hurry. The eighteen months I allowed may have seemed ample, but in hindsight another year in preparation would have been better.

The main reason for a very early start to any campaign is to secure sponsorship, essentially from a corporate body. In the end the commercial support I obtained fell far short of what I had hoped. Once again, in hindsight I should have put a lot more thought and energy into this. After all, although I was confident of my fitness to complete the task, I was going to be turning seventy-two years of age halfway round the 'course'. An earlier start in life would have been preferable, but fate and circumstances are fickle partners!

The title of this book has been chosen for several reasons. This outburst is one of life's verbal relief mechanisms. Bearing in mind my initial delay in making a start I needed a rallying call, and I was mighty glad to come under its influence as follows:

• I often found myself using the phrase as jump leads, to kick-start my enthusiasm for the project,

• When questioned on how they coped, many parents of children stricken with metabolic diseases would often use the phrase to brush aside any well intended but patronising praise.

• Nobody put a greater emphasis to this phrase than my favourite BBC radio comedian Kenneth Williams. Often when trapped in a moment of frustration with the studio cast or the script, he would interject loudly 'Oh Get On with It!'

New Year's Day 2008 arrived, and I did just that!

"Oh, Get On with It!"

At six a.m. raucous tones claim my immediate attention, but oblivious to the demands of the persistent alarm I slumber on. Then, the realisation hits me – it's New Year's day, the day I have been planning for two years.

Anxiously, I glance at my bulging rucksack. But why should I be worried? Yesterday I diligently checked its contents against a meticulously prepared list; now it holds my sole worldly possessions for the next twelve months.

My youngest son has recently come to live with me; moving in to take care of the house while I am away.

'Stewart,' I call out, 'I'm going to take a shower.'

No big deal in the normal course of events, but this will be the last dousing for me, at home, for some time. We have breakfast and then proceed with a hand-over procedure. Have we covered all eventualities? Time will tell.

The moment has come for me to commit. I am on a high. Why do proper athletes resort to using performance-enhancing drugs? Aspiration and inspiration are delivering the boost I need.

Stewart delivers me to the bandstand on the promenade at Bognor Regis an hour before the 'big push' begins.

Like the resort itself, the structure is modest in stature. Just a little ornate, it has had a recent paint job. Built on a wide promenade and having an elevation for public entertainment use, it is an ideal place to launch my 'Walk GB 4 Climb.

After two years of planning there is no going back: the finality of my decision is tantamount to having the 'snip'!

No one should get too concerned that I am overreaching myself. Going into space is not an option, nor is swimming the English Channel; bungee jumping is definitely out. Not on your life am I going to freefall from an aeroplane or even contemplate selection for Celebrity Come Dancing.

A septuagenarian, I'm taking a year's stroll covering four thousand miles around Great Britain, that's all! Miraculously I have no qualms about the task ahead. I am up for it.

At the bandstand a huge crowd – well, at least two hundred – has gathered and stands around expectant, rather as they used to do for executions. However there are no old crones knitting and no dangling noose within the structure. Everyone has gathered here for the right reason then!

The weather is a keen and bright; there is a buzz of anticipation. I sense the tone of remarks being bandied around:

'Doesn't he look pale?'

'He'll never reach Pompey.'

'You know, I think he's running away from something.'

'Men do funny things at his age.'

'Hope he's packed enough socks!'

The momentum quickens, and suddenly I am engulfed by a myriad of personal interviews. TV and local newspaper reporters lurk to get in on the act.

I am beginning to realise that only allowing an hour for the build-up is ludicrous – my first gross error of planning. Selsey, my first day's destination, is a long way off. Yes, we can all see Selsey Bill, but it is still ten miles away! I have to sweep round Aldwick Bay, plus there is the deviation of Pagham Harbour to contend with. It definitely requires an earlier start. Midday is fast approaching and it is January for goodness sake – the natural light will fade soon enough.

The back-slapping is relentless, everything is becoming a blur. Suddenly the clock has ticked onto 'high noon'. I haul my rucksack aboard. Before I have chance to check my bootlaces the caravan of family friends and well wishers moves off in a westerly direction to the sound of my brother Alan's jazz trumpet playing Gracie Field's hit Wish Me Luck As you Wave Me Goodbye. The whole show is now out of my hands and I shall have to do the decent thing and join in!

I am about to walk the longest footpath of my life. The big 'stroll' is definitely on, and I hope to be back in just under a year. At last I am walking out of this place. Never has the old king's phrase 'Bugger Bognor' felt so apt!

DAY 1

1st January 2008 – Bognor Regis to Selsey – 10 miles.
Kick-off at 12 noon – The Bandstand, Marine Drive, Bognor Regis.

At the end of the long Promenade many say their goodbyes. The remaining group, including my sons Martin and Stewart, stride onto the beach. We are soon driven back by the tide and noisily jaunt our way through to the elegant Aldwick Bay Estate.

Friends Tony and Joan Wells invite us all into their home to sample a huge uncut Christmas cake, to be washed down with cups of tea. This is all very well, but I have got to get going.

With a cry of, 'It's all right for you lot – I've only done two miles!' I harass everyone to stroll on to the last dwelling in West Beach Road facing the sea, the home of my plumber Lionel Voice. He and his family invite us all in for a glass of wine and another snack. Once again I have to break away!

I experience both tinges of sadness and pride as I stride out around Pagham Harbour, constantly glancing back to see everyone waving me goodbye. They finally disappear out of sight.

Setting out on New Year's Day, 2008. [Mike Parry]

I pass the deep Pagham Lagoon, remembering my brother Alan and me, with our school friend Eion Farmer, walking across its frozen surface during the bitter winter of 1947. Although the ice must have been a foot thick, I still shudder every time I think of it.

Striding around the harbour, an important bird reserve, I bump into walkers who saw me on TV the previous day. Also a group of birders appear. They have just seen a marsh harrier and point out little owls to me. Flocks of noisy brent geese are flying in to overwinter from Russia. I spent a lot of time out here as a kid and love the peace and tranquillity of this place.

My route around the harbour will come across the isolated St Wilfrid's Chapel just off the beach at the hamlet of Church Norton. It appears to be a simple cemetery chapel but has imposing Norman origins. Within its grounds lie my sister-in-law's mother Gwen Carter and Dave Munday, one of the larger-than-life characters in my life. Poignantly, the teenager whose early death is the inspiration for my walk has also been laid to rest at this spot I pause at this tranquil place and, then with great sadness and tears in my eyes, I say my goodbyes to them.

It's a long tiring walk across the extensive shingle of East Beach. The darkness is almost complete, except for a thin peach rim on the horizon still picking up the last light of the long-set sun. My lone boots crunch across the stones shattering the silence. I feel an intruder.

It was at this beach on a warm summer's evening in 1930 that the composer Eric Coates recalled that, as he 'gazed upon an incredibly blue sea, observing across the Aldwick Bay a distant Bognor tinged in pink, looking like an enchanted city, with a blue backdrop of the Downs', he was inspired to compose the melody By the Sleepy Lagoon. A blue plaque on a plinth records the moment nearby. This light orchestra serenade has been used as the introductory music for BBC Radio 4's Desert Island Discs for nearly seven decades. The programme's format will feature prominently as the tale of my journey unfolds.

I approach Selsey in the dark, clambering on to the sea defence wall leading to the lifeboat station. Street lighting allows a safe passage around Selsey Bill promenade, then on to the main road of the village where Jane Taylor collects me. We return to her home at Chichester.

It has been an eventful day: one down with 346 to go!

DAY 2
2nd January – Selsey to Bosham roundabout, A259 – 11 miles

Jane drives me back down the Manhood Peninsula to Selsey, where I have lots of memories. For five years in the Sixties my children Suzanne, Sonya, Martin and Stewart were brought up here.

I pick my way through what was once the largest holiday caravan complex in Europe, breaking out behind the sea defences leading to Bracklesham Bay. Even though it is New Year's holiday a sole excavator's engine powers away, its ever hungry grab shifting shingle in an effort to halt the sea's relentless threat.

My mobile rings, and a rendezvous with a Southern TV crew at East Wittering is hurredly arranged. After some sham strolling along the sand dunes for their cameras, I strike north to Itchenor. Here the harbour master has arranged to ferry me across the Chichester Harbour Channel.

At the end of a jetty I am perturbed to find a flooded Dory! A bucket and outboard ensure a safe crossing to the opposite shore at Bosham.

Jane rings. Southern TV wish to do a 'live' interview at her home. Later their outside broadcast unit will utilize her lounge as a studio. She picks me up on the A259. Their huge lorry arrives with its crew of four and transmitting lines. They install themselves. We indulge in small talk, waiting patiently, and at 5.22 precisely we go on air live. My interview with the station's charming female reporter Rachel lasts two minutes and they all pack up and leave.

It is all right embracing an early brief fame, but I am well aware that the starting pistol has only just been fired.

DAY 3
3rd January – Bosham to Langstone (Cobnor Point) – 11 miles

My schedule does not include islands (Anglesey the only exception), so I bypass Thorney and Hayling Islands, also the Chidham peninsula, and make straight down the A259 to the county border town of Emsworth.

After a tea and bun in the square I move on round the millpond and pick up the Solent Way Path. Crossing several fields I enter the imposing Warblington cemetery. Here rest two giants of sailing history. In 1968 Sir Alex Rose sailed around the world in 354 days, just a few more than it will take me round GB! Also laid to rest here is New Zealand's Americas Cup hero Sir Peter Blake, who was cruelly murdered by pirates in South America in 2001.

The day finishes at Langstone, south of Havant over the border in Hampshire. At least I have made it into the next county. Jane picks me up.

I feel OK. The 30Ib pack is comfortable so far, and the weather has been fine.

DAY 4

4th January – Langstone to Portsmouth Harbour – 13.3 miles

Once again Jane returns me to my start. I pass my only sewage farm of the year, close to the A27 and enter Farlington Marshes.

A bird-watching friend of mine, Chris Hyde, once told me that these marshes are frequented by little owls. He went on to explain that the bird has the ability to revolve its head 360 degrees. So, he said, the trick is to stare at it as you keep encircling; it stares back blinking in puzzlement, and eventually it is propelled up into the air like a coiled spring. 'Hoot's mon, I am away!' it screeches.

After pleasant banter with a birder we part only to meet again at a car park. His vehicle has been broken into and his walking kit stolen. It happens every day to somebody. (Thankfully it will be the only crime I come across during my year away.)

Soon I am on the eastern road bridge leading onto Portsea Island. Portsmouth is the only island city in the UK. A cousin of mine once told me that my grandfather Lashley had been a foreman of the gang constructing the original road and was known as Black Jack.

Following through Eastney I come out onto the five-mile Southsea promenade. The Solent spreads out before me; what a panorama!

At Southsea Common I pass the place of my birth. Standing on the spot now is a modern, ugly looking sheltered housing block for the elderly – another one of those so often unexplained planning decisions to come out of the town hall.

In 1936 the Bowlands Royal Naval Maternity Home stood on the site; my father was a naval petty officer. My mother told me that when I was fifteen days old she held me up at the home's front windows overlooking the common to watch the Queen Mary passing down the Solent on her maiden trials. To think, we two old wrecks are still around!

I proceed down the never ending promenade, past the little beach from where Nelson was rowed out to the *Victory*, a voyage that for him ended at Trafalgar. I ascend the Round Tower perched at the entrance to Portsmouth Harbour, from where countless women have watched their jacktar loved ones sail away.

I finish at the Harbour Rail Station where Jane picks me up. It is back to Chichester for the last time.

DAY 5

5th January – Portsmouth Harbour (Gosport/Hamble/Hythe Ferries) to Hythe – 16 miles

Jane drops me for the last time at the Gosport Ferry and we say our goodbyes. She has been an enormous help in getting me off to a good start.

The short crossing has a sobering effect. I am now irreversibly on my way, Portsmouth Harbour finally severing my links with home. With a last glance across to the outlines of *HMS Victory/Warrior* and the impressive Spinaker tower I move on, passing Haslar Hospital and to Gilkicker Point. At Stokes Bay the IRB Station had just had a 'shout', and I watch them kit-up and launch into the western Solent.

Further on is a café bustling with patrons. There's a great extended holiday atmosphere in the place, and bonhomie abounds. I find myself sitting at a table opposite a genial and well endowed lady. During a laughing fit she suddenly leans forward, the impact of her bosom against the table causing a minor tsunami across the surface of my soup.

The proprietors make everyone aware of my quest, and I walk out of the place with £40 of donations.

A walk along the beach brings me to Lee-on-Solent, past the hovercraft graveyard park and eventually to the Hamble ferry. Here a little man, dressed in a duffle coat, sporting a white beard and looking remarkably like 'Captain Birdseye' under his sailor's cap, operates a twee pink chug of a vessel. It is a quid to get cross.

CLIMB Families

All references to CLIMB Families in this publication means parents and relatives of children/infants/teenagers or adults who have been born with or have developed any of the known 715 genetic metabolic conditions and who have subsequently received support from the Charity CLIMB – Children Living With Inherited Metabolic Diseases.'

The Way follows Southampton Water through Netley to cross the Itchen bridge and onto the Hythe ferry. It is Saturday, and in the late afternoon the boat swarms with Southampton football fans returning from a home match. I wisely keep quiet about my Portsmouth FC affiliation. I can see the press headlines now: 'Elderly round-GB walker found floating in the harbour.'

Darkness has fallen. The ferry passes the moored-up and soon to be decommissioned *QE2*. In the rush of Saint' supporters at Hythe's pier-head I have no chance of boarding the oldest pier railway in the world. This historic boneshaker operates down the 700 yards of jetty, possibly the longest in the south. I am forced to walk down it into a chilly head-wind towards the lights of the town. It seems to take ages.

My hosts are Ken and Mary Endean, who live close by and greet me with great enthusiasm, spoiling me rotten. The Endean's are my first CLIMB family hosts. Mary's sister's two children were born suffering from the rare metabolic disorder Mucopolysaccaride Disease (MPS). Sadly John died aged seven years, but Chris survives although severely handicapped.

During the evening Ken and I discuss our military heroes. I stick with Nelson, while he settles for Wellington.

Ken and Mary Endean, my first CLIMB family members.

DAY 6
6th January – Hythe (via Bucklers Hard) to Lymington – 17 miles

My first really long day takes me via a road and forest lane for lunch 'on the house' at the Travellers Rest at Frostlane. I cross onto Beaulieu Heath fringing the New Forest where ponies wander everywhere without due care to traffic or anyone.

Just outside Beaulieu I meet a man in a pub who once lodged with my son Martin. This is the first of so many chance meetings and coincidences I am going to experience on my way round GB.

A long stretch of forest footpath leads me to Bucklers Hard. Here Georgian cottages flank a wide avenue leading to the former boatyard, birthplace of many Nelson's ships. A friendly chat with a couple culminates in a donation to my Just Giving charity website account, the very first while on the hoof.

Enjoy a long afternoon stroll. Outside Lymington I come across a roadside lectern notice, recording that the surrounding fields and buildings had been a D-Day advanced landing ground for squadrons of American P47 fighter bombers. I pause at this quiet spot and try to imagine the hectic activity that took place here for four months in June 1944.

Derek Gurney picks me up in Lymington. He is the first of many Rotarians who have elected to assist me along the way, an initiative started by my good friend David Garforth at Bognor Regis, a great servant of this organisation.

Derek's has arranged a dinner party at his splendid bungalow in Swale, inviting Jenny Simpson the 'lady' president of the Lymington Rotary and others. During the evening I am educated into Rotarian protocol and its motto 'Service above Self'. One of the constraints is the collar and tie dress code for meetings. I have to chuckle when Derek tells me about a branch member who persists in attending wearing shorts but has avoided being 'black-balled' as he is their indispensible ideas man!

Not being an IT geek, I am particularly relieved to hear that my Sony Eriksson is actually transmitting my blogs and photos through to CLIMB at Crewe. Amazing!

DAY 7

7th January – Lymington (via Keyhaven/Milford/Barton on Sea) to
Christchurch (Priory) – 14 miles

Derek drives back to my route from Lymington, and fortified with his
sandwiches I take the wet path south west passing Pennington Marshes.
By the lake at Keyhaven Marsh a lady is feeding swans with bread
pudding. No early take-off for them, then!

The weather is deteriorating and a strong headwind accompanied
by squally showers set in – my first taste of what the weather will throw
at me over the next month as I trek towards Lands End. Excellent all-
year-round cafés at Milford and Barton on Sea provide handy bolt-
holes. Here I look back over the Solent to the Needles Lighthouse and
the Isle of Wight.

I cut inland at Chewton Bunny Chine, using tree cover to consume
Derek's sandwiches. Going through the grounds of Highcliffe Castle,
another café appears. To explain, I already know these refreshment
stops from several trips along the Solent Way.

Rambling on, windswept and wet, I rendezvous with my next host,
Chris Rhodes at Christchurch Priory. We retreat to his home and meet
up with his wife Sam, an old friend of my daughter Sonya. We wine
and dine in their extraordinary conservatory – it's huge. I take great
pleasure in having a long chat with Sam, who has become such a good
friend to my daughter. They shared a house in Bournemouth years
before.

Today I realised how difficult lugging a large rucksack into prevailing
gale force winds is going to be.

Retiring to bed I reach for my iPod and set up the first of many
evening concerts. The search for my eight 'Desert Island Discs' starts
this evening. (See the 'Let's Hear the Music' chapter.)

For my debut I select Status Quo's 'Rockin All Over The World',
'Sidewinder' by Art Blakey's Jazz Messengers, Abba's 'Dancing Queen'
and Benjamin Britten's 'Young Person's Guide to the Orchestra'. My
'Wish' track is ELO's 'Mr Blue Sky'.

DAY 8

8th January – Christchurch to Sandbanks – 9 miles

It is a fine fresh morning. Chris delivers me to Southbourne from where I start a nine-mile slog along the continuous promenade around Poole Bay to Sandbanks. Without natural cover today I am constantly exposed to a cold head wind, which gets tiresome by the time I reach Bournemouth Pier. Some distraction is provided by huge 'Tonka Toy'-type levelling vehicles preparing another squeaky clean 'blue flag' beach at Bournemouth for the coming holiday season

The town, on its sea frontage anyway, has almost closed down, with just one tea outlet open. A billboard at the pier head announces future appearances of Marty Wilde and his Wildcats, the Bachelors and Chas and Dave. You don't expect Bournemouth to put on 'tribute' acts, so these veterans must be still alive, I think.

The cold wind persists and, although sunny, it's not surprising that I'm the only silly sod about. With great relief I pass off the prom into the protection of the well-heeled Sandbanks peninsula and its millionaires row. I wait in the ferry car park, shivering beneath my 'Desperate Dan' stubble, for my next host, Gill Cook. Gill is a relation of a CLIMB Family: her one-year-old niece Emma has the Medium Chain acyl CoA Dehydrongenase Deficiency (MCADD) metabolic condition.

DAY 9

9th January – Rest day – Poole

Gill introduces her young son Oliver, who enthusiastically displays his toys. Her husband Richard is away on business.

It is the first of my rest days, to be taken roughly every two weeks – whether I need them or not! Gill takes me on a tour of Parkstone, Poole and its harbour. Before enjoying a lunchtime snack we return to the Sandbanks ferry terminal for a photo shot and interview for the *Bournemouth Echo*. This is the first showing of local press interest, which continues spasmodically as I trek round.

During the day my permanent CLIMB Charity contact Lesley Greene rings to offer more details of walking companions and accommodation. It's all going well, but I haven't had to walk uphill yet. Not long now!

DAY 10

10th January – Sandbanks to Swanage – 8 miles

Gill waves goodbye as the Sandbanks chain ferry pulls me over to South Haven Point. I'm standing at the entrance to Poole Harbour, one of the largest inlets in the world. An impressive marker board announces the start of the 630-miles South West Coastal Path (SWCP), the longest coastal trail in the UK with a total elevation for walkers of 114,931ft – nearly four times the height of Mount Everest. It's my first major challenge, and I have allowed eight weeks to complete it. It will not be long before I find out whether the training has paid off.

I am met by Brian Oman (Retired Minister of the church related to my High School colleague Trevor Jennings) and Barbara his Wife who invite me to their home in Swanage for dinner later in the day.

At first the SWCP is but a short walk along the stunning Shell Bay beach. It then takes a sharp turn to the south-west, going round the curve of Studland Bay a section of which is set aside for naturists. There are warning signs for the squeamish, but this is January – surely no one is going to be foolish enough to be chancing skinny dipping today, or even a game of ladies' beach volleyball, are they?. The beach is empty of people, blast it. I am out of luck!

At the excellent National Trust café, after ample refreshment, I make a short detour inland before the SWCP makes its first ascent of Walk GB 4 Climb up to the Foreland. A couple of cyclists recognise me from

Waiting for the Sandbanks ferry.

a TV interview and stop for a chat. Soon I am following the Path to the Old Harry Rocks. Joining me are a couple who relate how for many years they helped their neighbours, whose son suffered from the neurodegenerative metabolic condition Battens Disease.

I press on to Ballard Point, into a ferocious wind and driving rain, making the cliff-top ascents extremely difficult. My poles are useless in this situation, so I resort to pulling myself up steep inclines using (carefully) the barbed wire fence and its stakes.

At each summit I can hardly stand up in the wind. Usually the sound of waves crashing on to the rocks hundreds of feet below is perceptible, but not today. The howling wind around by ears drowns out all other acoustics. At last I have a challenge – this is more like it!

I am pretty damp on arrival at Swanage, but Brian picks me up and I enjoy a splendid meal at the Omans. They have an evening appointment so my host address for the night is to be at Auberge (077 11 117 668) in the middle of the town. It's pitch black and still raining as Brian runs me down to the daunting rambling house that Pete Sedgewick has turned into a superbly appointed hostel. I am the only one staying for the night, and he looks after me particularly well.

The following 'Flek' chapter describes an unusual altercation announcing the surprise arrival of a mentor today!

I have now entered shipping forecast area Portland.

FLEK

'He was my perfect alter ego, cool and in control'
Henry Winkler

I don't suppose there are many individuals taking part in solo endurance events who have not fallen victim to a phenomenon both fascinating and self-illusionary. I refer to the state of talking to oneself. With a long lonesome journey ahead of me it is bound to happen. One can play along with this to advantage, but my initial reaction is how boring my own conversation is. I have to face the realisation that people have been listening to me for years ranting on about the ills of the world. Frankly it's embarrassing!

To my amazement, shortly into my long walk my ramblings began to elicit a reply. It happened like this . . .

On Day 10 I encounter my first battle against gravity. This occurs just after I leave the beach at Studland Bay starting the ascent up Foreland Point towards Old Harry Rocks. I press on to Ballard Point and encounter severe weather conditions. This is a sign of things to come and I start to mutter to myself. This aggravation graduates into words, then sentences and finally expletives. By the time I reach the outskirts of Swanage I am having a right old spat with someone or something.

What I have not realised is that there are ears taking in my every word. A male voice with a London drawl keeps butting in and I am forced to challenge it.

'Hello, who's there?' I enquire nervously, *'Who the hell are you. Can I help?*

'I think that it's going to be the other way round, mate.' comes a voice loud and clear, *'You are going to need me, Colin.'*

Really,' I answer arrogantly, *'How, on earth have you got here? What makes you think I can't handle myself? I'm on an escapade of my own choosing, if you don't mind.'*

The voice goes on: 'Listen sunshine, when things or people get tough in the months ahead you're going to need someone you can consult, confer with, seek an opinion from, extract a judgement or even share a smile with, savvy?'

I think that even if it only means I can maintain some sort of sanity, then the idea makes sense, but I'm not going to warm to this stranger just yet.

'So come on then, tell me – how did you get here?

'Well I've been at a loose end recently. The job centre have been cajoling me to take up a situation. It was put it to me that they had a cushy job on their books, helping a bloke out who was going to be on his own a lot during the coming year. They 'regretted' that the position would be unpaid but tried to reassure me. "Think of it as work experience – could pep up your CV no end," they said.

'Strangely the proposition appealed to me. Anyway, I like the idea of being carried all the way round GB. I'm looking forward to the scenery; I must be mad!'

I relent.

'All right but only on the basis that my decisions are final,' I reply.

I sense a knowing smile spread over his face: he is going to have none of it.

'Listen,' he says. 'When it comes to giving advice I call a spade a spade. It hasn't been unknown for me to agree or even congratulate a colleague.'

Then he softens his tone: 'I might just hang around.'

'Oh please yourself,' I reply, trying to sound cocky. 'If I have to put up with you, then you shall have a name.'

Thinking for a moment I come up with 'Flek.'

'It's a derivation of "reflection", you know' – trying to explain my reasoning.

'Sounds all right to me, guv,' is the gruff reply.

It's customary to shake hands on agreement, but this does not take place. He is only on probation after all.

DAY 11

11th January – Swanage to Kimmeridge – 13 miles

In mitigation I suppose that no enterprise has ever been undertaken without a hiccup, or should I say cock-up, in its logistical planning. As I set off towards Peveril Point little did I realise how personal doubt can influence an outcome.

For a start I ignore Pete Sedgwick's advice and take the lower cliff footpath, enduring the mud that he had warned me about – causing a delay that, as it turns out, I cannot afford. Against a strong wind but improving weather I arrive at the stunning Durlston Head Castle. Under restoration, it houses a vibrant café with a woodstove, providing a warm welcome on a stormy day.

The sun comes out but the gale persists. I slog head on into it for the next five miles to St Albans Head. I can hear the angry sea below thumping against the cliffs. The path turns north and I encounter the precarious Chapman Steps, about 200 down and 180 up. I get beyond Chapman's Pool and to my dismay the light starts to fade rapidly: I still have four cliff edge miles to Kimmeridge Bay

I resort to using the headlamp that my son Martin gave me, which proves invaluable. Only six months earlier I had walked this route, but this time I have not allowed for the seasonally advanced summer time and now it's pitch dark. I have not thought this out, and doubt sets in. Foolishly I decide to shortcut and cross a field towards a farm. I slosh through a stream and hack my way through a bramble hedge to reach its floodlit buildings.

'Now what?' asks Flek adding, 'Do you know what you are doing?'
My mentor is already mumbling in disbelief.

Unable to raise anyone, I enter the Farm Pen and push my way through the bemused cattle. I am now at the front of the farm but there is still no sign of life, not even a vehicle. Round the side I look through a window into a typical farmhouse kitchen of yesteryear – i.e. untidy, filthy and lit by a forty watt bulb. Prolonged banging on the door finally pays off and an emaciated old boy appears. This man is Albert Steptoe's double!

Without even glancing, he beckons me in. Listening to my plight (which include signal problems with my mobile), he offers his phone.

The receiver had once been a BT standard cream colour, but this has vanished long since under decades of grime.

While I am phoning my next hosts, Jerry and Annette Hole, Kimmeridge Farmhouse B & B (01929 480990), 'Albert' starts an extended bout of coughing, during which he produces an Old Holborn tin. As he rolls himself a fag I think he is going to die on the spot. Finally I make contact with Jerry and he picks me up. I rather sheepishly accept his hospitality. Soon I am in a beautifully appointed farmhouse, which is probably the best B & B accommodation of the whole trip.

Flek lambasts me: 'Frankly you don't deserve to be here, Col. Your hosts had planned an evening out with friends and your late arrival has ruined it!'

I have to stand and take it. This has not been a great night for my thought processes.

So what had gone wrong with the planning? Well, when I walked this way in October I still had another hour of light, which was crucial. I just had not allowed for British Summer Time. Victor Meldrew would have said, 'For goodness sake, I don't believe it! I had compounded the problem by not sticking to my planned route, which should have terminated at a host collection point in the Goulter Gap car park.

An hour ago I was soaked and plodding through slurry. Now I am wallowing in a luxury bath, still pondering on my foolishness.

Flek is fuming: 'You've got to buck up, Col, and concentrate. You've hardly started this adventure and look what's happened. You're not on an outward bound course, mate.'

Well, he did warn me he could be vociferous! He eventually calms-down and in mitigation admits that even Captain Scott made the odd error!

I consume the appetising supper that Annette had so caringly left in the room and question my actions. Despite all the preparation, am I up to this?

DAY 12

12th January – Gaulter Gap to Lulworth Cove – 8 miles

At breakfast Annette suggests that I strike north, climbing up on to the Purbeck Hills. From above I can enjoy unrestricted views of this unique coastline disappearing westwards beyond Worbarrow Bay heading for Lulworth Cove.

I puff my way to the top and catch up with lone walker on the ridge. She is Sybil, an American now living permanently in Dorset, and she becomes my very first single walking companion during the whole trip. We chat away for a couple of miles before she turns back.

A mile on I glance down towards Tyneham, which became a 'lost' village after compulsory Army take-over during the Second World War. A few miles further along the ridge in a valley to my right lies the Bindon army firing range, part of the Lulworth army camp. Surplus to requirement Russian tanks have been imported and emplaced everywhere on the Range so that the British Army Tank Corps hardware can then take regular 'pot-shots' at them.

A pale egg yolk of a sun appears as I finally drop steeply down to my destination at Lulworth Cove.

The Staff at Bishops Cafe/Hotel complex are waiting for me with tea and cakes. In an Annexe Proprietor Philip Ashley-Rudd has laid-on an enormous en-suite room heated by three two bar electrics fires.

After enjoying a long soak in the huge bath I pull the plug, nothing happens, except that the adjacent pedestal sink starts to fill up. I look at the toilet 'mincer' system to solve the problem.

'Don't even go there,' shouts Flek anticipating a Fire Brigade pumping out scenario. I was only joking; he hasn't detected my black humour yet.

The plumbing problem reported I sit down to a complimentary evening meal. Worn out and back in my room I wriggle and burrow like a snake in sand under a five foot duvet and pass out.

It has been an interesting if mostly lonely day. I am just getting used to the pull of the rucksack on my shoulders. As for my stubble, well it still looks grubby and very Sicilian!

Indentured

With over three hundred visits to sundry bathrooms during my trip, most of them in private homes, I unwittingly entered the puzzling world of bathroom fittings.

Visits often raise tricky operational problems, such as how to get a different make of shower each day to the right temperature, solving the workings of a Heath Robinson designed mixer system and, yes, even wrongly designated taps. I always asked for a bath as a good soak eases by aching limbs.

Many bath designs were luxurious, others were too short or deep and, when I was aching and stiff, difficult to climb out of. Pulling out the plug is never a guarantee.

Don't get me wrong – I am never ungrateful. All devices eventually eased my aching plight. However, coming to terms with some fixtures often meant relying on inspiration.

On completion of my journey I seriously considered myself to have become an honorary indentured apprentice of the Ballcock and Flushers Guild.

DAY 13

13th January – Lulworth Cove to Preston – 12 miles

I ascend the long concrete pathway out of the cove. Taking a westerly route, I am soon exposed to ferocious wind conditions again. With a sense that the day of reckoning is at hand, I look up: nimbus cloud as far as I can see.

Beyond Durdle Door are severe gradients made more difficult to negotiate by the muddy terrain and the surface resistance to the wind of my large rucksack. The trouble is that the elevating ground is so slippery. My recourse is once again to carefully grasp the barbed wire fencing and hand-pull myself upwards. Descending is just as hazardous. In the shrieking wind progress is slow and exhausting. Eventually the terrain levels out but the wind howls on. By the time I reach the ragged White Nothe Cliffs I can hardly stand up. It is necessary to dig the poles in and remain static sometimes for up to ten minutes at a time.

Shattered, I shelter behind a memorial plinth; I can no longer breach the impenetrable invisible wall of resistance. Two lads walk by, cutting through the wind with ease. Clad in skin-tight kit and beanie hats, they look ready for action. Sure enough they find it, getting out onto a break-away fissure of cliff which still has a World War 11 concrete bunker perched on top.

Stormy weather, White Nothe Cliffs.

I watch in amazement as in turn they haul themselves up on top of the relic and then, oh so carefully, stand up to face the raging gale. This is what they have come for, their 'kick of the day', akin perhaps to off-piste skiing or white water rafting.

Returning to my level, they constantly glance in my direction, keeping us in touch. I like to feel that, aware of my predicament, they are watching over me. Suddenly, however, they go over the hill and vanish.

The path descends steeply down into calm and passes through a copse. After my battering I find it difficult to keep my feet on the muddy path, falling over on several occasions. Try getting up with a thirty pound pack still strapped to your back! It ain't easy. At Osmington Mills I find a welcome café run by a Brummie couple.

Weary of fighting the elements, I take a lane inland and reach the A353. The view to the left across to Weymouth and the Isle of Portland is striking; it reminds me of Gibraltar. I stroll the two miles down to Preston where my host and ex-fire service colleague Roger Greet picks me up for a two-night stay. On a day when I have met the full force of nature, it is such a relief to put my feet up in his splendid home.

DAY 14
14th January – Rest day – Preston

I am staying with Roger Greet and his wife Jaqui. Roger's final appointment was as deputy chief fire officer for Dorset. We spend time going over our service experiences. Now retired, he takes me on a tour of his former 'fire ground'.

First stop is Poundbury, the Prince of Wales' pet project just to the west of Dorchester. Built to house six thousand people, it is an experimental town on land owned by the Duchy of Cornwall. Of a high density pattern, with a mixture of shops, business, private and social housing with no zoning, it is designed around people and not the motor car. Time will tell!

He whisks me around much of the county's' southern sites of interest. We finish up at Ferry Bridge, the narrow strip of road joining the Isle of Portland to the mainland at Weymouth. I am reminded of a past Southern Trails walking holiday around Portland. My party stayed at the Portland Heights Hotel perched on the top of this famous rock with commanding views down the amazing Chesil Beach.

The region will become the central point of the 2012 Olympic sailing programme. For three weeks the Portland Harbour will attract worldwide TV coverage, an exciting and prestigious time for the area. Back at his home I inspect his DIY efforts and Jaqui lays on an excellent meal.

DAY 15

15th January – Ferry Bridge to Abbotsbury – 11 miles

This turns out to be a day of compromise and running water. Roger recommends that I take the Rodwell Way, an old railway track going through the middle of Weymouth. This is a two-mile 'rail to trail' scheme terminating at Ferry Bridge, a chance to walk behind the facade of a town – a welcome alternative.

At Ferry Bridge I cross the main road leading to the Isle of Portland and start walking the north bank of the Fleet, a six-mile lake trapped behind the massif of Chesil Beach. The going is heavy, muddy and very slippery: progress is slow. I have made arrangements with my next host to rendezvous at Abbotsbury car park.

'Regarding today's schedule I think you are going to have to compromise on the route, Col,' pipes up Flek. 'With five miles of terrain like this you aren't going make it in time.'

He has started his mentoring in earnest. I am beginning to listen to him, but at this stage in our relationship I wouldn't dream of letting on!

He is talking sense, so I make a detour cutting north to pick-up the B3157 – one of many such compromises throughout the year ahead.

Two miles on I fork left, gaining a quiet lane running parallel with the main road. Leading through the hamlet of Langton Herring, I soon encounter water seeping off the fields from everywhere, I must have sloshed through three fords.I come across a 'theme farm'. At its entrance is a 10ft-high prancing horse made entirely out of horseshoes.

'There's enough luck in that pile to last the whole trip, but I shouldn't carry any,' advises Flek. As I splash along, it's welcome small talk.

A mile outside Portesham a gleaming Audi 4 x 4 pulls up behind me. A head pops out and says, 'Is that Colin?'

It is my next host, Jeffrey Ellwood, returning from Dorchester. With a promise that we will drop me back here tomorrow, I hop in and we journey back to his home at Uplyme House north of Lyme Regis. The building is a relatively new Georgian-style mansion complete with electronic entrances and peacocks roaming the grounds.

My hosting comes about because Jeffrey is the father of Guy, the partner of my niece Katherine. This is to be my staging post for the next three nights. I am going to enjoy my stay here, that's for sure.

DAY 16

16th January – Abbotsbury to West Bay – 19 miles

I fall out of my four poster bed and after breakfast place my booted feet into a plastic bag before getting into Jeffrey's super Mercedes sports car. He returns me to yesterday's pick-up location.

Abbotsbury is deserted. The place is noted for its tropical gardens but the famous Swannery has a shadow over it A dead swan has just been found here, triggering an avian flu scare (the H5N1 virus to be precise) throughout the British Isles.

I turn off the road and pick up the SWCP, again making for Chesil Beach. Here I meet Kevin with his splendid great dane Ben. He (Kevin) sports a bushy full-set beard and I take the opportunity of getting his opinion on my facial creation.

Kevin with Ben, Chesil Beach.

'Blimey, you have a long way to go,' he chuckles, boasting that his family have never seen him without his.

I join Chesil Beach, which is narrower here but continues for a long way yet. It stretches for 29km, the longest natural single shingle barrier in the world.

Picking my way along a gravel track running close to the beach, I eventually stumble on the Beach Café, Burton Mere. Open all year, it offers superb meals and snacks served up by handsome Filipino waitresses. I order Dorset apple cake and wash it down with two mugs of coffee. I have stumbled upon Shangri-La.

Pressing on to Burton Freshwater I get my first glimpse of a huge caravan site stretching down to the beach. From now on I am going to be constantly amazed just how massive this holiday industry is.

At West Bay I rendezvous with Jeffrey in Morrison's car park on the seafront. He has picked up his daughters from school. Following a heavy shop we return to the splendid Uplyme House. No rucksack to haul today– it's such a treat. I shall latch onto this arrangement, that is, hosts relieving me of this burden (referred to as 'free days') at every opportunity in the future.

After dinner I have a chat with Jeffrey. A self made man from industry, now retired, he shares his experience and expertise with the Dorchester Health Trust, is a governor of Brunel University (I informed him that I was a fire consultant at the university for several years) and serves on the magistrates' bench in Exeter.

We talk about British comedy, and it turns out he is a cousin of Alan Simpson, who with Ray Galton wrote the Hancocks Half Hour and Morecambe and Wise comedy scripts for many years.

We agree that scriptwriters are very much undervalued.

DAY 17
17th January – West Bay to Lyme Regis – 10 miles

It's another 'free' day (no pack on my back), and I make my way steadily upward along the Jurassic Coast in light rain to accend 'Golden Cap' whose summit at 191m makes it the highest coastal point on the south coast.

For the rest of the day it becomes necessary, because of continuous erosion along this stretch of coast, to strike inland. I stroll on through the centre of Charmouth, going north-westerly up and around the top of Lyme Regis golf course. Here I veer south on part road / part trail into Lyme. Once again it is bliss without the weight on my back. I could get use to it, but tomorrow it will be business as usual.

This evening Jeffrey arranges for me, wife Toni and daughters Jessica and Elizabeth to meet the lady mayor Sally Holman and mayoress Jane Whittington (her daughter) at the famous Cobb Arms in Lyme Regis. I am to meet eleven mayors before the end of the year.

After photographs and lots of chat, Jeffery treats us all to a meal. It is a most pleasant evening. On leaving I can just make out the Cobb. This

well known harbour wall found further publicity when used in the film The French Lieutenant's Woman, starring Meryl Streep and Jeremy Irons.

My legs have a holiday feel, as my overall fitness begins to pay off. Another night in the four- poster is going to help!

With the mayor and mayoress of Lyme Regis.

DAY 18

18th January – Lyme Regis to Seaton – 7 miles

Toni drops me at a car park on the west side of town and I finally say goodbye to the Ellwoods. Many of my excursions have been relatively easy, but not today. Shortly I am to disappear into the Landslip National Nature Reserve, a unique area formed by the Bindon Landslip.

This is where in the 1840s, after constant heavy rainfall, an estimated four millions of tons of rock fell towards the sea, forming an under cliff. This strip has self sown itself with ash – the largest example of its type in the UK – and provides habitat and protection for birds, in particular the relatively unseen cirl bunting. (More about these elusive birds later.)

The seemingly never-ending 'jungle' path is constantly hazardous to negotiate and becomes increasingly frustrating to those who enter. The way twists like a corkscrew and constantly changes levels. The ground is strewn with bare tree roots and rocks, and it goes on for four miles! There is no way out until the final exit.

As I stumble along, an irritated voice speaks up: 'Blimey mate, where you taking us? I'm being shaken up rotten.'

'I'd forgotten all about you Flek. Having a nice day out? I reply, seeking to placate,

'Never mind the sweet talk, matey. Is this what twitchers go through to find some reclusive silly little bird? They should have their beaks examined,' he angrily exclaims.

'Well it takes all sorts you know,' I react trying to calm him down. 'Bet you wish you were back in the dole queue eh?'

Strangely this doesn't dampen his temper.

'Well I'm not, so get us out of here pronto,' he bickers on.

I reassure him: 'Hang on tight Flekkie, we're nearly there' – deviously omitting to tell him that we are only half way.

The experience, though tough, has been fascinating. How claustrophobic must it be in summer when the dense leave canopy is on? I am mighty relieved to spill out at the other end intact two hours later.

I consume refreshments, then like a butterfly I am suddenly being rejuvenated by the sun's rays, adopting a prostrate 'recovery' position to take full advantage.

From here it is necessary once again to cut northwest, I swing round yet another golf course and cross over the River Axe on the Axminster Bridge into Seaton.

The town is typical of so many of our seaside resorts, old fashioned and free of vulgar amusements. It is definitely middle class.

I support a café until host Michael Horwood whisks me away to his substantial property up on the hill at the back of town.

Reunited today with my rucksack, I find that the terrain put my balance and perception to the test and I have just about come out on top.

Day 19
19th January – Seaton to Sidmouth – 11 miles

I am being hosted for two days by Michael Horwood (Rotary) and his wife Judy. At the Beer Head car park he arranges for me to be interviewed by the *Sidmouth Herald*. From here I go round the Head and after a mile descend several flights of steps down to the promenade at Beer.

Ascending the Hooken Cliffs, I stride onto Branscombe Mouth to find the busy Tea Cabin café and converse with the locals. Refreshed, I rise up again to the clifftop walk, discovering a Romany caravan which has been squeezed into a cliff-edge depression. It must have taken a remarkable feat to transport it here. Dire warnings scrawled on a trespass notice and the piles of logs clearly indicate it's occupied.

A couple of miles out to sea a part-wreck is still clearly visible – all that is left of the *Napoli*. (*See page 38.*) Standing alone on a cliff top bathed in milky sunshine and rustled by a light breeze, I hear the cry of a patrolling fulmar and find it hard to imagine the chaotic scenes that unfolded here exactly a year ago today.

Descending into Salcombe Mouth involves 247 steps down and a more palatable 187 up the other side. Some joker has scribed a subtraction equation on a stile gate, indicating a welcome gain if going west of course. Soon I am on Sidmouth seafront. Unlike Seaton this place appears a little run-down; it doesn't have the same confident air about it as its neighbour down the coast

Several years ago I discovered a band playing in a park on the outskirts of town. On a balmy evening the repertoire included music by Glenn Miller and Duke Ellington. You can never suppress culture! Michael picks me up and we return to Seaton.

The Horwards have invited Sandy Macfayden, a farmer friend, for dinner. The Romany caravan precariously stands on his farm land, and he tells me that its occupant on many a night crosses the fields to visit a hostelry. Despite any resultant inebriation, his return back to the cliff edge calls for spot-on navigation.

Flek's been quiet – still nursing his bruises I suspect.

The Napoli

'Oh please Lord, let us pray for all on the sea,
But if there's got to be wrecks please send them to me'
Wreckers' Prayer – Richard Larn

The owner of the Romany caravan I discovered on Day 19 must have had a birds-eye view of the scenes which followed an extraordinary event on the beaches below. Exactly a year before the 60,000-ton English-flagged container ship MSC Napoli beached two miles offshore here after suffering damage in heavy seas off the Lizard. Its stern section is still visible in the bay. Many of its containers broke loose and drifted ashore. News got around, and hundreds of people gathered from afar, descending on the beach to pillage the contents on a monumental scale. The media had also arrived and recorded the scenes live on national TV, to the astonishment of the viewing millions. Captured on DVD, this will surely become a collector's item.

The booty included wine casks, huge supplies of nappies, perfume, household effects and car parts, but famously it was the discovery of BMW motor cycles that excited the looters.

My host at Sidmouth, Michael Horwood, brought my attention to an amusing cartoon in a national daily, showing the unfolding drama illustrated in sequence with four cartoons as follows:

JETSAM   Vessel listing heavily, its cargo coming adrift.

FLOTSAM   Lines of containers floating ashore.

GET SOME   Figure breaking into beached container.

GOT SOME   Figure riding a BMW motor cycle across the beach at speed!

The scavenging of the Napoli's cargo caused a National Debate fuelled by the extraordinary tactics of the police, who only managed to stem the free-for-all four days later!

After much soul searching the relevant maritime laws were re-examined. It was eventually decided that the pillaging was the equivalent of 'theft' and the authorities encouraged those responsible to 'sign' a declaration form of goods removed. Some hopes!

It seems that any romanticising of 'wrecking' supposedly undertaken by smugglers in the past was possibly laid to rest that day in 2007 – no more getting up in the night to light fires on the cliffs enticing unwary mariners onto the rocks. Just listen to the shipping weather forecast follow umpteen news broadcasts/social networks and chance your luck. It could be a long wait.

DAY 20

20th January – Sidmouth to Exmouth – 13 miles

We all go back to Seaton and, accompanied by Sandy, walk out to the to the huge caravan site at Ladram Bay. Then it's goodbye.

It is mild, and the sea is azure blue and calm. To be honest, although I'm on a coastal path, some days I only sight it intermittently. Now the Exmouth Nature Reserve forces me to divert inland.

Crossing the River Otter it's only a short amble into Budleigh Salterton. Can't you just hear this name tripping off the lips of Noel Coward? I treat myself to a café sandwich, sit on the prom and ring my good friends the Aldertons at Bognor, who know this area well.

Passing The East Devon Golf Course, the SWCP reaches the endless lines of caravans within the huge Devon Cliffs Holiday Park. Filtering through these is akin to being in a giant maze. Path signs are often missing, or deliberately turned round; any progress becomes a compass job. Eventually I veer onto the River Exe estuary promenade and walk along Exmouth seafront. The place is packed with early-season day trippers. At the impressive clock tower I rendezvous with Peter Deane, my next host.

Peter (father of Dr Meryl Deane, Chichester Jazz Club) is now retired but was once a communications engineer at Goonhilly Down, Britain's pioneer earth satellite tracking station in Cornwall. The engineers were recruited from far and wide to service the station, and he has arranged for three others to host me.

After three weeks on the hoof I feel that my prime movers are now operating efficiently.

'Don't you get too complacent now, Col,' pipes up Flek. 'You still have most of the nation to circumnavigate.'

21st January – Exmouth to Topsham – 7 miles

I say goodbye to Peter, a gentle man and widower who has been great company. He drops me by the rail line on the east side of the Exe estuary. I stroll along the East Devon Way, ending up at the Globe Pub at Lympstone. Its bar walls are bedecked with cuckoo clocks. The trick here is to slyly fit a meal appointment between the striking hours to avoid the row.

'Let's get out of here before they all go off,' pleads Flek.

Once we had escaped I remember saying to Flek that it was going to be an uneventful day. How wrong can one be!

Forced inland to the A373 come I come across the main gate of the Royal Marine training establishment at Lympstone. I foolishly approach the sentries at its security guard room to wish them good morning. This is not a good idea. Some timely advice from my friend, Flek, wouldn't have gone amiss, but he must be having a snooze.

A uniformed civilian security chappie spots me with his beady eyes. He is a carbon copy of Mackay from the TV sit-com Porridge. Quite expressionless, he shuffles to attention and issues a challenge through clenched teeth. This acoustic obstruction, together with passing traffic noise, makes his words unintelligible. I persist with my greeting until from behind him appears the smallest marine I have ever seen, struggling to hold up an automatic weapon. At last, a voice of wisdom interjects.

'Col, for God's sake man, what are you doing?' shouts a frantic Flek, 'You have approached a sensitive MOD depot as a complete stranger with a heavy pack on your back. They are not to know that all you are carrying are some stale sandwiches and dirty underwear. Is the penny dropping, Col? This could be your Armageddon!'

The coin drops! With not a little panic I mutter the old music hall joke 'Armageddon out of here' and beat a hasty retreat.

Flek rants on: 'How bloody stupid can you be, Col. If this had been downtown Bagdad you would have been a blown away.'

Flustered, I speed up the main road but the Army are not finished with me yet. Still on 'red alert', they follow me down the road in the form of a one-ton truck. Heaving up an incline, the vehicle struggles past belching out noxious blue fumes which sends me reeling, tears streaming from my eyes. Are the Marines trying to take me out? Surely they wouldn't do it this way? Only the KGB, STASI or MI5 would try a stunt like this!

Hardly have I wiped my eyes when I spot a discarded audio disc lying on the grass verge, tossed like a frisbee from a passing car. Clearly a download, its title written in felt tip says Cradle to the Grave.

'Oh, how appropriate,' says a relieved Flek.

Pulling myself together, I reach a garden nursery. It's closed, but a man – probably the proprietor – stands by the entrance gate holding a golf bag. We chat and he becomes interested in my purpose. He suddenly says, 'I have two young boys who have the metabolic neurodegenerative condition Mucpolysacharide (MPS).'

I enquire as to their future, and sadly he replies that probably neither will reach their twelfth birthdays. As he is unaware of CLIMB, I furnished him with details. Suddenly his golfing partner drives up and he is gone.

'Bet that has blown you away, Col,' says Flek sympathetically.

He's right – for a little while I am taken aback. The experience abruptly reminds me that I am not on a holiday. 'Awareness' has got to be my constant buzzword. Some 16,000 families within the UK endure such uncertainty.

I turn off the main road towards Topsham. Passing through a small industrial estate I can't help but notice a three metre-high wicker sculpture in the form of a dancing ballerina. Balanced on one unit's front lawn, it is refreshingly unusual and cheers me up no end after a difficult morning.

A little further on, at some roadworks, I test out my highways perception for the first time, and fail – judging by the road gang's gesticulating. I will get plenty of practice during the coming year.

Somewhat unnerved I reach my destination.

I am to be the guest of landlords Dave and Liz Hodges at the Globe Hotel, Topsham. Putting my entire stay together is host Chris Beard, brother of John an old friend of mine who, with Daphne his wife, got me leisure walking in the first place.

We dine with Norman Croucher OBE, a legend in the climbing world. Norman lost both his legs in a schoolboy railway accident, but this hasn't stopped him climbing/exploring some of the world's greatest mountains.

I go to bed in disbelief. How did the day pan out like that?

Back came the answer: 'Because you didn't engage the grey matter son, that's how. Now promise me you will buck up tomorrow mate. Observation is one thing; intervention is another.'

Flek is on a tirade: 'Remember the old adage, Colin, "Shape Up or Ship Out." '

I need an evening concert to calm down.

Select: Stan Getz with 'Desinfinardo' and Grieg's 'Holberg Suite', followed by ELO's 'Now That Our Love Has Gone'. Wish Track is John Coltrane's 'My Favourite Things' (which would run for fourteen minutes).

DAY 22
January 22nd - Topsham to Shaldon – 8 miles

Planning this venture means overcoming the problems of crossing the plethora of estuaries in the west country, where the ferries do not run out of season. Today is the very first such challenge.

Chris Beard has come to my rescue and has fixed it with the ferryman at Topsham, Mike Stevens, to get me across the Exe Estuary. Although it's his day off, he gets me across in five minutes. This kind gesture saves me a seven-mile tramp around the top end of the estuary.

On the other side a canal (cut) runs alongside the estuary. Two fishermen have just hooked a couple of pike. Normally fishermen are sullen, but these lads take interest in what I am doing.   Co-incidence strikes again – one of the them informs me his brother lives a few doors away from my previous home at Nyetimber, West Bognor They search

With Chris Beard on the Topsham Ferry.

their pockets and gift a few quid for a drink. I start the long trail back down the estuary to the sea.

This is a wonderful place, rich with birdlife. A couple I meet say they will later donate to CLIMB by post. The silence is broken only by the trains, this time on the estuary's west bank – Isambard Kingdom Brunel's fast line to Penzance. At nearby Starcross the great man used a site to design and construct another kind of power (pneumatic propulsion), but this time he was unsuccessful.

I clamber up and get onto the seafront promenade into Dawlish. Here the permanent way track gets dramatically close to the sea. The massive locos are perilously near as I walk the lower prom. Along this open stretch, waves pound the sea wall, often covering the trains with spray – all part of Brunel's plan to master the terrain and mesmerise the lines passengers. This spray now causes problems with the overhead electricity conductors of modern train power units.

Climbing a railway footbridge on the sea front, I am enthralled as the powerful beasts suddenly swing out of the estuary from behind the town's facade. With lights on, they roar along the seafront track, waves threatening to engulf them, then pass beneath me – a thrilling experience.

ITV West has made contact and catch up with me at the Smugglers Inn on the Teignmouth Road. I survive another interview, and the reporter, David Lawrence, surprisingly donates a fiver, his expenses for the day!

It's a long haul uphill into Teignmouth and I pass onto the impressive regenerated Shaldon Bridge. Standing here and smiling is Rodney Bowen, whom I haven't seen for decades. He and I were in the SJAB Cadets together at Bognor Regis in our teens. Both of us went onto Chichester High School, where he became school captain. It is such a thrill to meet up with him and wife Wendy after so long.

From the school play Rodney developed a lifetime love of the stage and still selflessly gives up his time to ensure that the theatre in Teignmouth maintains productions.

Today I noticed that some daffodils and primroses are out, confirming the early moderate climate of the west country.

DAY 23
23rd January – Shaldon to Paignton – 14 miles

Rodney is going to accompany me for a couple of miles. I am so sorry to say goodbye to him, my visit having spawned a trip down memory lane. The Way is challenging, one of the hardest days yet, with considerable undulations. The sea is passive today.

A rock fall at Babbacombe Beach makes it look somewhat tatty. Lots of dogs are taking their owners out for walks. Making my way around the Hope's Nose promontory I end up at the TIO at New Harbour, Torquay.

Torbay has often been called the English Riviera. It is amazing how a generous landscaping of palm trees can transform a place.

Flek pipes up, 'I've been keeping an eye out for Fawlty Towers, Col, but no sighting. Plenty of Sybils tottering along the Prom, though,' he adds mischievously.

The TIO Staff recognise me from the IVT broadcast, as does a traffic warden. How long will this fame last? I stride out around impressive Torbay towards Paignton, to be hosted by Kevin and Nicky Jeffery's mum and dad, Doreen and Gordon Bird.

It has been a day to exercise 'fortitude'. Unaware of my hardship, Flek, the lazy tyke, dozes for most of the day. He wakes just the once, grunting his Peter Sellers impersonation from the Goon Show: *'Struth mate are you all right?'*

Then my guardian angel drifts back into oblivion.

DAY 24
24th January – Paignton to Brixham – 7 miles

After a splendid stay with Doreen and Gordon Bird, my route continues along the promenade. Down at the Paignton Pier I enjoy fresh coffee and muffin. The harbour seems deserted, but no – Flek spots Paignton's 'unofficial' beach wardens, i.e. four old boys sunning themselves on a bench stood against a marine workshop wall.

'Look at this lot,' he exclaims 'Nothing else to do but to chew the fat, probably reviewing all the things they talked about yesterday,' he presumes. 'Getting old, Col. Is this what life comes to? Tell you what, let's go over and give them the kiss of life,' he says with an eye to mischief.

I approach the old codgers, blurting out, 'It's The Last of the Summer Wine. Which one of you is Compo?'

They all immediately point at each other. I think they've been through this routine before. All retired, they comprise of two Yorkies, a Brummie and a Banbury Cross. They meet here most mornings when the weather is right, and yak about topics from the TV soaps to how

'The Last of the Summer Wine', Paignton.

they can get Northern Rock out of its present predicament. There follows some priceless banter.

An engineer covered in overalls appears from the workshop; they address him as Spanner.

'You lot still here. Why don't you all sod off, you're making the place untidy,' he yells.

The old boys retort with abusive answers amid raucous laughter. It is obviously a ritual played out most mornings.

'Why do they call you Spanner?' I enquire.

He smiles.

'It all depends on what I have in my hand. Tomorrow I could be called Wrench or Screwdriver!'

He offers them a gesture that I don't think I have seen before and disappears back into the works.

They quiz me as to my destination and purpose. The one I have nominated Smiler suggests a whip-round, and after much fumbling in pockets they come up with a total of £2.30, bless 'em. As one of them explains, 'Its emergency pay-outs like this which the government's fuel and light allowance comes in handy for.' Another admits he had been to Tenerife on his.

They all wave until I am out of view. Old boys! They had let on they were all younger than me!

Berry Head, upon which Brixham stands, is in view all day. Unlike yesterday the going is easy, and I arrive by 2pm.

I raid a tea shop; then wander around the 'tat' shops. On a bench at the foot of the Prince William of Orange statue I catch up on phone calls to home, CLIMB and also to Ruth Brooks my next host (she saw my article in the SWCP Journal and is to put me up for two nights). She picks me up with Colin. her friend, and we drive well inland to her home at Totnes.

For dinner the three of us plus her lady friend sit down to the best fish pie that I have ever tasted. It is cooked by Colin; his culinary secret is to use coconut milk.

I have now entered the shipping forecast area Plymouth.

DAY 25

25th January – Brixham to Kingswear (Dart Lower Ferry) – 11 miles

Ruth gets me back to Brixham. Free of the rucksack, I race away on a fine day passing memorial seats dedicated to John Snook and later John Alderton (same name as my good friend at Bognor). At Berry Head lighthouse I get my photo snapped by young girl.

'She must be impressed with the beard Col, can't say it does anything for me,' mumbles Flek.

I ignore his sarcastic remark.

I meet up with casual friends for the day – Beverley and Tony from Cheltenham, who walk with me half the way. This coastal stretch is classified as strenuous, but Bev sets a cracking pace, forging a head, The Path takes us via Sharkham Point, Scabbacombe Head and Outer Forward Point. There is a splendid stretch through Warren Wood, part of the ancestral home estate of Lt.Col. Jones VC, the Falklands hero.

The last mile reveals splendid views of the River Dart and Dartmouth. To finish I follow some steps leading through an arch down to the Lower Ferry slipway at Kingswear.

Waiting for Ruth to pick me up gives me a chance to view the Paignton to Dartmouth Steam railway station. The area is a tourist's dream. I shall have more to say about it tomorrow.

Now once again the long drive back to Totnes. Over the coming months many of my hosts will cover considerable distances to ensure my correct passage.

Metabolic Diseases – What Are They?

A dictionary definition of metabolism: 'The total sum of chemical processes that occur in living organisms. resulting in growth, production of energy and the elimination of waste'

The body depends on good nutrition for health, growth and function, digesting and absorbing the food we eat, and breaking it down to proteins and amino acids, carbohydrates and fats. In addition we digest trace elements and other food constituents. For the health, growth and development of our bodily functions (including internal organs such as heart, brain, kidneys, liver and muscles) we need a normal metabolic system.

All these processes are programmed by genes which direct enzymes to carry out them out. Enzymes are proteins which speed up chemical changes in the body. In healthy individuals all these processes occur automatically until something goes wrong. When there is a problem with metabolism, one or more of these processes are liable to go wrong and we become ill. Metabolism is closely controlled by genes and so when there is a genetic fault, or mutation – an inborn error of metabolism (IEM) – this may cause a metabolic disease.

Lorenzo's Oil

Possibly one of the most high profiled metabolic disease victims was Lorenzo Odone, the American son of parents who became famous throughout the world with the release of the 1992 film 'Lorenzo's Oil', starring Susan Sarandon and Nick Nolte.

It was clear from his earliest years that Lorenzo was a bright child. By five he was fluent in several languages, but at the age of six he was diagnosed with Adrenoleukodystrophy (ALD), a rare inherited metabolic condition which mainly affects boys and usually results in brain failure and premature death.

His parents Augusto and Michaela stubbornly refused to accept his diagnosis and began an exhaustive quest for affective treatment. They eventually enlisted the help of a British scientist, Don Suddaby, who came out of retirement to produce an olive/rapeseed extract which was to become known as Lorenzo's Oil. Driven by their son's rapid deterioration, they administered it. Lorenzo lived on long past the life expectancy age for the condition, but died aged 30 in 2008 after decades of loving care.

How do we inherit errors of metabolism? It is important to remember that one of the basic rules of genetics is that we receive half of our genes from our mother and the other half from our father. If we receive a gene that has an abnormality in it from one parent, but the gene from other parent is intact, then usually this does not lead to illness. This mode of inheritance is called autosomal recessive, meaning (1) that the defect does not depend on the sex of the person inheriting it, and (2) that people having only one copy of the defective gene are clinically normal.

However, when both parents are carriers of the same condition the chance in each pregnancy for their child to have a disorder is twenty-five per cent. There is a fifty per cent chance that the child will be a carrier like the parents, and a twenty-five per cent chance that the child will be normal, with no defective gene.

IEMs may begin early in life, even before birth, but they commonly become apparent after birth in the first few days or months of life. Others may show up only later in childhood or even in adulthood. An IEM can cause many kinds of symptoms. Children born seemingly healthy may develop epilepsy, loss of sight or speech, motor and mental disabilities before death – usually between the ages of five and thirty years. Treatments are available for some metabolic disorders, and a few others can be managed by diet. Much research is still needed to find new and better treatments.

Over seven hundred inherited metabolic disorders have been identified, some of them quite rare, and around 16,000 families in the UK are affected.

Day 26
26th January –Dartmouth to Torcross (Slapton Sands) – 10 miles

Ruth Brooks returns one last time. She has taken to the task with such great enthusiasm.

I catch the Lower Ferry early from the slipway I visited yesterday. It is packed with kids making for school on the Dartmouth side. The sun has come up, but much of the river valley is still in shadow. It is a short but idyllic crossing. Huge trees overhang the River Dart down to Dartmouth Castle at its mouth. Later I shall be quizzed on my 'unforgettable places', and the morning's departure from this jetty is going to be one of them.

This stage has a 'moderate' rating. Swathes of hydrangeas appear. I find a seat for a snack and hear the sea pounding into caves below me.

Past Combe Point the Path detours inland. I meet up with a large shooting party in all the traditional gear with guns stood down. and we exchange 'reports'.

'That's a joke by the way, Flek, a play on words – get it? He looks puzzled, unable to believe that I could be so inane.

The Green Dragon at Stoke Flemming provides a good value three-quid lunch.

I trudge into the Blackpool Sands, a resort which seems just a little out of place, but popular even at this time of the year. I take tea here and then head on. It turns out to be a very close-contour day, and I have to negotiate three stiff hills before Strete. Ahead of me is the geographical phenomenon which is Slapton Sands. It is not sand at all, but minute pebbles.

In 1944 this six-mile stretch of sands was chosen by the US Army to practise D-Day landings. During Operation Tiger here the troop ships were off shore when surprised and attacked by the fast German E-boats and nearly a thousand troops lost their lives. A recovered Sherman tank stands as a memorial to the disaster.

My hosts for the next three day are Bob (an old working colleague of my jazz club friend Ken Marshal) and Yvonne Ashling, who live at nearby Chillington.

The day delivers wall-to-wall sunshine. I complete the remaining three miles of Slapton. At 9.30am it is just me and a lone fisherman enjoying this lovely beach on a glorious morning. Passing through Beesands, I have a bite to eat at Hallsands.

Precariously perched at the head of the beach, this village of 120 souls was once completely lost in a storm – fortunately without loss of life. Excessive dredging off shore had removed natural sea defences and the place was swamped.

I walk a long way out to Start Point to view the lighthouse, but it's closed.

Flek gets peeved: 'It's a pity they didn't announce this on the entrance gate half a mile back. Col.'

'My sentiments exactly,' I reply in exasperation.

The first SWCP two-way mile post appears – Poole 168/Minehead 462 it indicates, so I am gradually getting there.

I meet a young lad birdwatching. He has ingeniously rigged up a tripod camera with binoculars strapped to the lens. Across a small field, marked off as a preservation area, he is observing the elusive cirl buntings in their habitat. I take a peep, then quiz him about several unusually light-coloured buzzards I have seen that day. He confirms that I wasn't seeing things. The buntings are not rare but are very much native to this coastal area.

Suddenly a group of people arrives at the spot. Our quiet chat is about to be shattered. They are in fact the lad's family, and one of them, his sister, lets their dog loose. It runs straight into the protected area and scatters the birds. The lad goes ballistic, screaming abuse at his thoughtless sibling. Oh dear! Wishing to remember him as I found him, I hastily leave them to their bickering.

'Don't these twitchers get twitchy,' sniggers a highly amused Flek.

Stopping at the Coastguard hut, Prawle Point, for a snack, I am offered a cup of tea by the volunteers.

In Portlemouth a girl takes a shot of me and forwards it on her phone to CLIMB

'Now they know where you are,' she says. It's a thoughtful gesture.

At the finish Bob and son-in-law Pete turn up on time. What a relief! It has been a wonderful day, but I am shattered. Pete gives us a white-knuckle ride home down miles of narrow Devon lanes.

In the evening his wife throws a birthday party for Yvonne, with all the family present.

The evening concert: Coleman Hawkins 'Hello Lola' (an unknown Glenn Miller in the ensemble), Jelly Roll Morton's 'The Chant', Caterina Valente 'The Breeze and I' and exerpts from Rachmaninov's 'Rhapsody on a Theme by Paganini'.

Early morning, Slapton Sands.

Day 28
28th January – Salcombe to Hope Cove – 8 miles

Today I will undertake some of South Devon's finest coast walking. A road walk out of the sleeping town leads to a viewpoint giving stunning views across to Starehole Bay. I yomp on to reach the rocky grandeur of Bolt Head, turning 90 degrees west. With the rucksack this stage is comparatively easy, far from its 'strenuous' grading. I stare out to the Ham Stone rock which put paid to a grain clipper in 1936. No such storm today: the sea is calm and very blue.

Soar Mill Cove presents modern horrors. On a breezy but sunny day I find the dazzling white sands are strewn with rubbish. It looks as if a whole skip has been has been tipped out. Particularly grotesque is a television set split into three parts which lie stuck into the sand. In this remote and beautiful place, it is doubtful if a land trip was responsible. This environmental outrage is probably the result of a dump at sea. The few people present walk about nodding their heads in disbelief.

Flek speaks out: 'One of the things that makes life worth living is the over-all sense of order, but, some people don't have a social conscience to join in. Who would deliberately spoil a beautiful beach like this?'

He shakes his head in despair. There is nothing more one can say.

Thankfully I am soon absorbing the beauty of this coastline again. I am virtually alone, getting into Hope Cove, a solitary figure sipping a pint in the Hope and Anchor. The barmaid yawns and declares that the village dies in January.

I call into the post office for chocolate and hear a gloomy forcast. It's under threat: will this mainstay of social need survive the coming government review and be granted its impending notice of renewal? More local nail biting! In the meantime the villagers are poised like spring flowers waiting for the new tourist season to trigger. It is very important down here.

Bob and Yvonne come and get me.

29th January – Hope Cove to Modbury – 10 miles

The coastal geography now gets difficult. The estuaries of three rivers, the Avon, Erme and Yealm, lie ahead.

At this time of the year my route can only be determined by the combination of three strategies. At the Avon is a seven mile diversion inland to a bridge. At the Erme a similar inconvenience can be avoided by wading across at low tide, while hailing a local boat out of season is the only option at the Yealm. All this in one day! Any tough outward-bound type with a stiff upper lip would wave aside such challenges but I am a naive, flabby-chinned nerk of a nervous disposition. I need a second opinion, and I get it.

'You've got your schedule to maintain, so be sensible, Col. Go inland and by-pass the lot,' advises Flek.

It makes sense, so I turn north, cutting across country to pick up the A379 and walk on towards Modbury. I ring my next host, Sonia Whitaker, and ask her to pick me up there.

On the way I call in to the Thurstone Hotel, a large holiday complex. At the end of a hotel management course at Chichester College many years ago my eldest daughter Suzanne spent some time here on work experience.

I enter the posh foyer and asked for the personnel officer. Now looking very much a 'man of the road', I get some wry looks from the well groomed guests, but I bluff it out. I needn't have worried. A charming lady arrives, arranges coffee for me and, to my delight, confirms that she remembers Suzanne as an energetic member of the staff. I depart a proud father with a spring in my step.

At Aveton Gifford I pass a couple of hundred ewes. Spotting me, they trot across field and start bleating. They think that my rucksack contains their grub. Their crescendo is deafening.

Covering his ears, Flek stretches his artistic ingenuity. 'Some of the best ideas come from the surreal,' he shouts over the din. 'It occurs to me that in a future Pixel cartoon movie this 'choir' could be shown appearing on Britain's Got Talent. Let's face it they would be up to the usual competitive standard of the programme.'

He goes on, 'For story tension there would have to be a baddie' involved – say their owner farmer acting as a greedy agent, fleecing them of their record deal.'

He pauses, and then adds 'I've even thought of a showbiz name for them. What about 'Sean and his Flockers!'

'Perfect' I reply trying to sound interested. 'Well, weirder plots than yours have already been thought up. What you need now is a producer and lots of money.'

His voice slumps: 'There are so many snags for us artistic types.'

By road traffic law all towns announce themselves by signage a few miles out. It is good tourist marketing if subtle hints are dropped to entice motorists pay a visit. So on the Continent we get 'Twinned with Ashenphalter' or 'Souffle dans le Seine'. For us Brits 'You are now in Banoffie Pie Country' is a prime example. Modbury has pulled out all the stops by stating its 'The First Plastic Bag Free Town in England' on it approach signs!

'Is that all they could think of,' taunts Flek, following up with, 'At least the council is trying.'

Sonia meets me in town. Embarrassed, I ask if we can retrace my steps as I have left my walking poles against a gate a couple of miles out of town. No luck of retrieval – some tramp has beaten me to it. So far on this journey I have also 'misplaced' two hats and a glove. Not a bad effort, in three months I may be naked!

I am to stay two days with Sonia, one of my oldest school friends going way back to the Nyewood Lane infant school, Bognor Regis, in the 1940s; she now lives at Ivybridge.

She has driven over to collect what remains of that five-year-old dirty, smelly little boy with holes in his trousers she once proffered a shy smile to across our classroom's ink-stained desks.

Those were inquisitive years for us boys, a whole decade before puberty. During respites from Cowboys and Indians we used to wonder why those soppy girls wore frocks. They also used a different toilet! What was that all about? Being allowed to sit near them in class was OK, but when the bell went being denied access in the form of a brick wall at playtime was baffling.

What happened to Sonia? She moved to another school in town and I didn't really catch up with her again. Well, shooting marbles, striking conkers or flicking fag cards with other spotty boys quickly softened the emotional separation and I soon got over it. You have to remember that all this predates Brief Encounter.

Besides, in our class I sat next to a Dick Whittington – his real name, honest. When he grew up he did go to London, but without a cat he never stood a chance of picking up the Lord Mayor's job so he became a police superintendent instead.

Day 30
30th January – Ivybridge to Wembury (back on the coast) – 9 miles

The South West Coastal Path Association, with its office at Ivybridge, is unique being the only national path organisation with salaried staff. Sonia accompanies me on a short visit, where I have a chat with Liz Wallis, its secretary. They had been kind enough to include some editorial about WALK GB 4 CLIMB in their magazine, resulting in several of its members offering accommodation.

Crossing the A38 I take the road down to Yeahampton (pronounced 'Yamton' by the locals) and I soon find myself on the Erme Plym Trail, a charming loop passing through woods and meadows while crossing streams. Wild garlic, crocus and polyanthus are out – spring is here! I arrive at the muddy seafront car park at Wembury.

On a little hill near-bye stands the parish church St Werburgh-on-the-Hill, where I later learn that my very good friend Daphne Ashton's parents had got married.

There are warships out to sea. I am now not far from Plymouth Sound. Sonia picks me up.

DAY 31

31st January – Wembury to Plymouth – 7 miles

As Sonia drives back into the car park at Wembury, Flek blurts out, *'Why did you have to mention spring yesterday? Just look – it's chucking it down out there.'*

The weather has turned. Thunderous seas whipped up by a near gale pound the rocks, accompanied by heavy rain. Sonia and I say our goodbyes, but I struggle get out: the wind catches the rucksack and I nearly go over. High foliage along the Path offers protection, but it is a wild morning and I get battered. Two miles on, at Heybrook Bay, I turn into Plymouth Sound. Magically the weather abates, the sun comes out and the wind drops like a stone.

It is my first ever view of the Sound, and how spectacular it is! A naval ship glides by and I can hear the captain addressing the crew on the intercom. Then I move on to the massive fortification at Bovisand.

Finishing at Mount Batten point, it is my intention to catch the ferry, but my next hosts, John and Margaret Desborough, have kindly driven round the Cattewater Creek to greet me.

They are SWCPA members who saw my appeal for accommodation in its magazine and contacted CLIMB. I'm taken to the Hoe and observe Smeaton's Tower – originally the top half of the first Eddystone Lighthouse. I am shall be staying at their neat bungalow for two nights.

The first month has seen me cover more than three hundred miles. I am becoming extremely fit, and the kit is OK, although I'm not sure about my Gregory rucksack. It's too clever by half, with seventeen adjustment straps! I will comment more about this problem later.

DAY 32

1st February – Rest day – Plymouth

The Desboroughs take me on a tour of Plymouth harbour and then out shopping in the town. I purchase some replacement poles and get another hat plus gas canisters,

We drive onto Dartmoor to view Princetown and its famous prison. What a forbidding place to do porridge. The phrase 'at her majesty's pleasure' surely adds further mockery to any sentence. No wonder the bloodhounds were given a run out so often in olden times.

I haven't sensed any height gain during our excursion up to the moor, but to my surprise children are snowballing.

Back at the house I tipped out the contents of the rucksack and take stock. Water is weight. With so many 'water holes' en route I reduce the fluid.

An exasperated Flek points out, 'Col you won't be camping out for weeks yet, so why did you add gas canisters at this stage?'

I tell him that the sooner I get used to carry the eventual weight the better. It's a futile answer and he knows it. Similarly, in hindsight I don't really need the bulky Freeloader Solar panel which arrived in the post. This device will keep me in touch when out of mobile contact, but I won't need it until I reach the Highlands months later.

The Desboroughs are perfect hosts, and have arranged a most interesting day. My head hits the pillow and I am soon away – but morning will come all too soon.

DAY 33

2nd February – Cremyl (Plymouth) to Portwrinkle – 13 miles

Time to amend my rucksack inventory again. Out will go slippers, some socks, tape recorder (old model that has failed), used maps and a fleece. My hosts have received fresh maps and dehydrated food packs. Frequent pre-arranged dumps of these items will arrive in the months ahead.

John drops me at Stonehouse to catch the Cremyll Ferry. I have now entered Cornwall, which has a Celtic history. Its distinctive black flag will be a constant reminder.

I pass into the Mount Edgecumbe Country Park, which holds the National Camelia Collection. Many of the buds have burst, creating a striking display. I leave this magnificent harbour through woodlands towards the quaint twin villages of Kingsand and Cawsand, sampling some apple pie and coffee on the way. From Penlee Point I see the Eddystone Lighthouse some twelve miles out. John Smeaton and, of course, the Stevenson family achieved incredible lighthouse engineering feats around the coasts of Britain. How on earth did they do it?

Swinging around Lillery's Cove I get to a deserted chapel on Ramme Head. I am not alone. Chris and Kate are sitting on its steps, and they share their coffee with me. It is bright and quiet save for the constant boom of the waves below. No red flag at the Tregantle Fort Ranges so I can later walk across the golf course into Portwrinkle.

My next Host is John Dyson who has driven twenty five miles from Tavistock to collect me. Tomorrow he will bring me back. It is another example of Host care.

John is from a CLIMB family. His son, now in his twenties, has Niemann Pick Disease, caused by enzymatic deficiency, and depending on which of three forms is present (A, B or C) can lead to early death. At present he is a paramedic.

In the evening we share a meal with a lady friend who expounds on the difficulties of working for the MOD at Plymouth.

Day 34
3rd February – Portwrinkle to Polperro (via Looe) – 12 miles

After breakfast we take the long drive back to Portwrinkle. I set out past the minuscule harbour into a howling wind. Keeping upright is difficult. Chris and Kate (acquaintances from yesterday) catch up with me again, and we yomp on to Seaton, escaping into a café for lunch.

Looe is still a long way off. Heavy rain continues: by the time I get to the bridge there I am soaked. I snack and take the inland route to Polperro, ending up at Talland village a little lost.

Mobile phone reception is out of the question in this area due to the many coombs (small valleys with steep sides) that stretch down to the coast. I come across at first hand one of the West Country's economic problems – a plague of second-home properties. I need a landline, so I bang on several doors, but so many properties are only occupied at weekends and school holidays. Passing through the West Country I am to hear many locals bemoan this holiday phenomenon for reasons of lost economy and neighbourhood depopulation.

Finally I rattle a gate and a friendly chap appears with his young son. I am invited in to meet his family over coffee and given access to a landline. My next host, Alan Leftly, says he is on his way. The couple take an interest in my project, and with good cause: their boisterous young son running around had open heart surgery when he was two.

Alan arrives and drives me back to one of the finest farmhouse conversions you will ever see. In two years this quiet plumber has worked wonders on the place. The Leftlys are a CLIMB family. He and wife Jackie have a son, Nick, who is twenty and has the metabolic condition of Congenital Adrenol Hyperplasia. A spirited lad, he has had to give up college. For monitoring his parents take him the long way to Bristol on a monthly basis.

It has been one of the most exhausting days yet, but I have arrived at a 'palace' fit for my needs, and I sleep soundly.

DAY 35

4th February – Polperro to Tywardraeth – 13 miles

Alan drops me off in Polperro, which geographically lies in a long fissure to the sea. Narrow streets are the norm. I wonder how the traffic manoeuvres during the summer months. The answer is 'by the tight discipline of the locals'. Unfortunately restraint does not extend to some of the 'emmets' (Cornwall's derogatory term for summer tourists: it means 'ant'). Alan recalls a bizarre incident when a motorist pulling a caravan tried to negotiate an impossible gap, getting stuck between two buildings.

I present less of an obstacle as I go north uphill to circumvent the village to pick up the SWCP at Frogmore Farm. I trek around two headlands to reach the River Fowey ferry at Polruan. On the other side I take in a heavy lunch. Immediate exercise after a large intake tends to induce a wearisome bloating effect. Stoic walkers just grimace and belch through it.

The Path goes out to Gribbin Head. Time is getting on, so I cut across this peninsular and pick up part of the Saints Way (this runs across Cornwall forty-six miles from Fowey to Padstow). The going is extremely muddy.

Passing some farm sheds I come across an appealing sight. A little girl of about four years, dwarfed by her gumboots, is with her grandma in a small enclosure tending five orphan lambs. Holding one in her arms, she tells me they all have names and proudly reels them off. Ah!

At Polkerris I pick up the coastal path again and march into Polmear. The CLIMB team have fixed me up with B & B, but unfortunately it is a little inland at Tywardraeth, so I slog on to the Elmswood Guest House (01726 814 221). The proprietors, Graham and Angela Hoskins, look after me very well.

The daily mileage has been rising, but my overall fitness seems to be coping. Graham drops me back to Par, and I proceed through an old china clay works towards Spit Point. Following the golf course, I am soon at Carlyon Bay. I have been here before and know of the row which has raged for years about a proposed futuristic development on the beach. It's a long, embittered story of warring local factions. In the car park stands a security kiosk. I asked the uniformed guard if there had been any progress.

'Don't ask me, mate, I only work here,' comes a terse reply.

The Path leads to the quaint harbour at Charlestown. The narrow entrance is clearly designed as a vessel refuge, but just how they pass in and out is difficult to envisage. A warm welcoming café serves me a big pot of tea with door-step toast and lashings of butter and jam. A Path collapse further on means a detour to Pentewan. Along the way I stop to chat with Dave and Rob of Cornwall County Council, who are installing improvements to the Path fence. Great blokes to chat to, they are the salt of the earth, and I take their photo.

This stretch is strenuous, so after a couple of hours I am glad to cut through a twitten past tumbling cottages that adjoin the long flight of steps into Mevagissey harbour. Here I purchase provisions for the night and walk out to Chapel Point. (This spot will for ever have significance for me: see the following page.)

On arrival at Goran Haven, two blows – the chippie is closed and my bed for the night is half way up yet another hill! My B & B hosts at the delightfully named 'Bumble Bees' (01726 842 219) are John and Patsy Bamford. She is a slight woman and he an amiable, cheerful old boy who is shuffling around on sticks awaiting a third hip replacement.

The ruler of the house is the largest Newfoundland dog I have ever seen. Chocolate brown, he is about a rug and half in size and sprawls across the kitchen floor oblivious to anybody. Patsy takes him down to the beach most days. Surprisingly for his breed, he doesn't take to water! It must be a monumental task for this small lady to persuade him up the hill again. It's lovely chatting to a couple clearly making the most of things. I'm made to feel very welcome.

JAN

'It is not what you have lost but what you have left that counts.'
– Howard Russell
(William Wyler: *The Best Years of Our Lives*)

I have made my way through Mevagissey and Portmellon. The Coastal Path then stretches away to Chapel Point along a private cul-de-sac approach road. To my surprise, into view comes a tiny isthmus housing several white-washed properties surrounded by trees that, despite their exposed location, are standing upright. It is an unusual sight: the place has a Mediterranean appearance about it.

It is a fine early February day giving up a watery sun, a stiff off-shore wind clipping off the tops of the waves, leaving an impressionist-like white hue as far as the eye can see. The scene has me transfixed. Opposite the tiny community I follow a semi- circular path at the foot of a tall grassy bank. Nothing could have prepared me for what happens next.

Wandering around the bend in the path I am astonished to see a woman in her forties sitting upright on the edge of a wooden seat staring intensely out to sea. I haven't seen anyone for several miles. Such is her concentration that she doesn't notice my presence until the very last moment.

We say our helloes. Her name is Jan. She enquires about the purpose of my journey and I relate my encounter with a teenager in respite care during the final stages of life. The woman reflects, and then her own story comes flooding out.

'Colin' she says, 'I am in respite myself.'

She explains that in her late forties she remarried. Just two months later her newfound happiness was shattered by a near-death car crash which left her husband a total invalid and brain-damaged. He has been in a near coma for a year, during which time she has become his full-time carer. She appears to have had little solace from her new in-laws and total indifference from the perpetrator of the accident. Her two children from a previous marriage have stood by her.

I become intrigued by her presence at this lonely spot so late in the day. Why is she here? Apparently she has come from Lincolnshire to stay at Mevergissy, and has then deliberately walked out to this beautiful spot which she visited many years ago as young girl. She has been struck by the panoramic beauty and solitude of Chapel Point, which has come to represent a consoling place – somewhere which she knows will offer her the spiritual uplift she so desperately needs in order to face the life-long task ahead.

She suddenly turns to me and says, with a half smile of defiance, 'Anyway, I still have him, Colin.'

I have become stricken with emotion but am struggling to conceal it.

'I've got to go now – best of luck on your trip, Colin.'

The circumstances of her story related in this idyllic place immobilise me for a while. I look back, but she has disappeared. I keep thinking that I have been on the location of a dramatic movie set.

I eventually get a grip and move off, but it is no good – tears continue to stream down my face. Have I dreamed this all up?

Without any doubt this is the most unnerving encounter of my whole trip.

Chapel Point, where I met Jan. [Photograph © Kath Featherstone]

DAY 37

6th February – Goran Haven to Portloe – 9 miles

Leaving my caring hosts, I climb over the dog and wave my goodbye. The Bamfords are a wonderful couple, the courtesies of yesteryear ingrained in them.

It is yet another strenuous jaunt today, but who cares? The weather is just great. A couple of miles on sees me at Dodman Point. I find a National Trust man, Dave, carrying out repairs to the impressive stone crucifix which dominates. This old timer explains that someone has taken the trouble to come all the way out here to nick the lightning conductor's copper. He is a philosophical individual, happily tending his task spurred on by a younger colleague who is content to watch.

Suddenly Dave takes a hard look at me and says, 'Beards make you more virile. Did you know that?'

I try to ward off his remark: 'So is that just another example of the witchcraft that goes on down here?' I reply.

He laughs, winks and we part, chuckling.

Flek comments, 'I bet they were all locking up their daughters when he was about in his youth. Did you notice the twinkle in his eyes?'

It is a tough five miles to Portloe, passing Portholland on the way. The cliff path has a number of challenging undulations, with more use of steps, but the views are so rewarding. I reach an old Coastguard lookout station now reoccupied by volunteers from the Maritime Coastguard Agency. They make me a cup of tea.

Portloe has been a long time coming! I shuffle up the road into the village and fall into the Ship Inn (01872 501 356), my home for the night. The landlord Peter Swannell, a Londoner, greets me heartily with a pot of tea, apologises for the present accommodation deficiencies and offers his personal bath. What hospitality!

I have a bar meal and with his wife Teresa and brother Mark, a partner in the business, discuss the vagaries of keeping the pub open in the winter.

Despite the renovations going on there is 'room at the inn', and I sleep well.

DAY 38

7th February – Portloe to St Mawes – 10 miles

The Place ferry at St Anthony is a summer service only, so my plan is compromised. Because of the geography I shall unfortunately have to bypass most of the St Anthony peninsula. Instead I make for St Mawes to catch a ferry to Falmouth tomorrow. My winter start means that I am always going to have a logistical problem with the ferries around the south-west coast.

First I trek three miles towards Carne Beach. The first section is excellent walking, but challenging in places until Nare Head is reached. Here I have good views of the impressive Gull Rock offshore.

One property up on the top of the cliff jogs my memory, and I rack my brains where I have seen it before. Finally I remember: of course, it was used in the memorable TV drama The Camomile Lawn. Sitting down for a break, I enjoy a bar of chocolate while watching a pair of buzzards in aerial courtship.

At Carne I divert inland, keeping me on the correct side of the Percui inlet in order to reach St Mawes. It's an uninteresting detour, although the hamlet of St Just in Roseland has a certain ambience – its very name raises my spirits.

On arrival at St Mawes I find that the CLIMB team have hit the accommodation jackpot. I am to be accommodated in the superbly appointed Idle Rocks Hotel at the invitation of the manager, Chris Skidmore. He and his efficient staff welcome me. I'm allocated the best room in the hotel, on the first floor with double-aspect windows overlooking the harbour. What a treat!

Later I am somewhat embarrassed: having discarded my slippers at Plymouth I have to go down to dinner in my socks. Up to now I haven't needed a change into casual footwear. Everything I wear is extra weight to carry. It won't be until I get to Morcambe in May that I properly address this omission in my inventory.

8th February – St Mawes to Mawnan Smith – 8 miles

I feel, as a scruffy walker, a definite feeling of intrusion when waking up in a luxurious bed.

'Its no good, Col, you've got to get up,' orders an envious Flek.

Taking full advantage of a top quality mattress, I vigorously squirm around seeking to massage my aching legs, then lower my whole creaking carcass onto the shag-pile carpet. Crawling across the room I haul myself into the en-suite bath for a soak. I am enjoying every minute of this.

On an idyllic morning the view across Falmouth Harbour allows to me to watch the ferry chugging away towards the jetty just below my window. Due to circumstances I find some fresh socks (I don't normally bother) and, unnoticed, pad down for breakfast.

After the bracing ferry trip I seek out an ATM. The charging of the mobile, provision of liquids, chocolate bars, bananas and regular chippie visits require constant visits to 'holes in the wall'.

'It gets you to thinking,' says Flek, now fully tuned it, 'Our grandparents would have been flabbergasted witnessing an ATM withdrawal. I suppose, first things first, they wouldn't ever have seen a plastic card before.'

I let him ramble on – not that I am ungrateful for social chit chat.

Bananas have become a talking point in this town. On the previous Saturday the 12,000 tonne motor vessel *Horncliff* had been towed into port after a battering from high seas off the Scilly Isles. She carried a cargo of fruit, including bananas, and true to their 'salvaging' heritage hundreds of locals gathered at Pendennis Point in the hope that a few more containers would slip off! Later I pass by the dockyard and hear the hammering out to repair the ship.

I sit down at the Point, peel a banana and reflect. Despite modern navigational aids and the Plimsoll line, in just twelve months the south coast has witnessed the Russian freighter *Sinegorsk* spill out thousands of timber planks onto the Sussex/Kent beaches, then the fiasco of the *Napoli* and now the *Horncliff* incident.

'You're doing a lot of reflecting these days' says Flek, 'Bananas won't charge your brain cells, so don't waste time on trivia. Using them to find your way around GB is more important, perhaps?'

'*Reflection is food for the soul, Flek, and don't you forget it,*' I chant, *rigorously defending my corner.*

It's another splendid hike today along the cliffs for six miles, stopping at Maenporth for a lunch snack and a pot of tea. I end up at Melanie Williams' superb B & B (01326 251 245) in the village of Mawnan Smith. There's a story here that I shall relate tomorrow.

DAY 40
9th February – Mawnan Smith to Porthallow – 13 miles

The Helford Passage ferry is summer only, so what now? Help comes in an unlikely way. CLIMB stalwart Lesley Greene's first attempt at finding me a B & B has been thwarted (the landlady broke her arm the previous day) but she has been given Melanie's number. Persistent Lesley has asked her whether there is any other way I can cross the Helford River.

'What day will your walker be here?' Melanie asked. When told it was a Saturday she exclaimed, 'Well that's all right then – the Giggers train on that day. They can take him across. I'll fix it."

What a stroke of luck! This is going to be my most memorable start so far. The sun is just rising and I take a two mile tramp down through the still hushed woods towards the Helford GIG Rowers Club House. I emerge onto the Helford River bank just as the mist is burning off. This is a beautiful setting.

The Gig Rowing Clubs

There are twenty five Gig Rowing Clubs in Cornwall. The six crew Gig rowboats were originally used to take pilots out. The first to arrive at a vessel got the job of piloting it around the rocky coastline to safety and the fee.

The Helford Club competes with others in the World Gig Rowing Championships, held every year in the Scilly Islands during April.

Lady 'Giggers' row me across the Helford River.

My route leads me across the tiny beach at Trabah one of the finest Gardens in Cornwall. I had paid a visit here several years ago. It is hard to imagine that from this tranquil beach setting American Rangers embarked here in landing craft for the horrors of the D-Day Normandy landings in 1944.

The Helford Gig Rowing Club has three Saturday training periods. The 11am session is for ladies training – naturally I choose to go with them. After a 'golly gosh' type of welcome I am bundled into stern of the sturdy Gig boat and five Amazons (Kate, Chloe, Ellie, Laura and Nicki), driven on by an unforgiving coxswain Dave, row me over to Helford village. It takes ten minutes, thus saving a sixteen-mile hike. I will be missing out on Daphne du Mauriier's Frenchman's Creek further up the River.

Disembarking from the Gig, I take my time wandering through sleepy Helford. A two-mile walk along the bank to Gillian Creek beckons to the mouth of the river, but I am not alone. On this peaceful waterway I hear 'Dastardly Dave' across the water barking out his orders. He now has the ladies rowing '42 at Chiswick Bridge,' as John Snagge (Snaggers) might have put it in his famous Varsity Boat Race commentaries. When the Amazons' pains eventually take the gig boat into the open sea, I can still hear him yelling at them!

At the Creek I miss the low tide and walk round the harbour. I end a wonderful day finding my B & B at the Gallen-Traeth guest house (01326 280 400), Porthallow. The proprietor, Clive Munday, is an amiable well-built fellow with a full set. I enquire about the Concord images on the wall and he explains that his brother had worked on the iconic aircraft at Bristol. The setting for my journey today has been nothing short of idyllic.

DAY 41

10th February – Porthallow to Cadgwith – 13 miles

In full sun I drop down to Porthoustock; the in-shore fishermen are busy selling their early morning catch. The Path moves inland, the map showing some 'giants' quoits' – and there they are, four huge round stones piled up in a field, a gesture to the local closed stone mine, apparently. Further on I reach the grey gritty beach at Godrevy Bay, and then suddenly the huge and ugly Dean quarry appears.

I arrive at Coverack for lunch. The friendly café staff offer me soup and rice pudding plus five pounds for CLIMB.

I get talking to a man about our national service days in the RAF. He is rotund, walks with a stick and finds it difficult to breathe. He is also two years younger than me.

'Be thankful for small mercies, Col,' says Flek.

'Believe me Flek, I really am.'

Moving towards Dolor Point I come across the unexpected. Taking a field path I am confronted with a couple of dozen large contemporary sculptures depicting animals and birds, all placed randomly around a field by the Terrance Coventry Foundation. His is a fascinating story of a man who farmed pigs until he was fifty then turned to sculpture and made a respected name for himself in the art form.

The final six miles of undulations seem to go on forever. The sun has well set by the time I reach the Cadgwith Cove Inn. Patiently waiting for me inside are my next hosts, Francis and Mike Young. After a convivial welcome over a pint we return to their home at Mawgan near Helston. Over the evening meal, the subject of the Goonhilly Down station crops up: there will be more about this connection tomorrow.

FIT FOR PURPOSE

'Listen, Mac, I'm a jazz musician, not an athlete.'
(Reported reply to an interviewer when asked if he
always lay on the floor when being interviewed).
Eddie Condon , Chicago jazz bandleader

In the beginning I devised an ongoing programme of training i.e. marching around immediate countryside at home, about eight miles each day, progressing to the Downs of West Sussex. I kept this up for eighteen months.

A break for a hernia operation stifled any activity for six weeks. Time came for tougher assignments, and in August of 2007 I embarked on the first of two prolonged proving exercises.

First Exercise – Lower Beeding to Seaford returning to Houghton Bridge, Sussex – 70 miles

I walk south-east, using the splendid Sussex Ouse Valley Way Walk, devised by Terry Owen and Peter Anderson, which terminates at Seaford. A return back into West Sussex follows, using the South Downs Way AND finishing at Houghton Bridge.

I need to confirm my overall fitness, do some 'rough' camping and check out my kit. The trip does not go without incident.

A Fall Nearly Puts Paid To It All!

Jane Taylor drops me at the village hall car park, Lower Beeding. I aim to complete the twelve miles on the first day. The Way is mostly flat via Furnace Pond and the fledgling Ouse, then goes north to Handross and south to Staplefield to end the first stage. Pressing on I pass under the Ouse Valley railway viaduct, carrying the London to Brighton line, the iconic image of the Way.

Near Ardingly I pitch my hired tent for the very first time. After several attempts I get the hang of it and heat up a dehydrated meal – another first. As the sun sets I consume it sitting on a fallen tree. My first night doesn't go without disturbance, because a tawny owl keeps me awake. In the early morning the sun beating down on the tent forces me to rise early.

I strike camp and make for Lindfield, wearily ploding onto finish at Newick. Here I find a stone plinth directing me to my find my hosts Louise and Simon Montebello who have a young baby daughter Josie. Simon is a stonemason. Over a meal I chat on about Louise's parents, my good friends Hugh and Daphne Ashton at Chichester.

My feet and boots are performing well but my sponsor's donated rucksack is short of capacity.

Next day I tramp on to Barcombe Mills, getting a meal in the Anchor pub by the Ouse. Later, leaving Lewes, I follow the river to Rodmell. Here I camped in the garden of B & B Sunnyside Cottages (01273 476876), run by Pauline Cherry, who is a member of the Lewes Jazz Club.

Walking along the roadside verge to Southease I have a nasty accident which at the time I think will put the whole project in jeopardy. A regular participant of the South Downs Way Walk, I have tramped this verge many times. I should have taken better care, but a concealed rabbit hole sends me sprawling.

In a flash I am prostrate on the slope of a deep ditch, my head level with speeding traffic a few feet away. What's more, I have wrenched a knee. With the rucksack still on, I somehow climbed out of the ditch. To my amazement a passing motorist has spotted my dilemma and a few minutes later has driven back to assist me – an unforgettable 'Good Samaritan' encounter.

The knee hurts, but thank goodness it is serviceable, although I know that it will take some time heal. I hobble by road to Newhaven, cross its bridge and pick up a path to the Seaford promenade. I make it to Bishopstone and erected the tent at windy Buckle caravan park. After a meal I lamely shuffle into Seaford to set up a venue for a forthcoming end-of-walk Southern Trails reception. Staggering back, filled with misgivings, I survive a fitful sleep.

The journey back via Rodmell picks up the South Downs Way leading to the Newmarket Inn. Via the pedestrian bridge over the A27, a long path leads to the crest of the Downs for a rough camp at Blackcap. I have a wonderful memory of sitting in the warm evening breeze watching from above as the villages across the Weald lit up as darkness fell.

In the morning I'm short of water! Struggling in heat of the day the considerable way to Ditchling Beacon car park, I finally get a couple of bottles from an ice cream van. Thinks: I will not be able to do this in the Highlands of Scotland.

The Devils Dyke Hotel provides lunch and I pressed on.

The times I have passed Truleigh Hill YHA high up on the South Downs Way – and now I am booked in to stay there. The facilities are excellent and the dining room on the first floor takes full advantage of the view.

Richard and his Polish girl friend sit at my breakfast table. They are on a cycling holiday break. He is a handsome, intelligent but a very restless fellow. He could spring a surprise at any moment, and he does! Asked about my purpose, I happen to mention my long fascination with the radio transmitting station's masts a short distance from the hostel.

'Do you want to go inside and have a look? he blurts.

'How can I do that,' I replied incredulously.

He then pulls a huge bunch of keys out of his shorts pocket and says, 'With these.'

I am aghast, who is this stranger about to tamper with a secured installation?

Noting my disbelief, he explains that his job as a BBC Radio 4 engineer means that constantly carrying keys enables him to perform random checks of equipment when the chance arises. As far as he is concerned that is now!

Soon we are at the foot of the 100m towers, and he struggles to unlock three huge padlocks. Gaining entrance to a transmitter room sets off the intruder alarm. I get anxious, foreseeing police or possibly military helicopters being scrambled. He dismisses my fears and without a care in the world lets the alarm ring while nosing around the equipment. He shows disappointment – the transmitter only serves the emergency and local services. With relief I share his frustration. Thank God there is nothing here of national importance!

After ten minutes we leave. Returning the padlocks he makes a couple of phone calls, presumably to tell somebody in the UK (GCHQ perhaps), who he is and what he has been up to.

Leaving down the approach road the following morning the pair pass me using gravity to pick up speed on their bikes. With bells ringing and legs outstretched they tear away, shouting 'Bye, Colin!'

I push on to Houghton Bridge where Jane meets me, and after tea at the riverside cafe she drives me home.

I conclude that my supplier should exchange the rucksack and provide more dehydrated meals. I will also seek out a recommended Hilliberg tent from 'Snow and Rock', who have a branch at Port Solent, Portsmouth.

My knee is very sore and, with the help of physiotherapy, it is several weeks before it comes good.

Second Exercise – Portsmouth to Lulworth Cove – 70 miles
Several weeks later, after a full recovery, I am at it again. This time Jane drops me at the Portsmouth-to-Gosport ferry. My first day's objective is the Royal Victoria Country Park at Netley on Southampton Water, where I will try to find somewhere to rough camp. The route is familiar to me, as I have completed the Solent Way with Southern Trails in 1999 and 2001.

A Scary Night In The Park!
Arriving at the Country Park before dusk I having some misgivings about camping here, killing time in a pub waiting for dusk to fall. I scout around for a suitable out-of-the-way site, as I may be breaking some bylaws. Then I have a bit of luck. I notice a van parked on the grass, with some equipment lying stacked nearby following a show in the park.

A man appears out of the van and listens to my purpose. 'Don't worry,' he says, 'I'm staying on for another night,' and he suggests that I pitch my tent nearby. He adds that if anyone queries my presence, 'Tell him you're with me.'

By now it is pitch black. On the other side of Southampton Water the Fawley Oil Refinery is lit up like Las Vegas, a tree line shielding the huge park area from its glare. I get the tent up unnoticed. Thankfully the total darkness will soon save me from real trouble. I settle down for the night, but then some yobbos arrive. From their noise and language it's clear that they are bent on mayhem. I have a very uncomfortable couple of hours praying that they won't stumble upon my tent; in the mood they are in I would be fair game. To my immense relief they finally move off.

I strike camp very early. All around me empty bottles are strewn across the grass;, and a park official is examining a large swing gate torn from its hinges. He guesses what I have been up to, but I nullify his admonishment by being able to confirm to him the activities of the 'vandals in the night'.

I shove off and trek on to cross the Itchen Bridge and catch the Southampton -to-Hythe Ferry, striding into the New Forest area through woods to Bucklers Hard to have lunch. Pressing on until darkness falls, I climb over a gate into a field of maize and find a tiny clearing out of sight east of Lymington. All this subterfuge is necessary: there are no rough-camping sites in the area.

After a fitful night I follow the Solent Way onto Lymington, the Pennington Marshs, Keyhaven, Milford on Sea, Barton on Sea, Christchurch and, finally, Bournemouth, where I am picked up by Bob Freemantle, my ex-wife Connie's husband. I stay with them for a couple of comfortable nights.

After a rest day exploring the Poole area, Bob runs me down to the Sandbanks Ferry. On another very long day I first I yomp along the beach at Studland Bay, then ascend to pass the Old Harry's Rocks and onto Swanage. My legs are not complaining" I am holding up well.

Finding some scrubland at Duriston Head I rough-camp. A hard frost ensures heavy condensation inside the tent – something to look forward to!

Somewhat dishevelled, I cook up breakfast. The day presents a long arduous trek along the cliffs to Kimmeridge Bay. Here I rough-camp close to the Cavel Tower.

Having previously checked that the Army are not exercising during the weekend on the Lulworth Bindon range, I am clear to proceed. Passing BP's 'nodding donkey' oil well, I push along a defined path between the MOD markers leading me along the ridge over the range to Lulworth Cove.

Jane has motored a very long way to take me back home.

My body has behaved itself, my knee standing the strain of considerable daily mileages while carrying in excess of thirty pounds.

Only two months now to the big event!

DAY 42
11th February - Cadgwith to Mullion – 10 miles

Mike Young is the second of four Goonhilly Down ex-staff to host me. Peter Deane at Exmouth has done me a great favour, kindly asking his former colleagues to follow suit.

Before returning to the coast, Mike takes me into the Goonhilly station to view its satellite tracking telescopes. One of them, Arthur (see below), is a listed structure.

The ten miles to Mullion Cove is spectacular. Attractive features constantly appear – in particular the rock stacks and headlands at Kynanace Cove. I am amazed to see that the Lizard lifeboat station is miraculously squeezed into a tiny rock cove. Because of the steepness of its approach steps, the crew reach the lifeboat using a gravity car on rails.

Goonhilly Down

With the introduction of earth satellites, this station, built in 1962, became one of the first three tracking sites in the world. It is positioned on the Lizard Peninsula for two reasons – its openness to signals across the Atlantic (a necessity that Marconi had originally deduced) and the need for a stable rock base for the receivers. In the early days the signals from the satellites were so weak that any movement at the receiver end would have distorted them. The natural bedrock here is serpentine, ideal to achieve the stability required.

The site's first dish, 'Arthur' (all the dishes were named after characters in the Arthurian Celtic legend), was a marvel at the time, its steerable dish based on the one at Jodrel Bank. My four hosts were radio engineers originally recruited for the project, and after retirement they made their homes permanently in the West Country. On our way back to Cadgwith this morning Mike takes us on a tour of the site;. I have my photograph taken with 'Arthur' – now a listed structure.

Reaching the most southerly café in the UK, horrors – it has run out of Cornish pasties!

'Time for another Victor Meldrew impression, Col,' says Flek.

'I don't believe it,' I respond to humour him.

One of the family staff members blushes in embarrassment. I settle for cheese on toast followed by plum tart and ice cream.

Moving on, I pass the lighthouse and then round Lizard Point. It is another four miles of easy idyllic cliff top walking before reaching Mullion Cove. Today I have seen shows of tiny tete-a-tete daffodils, grape hyacinths and wild violets, plus a magnolia tree in full bloom, and it's getting warmer. It has to be a 'wish you were here' day.

I wander into Mullion village from where Stina Nicholson, my next host, drives me to her home at Helston to meet husband Stephen and daughters Sophie and Emily.

With 'Arthur' at Goonhilly.

DAY 43

12th February – Mullion Cove to Porthleven – 7 miles

I haven't dwelt so far on my daily dressing and rigging routine but today I am proud to announce that I shall now discard my long johns!

Hurrah! for another free day – not having a burden on my back for this short stage graded as 'moderate'. Backed by a chilly wind I will be passing by three beautiful white-sand beaches under a cloudless blue sky.

At Poldhu the path runs along a fine cliff to the Marconi monument. From his pioneering radio station here in an adjacent field in 1903 Guglielmo Marconi tapped out his historic three 'S' signal which was picked up in Newfoundland. It was the first transAtlantic message and it changed the world. A few footings can still be seen.

Fascinated by my sudden discovery, I speak to a couple sitting on a bench close by, then decide to ring my eldest daughter Suzanne to tell her where I am. Damn! damn! and more damns! I can't get a signal. The irony of this failure in modern communications from such an historic signalling location suddenly strikes the three of us, and we burst out laughing.

I seem to arrive at Porthleven in no time. Visitors are indulging on an alfresco café lifestyle around the picturesque fishing harbour. I dive into the Atlantic Inn out of the wind for a pint. Host Stina Nicholson arrives to convey me back to Helston.

After we devour a plate-sized Cornish pasty, Stina's husband Stephen, a jazz fan, suggests that we cross Cornwall to the St Ives Jazz Club to hear the guitarist Louis D'Agastino who I had first enjoyed at the Chichester Jazz Festival. Musically it is an exciting gig. My previous hosts, the Youngs, also turn up – a most fulfilling day.

Stephen's grandmother Mary Kirk, the 'grand old lady' of the Chichester Jazz Club, had proposed him as a host and also his parents Bea and Ray, who I will be staying with later in the year near Berwick on Tweed.

I had a letter from Mary asking me how was it I going to deprive myself of jazz for a whole year. She was an ardent jazz fan, had a huge collection of record titles and probably had not even heard of iPods. Sadly Mary passed away while I was on the Walk.

DAY 44
13th February – Rest day – Helston

Helston is famous for the 'Furry' or Floral Dance held in May. In a carnival atmosphere thousands of visitors attend to watch four individual groups dance through the town. The children dance at 10am and, dressed in white and wearing their individual school headdresses, they shuffle through the streets in pairs to the town band playing the Floral Dance.

'They've got to sound better than the Terry Wogan version,' is the sarcastic comment from Flek.

Ignoring him, I idle through the town trying to imagine the scenes.

In the afternoon Stephen, a Fleet Air Arm NCO, takes me on a whistle-stop tour of the Royal Naval Air Station at Culdrose. Sea King and Merlin helicopters plus Hawk Jets for attack training all fly from this large air-and-sea-rescue operations base. He is responsible for the helicopters' air worthiness.

Back at the house my hosts' wary Doberman, Cujo, continues to snarl around my leg. Lesley Greene at CLIMB rings through with another list of host families.

I'm so whacked that I didn't hear the house fire alarm early this morning!

'Whacked are you? Well, you don't help yourself. You haven't had to use the camping gear yet, so why are you humping it about?' jibes Flek. 'You could have sent it on.'

I tell him again that it was an attempt to keep improving my overall strength. He had a point though!

DAY 45
14th February -Porthleven to Penzance – 13 miles

I go out into a cold easterly wind to encounter a series of ascents and descents on narrow cliff paths, allowing marvellous scenes to unfold.

I pass the disused tin mine of Wheal Prosper (1860). Heavy metal mesh covers protect abandoned mine shafts. I stop and try to imagine the hardships of the resilient miners who not only sunk the shafts but then routed them under the sea to find the seams of tin. Cornwall was possibly the only place in the world where the metal could be found.

At Prussia Cove an approaching lady, a bit of a dowager, asks me if I have seen her husband. In a hoity voice she says, 'We parted following a horrid dispute over map reading. He seemed resigned to our disagreement and walked awf,' she confesses. and then adds 'He is wearing a green anorak which I gave him as a Christmas present.'

When she has gone Flek, who can't contain his mirth any longer, bursts out with, 'He's probably jumped in the sea to escape her. I would!'

Smiling, I walk onto Praa Sands get my teeth into an egg and bacon sandwich. Later I round Cudden Point and get a wonderful view of Marazion. At this distance it resembles a Mediterranean coastal resort. The scene stealer here though is St Michel's Mount with it exposed tidal footpath.

Marazion has a certain antiquity and, like so many towns down here, has harboured many an artist. Before long I am striding along the very long promenade running parallel to the railway line. It delivers expresses from London to Penzance, the end of one of Brunel's great endeavours. I find it hard to believe that Paddington is so far away.

My next hosts, Peter and Pat Collins, drive me back to Porthleven for the night. Peter is the third of the Goonhilly Four. The Collins have just relocated from a home by the Harbour to one high out of town with wonderful coastal views

When first hearing about my route, Peter remarked that he had lived in Cornwall all his life but had never been to half the places I was intending to pass through. It was some admission from a Cornishman, and I was somewhat flattered to hear it.

'Brimming with pride now are we?' whispers Fleck. 'Remember what it comes before!'

DAY 46
15th February – Penzance to Porthcurno Beach – 12 miles

I follow a broad promenade for two miles to Newlyn, Cornwall's busiest fishing port. Walking through the town, I pick up the strong smell of fish that emits from many wharfside sheds now washed out after the day's catch has been sold.

Entering Mousehole a couple of miles on I reach an abandoned lifeboat station, now a commemorative setting. This was the slipway of the Penlee lifeboat. On the 19th December 1981 the entire eight man crew of the *Solomon Browne* lifeboat were lost answering a distress call from the freighter MV *Union Star*. Both vessels and sixteen people went down in hurricane force winds

With Richard Clark, deputy mayor of Penzance.

I soon return to the true SWCP. Wild daffodils, violets and campion show everywhere. The going is rugged, with steep ascents and descents and I arrive at Lamorna Cove. Getting into this famous cove (how many houses bear the name Lamorna?) the Path is rock-strewn and difficult. Fulmars sortie from their nests high up as I struggle on and arrive at a small café on the beach. I tuck into a dish of crab soup.

Getting out of the cove, sometimes on all fours, is even more of a challenge. The mini lighthouse of Tater-du appears. Further on the Path forces me to boulder hop along the beach. It is still hard going passing by St Loy, Penbert and Logan Rock until, with great relief, I finally drop down to the beach at Porthcurno.

Everything is shut down. I phone my next host, Richard Clark, deputy mayor of Penzance: he is on his way. Meanwhile I amble inland to a large deserted visitors' car park and wait. I am spotted by Terry and family from the first floor of a nearby holiday apartment block. He calls down and they invite me up for tea and cake! It was a kind gesture which was very welcome.

Richard arrives and points out the only original communications 'hut' on a beach left in the world. Standing on the sandy shore, it has a dozen communication cables terminating from all parts of the Empire. A vibrant museum stands nearby to tell this fascinating story.

In Penzance Richard and Lucia Clark have a rambling Edwardian house complete with an impressive first floor gallery. The wash basin in my room is so large and ornate that it resembles a font. In the evening the Clarks hold a dinner party for eight. One guest, Rory, is a heritage wildlife character who on this very day has been involved in retrieving a dead dolphin.

Today has been punishing and my legs unsteady.

16th February – Porthcurno – Lands End – Cape Cornwall – 15 miles

After a super breakfast we drive back to Porthcurno. Richard has one more curiosity to show me. Up an access road to the top of the cliff is the world famous Minack Theatre. It's early, and the premises are secured. Nevertheless I am able to get some idea of how exposed this cliff-edge open-air theatre is.

The cold easterly still chills my back. I strike out for Lands End five miles away. The compass turns northwest at Gwennap Head from where, swelled with anticipation, I can see my midday objective.

At Lands End I stroll into the usual tourist attractions of shops, cafés and a restaurant. It is out of season – only a few people around. Regrettably the place resembles a theme park.

CLIMB have informed me that I will be met by local dignitaries. Adrian Semmens, the chairman of Sennon Parish Council, turns up. He operates the 'last farm' in the land and has donned his best suit for the occasion: I am honoured. With him is Sylvia Smith, the outgoing mayor of St Just, the 'last town' in England. She is going to be of great assistance to me.

After a nice chat we go down to the famous multi-directional way-post for the obligatory photograph. Iike countless visitors before me I pose: confirmation of my arrival is now in the can. It will be another six months before the same agency will snap me again at John o Groats.

'I wonder how many well-meaning bods will be leaving this spot for John O'Groats this year,' Flek comments, and goes on, 'Well, it's only 874 miles – at least you're going all the way round.'

He almost sounds complimentary.

'Well, Flek, be charitable now – we all have our own personal objectives in life. Goodness knows how much money has been generated this way for the countless disadvantaged. Remember this is what we do. After all, we are British.'

'Blimey, it's Land of Hope and Glory time,' he taunts.

Sylvia is my next host, and she relieves me of the rucksack for the rest of the day. Now free, I swing round another 45 degrees and take the well-worn path north. After 470 miles I have now turned the first corner of Great Britain. Without a burden I am able to savour the moment and stride out with some purpose.

Now, I am your average bird watcher, so imagine my delight when a little later I am approaching Cape Cornwall and see a pair of choughs touch-down a few feet from me. I freeze and watch the large crow-like birds, native to the South West, with their distinctive long curved red bill and legs, as they prod around for food in a grassy knoll hugging the cliffs. I feel privileged. After all, the previous evening Rory had been bemoaning that he hadn't spotted the bird so far this year.

'Dont tell me, Col – you're chuffed!' says Flek almost apologetically.

I just knew he was going to say it. Have I ever been as crass?

The geography of Cape Cornwall is dramatic and in my opinion overshadows that of a few miles back. I am met by Monty Nichols, the present mayor of St Just, and after greetings he drives me to Sylvia's home at Botallack. Over a splendid meal in her beautiful home, formerly a tin miner's cottage, I talk to her husband Dave.

At Land's End.

He is a printer by trade at Hayle, near St Ives. In his spare time he champions the preservation of show/fair organs and is the editor of *The Key Frame*, a quarterly magazine on the subject. Interestingly he mentions that John Merrick the Elephant Man is linked to showground history.

Sylvia is passionate about her county and its problems with second homes (mentioned previously), its dependency on tourism leaving much out of season deprivation. She is a trustee of Age Concern, Cornwall, and they are a couple demonstrating true conviction in public life.

I have entered the shipping weather forecast area Lundy.

Starting at Pendeen three miles along from Cape Cornwall is a compromise. The decision will enable me to cover the severe terrain on this stage by 5pm for a reception at the Guildhall, St Ives.

Sylvia offers me a free day (no backpack) and confirms she will be in attendance when I meet the mayor of St Ives later in the day. (I should explain that I always carry a smaller day sack with me for use on 'free' days.) She warns me that the grading is 'severe' and as there are no food outlets she packs me up with provisions.

I have been on the move for six weeks now and have still not shaken off the maddening early day 'runny nose' disorder. My answer is to await the full dewdrop to form at the end of my proboscis and then blow it away. Hiding under a tramp's facade it's easy to shrug off the protocols of using paper tissues or even hankies. I calculate saving several packs of paper towels en route using this practical but despicable practice. This is hardly a scientific study, but my findings are not to be sneezed at!

A ninety degree turn at Pendeen points me in the east and then north-east directions for the first time. This stage is spectacular and remote. The paths are, often vague and narrow. with numerous short and steep ascents, and at times boggy. Now and then a stream tumbles over the cliffs. My Leki poles are now defective, which affects my progress.

As it is a Sunday there are other walkers about. The weather is holding. I wouldn't like to be exposed here when it's rough. The Path runs into St Ives at a low level and I arrive at the Guildhall with two minutes to spare.

What happened next?

An Evening with the Godfather

'I am going to make him an offer he cannot refuse'
– Don Vito Corleone

On Day 48, after a strenuous ten-mile struggle over difficult terrain, I arrive at St Ives. Sylvia Smith has told me that the mayor had 'instructed' that I arrive at the impressive Guildhall by five o'clock.

Bang on time I approach the building and the heavy front door half opens. In its frame stands a man of medium height, who has a full head of white hair and is wearing an immaculate Italian-style pinstripe suit. He would not look out of place in the Sopranos. With a finger he beckons me over and introduces himself as Bill Fry, the current mayor of St Ives.

'Watch it, Col, this man commands authority,' warns Flek.

I have to agree with his assessment.

Inside I am greeted by four members of St Ive's Council, and we all sit down in an ante-room. Bottles of wine appear, and in between healthy swigs this quorum wades into the current problems of the town i.e. second holiday homes (an old perennial), jobs and the economy.

Someone reminds the mayor that a photo shoot to mark the occasion is required. With the air of a 'godfather' he reaches for his slim attache case. My mind races back to the Hollywood black-and-white gangster films and to the inevitable scene when the prominent hoodlum (Bogart, Edward G. Robinson, James Cagney or George Raft, take your pick) clicks the locks and the lid springs open to reveal the pay-off – fifty grand! I am to be disappointed, for today only the mayor's regalia is inside his case.

I am sitting next to council member Richard Ryan, who whispers to me, 'Bill is full of it – loves these moments. He can't wait to put the gear on.'

'Everybody outside!' orders the mayor.

The photo shoot done, we all slink back inside to quaff more beer and wine. I say goodbye to the lovely Sylvia Smith who has helped me so much.

I am puzzled by the mayor's accent, so I lean over and, with some deference, I tackle him about it.

'You don't sound like a local,' I enquire.

'No, mate, I come from Kingston in Surrey and lived in Chessington for many years. I moved here and bought a small business then went into local politics, and Bob's your uncle.'

So that explains that, then.

I had arrived sweaty and am now getting cold. Plucking up courage I ask him about something to eat. He points over to Colin (the only member with a Cornish accent) and tells me, 'We are all going over to his son's place for a meal'.

The son runs a Mexican-style restaurant. We all traipse through the quaint and dark streets of the town, and Colin's gorgeous daughter-in-law offers up a great menu.

I am now quite merry and have to ask Mr Mayor for one more favour. He anticipates my enquiry.

'Your bed for the night is all taken care of, Colin. Richard there deals with holiday lets in this town and has fixed you up with an apartment.'

Bidding them all goodnight, Richard speeds me to his own two-floor pad which has great views across the town.

It has been an awfully long day. During my memorable stay I have been made offers by the mayor that I just couldn't refuse!

Day 49
18th February – St Ives to Hayle – 6 miles

Only half a day's excursion, so I wander into the town for a look around. I find Councillor Colin's emporium, just the sort of place to walk in and say 'have you got any fork (four) handles (candles)? Ah! It reeks of a good old fashion hardware store. Yes, if you want it, he has got it in the exact quantities you require,

'Mansion Polish, Mothballs or a Whitworth grommet? Certainly madam, step this way!'

An ATM is kaput, so I have to go inside the bank for some readies. Standing in the queue I still feel a little conspicuous carrying a large rucksack in winter.

My mind wanders back to another time long ago, standing in a similar queue. I was first married and skint. I asked my dad for a small loan. We walked down to the Trustee Savings Bank in Arundel Street, Portsmouth. It was busy with long queues at each teller's point. The lady cashier asked Dad a question. Being a little deaf he misinterprets and says out loud for all to hear, 'This is my son. He's a bit short at the moment, so I'm lending him three hundred quid.'

Oh for that trapdoor in the floor! Outside I felt like Harold about to strangle Albert Steptoe, but sense prevailed. Dad was from the 'old school' and never had any real money until he retired. When he handed it over to the bank he thought he had to justify his withdrawals each time. In truth it never dawned on him that it was *his* money, bless him!

Today I am going to be reunited with one of my Southern Trail walkers. Vanda Pawan. She has come over by bus to accompany me back to Hayle.

We meet and take a gentle stroll back, and it's not without interest. The first thing we spot is an exact replica of Del Boy's Reliant Robin which is parked outside a hotel.

Next up, a little further on, we come across a man diligently administering poultices of fibre glass on to what is probably the ugliest commercial vehicle ever produced. Citroen has never been a bastion for good design in the post war era. Just think of the 2CV or the big 6H used by Rupert Davies in the BBC Inspector Maigret series and you will know what I mean. This 'H' Van before us is something else.

Citroen 'H' van.

'What do you think of it Flek?

'Well, some bloke once told me that over thirty car models have had animal names like Beatle, Jaguar & Mustang etc. If I was asked to include this beast in the list it would have to be a Vietnamese Pot Bellied Pig.'

He is spot on!

The proud owner tells me with mischievous glee that having a top speed of only 40 mph, he has following traffic piled up in no time.

'Come and have a look inside,' he says.

Vanda and I glance in to see a bed, cooker and fridge squeezed in the back. It is a botched up mobile home with a difference.

The outside body work design is awful. The corrugated side panels do it no favours. It is, however, versatile in design, with spare parts cheap and easy to get and fit. Everything on this workhorse is light-weight to get the most out of its 1911cc engine, and more than 474,000 of them were sold.

'This brute can still turn people's heads,' the uncompromising owner proudly proclaims.

'*Flek, you can have the last word.*'

'*Well . . . come on, it is French!*'

We left him happily patching it up.

Further on there is a plaque on a 'Huer' house wall. These were early look-out posts for fishermen to spot shoals of pilchards coming in- shore.

On a short day we arrive at Hayle early. Vanda has a room in a sheltered home for the elderly. A spare room is kept for visitors, and fortunately for me it is vacant. We have a meal out. Vanda explained that Hayle had once been industrialised, but sadly the place is in decline: plans for re-development have never materialised.

It has been such a relaxing day and it is lovely to see Vanda again – a lady with such dignity.

With Vanda Pawan.

DAY 50
19th February – Hayle to Portreath Harbour – 12 miles

I reach two milestones today, having covered five hundred miles in fifty days. Each day I finish knackered, but my legs always recover after eight hours in bed. Usually the previous day's stiffness disappears after about a mile, and I am able to tramp along at up to three miles an hour according to the terrain: they are definitely up to the task and are getting stronger.

After breakfast Vanda prepares some provisions for the day. It is another sad farewell as I leave Hale across a big swing bridge.

I go round Godrevy and Navax Points. There is a long stretch of easy, flat cliff edge walking during the morning, and this allows time to watch some intense birdlife at very close quarters. Fulmars are much in evidence, constantly patrolling. I can closely observe their nests high up on the cliff face. A group of birdwatchers point out ravens and razor bills while, far out, gannets are plummeting into the sea.

At one cove I witness over fifty seals basking on a secluded beach below. A couple point them out to me. I am grateful as I would never have spotted them, they are so camouflaged on the shingle.

Somewhere I find a sheltered spot out the cold wind to eat my picnic. Battling on, I reach an impressive razor-edged rocky cove at Ralph's Cupboard two miles out from Portreath.

I find my digs, conveniently next door to the Portreath Arms. My hosts Simon and Viv Haywood of the Cliff House B & B (01209 843 847) have recently escaped the home counties to set up business here. They still have work to do, but I am made comfortable.

I seek an evening meal, and Simon recommends that I go next door.

'They do a great liver and bacon,' he says.

I take his advice, and friendly staff dish up the best plateful of this dish I have ever had in a pub. This includes red cabbage – and all for just a fiver!

Simon is going into Perranporth tomorrow and kindly offers to take my rucksack on.

DAY 51

20th February – Portreath to Perranporth – 11 miles

The going is strenuous to moderate today. The fine weather still persists and thanks to Simon it is a free day. Ragged cliffs often feature narrow stony paths with short, steep ascents and descents. Old mines and associated debris are much in evidence. Conical metal lids cover many a shaft. I first follow the fence of the Nancekuke RAF landing strip. Because of the quick access to the Atlantic the far south-west is sprinkled with disused air bases.

Several miles out I bump into another lone walker. He is Keiran and unfortunately a Manchester United supporter. We banter about the forthcoming clash with my team Portsmouth in the FA Cup. He seems confident, but neither of us can possibly foresee the drama that is about to unfold. He asks about accommodation and I recommend Cliff House. It is a chance to return Simon's favour.

I plod on mile after mile of dramatic cliff and cove scenery touching Porthlowan, then rounding St Agnes Head and onto Trevaunance Bay. Finally passing Shag Rock, I drop down into Perranporth.

My hosts Richard and Sylvia Howell look after me famously. Richard is the last of the Goonhilly Four and knew the other three who had hosted me. Interestingly he tells me that at some Goonhilly Marconi anniversary he actually met Marconi's daughter. He remembers her as being very large and dressed in black. What a link to communication history!

He had also just completed thirty one years as the officer charge of the local retained fire station It has been another of those super days without baggage or worry.

I spend much of the evening talking to Richard and his wife Sylvia about my purpose, walking progress and the fire and rescue service. They are a listening couple.

DAY 52
21st February – Perranporth to Newquay – 11 miles

Richard insists on donning my rucksack over the initial two-mile route along Perranporth's superb beach. It's a fine day and many people are enjoying an early season stroll along the firm sand. His fleeting favour soon comes to an end, and with his help I heave the sack up across my shoulders and shake his hand before the steep climb up onto Ligger Point.

Once again I come across many mine sites. The Path passes an ugly army camp and drops down to Holywell and its beach. On and around Pentire Point West, I arrive at Crantock Bay Hotel where I once had a great Christmas break and first met my very good friends John and Lyn Mercy. This splendid establishment has been in the same family for decades. The receptionist calls the proprietor Mrs Eyles Senior, who is gracious enough to say she remembers me. After I explain my presence I am treated to super afternoon tea supplemented by a sweet and given a £10 donation.

I continue along the beach and around the dunes to enter the River Gannel's estuary, finding a footbridge into Newquay. Cutting through the town, I reach the brow of a short hill and am amazed at the construction in progress, particularly along the sea front. I can't help wondering who is going to afford these expensive apartments.

The T.I.O. finds me a B&B address and I finish up with Sylvia Dunn at Trevillis House (01637 879 119). Sylvia is the very personification of an English landlady. Trading at the lower tariff end, she stoically accepts having to board dodgy guests. She is so cheerful I just have to take a photo of her in her lounge sitting next to that icon of boarding house history, a healthy aspidistra.

Fortunately I don't have to venture too far in town to find myself a chippie restaurant.

Sylvia and aspidistra.

Day 53
22nd February – Newquay to Little Petherick – 16 miles

The ebullient Sylvia serves up beans and bacon with an egg. I shake this indomitable lady's hand and set out early on a long stage. Another day of compromise will keep the schedule intact.

I walk through the town which has been described as the 'Blackpool of the West Country' and whose population at times swells tenfold due to its beach and surfing activities. For many of the retired locals this must seem an unenviable title.

It is February, and I note that the streets are full of half-clad youngsters milling around pubs, cafés, surfing gear outlets and a plethora of awful 'tat' shops.

'To be fair, Colin, despite the town's nickname these visitors are hardly likely to be candy floss and rock types,' says Flek in mitigation.

'How right you are old chap. Just imagine what this place is like in August, Flek. All the revelry of youth will be here sporting foul-worded t-shirts, 'mooning' out of bedroom windows, generating noise and throwing up into the early hours. I know all about it – Sylvia told me.'

'Yes but her view is probably jaundiced by memories of moonlight flits out of Trevillis House without paying.'

'Well, all right, but I've seen it all on the telly as well.'

It becomes necessary to distract him: my argumentative currency has run out.

I escape out of town to the north and get an excellent view of the extraordinary beaches and roaring surf. I walk on to the cliffs overlooking Watergate Bay and observe kite surfing, which looks fun.

A couple of miles further on I treat myself to delicious leek and stilton soup in Morgan Porth bar. Inland is the old RAF St Morgan which I am told doubles as Newquay's 'international' airport! Apparently Polish immigrant workers catch flights home from here for £40. There is little aerial activity this afternoon though, except for a lone Eurofighter cruising by.

It's another three miles to Porthcovan, and here I make the decision to turn east and cross country to my next hosts at Little Petherick. This means missing part of a coastal stage to Padstow. This is a pity, but I must keep to the schedule.

Using country lanes, I quickly swallow up the remaining four miles. My hosts are Larry and Audrey Pentice (she is a cousin of my Rotary friend David Garforth's wife). Their home, a former almhouse, has been beautifully converted. They are a charming couple, who have my welfare at heart.

In Memoriam – An Unsolved Mystery

During my diversion this afternoon I glance across to the transmitter towers on what was the old RAF Coastal Command's air base at St Eval. Memories of a past tragedy surface.

Like me, the likeable Les Swann was a member of the Bognor Regis Athletic Club. He was one of the older boys and a county class half-miler. He left for a career in the RAF and became a wireless operator. On January 11th 1955 he was a crew member in one of two Shackleton long-range reconnaissance aircraft which took off from St Eval on a training exercise over the Irish Sea. They never returned, and no trace has ever been found of either aircraft.

It has always been a complete mystery, and it is generally concluded that a catastrophic collision occurred, sending both aircraft into the sea. If my memory serves me right, the wireless operator on the other aircraft was also from Bognor Regis.

DAY 54

23rd February – Padstow to Port Issac – 11 miles

I ask my hosts about the second-home phenomenon. Audrey tells me there is little take up for the village newsletter out of season

They take me to Padstow. It is early, and the town is still sleepy. I take a shot of Rick Stein's famous restaurant. His influence on this place has been considerable and it's often referred to these days as 'Padstein'.

I say goodbye to the caring Prentices and catch the Rock Ferry. The Daymer Bay beach sand is firm and easy going, first up onto Trebetherick and then Polzeath. There are wonderful views out at Pentire Point.

The panorama is spectacular all day, but the going arduous with a continuous stream of undulations and more and more flights of those bloody steep steps every five miles!

I moan about them constantly ,but in truth they make it easier – although tripping on them with a full pack is a constant hazard. By now I have found that my equilibrium cannot always be fully relied on. I'm often teetering by late afternoon. Flek just smiles, of course. For him it's a normal day, cadging a lift as usual.

I arrive in Port Issac very tired and get a pricy hotel room, though keep the cost down by dining on dehydrated food. Mobile signals are non-existent. No sign of Doc Martin.

Vanessa Flook, the mum of a metabolic child known to CLIMB, has contacted me. Her daughter Anabel has the metabolic condition Medium Chain acyl CoA Dehydrogenase Deficiency (MCAD). Vanessa wants to walk with me from Boscastle. She is arranging accommodation for me for a couple of days, and her husband will pick me up tomorrow at Tintagel.

Day 55
24th February – Port Issac to Tintagel Haven – 9 miles

As the grading is designated 'severe' my intended progress calls for a risk assessment. The weather is OK, but I am not too happy about my balance and will have to be careful. Both the maps and Path guide show that the first half of the day will be particularly arduous, with a series of steep cliff-edge gradients. Sensing my apprehension, Flek issues some timely advice,

'Col, if I might say so, you are not a youthful athletic man any more. Please take the easier route today.'

'Thanks for your confidence old chap."

I must have sounded aggrieved at his prognosis, but he is right. I decide to go inland, and easily complete the six-mile road running parallel with the coast. I pick up a multifarious network of paths and lanes and get to Trebarwith Strand in the early afternoon, where I find a pub and order hot food.

After lunch the road rises steeply towards Tintagel, where I arrive without incident. The familiar landmarks of St Materiana's Church, the large out-of-place hotel and Tintagel Castle, associated with Arthurian myths and Tennyson's poetry, lie prominently ahead.

One has to grudgingly accept the inevitable commercialism that these sites attract. The first time I came here I was horrified to find two rows of 'tat' shops. There are no fears of frantic tourist activity today as it is the off season. I catch a café for a pot of tea just before it closes. There follows a long wait for my lift outside the Old Post Office, but at last Vanessa's husband Peter Flook arrives.

Peter is taking me to Widmouth Bay, where his friend Tim Naylor has a beach home called the Salt House: the vital commodity was stored here in the last century. I meet Vanessa and over an excellent meal have a chat with her about the difficulties of looking after a daughter who has MCAD.

Later I stretch my legs and take a stroll along the wonderful beach. My progress is halted by what looks like a coastal mist. It is In fact the fine sand being whipped up into high billowing clouds by an offshore wind. This is the only time I witnessed this phenomenon, a truly extraordinary sight.

DAY 56

25th February – Tintagel – Boscastle – Bude – 16 miles

Peter gets me back to Tintagel. I commence at the Haven and climb up to Barras Nose in front of the awful out-of-place hotel. At this headland sea birds are either on patrol or nesting everywhere, among them guillemots, razorbills and cormorants.

I move onto Bossiney. A further three miles along moderate terrain lies Boscastle with its unique harbour now mostly restored after the terrible floods of 2004.

After refreshment it is quite a climb out of the harbour up Penally Hill, and for four miles it is essential to keep to the Path to avoid the screes. High Cliff – as the name suggests, the highest cliff on the whole of the SWCP – is a head of me. The going is tough, but it levels out at Campeak

For some time I have been monitoring a figure who has been following me for several miles out of Boscastle. With only a plastic bag of possessions, he finally catches up as I stop to get my bearings.

'Hello. My name's John – pleased to see you,' he says.

'So what brings you here? On a walking holiday?' I enquire more inquisitively than usual.

'To tell you the truth I have never done anything like this before,' he says sheepishly, and goes on, "Had an argument with my father at Boscastle, so jumped out the car grabbed my bag, left him and took off along here.'

His story is not plausible and becomes even stranger when he reveals the contents of his 'bag', which include a tin of anti-freeze, deodorant and a spare string vest! He has obviously picked up the wrong bag!

He goes on: 'Got any idea where we are making for?'

'Well it's just a mile from Crackington Haven and I am hoping the pub will be open. I could kill a pint.'

'Good idea,' he says, and we descend into the Haven where the pub had just opened its doors.

I order some food and we chat. He indicates that he has time to spare and might stay in the area for a while. He then asks me if he can catch a train from here. I have to tell him that this part of Cornwall doesn't do trains.

His demeanour seems normal, but his story doesn't add up. Intrigued with why I am here, he suggests that I stay with his sister when I eventually pass through Swansea.

'She's a cracker,' he exclaims.

Unfortunately this arrangement is never going to reach fruition.

Time is getting on and I still have a long way to go, so I bid him farewell.

I puff up the steep incline from the pub to Pencannow Point and begin the strenuous ten mile slog to Bude. I'm feeling strong but it's a long, long way. I come to Widemouth Bay where I've stayed the night before.

Flek spurs me on: 'It's only four miles to Bude now, old fellow. You are doing all right, man.'

It is late afternoon when I get to Bude. My next host is Tim Naylor's father, who keeps the modern Camelot Hotel, where I have a luxurious stay.

I had originally been booked to stay at the Riverside Hotel back at Boscastle (this stage was originally scheduled for Days 56 and 57), but have had to re-schedule my day. My conscience bothering me, I ring the manager, Pete Templer, to apologise for not booking in, and I mention John. Pete tells me that John had aroused suspicion in several places and the police have paid him a visit at his hotel. It had indeed been an odd encounter. My perception was correct after all!

Day 58

26th February – Bude to Hartland Quay – 15 miles

Another stage that is classed as severe: I set my legs in motion and know they will not let me down.

Again, self-assessment is necessary. A route compromise today is difficult as I will be missing some stunning coastline. But common sense prevails, and I decide to cut inland and pick up a series of lanes running parallel with the coast, ultimately leading me to Hartland Quay.

The change of scenery is lovely, with picturesque cottages surrounded by early spring flowers. For weeks I have trekked around cove after cove with the sound and sights of the sea crashing against rock faces. It sounds blasé, I know, but it was all getting to be the same!

I tramp the six miles to Marsland Mouth before switching to the planned detour. After a stiff climb at the start, the going is comparatively easy. As the route gets tougher I forge on, taking in my regular refreshment – that is, snacking on a banana, chocolate bar and water at regular intervals. Close contours have been made easier by the provision of steps, hundreds of them!

At midday I descend into Marsland Mouth, cross a bridge and I am back in Devon. I spot the first human walking life for some time today. She is a weather-worn, completely self absorbed elderly lady clothed in what she has salvaged from the shore. She never says a word.

Studying my Explorer map 126 I work out a complicated PM route of initially twisting lanes. What a difference a lane makes! I am away from the jagged and noisy coastline at last. I rove through miles of quiet rolling countryside punctuated with hamlets, more cottages bedecked with spring flowers.

At Elmscott I find a youth hostel. A parked, powerful motorcycle indicates occupation but YHAs have their rules during the day and the premises are closed. I sit in the garden have a drink, admiring the view across a shallow valley towards my destination. Two miles up the road I turn left at and take the long dead end to Hartland Quay.

Just before the long descent down to the exposed hotel I chat to a farmer entering a field on a tractor, his two collies sitting on the back like a couple of book-ends making a charming picture. We talk of the weather (what else?) and he complains that dry spring seasons have become the norm.

The long curved descent to the Hartland Quay Hotel seems to go down for ever, but finally there it is, resembling a row of Coastguard cottages dumped on an exposed rocky platform. Whoever made the decision to build a hotel here? I have not booked accommodation, and for the first time spiel out a charity request for a room to the chatty barmaid. She thinks it will be OK but I will have to await the manager's decision.

I sit at the bar, and she explains that her husband, a farmer, is constantly loosing cattle to bovine TB. She has strong views on the matter of culling badgers. Chris Johns, the manager, appears and says I can have the room if I buy, breakfast which seems a very good deal to me.

This place is so exposed to the sea. I imagine gales howling around the first floor windows constantly during the winter months. But today the weather is in a benign mood.

I throw myself into bed, but annoyingly Flek wants to chat.

'You are pacing these lengthy stages without too much stress, Col. That's all very well, but it doesn't leave me space to moan.'

'Don't worry, you'll get a chance to drip sooner or later,' I tell him.

'Ah, that's all very well, but . . .'

His voice drifts into oblivion as I pass out for a full nine hours.

27th February – Hartland Quay to Clovelly – 10 miles

After a excellent hotel breakfast I grunt my way back up the hill, returning to the SWCP by the Old Rocket House. Shortly the ruins of a square tower appear and I have to sit down in the morning sun to catch my breath.

'Blimey, are you resting already? It's a bit early for that, mate,' mumbles Flek, who has just woken up.

'Remember, my friend, that I do all the kit carrying.' I reply angrily. That includes you, got it?'

Over the next two miles there are some steep valleys before I reach Hartland Point's lonely lighthouse. The route turns abruptly from west to east. The Path moderates as the Way continues along wooded cliffs and I go across fields which, surprisingly, have stiles.

'You haven't cocked your legs over these for a long time, Col. They're great for pulling a groin muscle!'

Has Flek any concern about my physical welfare at all, I wonder?

My mobile goes off. At last I have made contact with my next host, Ivor Cooper, a past fire brigade colleague. We fix a rendezvous point on the hill behind Clovelly..

Ivor drives up. It's great to see him again after such a long time. He has come a considerable way from Barnstable to pick me up. At present he holds a job at a local hospital but he is dabbling in property development. Marion, his wife, prepares a splendid meal.

Going to bed I remark to Flek that I haven't spoken to a soul for ten miles today. My remark triggers the predictable reply.

It's time for an Evening Concert. I decide to dedicate the evening to the jazz of Duke Ellington, particularly his composition *Take the A Train*. I have his track of it, plus Dave Brubeck's version. My Wish Track is The Duke, the latter's tribute to Ellington whose composition output to the genre is unassailable.

DAY 60
28th February - Clovelly to Westward Ho! –11 miles

It is going to be a significant day as my eldest daughter Suzanne, husband Rob and grandchildren Lewis and Lauren are going to rendezvous with me at Westward Ho. We are all staying with Rob's parents, Barry and Pat Powell, in Barnstable for four days, my longest stopover of the whole walk. It is not a complete break – I shall be walking for two of the days.

Suzanne and Lauren at Westward Ho!

We leave early, because Ivor has a long return journey to Barnstable. He's a gentle man, and I am so pleased to see him and Marion again.

I leave Mount Pleasant and follow the Hobby Drive along a fine woodland track. It's a pleasant stroll on muddy paths; the leg muscles warm up to allow maximum efficiency. The going includes a series of short, steep undulations, finally leading to the Westward Ho! seafront.

I take shelter in a deserted amusement arcade. Its robotic machines are all blazing away in a cacophony of sound and sequential flashing coloured lights. There's not a soul about. The rain beats down, the wind blows and the sea frontage is deserted. .

Flek, trying to impress me with his literary knowhow, comments, 'Is this really the place Charles Kingsley wrote about?'

'Yes, it is. After his novel had become a best seller the place was romanticised and then became ripe for property investment. I must say it looks somewhat drab today.'

Venturing out into the wind I am ambushed by my family. We take a few hurried photo shots, all squeeze into the car and Suzanne whisks us back to her in-laws. Her father-in-law Barry is a 'Brumee' with an attitude, and a very amusing one at that. In retirement age he has had a part-time job at the local hospital, and Suzanne jokes, 'You just get the feeling that he runs the place.'

Mother-in-law Pat fusses around me and I soon feel very much at home.

Lewis and Lauren are amused to see Granddad with a beard. It soon becomes noisy, and Flek, anxious not to be left out, says, *'Just think – a nomad like you staying in one place for four days. You're going to get itchy feet, Col.'*

'There's no fear of that my friend. I think I've earned some convalescence entitlement though, don't you?'

Day 61
1st March – Westward Ho! to Barnstable – 19 miles

Suzanne runs me back to Westward Ho! I have a very long free stage today along broad, clear tracks and pedestrian paths for most of the way. With no ferry running, a lengthy detour is necessary along the banks of the River Torridge from Appledore to Bideford and then back to Instow on the other side. This bumps the mileage up to 19 miles.

After leaving the amusement arcade, the SWCP wheels around the weather-exposed Royal North Devon Golf Club. Then it circles Appledore's ship building sheds before the three-mile riverside boulevard leading to the Long Bridge in Bideford.

In delightful spring weather the riverside is packed with people sitting out in the sun, and I join them to for an alfresco lunch. Once over the bridge I follow the three miles back up to the rivermouth to stop at Instow. A very old railway signal box has been preserved here, a Mecca for rail buffs with a Grade II listed status.

The Way now utilises the old railway line with fine views across the estuary along the six miles to Barnstable. If it had not been for meeting several interesting people over this last stretch, the afternoon would have been a bit of bore. Perhaps I have come to expect a real physical challenge every day!

I have a rest day tomorrow. I can do with it.

Determination
'Do your thing'
Ralph Waldo Emerson

Any one competing in an endurance event has to obtain by hook or by crook certain attributes if they are to get through. A couple of words sum up the determination required to achieve success. They may sound a little old-fashioned now, but they still maintain their authority:

Fortitude requires the strength and endurance in a difficult situation or the ability to recover quickly from setbacks. The words 'courage', 'guts' and 'staying power' come to mind, but these days it might be hip to substitute them with 'up for it', 'gung ho' and ' hanging in there'

Resilience is the ability to recover quickly from any setback. Here key words that might fit could include 'spirit', 'hardness' and ' toughness', the modern counterparts perhaps being 'guts', 'no pain, no gain' and 'butch' .

It seems there are brief windows in life when personal physiology, fitness, ambition, stamina, will and endurance come together. The trick is to whistle up these building blocks of character at the exact time when the body and mind are in unison to tackle the objective.

There is, of course, an endless list of role models. Every day someone comes on the scene who has somehow bound all these traits together, among them:

Dee Caffari, whose circumnavigation of the World against prevailing winds in 2006 took just 178 days (half the time it took me to walk round GB).

Ranulph Fiennes, veteran explorer and circumnavigator of the world, who at 65 got up the north face of the Eiger in 2008 for charity.

Jane Tomlinson CBE, a Yorkshire mother and athlete who, despite suffering from terminal cancer, completed a series of athletic challenges and raised nearly two million pounds for charity before succumbing to her illness at the age of forty three.

Mark Beaumont from Dundee, who created a record by cycling around the world, covering 18.297 miles in 194 days despite vehicle crashes, being robbed and suffering dysentery.

I am particularly impressed by David Walliams of 'Little Britain' who found out that the only sport he was good at when growing up was swimming – so in 2006 he swam the English Channel in 10 hours 34 minutes.

These days there is a plethora of sports psychologists, personal trainers or so called 'life' coaches trying to induce the maximum physical output out of those prepared to pay for the 'pain to get gain' experience. On the other hand there are those who somehow get away with it with comparatively little effort. That's me folks!

DAY 62 –
2nd March – Rest day – Barnstable

It's a rest day with a difference, in the company of my family. Will it promise to be a laid back experience without incident? I doubt it – I bet Suzanne has got something up her sleeve!

After breakfast we leave her in-laws and saunter down into the town. As we pass the fire station the duty officer suddenly appears and invites us in. Before long I am being hoisted up on the hydraulic platform appliance, giving a bird's eye view of Barnstable. My daughter has arranged a 'busmen's holiday' for me: nice!

We later spend some time in Boots sorting out my SIM card photographs, and the rest of the day I relax with the kids. My presence is a little confusing for them because they now have to put up with two grandads. They are very brave about it!

Kit – State of Play

By now I think I am carrying everything that I am ever going to need. What I mean is that I have been away from home long enough to have embraced self-sufficiency, and so now (whether I like it or not) will have to depend on what is in the rucksack.

The important point here is that the talking is over; the crunch will really come when rough camping becomes a necessity. So far the only really niggling problem is the rucksack, which sooner or later will have to be replaced.

There have been real life changes of sorts. Not one 'Fisherman's Friend' have I sucked so far. It's not that I have a dependency: normally I am regularly bothered with a throat irritation but after two months I seem to be free of the problem. I'm off drugs!

DAY 63

3rd March – Barnstable to Croyde Bay – 14 miles

Another free day, and with Barry and Pat's provisions in my day sack I set off from the Long Bridge in Barnstable down the River Taw path.

The easterly wind still hasn't eased; it's mainly behind me. I get to the Chivenor Barracks and Airfield. Not a lot of activity today, but this is where the Army beach-landing assault 'squadies' do their training.

At Braunton the SWCP turns south to join the Tarka Trail and runs two miles out into the Taw/Torridge Estuary. A few 'on the fringe' lifestyle followers cling to an existence here in old caravans. At the bottom, an oblique turn north sends me through a semi dune area and I veer onto the Saunton golf course, passing the club house to the B3231. It's a Monday and there is hardly anyone around.

I cross the road to ascend Saunton Down, where I pause at an abandoned farmhouse on the hill. Its roof caved in, it is a sad sight. There are superb views here across several estuaries. A short walk along a cliff edge descends onto a narrow road without escape opportunities so I have to be wary of any traffic. I arrive at the popular Croyde Beach, popular for surfers. Here there are much needed refreshment facilities. I've not spoken to anyone today: a lucky break for someone!

Now Barry's last trip back to Barnstable and the family.

DAY 64

4th March – Croyde Bay/Woolacombe/Ilfracombe – 13 miles

A wistful goodbye to Suzanne, Rob and the grandchildren, who cheerily wave me off: four days of Grandad are enough. Barry takes me back to Croyde Bay. A big hug for Pat and a hand shake for Barry. They have been great, and I am off – rucksack and all.

I walk a mile along to Baggy Point to round this small peninsula. Further on, the path bends back again, and from the cliff head here I get a magnificent view of one of England' s most popular beaches at Woolacombe. Just one person with a dog is the only human presence on this two mile stretch of pristine sand.

'Look how clean it all is' exclaims Flek, 'Just think that in a few months time

it will be packed with sun worshippers, most of whom will have layered themselves in potions claiming protection from factor nought to fifty. They will all be sprawled out like basking seals. It's a tribal ritual, that's all it is.'

'I agree – and what about the cost of it all?' I reply. 'There was no Ambre Solaire when I was a boy. My mum ran a guest house in the 1950s and when the paying visitors came back from the beach at the end of a sunny day they were smothered in calomine lotion!

'Oh very alluring,' he replies, and we laugh at the absurdity of it all.

The beach looks very tempting, but it's a 'no go' area. Carrying thirty pounds over the soft sand will tax my energy levels in no time. Alas, this need for restraint applies to most of the beaches I encounter.

There are rewarding views along Lee Bay The first mile to Morte Point is easy but a rollercoaster and a flight of 92 steps awaits. After the Bull Point Lighthouse and some steep valleys the Path drops down into Lee. I get a drink at the Grampus pub. The remaining three miles are moderate to easy.

I am finally making for the upturned bucket-like towers of Ilfracombe's Landmark Theatre, and with some relief I descend into the town.

DAY 65
5th March – Ilfracombe to Coombe Martin – 5 miles

Jemma Lowin, a student, answered my appeal in the SWCP magazine and is hosting me for two nights. She shares a flat on the edge of town with a male colleague.

With just five miles to cover, this is really a rest day. Jemma drops me back in the town and I exit past the tiny secluded beach in the harbour and its wharf buildings. A steep circular path winds its way up a prominent landmark, the Hillsborough, topped with the earthen remains of a hill fort and now a nature reserve. Noisy bird activity here and fine views back to Ilfracombe.

Because of tidal restraint I have to resort to some dodgy coast road walking to Combe Martin's village high street, said by some, to be the longest in England.

To say that these short and FREE DAY stages are a luxury is not idle talk. The absence of pressure is calculable.

DAY 66

6th March– Combe Martin to Lee Abbey – 12 miles

Jemma drops me back to Coombe Martin, which stands at the western end of the Exmoor National Park. I thank her for acting on my story in the SWCP magazine. I buy provisions: there is little chance on this stage of purchasing refreshments.

Among the challenges today will be a couple of deep valleys with sharp ascents, a stretch of moorland and some cliff top hikes. One thing for sure – the scenery will be spectacular.

I have now been on the hoof a couple months and two things are becoming apparent: the days are getting longer and I meet more people on my travels. They look intriguingly at this scruffy individual approaching, but many stop and ask questions. I have begun to develop a blurb about what I am doing and the intention of it all. This has to be carefully managed, though. Flek offered advice the other day on how to overcome my shyness – or was it a dressing down?

'Now, Col, don't get too technical with these people. Watch for any yawning. Measure your message to finish before they start slipping away and, above all, allow them time to ask questions. I reckon about three minutes is your limit, with some time added for Q & A.'

He rattles on and on, and finally adds, 'Remember, I'm also here as your back-up monitor, so make my day and get it right.'

In other words, he is hinting, 'Keep me out of it.'

It is late afternoon when I reach the long uphill approach road to Lee Abbey. Here my hosting is due to an arrangement made by the helpful Heather Hyde, a member of the Chichester Jazz Club.

I am taken aback, because the building it is not what I thought it was going to be, an abbey! Structurally it isn't really true to its title. Built in the 1850s in a dramatic setting, it was first used as a private home and then a hotel. It is now a Christian conference retreat and run by the International Interdenominational Community. The place, in hotel speak , has a four star setting and comfortably attains a three-star accommodation standard.

Although treated politely I never really feel a part of the assembly, probably because I'm not here seeking spiritual guidance. Or, is it because the mainly mature students sense that here is a secular chap with whom they have little time to spread the faith. During breaks in the evening's programme small groups gather in corners and murmur seriously out of earshot. I wonder if they are actually talking about God. Except at the mealtime thanksgiving, I never hear anybody mention him at all. Strange that!

I am treated very courteously by the staff during my stay but am never approached by any of the delegates. The setting and grounds are wonderful.

DAY 67
7th March – Lee Abbey to Minehead – 20 miles

This is the last day of the SWCP, and the longest day for me so far. After an excellent, very early communal breakfast, I leave my temporary spiritual stop-over and step out towards the famous Valley of the Rocks just up the road.

It is a superb morning as I enter the valley, the sun rays just reaching the tips of its striking geological features. There is not a soul about as I follow the road through the one-kilometre dry valley. Its permanent residents, a herd of feral goats, are already browsing. Grazing on semi-sheer terrain holds little fear for these hardy animals.

Soon I reached Lynton, find a café open and take coffee and cake in alfresco style. The Lynton to Lynemouth cliff railway is closed for the season, so I negotiate a flight of never-ending steps down to the seafront. Just a few strides at the bottom and I arrive in Lynmouth.

It's a place of serenity now, but In 1952 the harbour was wrecked by a devastating flood after thirteen inches of rain fell on Exmoor overnight with the loss of over fifty lives. I steadily ascend a long, gradual hill and take the Path out towards Foreland Point. A hard twisting slog of seven miles awaits me.

After eight weeks of the SWCP I have had enough of the coastline. Although it is the last day of the Path I decide to cut inland to the A39 for two reasons – there is still a very long way to go and this road offers the shortest route; and I will have a chance to satisfy another objective i.e. to walk down the steepest 'A' road in the UK at Porlock.

It's the middle of the afternoon when I reach the A39. After a couple of miles I begin the descent of Porlock Hill, which drops 1300ft in less than two miles. This is no place for faulty brakes – or legs, for that matter. With its gradient plummeting to a severe 1-in 4-in places and some hairpin bends it is not surprising that vehicles breach walls on their descent. Half way down my calf muscles begin to tell me that I have made a reckless decision. Stumbling into Porlock I find a seat and put my legs up for fifteen minutes.

Still with five miles to go, I ring my next hosts Dave and Pam James. Dave comes out to meet me a couple of miles from Minehead. I refuse a lift, but mercifully he relieves me of the rucksack. Later he walks out to meet me again and we soldier back to his home.

The James, friends of my colleague Ivor Cooper from Barnstable, will be my hosts for two days. Later we are joined by a friend of theirs and all sit down for a super meal, spending a most convivial evening.

'So you have now completed the South West Coastal Path in 56 days – you should be proud of yourself,' says Flek warmly. 'Well done, Colin.'

I smile with contentment, but can't help wondering whether it is the wine talking!

It's been the longest day yet, and frankly I am knackered. Thank God I have a rest day tomorrow.

I yearn for my day off every fortnight. After a leisurely breakfast I wander down into Minehead, buy a *Telegraph*, enter a café for a coffee and read. It's not long before I progress to a pub for lunch and read on. It may sound silly but, believe me, the sense of freedom is quite overpowering!

Once again Dave and Pam look after me splendidly during the evening.

The Evening Concert: Bill Withers *Lovely Day*, Jimmy Smith *Walk on the Wild Side*, Brad Mehidau *Day is Done*. Wish track is Oliver Nelson's *Stolen Moments* – timeless and romantic as the title suggests.

MINEHEAD

This is the place where, in his hilarious book *500 Mile Walkies*, Mark Wallington records memories of sitting disconsolately on the murky seafront. He is at the start of his South West Coastal Path journey, pondering how he is going to control the unruly 'mutt' he is taking for walkies.

I burst out laughing when I read this comment on the first page: 'At the other end of the promenade the machine gun nests of Butlins loomed out of the mist and were gone.'

It reminded me of Bognor!

DAY 69

9th March – Minehead to Williton – 12 miles

Dave and I walk down to the IRB lifeboat station. A shower appears out of nowhere and I shelter inside until it blows over. My pause allows a chance to meet the crew. Like so many male close-knit groups, they jibe away at each other, injecting humour the likes of us wouldn't understand. I will come across more of this conduct later in the year.

Saying goodbye to Dave and the crew, I locate the magnificent commemorative marker which celebrates the South West Coastal Path. It comprises a large metal map sculpture held by huge hands and marks the start (or end) of the Walk.

In good hands – the end of the SWCP.

At last, after eight weeks of climbing practically every day, the going will be flat for miles and miles. What a relief!

I walk up into the town to the holiday village (Butlins), veering away from the soft sand beach, and go inland to the A39 to trek along to Carhampton. Here I turn left and return to the beach at Blue Anchor.

I discover the Blue Anchor Platform Museum on the West Somerset railway line. Running from Taunton to Minehead over a distance of twenty-three miles, it is the longest privately owned railway in the UK.

I am in luck, as there is some sort of event going on. A large crowd of railway anoraks, most with at least two cameras round their necks, are all waiting excitedly for a steamer to come through.

Unloading the rucksack, I hang on for the great occasion. On the narrow, crowded platform this turns out to be a wise move, because as the 'beast' puffs in there is an almighty push and shove by the enthusiasts to get their shots. I could have easily been tipped on to the line. You can imagine the press headline: 'Lone Walker Tragedy – Well He Got This Far!'

As the GWR 454 x 4-6-0 No. 7820 Dinchmore Manor (see how infectious train spotting can be) steams away, everyone contents himself with the excellent, but tiny, museum in the waiting room.

'Talk about an obsession. I don't suppose any of them has got an allotment,' remarks Flek.

'That's an interesting turn of thought, Flek,' I answer, struggling with his logic.

Just a few miles away is busy Watchet, invaded with weekend trippers. Now for a three-mile walk inland to reach the hamlet of Yarde, where Dick and Liz Mayes, friends of my colleague Doug Murgatroyd of the Cicestrians, are my next hosts. They live 'the good life' in a sprawling and cluttered bungalow.

Before an excellent evening meal Dick drags me around the small-holding to see his pigs. Hearing us, two spotted porkers pound across their enclosure and stand in their trough, expecting grub. He tries to re-assure them that it is not quite time for scoffing ,but they just squeal and squeal in a temper. He is so proud of them!

DAY 70
10th March – Williton to Holford – 12 miles

Dick and Liz take me back to Watchet and we stroll along the harbour promenade, pausing to view the statue of the Ancient Mariner. This is a tribute to Samuel Taylor Coleridge, who wrote the epic poem when living in the area.

We part and I head off out of town on a B-road, crossing the West Somerset Railway on my way to pick up the A39 again. I keep to the main road until just after the village of Kilve, when I get a chance to pick up a path which runs parallel with the A39, and I arrive at Holford. A pleasing diversion through a long dry wooded valley brings me almost direct to the home of my next hosts, Stewart and Elaine Tavner. Arriving a little early, I wait their return from daily teaching occupations and receive a warm welcome.

The Tavners are a CLIMB family, having lost their infant boy Jamie who had succumbed to Battens Disease several years ago.

The Tavners are marvellous hosts, and during the evening I am able to explain the circumstances that led me to become interested in metabolic conditions.

DAY 71
11th March – Holford (Coombe Witch) to Burnham on Sea – 13 miles

It's compromise time again. I need a catch-up day to maintain my schedule. Stewart agrees to drive me on a few miles into Combwich on the River Parrett. It's raining steadily as he drops me off at a riverside car park.

The trail I follow takes its name from the river. Across to my left I get my very first sighting of a nuclear power station at Hinckley Point; there will be a few more of these along my route. A couple of miles later the trail leaves the river and goes south across country, wending its way into the suburbs of Bridgewater. After a mid morning café break I cross the town's bridge and hike along the A38 to Burnham-on- Sea. Progress today is via three long, straight stretches and although they represent the shortest route it makes for a tedious journey.

My hosts for the next two days are Trevor and Elaine Mapstone a CLIMB family. Their son Adrian suffers from the metabolic condition Citrullinaemia. They live at North Petherton in the reverse direction on the other side of Bridgewater, and so Trevor is going to be ferrying me long distances to keep me en route.

On the phone we agree a rendezvous outside Burnham. Because of work he will be delayed, so I spend an hour sitting in a traditional enclosed glass bus stop complete with its traditional smashed pane of glass. I finish up my provisions for the day and bask in the sun, a wonderful tonic for the legs.

Several buses make the stop and I glance up from the greenhouse-like structure to see the curious stares of passengers. I sense that they are relieved that this worn-out tramp clasping his worldly belongings is not getting on board. Perhaps they're thinking that I am waiting for nightfall so I can doss down in it! Let 'em think!

As the umpteenth bus pulls away Flek unloads what has been puzzling him for some time: 'You have tendancy to fantasise a lot, Col. Some of your thoughts border on the surreal. How come?'

'Well, my friend, my formative years were dominated by radio's The Goon Show and Round the Horne, followed by TV's Monty Python and Spike Milliagan's 'Q' series so it became the norm to embrace humorist fantasy bordering on the surreal. Being a fan of Michael Bentine's Potty Time meant that there was always the possibility men in white coats would soon turn up and carry me away! You had to be a complete nutter to graduate in the first place, there aren't many of us left now, Flek.'

'People still laugh today, though', he says. 'The discourse to amuse is still alive. Each generation's perception of humour are poles apart, aren't they?'

'Well, be that as it may. In my opinion the art to amuse is today largely dominated by stand-up comedians who resort to profanities to get a laugh. It seems to me that the audiences of today are responding to expletives rather than to the content. Perhaps you would allow me to be a little more precise about

English humour, Flek. It's best described as "having a strong sense of sarcasm and self depreciation running though, with just a smidgeon of smut and innuendo." Got it?'

This was a little highbrow, and it startled him. To be honest, my pompous outburst surprised me as well!

Determined to make a point he goes on: 'There's a theory that the English joke to hide their embarrassment.'

'Well, Flek, I think you've knocked another nail on the head with that one.'

A cheerful Trevor finally picks me up for the long trip to North Petherton, where Elaine greets me like a long lost son.

Elaine and Trevor Mapstone, CLIMB parents, North Petherton.

DAY 72

12th March – Burnham on Sea to Weston-super-Mare – 12 miles

Trevor gets me back to Burnham. It is another free day. As the terrain is flat and easy going, I have a chance to look at the town's unusual structures. There are three lighthouses here. Identifying them can be confusing to a non-native. They are the 36ft Low tower on the sands, the Round Tower (1764–1832) and the 110ft High Lighthouse (1830–1992), once bought by the Rothschild family but now converted to residential use.

As I look up at this one, Flek jokes, *'Last one here gets the top bunk.'*

Not satisfied with this one-upmanship, the town also claims to have the shortest pier in the country. It seems that some councils will stop at nothing to get on the tourist circuit!

Returning to the Berrow Road leading to Weston, I catch two blokes maintaining street lights. I use the word loosely, as Stewart the cage operator says he has had to retract the hydraulic tower because the wind has got up to force two. Health and safety, he adds – and winks. He is, of course, having me on. I reckon it's blowing at least a force five.

Standing on the pavement is Derek, who is obviously the gaffer as he had a spanner in his hand. Stewart, an ex Para, will shortly be doing his own yomp for charity over the Brecon Beacons. It is an uplifting encounter with men of the countless army who sustain the nation's utilities and the quality of the banter is top-hole. We wish each other luck and I battle on, catching the full wind blast at each side-road I cut across.

I am now following a coastal access road for five miles, passing umpteen caravan/camp sites. There are wonderful views across the Bristol Channel to the islands of Flat Holm and Steep Holm, both important bird reserves. The wind is incessant and I am so glad that the Mapstones have relieved me of my rucksack.

Finally I reach the suburbs of Weston and stride out the last couple of miles along the front to the tourist information office.

Trevor comes an awful long way to pick me up, and once again it's miles back to his home.

The Kit

'The reason the Romans built their great paved highways
was because they had such inconvenient footwear.'
– Charles de Meontesquieu

I could submit the list of my requirements and eventual choice of kit, such as how many pairs of socks I took, but I won't. I'm going to concentrate on the main successes, disappointments and failures.

Firstly I never used Fisherman's Friend throat tablets (yes, I have heard the joke), water bladder/reservoir and tube system and first aid kit (not once in the whole year: how is that for luck?).

I had a tenuous relationship with my kit supplier/advisor. I enjoyed a discount on the equipment purchased, but they showed little enthusiasm for my project. Although agreeing to some sponsorship, the body language of the staff, with one exception, said it all. My advice is seek out a big player in the leisure equipment retail world and make your mark, allowing two or even three years' notice. Everybody is after sponsorship!

Personal kit must be fit for purpose, doing what it says on the tin! The first priority is to restrict the total weight to be carried at all costs. I aimed to carry 25lbs (11.3 kilos) at three miles per hour in Wales and England, and 30lbs (13.5 kilos) at two-and-a-half miles an hour in Scotland. In military terms these payloads sound modest, but try carrying them up relentless gradients for a year. Water and gas cylinders make considerable in-roads into the total weight allowance.

Disappointments
• Tracker device.
• 'RAB' top Jacket – had fiddly hood 'pulls'; early loss of breast pocket, zip pull; became detached. (All my grandkids' key ring photos were attached, and daughter Suzanne went to a great deal of trouble to get these: a shame!)
• 'RAB' waterproof trousers - started to come apart after just a few wears! Had the annoyance of claiming on guarantee and arranging delivery to host address. (Always take purchase receipts on the trip.)
• Gregory Rucksack (American apparently) – too clever by half. (Too many adjustment straps, seventeen in all! I ditched for Berghaus replacement in Wales.)

Failures
• Sleeping bag. This was my fault. Because I arrived in Scotland during the summer months I ditched my -10°C-rated bag and at Fort William foolishly replaciing it with a -2°C rating, a big mistake.

• 'Thermorest' inflatable mattress. This developed a puncture, supposedly repaired by my kit supplier. I was saved by John Hutchinson, my excellent host at Fort William, who gave me a length of thick, hard foam bedroll. I really needed it.

Successes
• Hilliberg tent – stood up to the weather
• Hanweg boots (German and possibly a 'promotion'). I used three pairs. Receiving the third pair turned out to be quite a saga. It's a shame that it was the only problem that my retailer/sponsor ever bothered to contact me about on the whole trip. They failed to show up on my walk's departure or arrival!
• All my body layers worked as well as could be expected. I became very wary of manufacturers' claims about the 'wicking out' of perspiration.

Little Things That Helped Me a Lot
Strangely a number of small items were invaluable:
• Silk liner insert – for the sleeping bag. Expensive but feather-light. The claims of upgrading the bag's insulation by three degrees rang true.
• Crocks – very light, providing me with a much needed change of footwear in the evening. What a bargain at £2.50 in the seafront market at Morcambe!
• Kitchen rolls – Multi-use and invaluable;. Wrapped inside a shoe bag they made an excellent pillow.
• Underwear – 'Icebreaker' base underwear sold as 'no odour' garments. Pricey, but manufactured in Merino Wool: the concept worked. The sales person said that one customer claimed sixty-three consecutive days in the pants. I felt a bit of a failure, clocking up just ten. One of my pairs went missing from the Inchnadamph hostel drying room, meaning that I had fifteen hundred miles to go in my remaining pair. Many of my hosts laundered them – whether they needed it or not!

Finally, I calculated that I shipped the 15kg rucksack onto my shoulders over two thousand times. Whenever possible, the trick is to first hoist it on to a wall, somebody's wheelie bin or even a telephone street junction cabinet – all manoeuvres making it easier to transfer on to the back.

I made considerable efforts to consult experienced people on how best to kit myself out. However, unless you are a regular outside trail blazer there is always the chance of hit-and-miss results, and that's how things turned out.

DAY 73
13th March –Weston Super Mere to Clevedon – 13 miles

Farewell to the Mapstones. They are a typical CLIMB Family, for years suffering all the tribulations of care for their son. It was a privilege to meet them. Trevor gets me back to Weston, a long trip.

There are going to be some days when going from A to B is not straightforward, and today is one of them. The coastal route will include road, a sandy bay and a further four miles of exposed sand with no discernible footpath showing on the map.

The normal tide limit (NTL) is up, which probably means a slog along soft banks/dunes. I also have to find some way to get across the River Yeo, so I opt for the longer inland route. It's going to be on the road all day, but I will be on a firm footing and I am used to these mileages by now.

I wend my way out of Weston, crossing Junction 21 of the M5 and three miles later re-crossing the motorway. Entering the outskirts of

The Bird family.

Clevedon, I visit Tesco's. A phone call to my next hosts, Neil and Nita Bird, confirms that their home is a only a few hundred yards away. Soon I am having tea and chat with a most delightful family and their dog.

The Birds are another CLIMB family, their little boy Sam having the generic metabolic disorder Tyrosinaemia Type 1. He is your usual noisy little lad, and careful diet and expensive drug control stabilises his life. His sister Lauren has sacrificed her bedroom for me. Tonight this butch adventure is going to slumber surrounded by pink accessories and cuddly toys!

DAY 74
14th March – Clevedon to Avonmouth – 13 miles

After a great stay over I have to move on. The kids go to school. It's a day off for Neil, who decides to walk with me to Portishead where Nita will join us later for a pub lunch.

With their dog Mercy we set off on a miserable morning, this time on the proper coastal path. Weather conditions prohibit us from seeing the Welsh coast, but we plod on at a brisk pace.

After four miles we arrive at Black Nore, where an extraordinary structure confronts us. Anyone passing would be forgiven for thinking they were viewing either a giant rocket firework stuck in the sand awaiting someone to light its blue touch paper, the Tin Man from the Wizard of Oz or a Dalek on stilts – or, best of all, a crude spaceship prop from a 1930s Hollywood epic. Is it any of these things?

Of course not: it's the Black Nore Point lighthouse. This strange structure was erected in 1894 to serve the Bristol Channel shipping traffic. At just 11 metres in height, it has a range of 15 miles.

The Priory Pub at Portbury is packed, but we finally secure a table and have a splendid lunch in a bustling atmosphere.

I'm not going to say goodbye just yet. Such is this family's loyalty to my cause that they are prepared to collect me tomorrow beyond my next host's territory, an extraordinary gesture.

I ring those hosts and Emma Clare arranges a rendezvous at a pub close to the Avonmouth Docks. This pub upholds a fine English tradition, that of being a midweek meeting house for all those on social benefit. I wade through the fag ends, push past the itinerants on the pavement outside noisily swopping jokes, some at my expense, and enter. It is like being in a 'Western' i.e. stranger enters a bar and the critters go silent and look up. In shorts and unloading a backpack, I'm a little conspicuous but then some inquisitive Charlie asks me what I am doing and all of a sudden I become a celebrity.

With a pint in my hand I am paraded outside to the same lot who had reluctantly stood aside a few minutes earlier, and an infection of amusing banter breaks out. Most of them find it impossible to comprehend that I have been walking for two months. They talk to me as if I am an 'experiment' It's an hilarious encounter.

Some time later Emma Clare drives up in flash limo. She is on a 'high' having spent the day with her girl friends at Cheltenham Races. The pub crowd give her what can only be described as an 'unsophisticated' roar of approval as we speed away to her splendid home somewhere in the suburbs of Bristol.

The Clares are a CLIMB family, their daughter Millie having the metabolic condition Cystinosis, which has meant a poorly start to her life. With the support of her mum and dad, Emma and Darren, and her brother William, she is lively young lady who accepts her treatment with innocent casualness, as I am to experience during my stay.

Down in the kitchen next morning her mum makes up a liquid meal then loads it into a pump device. Then, as cool as you like, young Millie places it into her tummy externally and has breakfast in her own way. This procedure is all part of her special diet, and like kids all over she takes it in her stride before going to school.

15th March – Avonmouth to Severn Bridge (M48) - Aust - 9 miles

Following my own 'orthodox' breakfast, Darren drives me the long way back to the Pub at Avonmouth and I am ready for another nine miles. I am heading towards the Avonmouth Docks and onto the Severn Way Coastal Path, passing a vast area of heavy industry including the Seabank Power Station. These areas are never pretty, and the deteriorating weather adds to the gloom. The M4 Severn Bridge now looms ahead. It starts to rain heavily and I escape to a pub in the village of Pilning .

This is just what I dream of on a wet day, i.e. a bar with raging fire, friendly landlord and a plate full of great grub. I am not alone, though. The bar is empty save for a group of men all standing in a corner arguing the toss over this and that. One of them is holding court using expletives continually to make his point. This time nobody even blinked as I entered, so no 'Wild West' stand-off on this occasion then.

With enthusiasm Flek butts in: 'There have been few Westerns that have not included 'stand-off's ,Col,' he says, 'I love them, especially if Clint is the gunslinger. It's so predictable that he's going to take at least three gunfighters out at the first 'pull' using only one barrel! What a success rate. My favourite scene though has got to be the Earps and Doc taking on the Clantons and McLaury's at the OK Corral.'

'So I gather you are a Western Fan then, Flek. I like a good 'kitchen sink' drama myself.'

He laughs in derision.

The rain persists as I find a B road which crosses the M4 on its way to the M4 Bridge. In a mile I am back on the Severn Way Path, which is now the Severn Estuary bank approaching the M48 Severn Bridge. I have to cross the second of the two bridges, as it has a footway across it. Just one-and-a-half miles separate these two mighty suspended structures.

I ring Neil Bird. He motors the very long way from Clevedon to fetch me from the church standing adjacent to the bridge in Aust village. In the last couple of days two CLIMB families have shown great commitment, covering many miles to ensure my accommodation.

DAY 76
16th March – Aust (M48 Severn Bridge) – Portskewett in Wales – 10 miles

The Birds get me the long way back to Aust, what a generous family! My charity CLIMB have arranged for me to meet Nigel Eaton, chairman of its board of governors, who lives in the Bristol area with his wife Jane and their daughter, Issy. It's another dreary morning as Neil drops me at the local church after a long drive: brilliant! The Eatons have taken shelter in the church porch.

Nigel's involvement with CLIMB stems from the loss of a son, Henry, just a few days after his birth from the metabolic condition known as Hyperammonaemia Ornithine Transcarbamylase Deficiency. Issy has inherited the same condition but is a boisterous six year old and seemingly in good health. She constantly harasses me for details of my walk for use in a class project at her school. I sign my first autograph!

With Nigel Eaton and Issy.

We have a grand chat. I very much appreciate they have made the journey from Bristol so early to greet and encourage me. Our parting is particularly significant, as I shall shortly be leaving England for some time.

I can hear the drumming of traffic approaching the M48 Bridge, it is so near. I cut up the short lane to the bridge, its towers rising 445ft above me into the morning mist. The Queen opened it in 1966. At 1600 metres long, the suspension is achieved using 18,000 strands of wire.

The Anglo-Welsh bard Hari Webb wrote an *Ode on the Severn Bridge* which goes:

> *Two lands at last connected*
> *Across the waters wide,*
> *And all the tolls collected*
> *On the English side.*

This cosy arrangement was made to counteract traffic congestion! Well, that's what the English said!

I pass on to the footpath with the roaring traffic just a few feet away. At a couple of miles to my left is the equally massive M4 Severn Bridge.

To celebrate my first major bridge crossing I get out my ipod and select three tracks. The first is 'The Chant', recorded by Jelly Roll Morton and his Red Hot Peppers in 1928. For the uninitiated, Morton was one of the great characters in jazz history and went round New Orleans boasting that he had invented the music idiom. My second choice is Bach's 'Toccata & Fugue', for two reasons: first it seems so majestic for the occasion, and secondly I imagine that the hundreds of vertical suspension wires around me are organ pipes. Seeing that I am fleeing from my home country, I finish with Queen and Freddie Mercury belting out 'I Want to be Free'.

Despite the traffic noise and the ipod distraction, the experience leaves me strangely isolated. Flek however gets quite excited and blurts out: 'Wouldn't it be great today if scores of surfers riding the Severn Bore passed beneath us?'

'Dream on mate, don't get carried away,' is my reply to his preposterous suggestion. This is an agitated reaction and unfair, for he is only trying to bolster the occasion. He just whistles a tune and ignores me.

In twenty minutes I arrive in another country and, with no passport control, I pass down the exit steps cross a railway bridge to pick up the B4245. I enter Wales, and soon I am with my next hosts Joe and Margaret Cowley and granddad Ernest.

For this hosting I have to thank my jazz club colleague Ray Pratt back in Hampshire who has known Joe for many years due to their shared interest in classic motor bikes.

Joe commutes to work over the bridge to Bristol daily but doesn't part with any cash as motor bikes are exempt – a cunning way to thwart the English!

I have a great stay and am becoming an authority on bathroom fittings. At the Cowley's I have spotted a collectors' item, i.e. I get into the only corner bath during my entire walk.

Crossing the Severn Bridge (M48).

Legs (1)

'A brief moment when we are given the opportunity of performing
at our best'
- Michael Johnson

All parts of our bodies are dependable on each other, this is what we are. For the sake of emphasise, though, it is the limbs, particularly the lower ones, that deliver the motive power necessary to achieve physical targets The brain, our control and command mechanism, issues instructions. However, I am convinced that on many occasions, my legs simply did not obey; they had temporarily expired. This was a first for me!

One day during a storm I sought protection in a bus shelter. It was summer and I was in shorts. The rain persisted, and after refreshment I looked down at my legs. The lower limbs gift us with at least seven essential manoeuvres and since our birth have grow to the full human potential: they are our first and only issue. They also have a history, and as the rain ran down the shelters glass panes, mine started to flood back.

Our memories develop at different speeds, but most of us have can remember snatches of childhood. Sometimes they are so vivid they stick and are instantly recalled in detail when triggered

My very first memory of how important my legs were to me occurred on the night of the 10th January 1941, I was four years old. I was born in Portsmouth and during that night the Luftwaffe paid the city a visit. The air raid siren went and I remember the next door neighbours banging on the door. My mother was just recovering from a serious operation and she had asked them to help her in any emergency. My father was away at sea in the Royal Navy.

Our neighbours picked up my brother Alan, and Mum grabbed my hand. I vividly remember my little legs trying to keep up with hers as we hurried to the brick air raid shelter allocated to the householders at one end of Nelson Road in the Landport part of the city.

For the record, three hundred bombers dropped 140 tons of high explosive and thousands of incendiary bombs which set large parts of the city alight, including the Guildhall which was badly damaged. Over 170 people lost their lives.

My other abiding memories of that night are of my mother's terror as the bombs fitted with whistling devices rained down. When we left the shelter after the 'all-clear' siren, the early morning cloud cover had a vivid pink hue, reflecting the scores of fires raging across the city.

That is the first time I remember using my legs!

DAY 77
March 17th Portskewett (Wales) to Langstone – 10 miles

This address is a map dump, and armed with a fresh supply I strike out along the B4245 towards the town of Magor. For some inane reason I keep pondering who is the Welsh equivalent to Victor Meldrew in tone of voice? Philip Madoc is it?

After mid-morning café refreshment I slog on in fair weather. On approaching Langstone I notice banners swinging from lamp posts announcing that the Ryder Cup is to be held at the local Celtic Manor Golf Course in 2010. Not being a golfer, I find it hard to believe that this prestigious world sporting event is to be held here in Wales and not on one of the established championship courses. But it is!

The host connection in Langstone has come to me in a roundabout manner. My next door neighbour Sue Black is a driving instructor. She mentioned my project to her boss at Chichester, who not only donated but introduced a friend of his, Steve Cheesewright, who lives in this area.

A knock on the door triggers much barking and Steve's wife Ingrid appears with a couple of Pointers. These naturally energetic dogs eventually settle down – and so do I in a splendid residence.

Steve, a member oft the Celtic Manor, later solves my golfing enquiry. It appears that a local who made a fortune in the USA returned home with a determination to bring the Ryder Cup to Wales. So he financed the building of a course to fit the occasion, as you do! So the mystery, for me, has been solved.

This is another enjoyable stop-over.

DAY 78

18th March Langstone to Barry – 22miles

I say goodbye to Steve and Ingrid early, as I have the longest stage so far. For the first week the Welsh coastline is not blessed with paths which allow my walking pace of two-and-a-half miles per hour with a 30lb rucksack or three miles without. There is no time to deviate today: it is going to be road all the way. I follow the A48 to Junction 24 of the M4. On the way I can see to the south the vast Llanwern steelworks, now sadly in decline.

Next is the B4237, which dissects Newport, and it's time for a café stop. I press onto the A469 and enter Cardiff city centre. Getting a little tired now, I flop down into a café.

I stroll down the one mile-broad and straight Lloyd George Avenue, created as part of the Cardiff Bay development. On one side are up-market flats, and on the other an open prospect has been retained. Landscaped with trees and flower beds, it leads down to the Millennium Centre and the National Assembly of Wales building.

The impressive unusual design of the former, a major arts centre, has affectionately attracted the nickname of the Armadillo. The Assembly building, in contrast, has had its detractors calling it 'a large shed with a chamber in the middle'. From the outside it doesn't look anything special, but no doubt the interior meets its purpose. The cost of all this must have dug very deep into this nation's GNP.

Flek is fed up: 'Enough of this sightseeing, Col. It's late afternoon, you still have to get to Barry,' he urges.

Most of the main roads I follow today are lined with Sustrans National Cycle Path Route 4, allowing ample pedestrian separation from the traffic. However, for the last three miles I have no protection and my progress in what is now the evening rush hour is 'hairy'.

By now I am knackered and drop the dreaded pack off my back by an approach roundabout to Barry, waiting for Lorraine Powell, my next host, to pick me up. I have covered twenty-two miles.

She and her husband Ivor will be looking after me, thanks to the intervention of my old jazz club friend Ken Marshall, who arrives later. He has come all the way from Spalding in Lincolnshire to stay, and will be my walking companion for a couple of days. What a pal!

Ken Marshall's career was with the immigration service. This means that many of his former retired colleagues still live by the coast. So he, with several others, notably Dough Murgatroyd (Chichester High School) and David Garforth (Rotary UK), have turned out to be key sources of hosts for me throughout the year. Invaluable!

DAY 79
19th March – Barry to Llantwit Maor – 14 miles

I set off with Ken Marshall through Barry, avoiding the dock area. We join the Valewood Millennium Coastal Path. It is cold, overcast and breezy. The beach is a mixture of rocks and pebbles, not very inviting today. A lone walker appears. Apparently he is doing the same thing as I am and hopes to get to his finish at Portsmouth in a couple of months' time. Hope he makes it.

We pass Cardiff International Airport at Rhoose. Not a single air traffic movement occurs during the two hours we are in vicinity! Normally these regional airports have regular winter breaks flights, but let's face it, who wants to leave the Vale of Glamorgan for an out of season holiday in the Canary Islands on an indifferent day like this?

This is the first of many day walks with Ken during the coming year At eighty years old his walking ability hasn't diminished, and he is great company. Humour and jazz talk sums him up.

We come off the Path at Stout Point and walk north a couple of miles to Lllantwit to call on next hosts Neville (Rotary) and Janet Farthing. Ken is picked up: I shall see him again tomorrow.

Later a Rotary friend of Neville's takes me for a drive to view the nearby St Donat's Castle It was to here in the 1920s that William Randolph Hearst, the legendary Californian newspaper magnate thought to be the Orson Welles model for Citizen Kane, brought his mistress, the film star Marion Davis, on a vacation. He spent a fortune on the place for her – I'm sure she thought she was worth it. Then the depression came, he went bust and that blew the lid on their deception. Apparently their presence was not to the liking of local moralists. It's now the seat of the successful international Atlantic College.

My hosts are great company and their small talk is of much interest.

DAY 80
20th March – Llantwit Magor to Monknash – 6 miles

The Farthings have looked after me so well. Ivor delivers Ken back and we set off on what is to be a short and leisurely 'free' day. On a brighter day we soon get back onto the Coastal Millennium Trail, and after a couple of miles arrive at St Donat's College, where I have been the previous afternoon.

At Cae'r Eglwys it's necessary to cut inland to our destination at Monknash, where I have been informed that an agreeable pub awaits us for lunch – and we are not disappointed.

The Plough and Harrow dates back to 1383 and was originally a monastic farmhouse. It boasts a food and drinks menu which is constantly changing, with fresh and unexpected delights. It's one of those pubs we all dream about, i.e. it has an ancient history, a huge fireplace, no-nonsense furniture, a young chatty landlord and super grub. Most importantly, it has never been 'tarted-up'. Ken and I have a

most comfy and congenial time for a couple of hours: frankly, we did not want to leave. However, our time was called when Neville Farthing arrived, and after another drink we returned to Llantwit.

I say goodbye to Ken for the time being. It will be another seven months before we are to meet again in Lincolnshire.

With Ken Marshall at Monknash.

DAY 81
21st March – Monknash to Ewenny – 6 miles

Neville delivers me back to Monknash. It will be a short journey on the road today.

Still on the Millennium Heritage Trail, which has now passed inland, I head for the attractive town of St Brides Major for an early lunch. I pass through the short Pant (valley) St y Brid safe from the traffic on the generous roadside grass verge. A cutting entrance appears in the roadside high bank to my left. Through huge gates I look into what is an enormous limestone quarry.

It's not far now to my next hosts, Colin and Pauline Karp. These are the parents of Trish, the wife of Jane Taylor's nephew Darren Grafham. Host Colin turns out to be a very precise but interesting character, the exact opposite of his namesake who is staying the night!

A little later Darren arrives with his wife Trish, my hosts' daughter, and their young son Ewan. I am privileged to part of an affectionate family get-together, with grandson Ewan being the centre of attention. Before an evening meal we retire to the garden for photographs and then have a grand chinwag.

The Karp and Grafham families, Ewenny.

DAY 82

22nd March – Ewenny to Port Talbot – 15 miles

Parting company from the Karp family I stride out cross the Ewenny Bridge and take the secondary road up to the busy Bridgend Bypass.

Flek makes himself known. He apologies for his silence during the last few days, saying it is because I have had company. He can be very thoughtful at times.

'That's OK Flek but keep alert, I still need a cutting edge councillor, guru, sage, buddy and . . .'

'All right, Col, keep your hair on,' he splutters in embarrassment. 'Normal service has been resumed.'

Walking the trunk roads is noisy and tedious but is necessary. This strategy comes about for three reasons. Firstly there is no defined coastline path in this part of South Wales. Secondly the uneven course and constant change of direction of existing paths hampers progress, and finally I have to honour the original schedule in order to keep faith with my Hosts.

I'm pushing north now, and at Mawdlam I cross and re-cross the M4. I go through the small town of Margan, the location of the second massive steel works in South Wales.

Eventually I locate the address of my hosts Dennis and Chris Dyer in Port Talbot. This contact is due to my benefactor of yesterday, Colin Karp.

The Dyer's house is in chaos. In view of their recent holiday engagement I am amazed that they took me in at all. They have just arrived back from a month's holiday in Australia only to find that their rugby playing sons haven't done any laundry during their absence. Chris toils away constantly loading the washer. I find it difficult to comprehend that this dedicated wife and mother had, just a few days previously, clambered to the top of the Sydney Harbour Bridge.

Regardless, I am made very welcome. One of her boys has sacrificed his room for me. As I settle into bed I glance up to his extensive library shelves. Guess what? Rugby literature from end to end!

'What is it with the Welsh and this game Flek?

'Dunno,' he says. 'Perhaps it gives them a break from the singing!'

Let's Hear the Music

'The English don't understand music, but they like the sound it makes.'
— Sir Thomas Beecham

Despite the physical targets set for each day and the time consumed in achieving them, I still had hours of idle evening 'leisure', when either at a host's home or, more importantly, in the tent. Carrying books would sap my energy, so how am I going to combat boredom?

My itinerary runs thus: pitch the tent, prepare a meal and brew up a drink. Later I leave for a 'comfort' break and return, make up my 'bed', edit a blog to CLIMB and then phone friends and family on a rotation basis. With a host family I would be tucked up in a warm bed, but what do I do now?

Problematically most camping took place in the north and in Scotland during the summer months. Here the daylight hours persisted well into the early hours of the morning, the continued light making getting to sleep an issue. Although I marvelled at the evening sky I still had many hours in which to provide my own entertainment.

Early on the Walk I remember Flek goading me on: *'Go on, Col, shove some wires in your ears – pick up the vibes man.'*

He was trying to sound like a Rasta; it was his way of keeping my spirits up.

The problem is solved by using the iPod that my brother Alan had bought me as a birthday gift. The task of loading my music selection fell to Malcolm Oliver, my fire brigade colleague of many years. Alan, with Olly, spent an afternoon loading up a selection of tracks from tapes and CDs. Olly has a master collection of radio humour avidly recorded over several decades, and he added eight episodes of Round the Horne. I had left this option to the last moment so only a fraction of my preferred tracks are included.

It is going to be an eclectic choice. There is Jazz of course, with some classics and pop. These genres made up the bulk of this mobile library but some 'miscellaneous' tracks were also included. As I went round I would yearn for performances that had not been downloaded. Annoyingly I had to compromise and added these as a postscript to each concert classifying them as my 'Wish' list.

For obvious reasons, tramping the roads using earplugs in't a good idea. Although pathways offered a safer alternative I still needed to concentrate on my footing, but occasionally I relented. Waves crashing against the cliffs meant the accompaniment of 'Fingals Cave' was called for. South of Hartlepool on the road to Middlesbrough I pulled out Chris Rea's 'The Road to Hell'!

I devised the Evening Concert, which eventually became a spiritual need and, thanks to hosts who kindly charged up my iPod, I was able to enjoy some of my favourite music on demand. Utter Bliss!

I think it is time to let everyone in on an indulgence of mine. I am still playing out an entrenched fantasy here. It involves Desert Island Discs and goes like this. For years when soaking in the bath I would listen out for the phone – no mobiles in those days. I used to dream that it would ring, where upon I would then rush clutching a towel to the receiver, pick it up and a voice would say, 'Is that Colin? This is Sue Lawley here. I understand you are an avid listener of Desert Island Disc. Now you must be aware of the format, i.e. that each week a well known personality announces their eight favourite tracks. This week's invitee has had to call off at short notice so the producer, anxious to hurriedly find a replacement, has decided to hold a lucky dip into the BBC's TV licence holder register and your name has come out. Can you get up to Broadcasting House on Wednesday so that we can record you for this week's 'Programme'?

Of course her call has never come, so during this 'solitary' trip I will use my 'off duty' time, in part, to fulfil the dream. I refuse to be thwarted because on a day to day basis I always adjust my list of tracks anyway.

May I add that one of the disappointing aspects about modern popular music is the exclusion of any instrumental solos. It's a voice-only culture that now prevails. Here is my current list:

"How High the Moon" – Les Paul and Mary Ford
"Savoy Blues" – The Saints Jazz Band
"Piano Concerto in G" – Ravel
"Stolen Moments" – Oliver Nelson
"Balcony Rock" – Dave Brubeck Quartet"
"Requiem" – Lennie Tristano
"Fantasia on a Theme by Thomas Tallis" – Vaughan Williams
"Bohemian Rhapsody" – Queen

If I am going to play this game, then I suppose I had better answer the programme's other obligatory questions. Here goes:

If I have to select one track then it has to be the Dave Brubeck.

My Book choice is probably Lawrie Lee's *Cider with Rosie*.

Luxury Item – An inexhaustible supply of disposable electric tooth brushes with toothpaste. Can you imagine not be able to clean your teeth year in, year out.

I don't suppose I am the only one who wishes that dear old Roy Plomley had settled for ten discs. These days it would mean a whole hour with the delectable Kirsty Young!

I am pleased with my choices, but then Flek unsettles me: *'So is this it then, Col? Are you sure that this really is your definitive list? After all, tomorrow is another day!*

DAY 83
23rd March – Port Talbot – Swansea to Mumbles – 15 miles

Port Talbot is part of a former industrial heartland which is experiencing a steady decline. However, it has another heritage. Both Richard Burton and Sir Anthony Hopkins were born here, and Newport-born actor Michael Sheen was brought up in the town from an early age.

Dennis runs me up to the nearest A48 junction. A mile on is a junction onto the A483 to Swansea. Luckily this is also Route 4 of the Sustrans National Cycle network, allowing me to walk for miles on its cycle paths and so keeping me a safe distance from the traffic.

I journey on for five miles and enter Swansea, passing a modern hotel where, unknown to me, I will be staying the night in a few days' time. I make my way onto its seafront esplanade walk. This sweeps seven miles around the impressive Swansea Bay all the way to the Mumbles, the most memorable promenade stroll of the year.

I am surprised to find that the Mumbles is not just a lifeboat station but also a bustling retreat for those seeking a day out with a string of restaurants to rival any city. The place is packed, and I push my way past the RNLI Station post and around Mumbles Head to the quieter and well kept residential suburb of Limeslade.

Here I was originally going to be hosted by the Coates family. Phil Coates has rung CLIMB to say that their holiday dates now clash with my arrival, but he has made arrangements with their next door neighbours, Mr and Mrs Rance, to put me up. This splendid couple have stepped in to give me shelter, and I am interested to hear about Mr Rance's a career as a salesman in the toy industry.

As an industrial and commercial history exercise, this day has had everything. Starting with an escape from a town still coming out of a state of industrial decline to one which is clearly re-inventing itself and finally onto a bustling day-trippers' leisure venue at a startling location.

Also this is the gateway to the famous Gower Peninsula, the very first place in the UK to be designated a 'site of an area of outstanding beauty.' I am about to hike round 34 miles of its heritage coastline.

24th March – Mumbles to Port Eynon YHA – 13 miles

As I leave, the Rances tell me that at the end of the road I will pass an unimposing house hidden by a high fence where the Welsh-born Hollywood actress Catherine Zeta Jones returns home to visit her parents. As I pass by I can't resist a quick peep: she isn't in!

'So in the future you might be resorting to name-dropping. That's a bit desperate isn't it.'

Flek's sarcasm is back with a vengeance.

'My granddad was brought up in the East End,' he goes on, 'and knew a friend of the Kray's mother but he didn't go on about it – well, only after several of pints.'

'He sounds like Alf Garnett to me. Did he make you all stand up when the national anthem was played late at night on the telly?'

'Watch it, Col, we are supposed to be pals,' he grumbled.

As they say, this line of enquiry is terminated.

I have walked just a few hundred metres when another chance encounter occurs. A Land Rover pulls up with a 'Ranger' sign on the door. A lean, fit individual replete with wide brim hat and wearing bush gear jumps out and asksd me where I am going. Having heard my story he enquires as to my accommodation needs. I tell him that I may have to pitch the tent on Tuesday.

'Don't worry,' he said, 'I've got a caravan at LLanrhidian on the other side of the Gower. Stay with me.'

He added: 'I'm working on the beach at Port Eynon at present, so if it's your rest day there tomorrow seek me out and we can have a fish and chip lunch in the village café and talk about it. I'm Martin Cook by the way, and work as a heathland ranger for the local authority.'

What another slice of luck!

In fine sunny weather this is a momentous day walking the cliffs of a magnificent coastline with its imposing beaches offering fabulous stretches of golden sand, several backed with dunes.

The youth hostel at Port Eynon is a former lifeboat station in a superb location. Its slipway down to the beach is still in situ. The warden, Mags Attwell, a bubby person, waives the charges.

I appear to be the only resident in the hostel at the moment. I fix myself some breakfast. Mags tell me that the hostel is the base for a 'reflexology' practice. She has arranged and paid for me to have some treatment this very morning. I find myself at the head of a stream of clients.

The practitioner, a strapping German lady, sets about my feet and soon I am wincing.

'Don't worry" she says. 'When you leave tomorrow you will be walking on air, I promise you.'

Of course I experience nothing of the kind. Call me a sceptic, but frankly a good soak in hot water would have had the same effect. I have always thought that with many of these health practices a sort of placebo effect kicks in. In fairness, the two ladies have put themselves out for my welfare and I really am most grateful.

At midday I walk along the beach and find Martin Cook and a colleague carrying out remedial sea defence with a JCB.

We retire to a nearby café, and over a fish and chip lunch Martin outlines the directions to his caravan site. His colleague smiles knowingly – aware of what I will be experiencing the following night!

I spend the rest of the day relaxing at this wonderful location: after all, I *was* now 'walking on air'! Mags, her partner Fred and baby Josh appear, and I eagerly snapped this loving family.

I am to find out that some of the most helpful individuals about are hostel wardens, and Mags is a prime example.

DAY 86
26th March – YHA Port Eynon to LLanrhidian – 14 miles

I give Mags a well deserved smacker on the cheek and strike out along the dramatic cliff path of South Gower. At midday, after four miles, I find myself at the south-west tip of this outstanding peninsula. At an information post I chat to a man with a splendid dog. We I will meet again later in the day.

To my left is the imposing Rhossili Beach, which stretches away dramatically for three miles. The most westerly of the Gower's many beaches, it is often at the full mercy of Atlantic gales. It's popular for surfing, once being voted the best in the UK. On this sunny mid-spring day hardly a soul has set foot on it.

Flek is ecstatic: 'What a wonderful view! You're bringing me to some outstanding places. Col.'

I wince with satisfaction. I suppose deep down we do share the same values after all.

Hauling myself up the long gradual incline to the top of the 500ft Rhossilli Down I get an overall view of the whole bay at the tip of the peninsula, an impressive sight. After two miles along the ridge, I drop down the steep slope to the village of LLangennith.

Falling into the Kings Head for a pint and sandwich, I meet my recent acquaintance with his faithful friend. The pub is crowded and we sit outside in the sun discussing dogs. He is very knowledgeable on canines, and it soon becomes clear where the animal stands in the hierarchy of his family.

Llanrhidian

'Freedom is just chaos, with better lighting.'
– Alan Dean Foster

I answer Martin Cook's invitation and go looking for his caravan at LLanrhidian. His directions were a little hazy. I remember knocking on one door and a woman answering. When I describe my quarry she says, 'Oh them!' – pointing up the lane opposite and slamming the door! I walk up the lengthy approach lane flanked with builders' debris and derelict cars, passing into a field. Martin spots me, but is busy trying to catch a pig which has escaped from a pen located in the centre of the field.

'Hi Colin, glad you've found me. I'll see you over there shortly.'

He points to a poly tunnel in the corner of the field. It has a small caravan standing inside. The ground has a high water-table, so it is necessary to walk on timber pallets to approach the unique accommodation arrangement. It is also necessary to cross a man-made pond by way of a couple of planks. This facility is also used by geese that spread their waste on it, as geese do. Having got across with care a closer observation reveals that the plastic tunnel not only covers the van but is extended at each end allowing further accommodation of sorts open to the elements.

There is absolutely no attempt to keep any order. The front area is strewn both inside and out with detritus. Cutlery, crockery, tools, nuts and bolts, fire extinguishers, tyres, old deckchairs and countless items of junk lie all around, many half-buried at random in the ground both inside the tunnel and out. The rear plastic covered area behind the van houses a Heath Robinson heat exchange water system, a battered two-piece suite and an indescribable kitchen area.

Flek is almost speechless.

'Crikey what have we let ourselves in for?' he whispers. *'Health and Safety would have a field day here.'*

Later I learn that the van has been covered to avert the prying eyes of the local council when on aerial reconnaissance!

Strangely I quickly develop a more philosophical attitude than Flek's. Martin and a couple of others on site maintain a clean personal image – they aren't hippies or travellers, but have deliberately chosen an 'on the edge' existence. There are no modern comforts here. In the absence of electricity, running water or normal sanitation, they are making it work. Martin Cook is an affable fellow and is proud to invite me into his environment.

'I hope your risk assessment is right, Col – only time will tell,' Flek warns.

Martin is chuffed with his bottled gas water heating contraption which has been on most of the day and produced enough hot water to fill a washing bowl. I am invited to soak my feet. Such care, I am touched.

'I was going to cook you a meal tonight, Colin ...' explains Martin.

I hear Flek imitating a 'throwing-up' noise.

'... but an alternative arrangement has cropped up.'

Flek sighs with relief.

'Gareth who owns the field has invited us for a meal at this place. His lady partner, who recently starred in a TV cooking competition, is going to feed us, so when you are ready lets go.'

His Land Rover crashes down several hundred yards of lane over deep pot holes and, shaken up, we speed away to another caravan a couple of miles away. And what a difference! The door opens into a living space lit up like a Christmas grotto in a departmental store.

In these convivial surroundings we all sit down to a shank of lamb with all the trimmings. A genial mood is sustained with the help of a bottle of wine.

B & B at Llanrhidian.

Gareth reminds me of Simon Callow and is an interesting character. He hasn't quite opted out of a normal existence and is occasionally tempted back to his profession as a structural engineer when necessity demands.

All good diversions come to an end, and back at Martin's field windup torches allow us to cross the planks without mishap. Martin selflessly offers me his bed inside the caravan, a kindly gesture. Snuggling in under a thick duvet I hibernate like a dormouse. He settles down under the open front of the poly tunnel. A battered chez long, which must have in earlier times graced a proud home, is his bed for the night

The following morning I use the' open air' toilet facilities in the next field. Martin's colleague, who I met on the beach at Port Eynon, turns up. As the sun rises and the air warms up we all sit outside in clapped-out chairs sipping tea and discussing the day ahead. He knocks me up a breakfast of beans and bacon.

'You will not want to inspect the pan he used, – worse than a transport caff,' reports Flek.

'Come, come my friend, I think you are panicking without due cause. If Martin can survive then why can't I?'

Secretly I was banking on a myriad of tetanus injections to stave off any infection.'

Before I leave, Martin takes me on a tour of this chaotic site. I observe many hundreds of five-gallon cans containing old cooking oil. Gareth has learned that one day there might be a use for it as bio-fuel for vehicles. I notice a couple of pink elephants in a hedge.

Martin explains: 'Arriving home pissed one night we yanked them off the kiddies' roundabout parked over there. Apparently Gareth had bought it as an investment. In our stupor we attempted to ride them – I must fix them back on some time.'

'This will never ever happen,' prophesies Flek.

Soon this ranger will be operating his JCB again on he beach. He drops me on the exit highway from the Gower, and with a genuine friendly handshake we part.

Striding down the road leading off this wonderful peninsula towards Llanelli, Flek mellows and sums up: 'We're never going to experience a stop-over like that again,' he says. 'The hospitality rendered under difficult conditions was so genuine I'm sure the memories will linger on.'

DAY 87

27th March – Llanrhidian to Llanelli – 15 miles

The road leads five miles to the exit of the Gower. It takes until midday to reach the minor road on the map, a short cut to the mainland. Following this link I come across a large caravan site. Seeing a picnic area with bench type tables I enter and seek permission at the site office to sit and eat. 'No bother at all,' is the reply, and a lady from the office kindly brings me out a cup of tea.

'That's a nice gesture. You do melt some hearts, you rascal Colin,' says a condescending Flek. For a moment I think he is speaking to me!

I pick up the A484, returning me in a westerly direction for another five miles to Llanelli. Major road works are in progress on the town's outskirts. Passing a road crew constructing a roundabout, I test their curiosity with a salvo of entertaining banter. Well, I had hardly talked to anyone during the day so I took my frustration out on them!

My next hosts are Sue and Ken Roberts. This time the link is their daughter, who works in Chichester and heard about my escapade via the jazz club. Ken picks me up at Tesco's on the park.

We drive to his home up a hill on the outskirts. He apologises that Sue is away visiting their daughter. Over an excellent meal he tells me he was born and bred in Llanelli and is an engineer with the Swansea local authority.

His wife and daughter like West Sussex, and he is considering a plan to move down. So may I in future see him at the Jazz Club?

DAY 88

28th March – Llanelli to Kidwelly – 9 miles

As Ken runs me back to down to the sea front he sings the praises of the huge millennium investment to rejuvenate the old Llanelli dock facility. The works include an impressive promenade, the laying of a Nicklaus-designed golf course and inclusion of a superb Sustrans Route 4 cycle track which allows pedestrian passage all the way to Burry Port. It's a remarkable vision.

Because of a river I shall have to retreat inland for a considerable way. I follow the A484 to Kidwelly for several miles. Along the way I can hear, but not see, motor racing cars practising on a disused airfield to my left. RAF Hawk training jets, probably from Valley, constantly buzz overhead.

I turn off the main road into the town of Kidwelly and enter the first pub. Standing behind the bar is the proverbial peroxide ice maiden. There is no smile or welcome from this barmaid for a man of the road.

'A pint is it? she asks, forcing herself into action.

I pluck up the courage to ask about food.

'We don't do food, try the Chinese next door,' she says with all the coldness of Hi-di-Hi's Gladys Pugh – only worse.

I plonk down at a table and quaff my ale, trying desperately to admire the indifferent decor and fittings. What a depressing hole! The place is empty save for three old blokes. One of them is spouting on about what is a wrong in his social life, while other two are faking an interest as he goes on and on.

Suddenly 'Gladys' is distracted and I seize the moment and escape to the Chinese next door.

What a different atmosphere: several cheerful female staff scurry around, and the air is full of loud Mandarin speak and expectation.

Suddenly the reason for their excitement arrives as a car draws up outside. They desert the café to help an elderly Chinese man from the vehicle, and he is assisted inside amid palpable joy. He is obviously the patriarch and godfather of the business and their affection for him is unbounded. The ambience spills on to the customers. Some actually break into a smile.

I wander down to the end of this drab town and enter another pub. The inside layout doesn't conform to the norm of a drinking house. The bar has been superimposed to divide the drawing rooms of a private house. I ring my daughter Sonya to confirm my location.

The place is empty, but the landlord eventually appears. He is a striking, weathered individual with a half-beard, and he has a trans-Atlantic accent. I asked for a coffee.

We get chatting. It turns out that he'd been living in Canada for the last ten years.

'All my relations are here, though. In fact my cousin is in the *Daily Mail* today,' he reports.

Flek cuts in, '*The* Daily Mail, *It must be someone famous. Go on, ask him who it is.*'

The answer is Greta Saachi, the rather gorgeous film actress.

'She doesn't appear in many films' I comment.

'No she's a picky cow with film parts, but seems to be doing all right at the moment on the stage.'

He hands me the *Daily Mail* and, sure enough, I read that she is getting rave reviews in a revival of Terrance Rattigan's Deep Blue Sea in the West End.

A car pulls up outside. Sonya and partner Simon with my grandson Jack have arrived. As a treat for her Dad she has come all the way from Solihull, booked into the hotel at Swansea I passed a few days earlier and then motored out a further twenty miles to pick me up. I am so pleased to see them all.

Thanks to her I am about to stay overnight in a luxury hotel.

We have an early breakfast at the hotel. The weather is lousy, with heavy rain. Simon drives the twenty miles back to Kidwelly.

What a tremendous effort he and my youngest daughter Sonya had made – following in the footsteps of her sister Suzanne's endeavours back at Barnstable.

'The place hasn't changed since yesterday' remarks Flek, *'Pity the sun hasn't come out. The Met Office often reports a sun-hours league list. I reckon poor old Kidwelly is about to be relegated.'*

I don't know where he drew his analogy from, but it was about right.

Booted and spurred to take the weather on, I get out of the car to face another day. Sadly I wave them goodbye, and in pouring rain wend my way out of the town towards the A484 to Carmarthen. Fortunately I pick up a couple of country lanes which allow me to get off main road for several miles

A farmer comes by, listens to my story, and produces a pound coin for me.

'Every little helps,' pipes up Flek. *'By the way, I'm getting soaked back here. Any chance of giving "Sarah the brolly" an outing?'* It was not unreasonable request – after all, I did have my hood. So I spread her wings over him.

The weather has not abated and it's still bucketing down when I reach a roundabout on the outskirts of Carmarthen. CLIMB has found me a B & B, and luckily I make the right choice and turn right here towards it.

I go into the town centre for money and Millets for a couple of walking items. Rather wet, I take the long walk out to Price Street and Mr and Mrs Bowyer's homely terraced house. I am shown to a comfortable bedroom on the second floor with bathroom attached. After a good soak I make myself a meal using one of the dehydrated meal packs, followed by some pastries I bought in the town.

There is some paperwork/map reading to do and emails/blogs to send, then I watch some TV, catching up on the national news.

Thinking a couple of days ahead, I try unsuccessfully to get accommodation at Laugharne (location of Dylyn Thomas's boathouse home) but there is a book festival going on. Tomorrow I shall have to settle for a Travelodge at St Clears.

It seems a long way from the Swansea Hotel's sophisticated service of last night, but these are smashing digs.

With Sonia and Jack at Swansea.

DAY 90
30th March – Carmarthen to St Clears – 14 miles

At last I can cross the River Towy. I follow Sustrans Route 4, disappearing into a labyrinth of country lanes south of the A40(T). A few miles on I catch up with a family walking out for a pub lunch with their dogs, Ruby and Robbie. Daughter Amy rides her horse, Stella, and we arrive at the Wern (Marsh) pub;. Dad Gwyn buys me a pint and donates a fiver to CLIMB. Talking to wife Bev, I hear she has in-depth knowledge of inherited metabolic diseases.

I struggle the long way to St Clears with an annoying groin strain which eases. This little town is deserted: why *is* a Travelodge located here?

I book in. The young manager shows considerable interest in my quest, but this may be a ploy as he has to relieve me of £50 for the night and he knows there aren't any frills here.

The building is new, just functional but faceless. Breakfast is offered in a presentation box. Such is his embarrassment that he gives me two. The room has no wardrobe as such, and only a 4ft bath, the smallest I encounter on the whole trip. Normal complimentary soaps and shampoos are not included. Travelodge does what is says on the tin – it 'budgets'!

In bed I give some hard thought to tomorrow. Going via Laugharne is not a practical option. I shall have to opt for a very long day and get to the Manobier YHA. Missing out on walking the Pendine Sands, scene of world record motor speed attempts in the 30s is disappointing, but there you are.

31st March – St Clears to Manobier YHA – 16 miles

Another long day is inevitable, but the task isn't daunting. I take to Sustrans Route 4 route and am swallowed up in lanes for eight miles. Anyone reading this narrative might think I am somewhat blasé about the mileage claimed, but it's real enough. I am now fit enough to just put my head down and get on with it. I do believe I have lost seven pounds!

I call into the New Inn at Amroth for lunch, having covered nine miles. The ploughman's is disappointing, thrown together on the plate and tasteless.

'I ask you, Col, how can they foul up a ploughmans? Flek meditates.

'Anything is possible if you try hard enough,' is my despondent reply.

Outside is a plaque which commemorates the opening of the Pembrokeshire Way Coastal Path in 1970 by the distinguished Second World War correspondent Wynford Vaughn Thomas. I am now on the second longest coastal path of my Walk. It twists and turns its way 186 miles to St Dogmaels and has a total ascent of 35,000 ft.

Saundersfoot is surprisingly busy, with early season visitors. I get a refreshing pot of tea. The path to Tenby is challenging. Sweating profusely, I discard my top coat for the first time. Dehydrating in Tenby costs me a quid for a bottle of water. The price of this commodity varies so much.

'You ought to carry a huge funnel, mate, and catch the H_2O as it falls out of the sky.'

Yes, it's another one of Flek's impractical suggestions. What would I do without him?

At Tenby I walk along the South Beach. I have been here before with my kids on holiday and remember the sand to be firm, but I turn off the beach towards the road, making faster progress – it's getting late. I find a bloke who is holding out on the dunes until dark so that he can camp contrary to the local bye-laws.

'A rambling hobo,' I hear a tired Flek mumble.

The last three miles are a weary slog. I turn off down a lane, cross a sports field and, thank god, there is the Manobier YHA. Absolutely worn out, I enter and receive a great welcome from Martin, the manager. The chef has saved me a massive evening meal.

Taking a power shower, I have just enough energy to stand up in its relentless flow. Although the hostel is pretty full, they have kept a single room for me. As with so many YHA hostels, my stay here is on the house.

Shattered I send my daily blog to CLIMB and turn in early.

1st April – Manobier YHA to Stackpole Quay – 8 miles

At breakfast the staff are coping with more than sixty hostellers. Making a great deal of noise are an 'A'-level field party, a group of German students, some individual families and an individual Joe like me.

I bid a fond farewell to Martin and pick up the Pembrokeshire Coastal Path again. It is going to be a lot more forgiving than the SWCP, with fewer steep accents and softer paths. It's so much easier today, and I amble along without effort to Freshwater East and enter the Fishermans Arms. The landlord treats me to lunch, and I spend a pleasant hour talking to a few regulars.

A continuous battering from a strong wind forces a detour, using an inland parallel lane.

'T.S. Eliot said that April is the cruellest month, did you know that, Flek?' I shout over the wind.

'I am not familiar with the geezer's name, Col. You're name-dropping again.'

'My remark is only in the context of the weather, my friend.'

'Being April, my guess is that he wasn't looking forward to his tax bill dropping on the mat,' is his pragmatic answer.

At Stackpole Quay there seems little chance of anywhere to camp. I am fortunate to persuade Pat and Peter Sherwood, proprietors of some well appointed holiday cottages, to let me stay at a reduced rate. In no time at all Pat produces a tray of tea and scones, which I enjoy on the patio. They are an attentive couple offering splendid accommodation.

Sitting outside, my mind turns to aspects of physical well being. My extremities are taking a long to time to warm up. The hands are not too affected – I have hardly had to wear gloves at all – but when the walking stops the feet circulation fails forcing me to wear two pairs of socks in bed. To make matters worse, I still have no alternative footwear. I'm still shuffling around in two pairs of socks when 'off duty.'

It doesn't help when Flek pipes up with: 'So much for your planning, Col! You're going to have to really think things out mate.'

'A thought from Sir Joshua Reynolds, perhaps Flek. I don't suppose you've heard of him either. He said, "There is no expedient to which man will not resort to avoid the real labour of thinking." I'm your man!'

The Hard Slog

'Dear Lord, if you pick'em up, I'll put 'em down.'
— Lord's Prayer for Hikers

Armchair-bound when reading about or watching any marathon physical effort on TV, it's easy to be seduced into thinking that it has been a simple task. Most endeavours are presented only to emphasise the pleasing or conquering aspects of the achievement.

Too often not enough emphasise is given to the mental or physical hardships endured along the way. It makes for boring reading or viewing. So how do you write up pain, aching, soreness, hurting or mental stress? It's rarely possible. With a physical endurance test, it's the pain in the unseen middle of a journey that has to be overcome by the individual alone.

In walking, trekking, yomping — call it what you like — the definition of a 'hard slog' is, 'progressing on a long and exhausting march with a heavy pace against the natural resistances of gravity, wind speed and terrain'.

These restrictions form the bulk of the effort, can't be avoided and are often performed out of sight. To give an example: when Eddie Izzard embarked on his series of marathon runs it was naturally his stops and adventures that entertained the TV viewers. The loneliness and sheer exhaustion between camera shots were his alone, and he did a great job in driving himself on.

I think it is fair to say that anyone who gets involved in an endurance event is entitled to say 'I've been there'. Strength and resolute endurance with firmness of mind (i.e. 'fortitude') is always part of the equation.

Against strong winds balance is always king: keep reminding yourself that giving up is not an option!

Bearing in mind that I was carrying thirty pounds, it's not surprising that defeating gravity caused the most problems. I continually set bearings on objects and methodically 'staged' myself up the ascent. If this wasn't possible, then I would take climbing steps in multiples from ten up to a hundred (depending on the gradient) and then rest. (Descending was easier, although pressure on the thighs and knee joints is always present — anyone who has been skiing will know this.)

It became very important to me to maintain this system and to engage in a continuous dialogue with either my inspiring 'teenager' or my lost walking pal Bill Bloy — not without a few tears on many occasions. If I was desperate, I sometimes called upon Flek to rally me, although any resort to him for sympathy was always met with 'Oh get on with it!'

What an indifferent mutt he can be!

DAY 93
2nd April – Stackpole Quay to Angle – 15 miles

There's a lot of ground to cover today, so I hope my groin strain doesn't play up. A mist has drifted in along the coast; it's called a 'fret' down our way.

The path turns inland in order to bypass the enormous NATO artillery range at Castlemartin. During this detour at Stackpole Warren I skirt two lengthy stretches of water known locally as the Lily Ponds. It's a charming recreational area, and I pass a group of noisy children on an educational field trip with their teachers. At a National Trust hut a warden informs me that the pub at Castlemartin is now closed, so I get lunch early today at the nearby Boshington pub. Although scruffy, I seem to melt into bar crowds.

On a secondary road I now have to walk the full length of the Army's Merrion Camp and its artilllery range into Castlemartin. I remember reading that Spike Milligan, on hearing that Harry Secombe was an artillery man in the war, called him a 'six-mile sniper'! Well, there is no sniping today. Firing has been cancelled due to fog.

Entering the Freshwater area, the road passes between the highest sand dunes I have ever seen. Sand is everywhere, much of it blowing across the road. I turn north at Rat Island into West Angle Bay and get my first glimpse of Milford Haven, one of the deepest natural harbours in the world.

Lesley rings from CLIMB to say that there are no digs available at the approaching village of Angle, so for the first time since the start of the Walk three months ago I am going to have to pitch my tent. The payment for the use of my first field, which doesn't appear to have the usual facilities (a great start to a camping strategy), is three quid, but nobody turns up to claim it.

I entered into a routine to be followed many times in the coming months. Get the tent up; heat up a meal with a cup of tea; send to CLIMB my blog for the day; phone members of my family or friends; and, finally, listen to an Evening Concert.

It is my debut under canvas and, surprisingly, I sleep soundly.

DAY 94

3rd April – Angle to Windmill Camping site, Maiden Wells – 10 miles

Camping when the seasonable temperatures fluctuate wildly can be annoying. The problem is condensation in the tent. There's nothing like starting the daywith a heavy shower as your head touches the inner sheet. The experience creates an overwhelming reluctance to get out of a warm sleeping bag.

'Wakey! Wakey! yells Flek with well meant enthusiasm. 'You're going to have to show more grip than this. It's a new day, so come along, there's a good walker.'

I think my reply is, 'Do I have to?'

The reply is an emphatic: 'Yes, you do!'

I make up some breakfast and squeeze what looks like the remnants of a car boot sale into a 15-litre rucksack.

I set out on the hottest day yet, and physically the hardest so far this year. My legs, particularly my hips, ache all day. But the sights and contrasts down the southern sweep of Milford Haven temper any discomfort.

On the map the shape of Angle Bay reminds me of Lulworth Cove. I trudge around it on muddy paths, getting wet under foot. Always ahead of me is the huge Chevron oil fefinery dominating the skyline. Walking through a wood on the shoreline I tread past clumps of primroses. In sharp contrast, just through the trees a few yards to my left massive moored-up oil tankers constantly top up the tank farms with liquid gold via arteries from the many jetties. Flare pipes complete the picture of human exploitation.

The PCW path now passes inland behind a power station, and I head for my overnight sanctuary at Maiden Wells. Lesley from CLIMB tells me that the owners, Richard and Jane, will make no charge. It's a lovely sunny evening on my arrival, and I pitch down adjacent to the only other occupants on the site.

'Good decision, Col' says Flek. 'I'm a poor substitute for real company. What you need is stimulating conversation with laughter. The change will do you good.'

He is becoming a master at layering on advice with a trowel.

The 'company' are mum Heidi and her children Oz and Evie from Hertfordshire. They welcome me with open arms and we all sit around a bench table in the evening sunshine. I share their huge meal of pasta/chicken washed down with wine. It's a memorable time with a happy-go-lucky family of enormous energy.

DAY 95

4th April – Windmill Caravan Site to Upper Neeston Lodge
near Milford Haven – 12 miles

On waking, my body feels good. An eight-hour sleep has done its job. Condensation in the tent again but I am getting quicker at packing up my kit. Oz is also up early. He makes everyone tea and I rustle up some porridge. Camp site bench tables, not always provided, make camping chores so much easier. I am so sorry to bid farewell to my temporary neighbours an ebullient family if ever there was one.

Two miles on I wander into Pembroke and the first pub offers a 'full monty' breakfast, so I go in and have one. I refuse the sausages, as they seem to hang around all day.

I go north through the town. I am now at the far eastern end of the Haven and cross the impressive Cleddau Bridge. Descending steps down on the other side turns me west along the north shore of the Haven, passing Neyland. This quiet neighbourhood with its terraces of early 20th century houses leaves quite an impression on me.

Just before the Northern oil refinery I enter a pub and am soon joined by an American, Ed Brown. Noticing the print on my rucksack cover, Ed questions me. He has done some fundraising for Cystic Fibrosis back in the States and is interested to hear that metabolic inherited diseases are also caused by a faulty gene from both parents. He goes on to tell that his wife, an engineer, is working on the intended massive NLG liquid gas installation here, mentioning that he is just a number cruncher on the project.

The PCP passes the refinery via a temporary bridge crossing over huge pipes that come up from the tanker jetties. Soon I am in Milford, a rather dour and old fashioned town, and make for Tesco's for provisions. Afterwards I prefer a local café for a cake and two mugs of tea.

I notice a small open park area opposite. In it, adjacent to a road junction, there stands a magnificent umbrella-shape cherry tree in full bloom, under-planted with pink tulips. It looks out of place in this dingy part of town, but what a picture it presents! I have to take a shot.

My digs for the night are two miles on. My host, Sean at Upper Neeston Farm, has followed a current trend to convert unused outbuildings to bunkhouse-type holiday accommodation. Persuaded by Lesley at CLIMB (she seems to get around nearly everyone), he has opened up out of season for me. Recently finished to a high standard, this six-berth area is impressive. I have the place to myself. Although I provide my own food, the tariff of fifteen pounds is a bargain.

DAY 96

5th April – Upper Neeston Farm to Marloes – 8 miles

A short passage today, and it needs to be. Why? Well, something is up! I march off into a stiff westerly. At Herbrandston, two miles from Marloes, the PCP splits and, ignoring the coastal route, I turn north. The road to my left leads to the spectacularly diverse Dale peninsula. (It lies on the port side of the tankers as they ease into the mouth of Milford Haven, and I walked around it several years before.) From there the PCP stretches out towards Martins Haven and Skomer. Not going this way means that I shall miss out on a dramatic coastline. However, I am irresistibly drawn down the road ahead to Marloes.

Why? Well, my football team, Portsmouth (Pompey), are playing West Bromwich Albion in the F.A. Cup semi-final this very afternoon. I have rung my hosts Phil and Sue Twidale (proprietors of the Clock House and friends of a friend) and made sure that I have a room with a TV in it so I can catch the second half.

The Clock House is a unique combination of guest house, tea room and restaurant. On arrival Sue rushes me a pot of tea and some cake and I speed up to my room. I put my Pompey shirt on (sent on by my son Stewart) and lie on the bed to watch my team make it to the FA Cup Final with a one goal to nil victory.

Exuberant, I return to the crowded café downstairs.

Flek says: 'Go on, Col, let your hair down and give it to 'em. I won't tell that you skived off half the day's schedule – mum's the word!'

'Yes they have done it!' I shout to everyone in the restaurant. 'I was three years old the last time they got to Wembley, in 1939.'

A professional photographer happens to be present and he takes a shot of me in front of the impressive village clock tower which stands opposite. The image goes onto my blog to CLIMB that evening and remains there for several weeks after.

My hosts are terrific and produce a splendid evening meal. I retire to bed and the only football speak phrase I can think of to describe my mood is 'Over the moon, Motty!'

'Play up, Pompey!' By the clock tower at Marloes.

DAY 97
6th April – Marloes to Broadhaven – 8 miles

A sunny day, but snow showers are predicted. The weather forecast for the next few days looks dire. With no fixed accommodation tonight, it is with some unwillingness that I put my boots on to face the day. All the euphoria of the previous day seems to have vanished. Leaving the comfort of the Clock House is going to be a blow –my mood has changed.

As always Flek has to make comment: 'Col, be brave, man. Get off your butt and get going for God's sake.' He can be so blunt.

With some reluctance I step out into a cold northerly. Soon I am back on the PCP. The going is flat and easy. Right on the coast is Brides Church, where I discover the photographer of yesterday on the beach searching for worthwhile natural history subjects to record. Out at sea a group of tankers are anchored up and I spot the expected snow showers on their way. Fortunately I reach the protection of some coastline woodland just as they come ashore. This is April and I'm experiencing my first snow on the hoof: amazing! I drop down into Little Haven and suddenly realise I had been here before on a previous holiday trip. A lunch of fish and chips washed down with a mug of tea puts me right.

At Broadhaven the YHA is full and as it's a Sunday out of season the two camp site receptions are closed. The snow has turned to rain and, getting a little desperate, I spot a B & B. A welcoming landlady shows me up to a room with a great view of the bay and I soon revel in the benefit of the full-on central heating. I have a short snooze, then enjoy a bath and the tasty packed lunch SueTwidale prepared for me. I down it with the sixth cup of tea of the day!

I am getting used to short mileages and early finishes. Not having to pack up on camp sites and having more time to rest tired limbs in civilised surroundings are treats I could become accustomed to. Normal routines will become psychologically important during the coming months.

From my first floor vantage point I watch a wonderful sunset over the moored-up tankers and spot more approaching snow showers. It has been a trying day but, despite the re-emergence of my groin strain, I have come through. I get my iPod and listen to some romantic Rachmaninov. What a nightcap!

7th April – Broad Haven to Newgale Sands – 7 miles

I have a comfortable night at Mrs Morgan's, and she kindly makes me up some sandwiches. I wait for a heavy shower to pass over and leave on a bright, windless day.

After traversing to cliff height I get a mobile signal at last. From here I have little difficulty in transmitting emails to CLIMB. As I am doing so a small herd of grey and brown patched Welsh Cobs wander over and corral me to the spot. Not content with that, they subject me to gentle nuzzling, their exhaling warming the back of my neck from the chill of the morning. Three mares and their days' old foals keep their distance. It is one of those never to be forgotten magical experiences, but just in case my memory fades, I take some snaps.

A little later I spot what I think is an ancient 'barrow'. But wait a minute – this grass mound has a steel ring around the top and sliding patio doors on two aspects. Puzzling? I suddenly realised it is one of those TV 'Grand Design' projects.

A beguiling moment.

The path descends to the 4km Newgale Sands, one of Wales's great beaches. My camp site is having off-season remedial works carried out: the charge is waived as the toilets are yet to being fixed.

Next to the site is the Duke of Edinburgh pub. I try some 'cawl', which is Welsh soup with lamb added to it, so making a stew – mmm, quite tasty! The campsite shop is surprisingly open. I buy some much needed gas and a *Telegraph,* then relax in the tent waiting for the pub's later opening time.

In the evening I stretch my tired limbs just a hundred yards to re-enter a packed Duke of Edinburgh for scampi and chips. I have read in today's paper that the 'real' duke has just been discharged from St Georges Hospital in London following a chest infection.

'Goodness knows what Britain's most famous curmudgeon would say about this place which carries his name, currently infested with screaming kids, running amok,' grimaces Flek.

I have to agree, and as the last chip slips down my throat I flee back to the 'Tent and Telegraph'. Now, that sounds a good name for a pub. I find that the toilet has now been overhauled – good timing and a fitting gesture to celebrate my arrival.

I have managed to get my blog away to CLIMB. At my age most of my physical assets have mostly weathered away – it's called wear and tear. So I pull everything on, including four pairs of socks, in an effort to maintain what parts I have left, and amazingly fall asleep.

I'm looking forward to meeting up with a very good friend of mine tomorrow.

Let's hear the music? I'm too tired.

DAY 99

8th of April – Newgale Sands to Ocean Haze, St Davids – 8 miles

I spend a very comfortable night but am still plagued with condensation in the morning. I seem to spend a long time breaking camp, but finally get away and haul myself up onto the PCP cliff walk, which is easy going. As I approach Solva a few miles on I am caught in a heavy downpour, and on arrival at the Harbour sheepishly enter a very smart café dripping wet.

I struggle to shed the wet gear, but it's not a dignified exercise to observe. On hearing of my venture the proprietor offers me a meal on the house: I choose a Panini. The presentation of the food is impeccable and the standard of the all-round attention to customers is faultless. Sadly these attributes are so often missing in many British food outlets. It's a long standing gripe of mine that there is little understanding of real service – emphasis is placed on the ascetics of premises at the expense of training the staff.

I have a lovely chat with an old Manchester United supporter who actually lives in Stretford. After thanking and congratulating the proprietor on her standards of service, I don up and make my way.

The bad weather has cleared and I enjoy a wonderful afternoon's walk in terrain akin to Cornwall, i.e. dramatic. The difference this time is that wild flowers are beginning to show. Drifts of the pink thrift are everywhere.

I have to turn off the path and head north through disused quarries to meet the A487. My objective is the Ocean Haze accommodation, part of a Texaco garage complex. Its outside appearance gives little hint of the excellent standard inside. I am here for two nights, paid for by someone unknown to me. The view from my room patio goes right across St Brides Bay, which has taken me three days to walk around.

Birthday cards have arrived from my friends at Worthing, Brian and Beryl Coote, and also from Jane Taylor.

DAY 100
9th April – Rest day – St David's

I am the only resident at Ocean Haze, but a special friend will arrive today. Chris Morris, the proprietor, serves up a superb breakfast. I fuss around for a couple of hours, giving attention to my schedule and drying out my tent over the line on the patio.

I walk the mile into St David's and am delighted to hear a familiar voice. It's my good friend Hugh Ashton calling my name. After heart-felt greetings, we get a drink. He has come all the way from Chichester in West Sussex to add his support. We visit the cathedral and check out a pub in the town square for a lunch of faggots.

Hugh is pretty tired, and I'm not surprised. He is chairman of the Chichester Jazz Club and last night he was at the Pizza Express, Dean Street, Soho at a gig. Then, having returned the sixty miles to his home in Chichester, he got up early this morning and drove all the way up here, some two hundred miles-plus, to make this reunion. He had expressed a desire to join me for a day's walk on the PCP and, true to his word, he is here. What a pal!

We walk back to Ocean Haze, having a chat about my progress so far. He retires for a well-earned sleep while I sit on the patio in the sun and catch up with news in a national paper. I sometimes gleam some idea of how the country is coping by snatching occasional peeks at TV. However, I must explain that reading a newspaper on my rest days is a luxury. It seems strange that something which is normally an everyday occurrence at home suddenly becomes a guilty act of indulgence.

The evening starts with a drive, Hugh taking me out on a recce for tomorrow. Returning to St David's, we are fortunate first to find a parking space in the middle of the town and then to get a prime table, i.e. opposite a large-screen TV in a packed Farmers Arms. We enjoy a meal watching Man United playing Roma in the Champions League. There's just one snag: our line-of-sight is constantly interrupted by delightful young ladies passing to another bar. Being reserved and British, we cope with this annoyance admirably!

Returning to the Ocean Haze, I find getting to sleep no problem.

DAY 101

10th April – St Davids (Whitesands Bay) to Trefin (Hostel) – 12 miles

Hugh drives us out to Whitesands Bay. A passing walker is coerced to take our mugshot, and we set off in uncertain weather. This stage is difficult underfoot, but with the weather brightening up we enjoy a seven-mile hike to Abereiddi Tower Bay.

There is a hive of activity on the beach here. A large party has arrived on a marine study course, the instructors strutting along the waterline seemingly to confirm their status. Challenging geographical features abound, including caves and waterfalls.

'So I imagine that a two-hour health & safety course for the students is on the cards for starters,' mocks Flek.

Many day trippers swell the numbers at this charming little bay as Hugh and I refresh at a kiosk run by a happy and chatty couple, Kim and girlfriend.

Hugh needs to leave me now, but he has a problem – he can't get a mobile signal to call for a taxi back to his car at Whitesands. In desperation he decides to tramp to the nearest main road a mile away with the hope of hailing a lift and sets off.

With Hugh Ashton at St David's.

Kim suggests that elevation up the cliff path will cure the signal problem. I try it and it does. I shout across the bay, and Hugh returns to make his call. We patronise Kim's kiosk again for drinks, and the taxi arrives at last. Later Hugh tells me the fare cost him an arm and a leg, but at least he was going home.

It's an emotional goodbye to a true friend. I find it difficult to describe this boost to my morale. Hugh has made a round trip of five hundred miles to bolster my confidence. He returns to West Sussex with the news that I am alive and well, having completed the first thousand miles!

I have only three miles to go today along this outstanding coastline. I pass through Porthgain, a charming spot where (not surprisingly) artists are at work. The hostel at Trefin is the old village school and, released by the YHA, it is now privately run by Sue Whitmore and her German volunteer warden. I am invited to dinner and get talking to hosteller Mark (ex-Home Office) who is one of those interesting people who passes on his camping skills. Fortunately our paths will cross again in the near future.

DAY 102

11th April – Trefin Hostel Aber Draw to Goodwick (Fishguard) – 9 miles

After one hundred days on the Walk I find myself once again getting back onto the PCP super coastline, where the sea's 'white horse' waves are crashing in. I cross Abercastle and on to an unusual man-made shingle barrier fashioned from circular stones and slates.

Turning in to Woollen Mill for something to eat, I meet a couple returning from the shore to their car. After the usual salutation I mention Battens Disease. The man turns out to be a retired Great Ormond Street consultant and knows all about the condition. He reminds me that the present prime minister, Gordon Brown, has a son who has finally been diagnosed with cystic fibrosis (a metabolic condition) at the London Hospital. He says he will follow my blogs.

Strange, I had been encouraged by CLIMB to catch a bus from St Nicholas to Goodwick, but as I am early I decide to walk on the further three miles to my destination of the night. I settle in with my B & B proprietors Ann and Gary Strawbridge, who – as I am soon to find out – are in on a plot.

Later my bedroom door bursts open and in walks my youngest son Stewart with his partner Chris and her children Lauren and Amy. They are staying for a couple of days, and I am to be their guest. Ir's my birthday treat and a wonderful surprise.

I have now entered shipping weather forecast area Irish Sea.

DAY 103
12th April – Goodwick to St Nicholas – 9 miles

It is my 72th birthday. For logistical reasons today's stage is done in reverse. Stewart, Chris and the girls accompany me along the cliffs for the first two miles. Lauren and Amy love the freedom and get their clothes rather dirty while Stew clicks away constantly with his camera. They leave and return to Goodwick, and I continue along the jagged coastline.

I arrive at the Stumble Head lighthouse, sit down and enjoy the stunning views and a chocolate bar. The cliffs now head south, and a couple of miles on I stumble on the remote Pwll Deri YHA, which is closed for renovation. I manage to get to the Trefasser crossroads and

With Stewart, Chris, Amy and Lauren at Goodwick.

call it a day, so ring Gary Strawbridge to pick me up. On the way back we drive through a pleasant rural suburb of Goodwick for which he is the permanent 'Postie'.

My family ventures out in the evening for a meal. However, Amy is tired and gets bored, which mars the occasion. We return to Seaside Steps, the Strawbridges' B & B. The two families sit down in the lounge and we all get drawn into an evening of laughter and chat. They and their children permeate such a friendly atmosphere and treat us as if we were their own. I ask Gary how come that, although living on the west coast of Wales, he is a fan of Wolverhampton Wanderers? Apparently it boils down to geography: surprisingly, Wolves are the nearest Football League team to go and watch!

During the day mobile wishes come in from my daughters and cards from Jane Taylor, my good friends Hilda and John Alderton, John and Daphne Beard (by phone) and CLIMB.

Retiring to bed I get out the iPod and treat myself to an evening concert. I click onto the 'random' function and pull out Chris Rea, Vaughan Williams' 'The Lark Ascending', Lennie Tristano's 'Requiem' (a stunning tribute to Charlie Parker following his early death), finishing off with Al Gerrau's 'Easy'.

That's another year gone.

Day 104

13th April – Goodwick (Fishguard) to Newport – 11 miles

With great reluctance we bid farewell to the Strawbridge family. They have been so friendly, and it has been a memorable stay. Lauren and Amy loved taking their dog for a walk.

Stewart accompanies me along five miles of the PCP to the restaurant at Pwllgwaelod just before Dinas island. The route takes us past the ferry docks at Fishguard, and later the coastline is stunning.

Chris and the girls motor on and join us there for lunch. The restaurant is packed and very noisy. In these circumstances, as often in this country, the service deteriorates, but we eventually get something to eat.

I collect the rucksack from Chris's car and have an emotional farewell with my family who have made my birthday occasion so memorable.

Bypassing Dinas Island, I continue along the PCP until I arrive at the Morawelon camping site, Parrog, Newport, which has the Preseli Hills as a backdrop. A CLIMB enquiry has resulted in the Owner Mrs Watts and her son Richard hosting my stay. I look them up in their splendidly appointed adjacent restaurant and have a chat. Mrs Watts has kindly arranged to collect sponsor monies and will send them on to CLIMB.

I wander into the camp site to pitch the tent and, lo and behold, there is Mark, my acquaintance at Treffin a few days ago. He is touring by car and has a superb tent layout. He shares his evening meal with me and we spend time discussing life in general. He introduces me to 'crocks' as a change of footwear. Although not waterproof, they are extremely lightweight – ideal at the end of each day. I must get a pair.

14th April – Newport to Poppit Sands YHA – 9 miles

Its goodbye to my recent friend Mark, who has been great company. I pass through bustling little Newport to get some provisions from a Spar. This shop chain is particularly strong in Wales, and I find their outlets in some of the tiniest villages.

'This means,' says Flek flippantly, 'you are never far from a Spar for a chocolate bar.' His weak giggle matches the ode.

'If I wanted the Poet Laureate on board I would have invited him' I say.

'Please yourself,' he says and pretends to sulk.

'I'm only joking, Flek. It's just that you have been a bit quiet for a couple of days. Yes, I know – I've had company.'

For the first part of the day I am going to skip the PCP and take a parallel road inland. At Blaen-Pant Cottage I find that Rob and Jane are building a wall. They spot me and make a tray of tea. He is a former lecturer at Anglian University and they have been knocking this place into shape for three years. Jane tells me she will sponsor CLIMB.

The road is undulating, and on a hill I come across a private Welsh cemetery. I pass many of these, and find their plain black marble tombstones in neat military rows somewhat forbidding.

At Moyle Grove I revert back to the PCP and rejoin the easy but spectacular cliff top trail. I get around Cemaes Head and reach the YHA, which is perched wonderfully high overlooking the rollers washing up the Poppit Sands. The building was a gift to the YHA in memory of an RAF pilot killed in 1944. It's locked up, so while I wait for Stewart the warden to arrive, I brew up some tea. I find an old wicker armchair in the sun drenched conservatory at the rear. It's very warm and I doze off.

I am the only resident tonight, and Stewart has kindly opened up especially for me. A shower is just what I need, and I use up the remaining provisions I find in the sac. I give daughter Sonya a ring. To do this I have to climb further up the hill, giving me an even better view of the sandy bay on a lovely sunny evening. She has news of a further substantial donation to CLIMB.

I fancy an Evening Concert and make a selection. My Wish Track tonight is Sibelius's Violin Concerto in C.

DAY 106

15th April – Poppit Sands YHA (St Dogmaels) to New Quay – 19 miles.

I leave a thankyou note for YHA warden Stewart, lock the place up and stride down to St Dogmaels, passing the Wynford Vaugham Thomas plaque denoting the start of the Pembrokeshire Coastal Path at this end. So that's approximately another 180 miles done then!

This is going to be a punishing day, so I take the easier long hike along the A467, turning off at the West Wales Airport, then along the lanes to Aperporth back on the coast. CLIMB has arranged for a publicity picture and progress report. The photographer turns ups to cover the assignment, then runs me a mile down the road to Tresaith.

This is splendid countryside, but a combination of 'misleading' road signs lead me into a labyrinth of country lanes, delaying my progress. It's getting late, and as I am negotiating a steep hill climb through the village of Penbonrhydyfothau (gulp! I have just gone through Cwmhawenfach and Ffynnonlefrit. Try pulling these out of your dentures!) when a car pulls up behind me.

'Are you Colin? I'm George Legg, your host at New Quay. You're still a long way off, so you'd better get in.'

Given the wrong information about which route I was coming from, he has found me by a combination of chance and deduction.

Soon I am being greeted by his wife Jean. She lays out a much welcome afternoon tea in the kitchen of their charming terraced house overlooking New Quay's delightful harbour. George, a jovial Harry Secombe look-alike, points out his moored yacht down below. The contact has been secured by their friend Ann Lee from Condicote in Gloucestershire, one of my regular Southern Trails walkers.

Over dinner George lets on that he is a second cousin of Dylan Thomas, the legendary Welsh poet. He points out that Thomas was often the worse for drink and relied on others to help him out. It was his family, the Leggs, who secured for him a dilapidated bungalow on the coastline at the other end of the town. There seems little doubt that during his stay in New Quay, Thomas wrote 'Under Milk Wood', basing many of its characters on local townsfolk.

'You've got to go past the site tomorrow morning, Colin,' he says. 'I'll take you down there.'

DAY 107
16th April – New Quay to Llansantffraed Campsite – 10 miles

George runs me down to Majoda (acronym of a previous owner's children's names) a modern bungalow on a superb site looking across the New Quay Bay. There is a blue plaque on the drive recording that Dylan Thomas had lived on the site in 1944. The original building was described by Thomas as 'this shack of wood and asbestos' and it had a corrugated iron roof. He rented it for a pound a week. A wooden ladder he used to facilitate a short cut to the beach and the Black Lion pub in the town is still there.

While we are there the present owner turns up and tells us about the filming of 'The Edge of Love', the story of a possible love triangle involving Thomas, starring Keira Knightley. A replica of the original 'shack' was rebuilt on the adjacent field to maintain authenticity.

George recommends the coastal path, which I take to Aberaeron. It's superb walking. The town is a delight, with an architecturally beautiful square designed by Nash before he was known. I grab some lunch.

The coastline to Morfa Farm is equally as good, but I use the A487 for the last few miles. The campsite is almost empty, but it's free of charge. It is cold and blowing a gale. I get the tent up ,make some tea and consume the sandwiches prepared this morning by Jean Legg,

Dylan Thomas lived here.

175

This may be a good time to reflect on typical preparations for the night. The inventory includes:

Two tent under-layers – blow up mattress and lay out –10°-rated sleeping bag with silk liner.

Personal wear – according to the weather temperature this can include long johns, trousers, four pairs of socks, two tops and a Benny Hat.

My feet are cold for some time, the bad circulation of old age, I suppose. There are no phone calls or signals today, so switching on my powerful headlight I settle down to read a *Telegraph* which I found in a village shop on my journey.

The cold easterly blows all night but, protected behind some caravans, I held off the worst.

My Evening Concert: Swing section included Duke Ellington's 'Take the A Train', followed by the pre-eminent 70s jazz fusion outfit Weather Report, which lasted sixteen years, with their version of 'Birdland'. The concert jazz pianist performer Errol Garner chipped in with 'I Remember April', and pop was represented by Queen's 'It's a Kind of Magic'. The romantic 'Samson and Delilah' by Camille Saint Saens is a delight. The evening chuckle by courtesy of Round the Horne is always going to be the finale to these concerts. Tonight's Wish Track: Erich Korngold's violin concerto.

Cocooned in the prementioned gear, I sleep warmly.

DAY 108
17th April –Llansantffraed Campsite to Aberystwyth – 10 miles

Knocking up porridge and tea, I thank Mrs Jones (the owner) and move off. I get coffee and toast in the service garage café at the end of the lane. One thing I've learned during my long spells in the sticks is to top-up with nutrients at every opportunity

Once again I ignore the coast and the main road and turn to country lanes for easy walking and contemplation. This is a longer route, but what the hell – my legs are up to it by now. In the late afternoon it is very cold (blasted wind). I head back to the main road and, two miles on, enter Aberystwyth.

My host, Gareth Harvey, lives just off the seafront. His generosity comes to me via Ann Cripps, a Southern Trails walker. A mature student, he is studying international politics at Wales University and is preparing a dissertation on Ruanda, of all things.

Gareth is an amiable and chatty bloke. Like me, he was born in Portsmouth and is a fanatical Pompey fan. He has high hopes of getting to the Cup Final to see them take on Cardiff City and appears most impressed that I am carrying a team shirt.

We go for a pint on the sea front. The sun pours through its bay front windows. Later I enjoy a meal and a chat with some of his friends.

I'm looking forward to being back in a bed tonight.

DAY 109
18th April – Rest day – Aberystwyth

Ah, the luxury of a leisurely breakfast! While Gareth goes about his business I venture downtown to top up provisions and gas. Yet another indulgence, I treat myself to a *Daily Telegraph*. Well, it's only once a fortnight. This is a map dump, so I post my redundant ones home.

In the afternoon I wander onto the seafront. The promenade is wide, and terraces of four-storey Victorian apartments dominate. There is a pier, castle ruins and a cliff railway (closed), and that's about it. The population is swelled by seven thousand students attending the University of Wales.

Gareth has taken time off from his studies to get a couple of sirloin steaks for our evening dinner. After taking an inventory of my rucksack we go out for a drink and more chat. He has seen to my domestic and social needs admirably.

My complacency is to be thwarted when, as I turn, in for the night. Flek pipes up, 'Just to remind you, Col, that I'm still here to comment, administer good advice and issue reprimands when necessary, all right?!'

'Roger and out, to you my friend!'

DAY 110
19th April – Aberwystwith to Ty Mawr Campsite, Borth – 11 miles

Gareth and I bid farewell in the only way appropriate: 'Play-Up, Pompey!' is the chant. Rather than face a torturous hike to the top with the rucksack I circumvent the Penglais and golf club area, turn left at the Llangorwen crossroads and return to the Coastal Path that way.

It's a challenging and windy three miles to Borth, which lies next to a long beach and is sandwiched between the through B4353 road and the Cambrian Line railway. As I'm camping tonight I make good use of the general store.

Another three-mile hike now to Ty Mawr, reached when the road turns sharply to the east. The proprietor, Paul Beech, greets me and I can't help noticing his Ferrari. I mention that I live close to Goodwood, and in no time we are talking about motor sports history. He used to race and manage Formula 3 cars.

He listens intently when I tell him that during the mid-Fifties, while on St John Ambulance duties in West Sussex as a cadet, I had access to the service pits on race days at the Goodwood circuit. This allowed me to mingle with the team drivers of the time who included Juan Fangio, Stirling Moss, Albert Ascari, Reg Parnell, Prince Bira and Archie Scott Brown. Fangio went on to win the first five F1 Championships. Motor racing was on the brink of greater things, and predictably the small Goodwood circuit was dropped from the F1 season. I had little idea of the significance of it all at the time!

The camp is deserted and my tent is exposed. As the wind blows throughout the night I get only a fitful sleep.

DAY 111

20 th April – Ty Maur Holiday Park, Borth to Aberdovey – 18 miles.

How many times have I predicted that it's going to be a long, hard, gruelling day today? Ahead lies the River Dovey; there is no ferry. To cross it I am going to have to slog inland for ten miles to reach the first bridge at Machyynleth and then another ten miles return to Aberdovey on the coast. All roadwork: I am so looking forward to it!

Fortunately this is West Wales and there isn't a lot of traffic at this time of the year. I pass through hamlets, the houses looking bleak and deserted.

'They may be a home to someone,' offers Flek.

The railway has also had to swing round, and I discover at intervals parties of linemen maintaining/improving it. One of them tells me that there is a £19 million pound upgrade going on.

I find a nice pub at Derwenlas and treat myself to a roast dinner because, frankly, I deserve it. I alert dogs in practically every house and finally reach Machyynleth at last. As it's a Sunday morning in West Wales, it's not surprising to surmise that the place is in hibernation – or are they all at chapel? There is not a soul about, look-you.

I cross its bridge and grudgingly start back on the ten mile return to the coast. The journey is unrelenting and I am forced to enter a hotel at Pennal for refreshment. The last three miles into Aberdovey have been hewn out of solid rock in the true tradition of the pioneering railway companies.

I reach Sea Breeze, my B & B, exhausted. I say this, but there is always a force holding me up: is it mental or physical?

CLIMB has fixed up this accommodation and has passed on the security code to obtain entry. I find a welcome note with keys to a single room on the 2nd floor. Just what I need is two flights of stairs, which I crawl up. The place is well appointed. I have a soak and start nibbling away at a snack I just happen to have. Tired or not, there is work to do, and I get away two days of blogs to CLIMB for my website.

I am startled by an almighty racket going on outside. My room overlooks a seafront car park now empty. I observe that several squadrons of sea gulls have flown in. Strangely a single bird has alighted on to each parking space. Birds continually encroach on their neighbour's patch, only to be noisily repelled. Several spaces are particularly desired, and I conclude that the birds have deduced it is these where motorists discard the most food. I have been watching nature's pecking order in action. David Attenborough would be proud of my observations. I clean my teeth and put my legs to bed.

DAY 112

21st April – Aberdovey to Barmouth – 17 miles

Sea Breeze is run by Ian and Linda Hinton. He sees to my every need at breakfast. Sitting at my table is a rail man who confirms the railway's activities. On this occasion I pay my dues and make an early start.

I set off for Tywnn four miles away. The local TIO has confirmed my fears that there is no ferry over the approaching River Dysynni. This means another detour inland – a round trip of 14 miles to a road bridge near Bryncrug and back. Deja vu!

The pub is closed, but at another Spar I get a Stella and an egg sandwich. I have returned to the coastal road which takes leads into the village of Llwyngwril. In it two ex Brummie's are chatting away cutting a hedge, their wheelbarrow dumped in the middle of the road. I comment on the 'serene peace' of the place.

'Yeh,' says one of them, 'my mate back in the Midlands often says I have come here to die.'

'Is this the biblical role for West Wales then?' comments Flek. 'To be a sort of elephants' graveyard for Brummie's?'

I don't think they will be able to figure out the analogy, and we leave.

'There you are, Flek, you've left them open-mouthed and confused.'

'It was just a thought,' he said, almost apologetically.

This village is all a bit rundown, but I suspect that they could rustle up an emergency committee if pushed.

A further three miles on I reach Fairbourne narrow-gauge railway station. There is a faint hint of early tourist activity. After refreshment I venture towards the Barmouth Bay estuary where the miniature railway track takes a loop to return.

The much photographed half a mile long Barmouth Foot (toll) and Railway Bridge is in full view, and I cross the estuary's raised dyke paths to reach it. Now and then a train rattles over. I cross this famous dual train/footbridge alone and see my first swallow of the season.

At the town end I have to pay my 70p at a booth. From the darkness within, all the intonations of the Welsh language come flooding through the tiny pay point's window as the attendant and her husband prattle on. She sounds like Gladys Morgan – remember her?

At the Hendre Mynach caravan park I am expected and made most welcome. I am directed to a pitch which is just fifty feet from the railway track.

Operating on this single-track permanent way are scheduled trains whose carriages are covered in colourful graffiti, the exact reverse of England where Banksie and Co express their talents on the station approach cutting walls. It's a welcome alternative to this controversial culture.

The camp's facilities are not yet fully open, so I make up a meal with what I have.

Tonight's Evening Concert is classical. First up is the 3rd movement of Saint-Saens' magnificent Symphony No 3 the 'Organ'. then Mendlelssons's Scherzo from his 'Midsummers Night's Dream'. I select Rachmaninov's No.2 (the Brief Encounter bit). This will have some relevance later in the Walk. I am a great lover of Vaughan Williams' music so I pop on his Fantasia on Greensleeves. The evening winds down with another hilarious Round the Horne.

Legs (2)

'I haven't got time to be tired.'
– Emperor Wilhelm I

Apart from the motive power that legs provide in normal movement they come in useful for activating specialist bursts, as in sport.

People's prowess at sport generally falls into three categories. First there are born athletic giants; second are those whose sheer determination and dedication pulls them through to success; and then the rest of us, who just have a go. The pedigree of the legs is crucial.

Sporting ambitions, e.g. such as becoming a striker for your favourite league soccer team or breaking the world mile record, gradually dissipate as the realisation of your limits sets in.

Having a go usually starts at school. In my case I won the school sports day intermediate 220 yards and progressed up the school soccer teams, i.e. Colts, 2nd and 1st elevens, earning castigation in the *The Martlet*, the school magazine, from Frank Haille the sports master for lack of skill. I only had the speed of my legs to call on: any physical dexterity shown on the pitch was purely accidental. Playing for my house team, St Richards, alongside another pupil Alan Arnell, who went on to score 74 goals for Liverpool, didn't help. Liverpool played in the FA's Second Division at the time.

I have wonderful memories of Bognor Athletic Club in my youth, competing for several summers until called up for National Service. I had joined the Air Training Corps, going up to Uxbridge to win the national discus event.

On demob I joined the London Fire Brigade, which ran its limited athletics championship programme at the White City Stadium: I won the 100 yards. In those days I 'lived' athletics, and having a chance to race on this famous cinder track, scene of so many great performances and world records, was a thrill. I kept up my interest by sprinting and throwing for Thames Valley Harriers, training out at Alperton and Hurlingham.

It was about this time that I started to play volleyball, an exercise medium used on most fire stations to promote fitness. I came to the attention of Don Anthony, the British hammer throwing champion and also chairman of the fledgling Amateur Volleyball Association. The AVA put together the very first national representative team comprising mostly experienced players from new UK residents coming in from Poland and Estonia, plus Hungarians who had escaped their country following the 1956 uprising. A couple of us Brits were also included in the squad.

We took on the Russian embassy at the Swiss Cottage Centre, north London and were crushed three sets to one, but it had been a great experience. The

AVA then secured a game against the United States Air Force held at the Harlow Sports Centre. The BBC took an interest and used the game for an outside broadcast on Grandstand, with Alan Weekes commentating. Underdogs once again, we went down to the Americans but the taking part was paramount. Later we had another go at them at their Upper Heyford airbase. A couple of years later I brought the Russian embassy team to Bognor Regis for an exhibition game against AVA Team. This was a very difficult event to organise – well, the Cold War was still on!

In my thirties I still liked kicking a ball about, and back in West Sussex I played for Selsey FC, getting in the third team. My leg speed was still there, and in one season I notched up twenty eight goals – the highest tally of the club's three teams.

I continued to play volleyball, but had one last athletic outing and travelled to the Aldersley Stadium in Wolverhampton to win the British Fire Service discus event. It turned out to be my last fling (excuse the pun).

I must emphasise that all these sporting outings produced very average performances. My legs had done their best, and I'd had a go.

There is always a case for what *could* have been. During my teens I was selected to attend an athletics training course at Motspur Park in Surrey. We listened intently to an English national coach. He explained how he had solved a muscle weakness in the country's internationally renowned sprinter. He coached the athlete to work on his back muscles by suspending him from a bar by his hands and getting him to run in mid air. This sounds pretty rudimentary now, but it worked, helping to solve a problem of bad starting.

The sprinter involved was E. Macdonald Bailey, a Trinidadian who elected to sprint for the UK and who came within a whisker of winning the 100 metres sprint title at the 1952 Helsinki Olympics. He was also joint holder of the world record 100 metres' time of 10.2 with several others, including Jesse Owens.

The point I am making is that as a young keen athlete I also had a problem, one of my leg's muscles being weaker than the other. At about 80 yards into a sprint I started to wander off-line like an itinerant supermarket trolley! This is still the case at the end of a long walk, all because one calf muscle is less developed. With proper coaching and remedial training I am sure my classification as a club athlete would have risen from 'average' to 'useful!

But this is now: I hung my boots and spikes up years ago. I have no idea what the future holds for my lower limbs, but they are certainly not on a casual stroll around the park!

22nd April – Barmouth to Harlech (Cae Cethin Camp Site) – 15 miles

It is 5am, and I am awoken by a thundering sound which is getting nearer. Swiftly coming out of my post sleep stupor, I realise that a train is approaching. Its clattering becomes louder and louder and then deafening. For a split second I fear that the contraption is going to run us over in the tent.

'Struth, Col, I thought we were a goner" splutters Flek. 'That's got to be the ultimate morning alarm call.'

Still shaken, I fall out of the tent. It is cold but bright.Time for the earliest breakfast I have had yet. I boil up some packets of honey flavoured porridge then dunk a few chocolate hob-knobs in my tea.

Looking at my map I see that I can follow Sustrans Route 8, which runs along the mean high water mark of the Morfa Dyffryn National Nature Reserve. I soon pick it up, but although the sea views and sand dune landscape are stunning it is hard going. Near to the end at Shell Island I cut sharply across the top of a former airfield to the A496 and the village of LLanbedr. Sitting on a wall, I have a long chat with Lesley Greene who tells me that to break up the sequence of site camping she has booked me into Snowden Lodge at Tremadog tomorrow.

On a back lane I see and chat to a council worker whose sole job is to collect animals killed on the roads. He is bagging up a dead badger. Well, someone has to do it!

'You know, Col, the only way to know what's going on is to be out here,' utters Flek.

He is so right.

There are great many dead bumble bees along the way. A logical explanation is that they have ventured out to forage too early and been caught out in this recent cold spell.

I call in the busy Queen Vic at Llanbedr. Sitting in the garden I chat with an ex-station fire commander from Liverpool and his wife. I share views of the service with him while devouring a tuna melt.

Two miles on I arrive at the Cae Cethin caravan site, which in the season also operates as an animal theme park for children. The owner,

Rob Owen, appears from his bungalow and offers me the field for nothing. At first the site appears deserted, but up on a plateau at the back of the field I discover a smashing café. Ladies there ply me with tea and cake, and we banter on.

No music tonight. Today the weather has got warmer and tired me out. Like a snake in sand, I quickly dissolve into my sleeping bag, but it is going to be a disturbed night? The truth is that I have drunk too much beer in a pub today, and keep having to crawl outside for a pee.

On the third occasion an irritated Flek stirs and shouts.

'What's up?' he blurts.

'When you have got to go, you have got to go chum,' I mutter.

'My Dad had a prostrate operation to stop that kind of thing' he commiserates.

'Yes, yes I know all about that. I used to get up sometimes eight times a night before my op. Don't laugh, Flek, your turn might come,' I warn. 'Between you and, me the trouble is the procedure can mean the end of . . . well, you know.'

'No, I don't, Col. Spit it out, man.'

Looking over both shoulders as if in a doctor's waiting room I whisper, 'It's got something to do with manhood.'

'Sorry mate, you've got me.' He pauses, and then the penny drops – or so he thinks. 'Oh, you mean like a sudden increase in body hair,' he says with a broad smile.

I shake my head and speculate: is he being deliberately naff?

By now nature can't wait. I frantically unzip the tent and skedaddle into the night to burst forth!

DAY 114

23rd April – Harlech to Snowdon Lodge, Tremadog – 12 miles

This was going to be just another day. I have made no specific plans and have hardly perused OL18, the OS map for the area. As it turns out I am about to experience a series of historical and heritage treats which just keep popping all day.

About a mile on the road I come across two more Brummies who are repairing a stone wall outside their homes on the main road.

'Another bloody lorry has hit it,' grumbled one of them. 'We always seem to be putting the same rocks back into place.'

'This part of Wales is teaming with you lot from Birmingham – how come'? I enquire.

'This is the nearest and easiest foreign land we can travel to,' says the other chap with a tongue in his cheek. 'Besides, it's evolution, isn't it? I mean, without knowing it in time we could be improving the local twang no end.'

'He's taking the proverbial,' says Flek. 'Let's move on.'

We all have a laugh and I push on the mile up the road to Harlech where a café owner is just opening up. Starving, I have to wait fifteen minutes while his missus fires up the stove, but it's worth the wait. Sitting at the rear of the premises I glance out and Harlech Castle towers up – I can almost touch it. This is to be my first unexpected culture surprise of the day.

Later I enter the town of Penrhryndeudraeth. My brain, without a conscious prompt, reminds me that this was the home of the mother to one of my earliest girlfriends over sixty years ago. Now why should I remember that?

I purchase an indifferent fish and chip lunch at the Griffin pub, open my map and spot that Portmeirion is just up the road. Shortly I am puffing up the hill of its entrance drive. A van stops behind me and a steward in a smart grey suit jumps out, asks me what I am doing and then invites me hop in.

'Don't worry about the entrance fee – we're Portmeirion staff and will take you straight in,' he says.

Their lodge is a bustle of activity. They fuss around, taking care of my rucksack, and invite me to enjoy the site. This amazing village was designed and built by architect Sir Clough William Ellis from 1925 onwards in the Italian style. Many will remember it being used in the TV drama The Prisoner. It commands an outstanding view across the Traaeth Bach estuary.

Visit over, I return to the porter's lodge. One of them asks where I am staying the night. When I tell him Snowden Lodge he informs me that it was the birthplace of Lawrence of Arabia. They present me with bottled water and I'm escorted to a short cut through a wood and out of the estate on to the road to Porthmadog.

Portmeirion.

Up ahead is the footpath of the Ffestiniog railway bridge. I go into the harbour station for a drink in the period waiting room bar. I can hear a loco getting up steam, and just catch the gift shop for some cards to send home.

I depart out into Porthmadog's Penamser Road and go up to the A487 roundabout and onto Tremadog. Entering the village I see a plaque on an unimposing detached building which is in need of decorating. This is the birthplace of T.E. Lawrence, in 1888.

Karl, the warden. books me in. It is a rambling place inside but very functional as a hostel. The spot where Lawrence was born is now a toilet!

A room has been set aside as a small museum and contains all the classic photos of Lawrence in the Middle East, plus the one sitting on his Brough Superior motorcycle talking to George Brough, its designer. This was the powerful beast on which he was fatally injured in May 1935. I have visited Clouds Hill in Dorset, where he lived, and also his grave at Morton, but until now I never realised he was Welsh born. A controversial figure, his funeral at Morton in the New Forest was attended by Winston Churchill.

It has been an extraordinary day for me, the itinerary of which came together purely by chance.

Once again it's down to the chippie in the village to collect supper.

DAY 115

24th April – Tremadog to Abererch Sands Caravan Site – 12 miles

Geographically Tremadog is quite a spectacular village. The square backs onto a sheer 400 feet escarpment covered in trees. With its church perched on a rise the place has an Alpine feel.

The walk to Abererch is uneventful. I pass the old Butlins Holiday Camp on the way. I have a lousy night in the tent. The ground seems especially hard and I doze intermittently.

DAY 116

25th April – Abererch Sands to Abersoch – 12 miles

I set off to Pwllheli two miles down the road and get myself breakfast and a Lleyn Peninsula map. The weather deteriorates, so I keep to the A499, which with long straight stretches is boring, especially in the rain.

The half way pub at LLanbedrog is closed, so I trudge on to Abersoch. I enter a café and its friendly owner offers me tea and cheesecake. I get some provisions and complete the last two miles to the Deucoch caravan park. Owners Ruth Pullan and husband Andrew welcome me with open arms, their hospitality second to none – first some tea, and then the use of the best shower block yet. They get my clothes washed and invite me out for a pub meal with the whole family. which includes daughter Rebecca (plus her three dogs) and grandparents Norman and Audrey Winteringham.

My mobile and iPod are also being charged: it's all rather overwhelming. The rain persists but I settle down in the tent and take stock.

Kit at this Stage: Boots are starting to go home. Top coat OK but very smelly. Waterproof trousers still functional. Socks show no sign of real wear. Rucksack beginning to wear (I have never been satisfied with it). iPod is stuck in 'pause' mode, so no music tonight.

Me at this Stage: Legs are OK. (They are always ready to go). Feet complain now and then. Have lost some weight (no surprise there). I am trimming the beard occasionally. Nose is weathered and red. Not sure that I have the physical elasticity for a tent life.

Appraisal done and noted, it's 'Good night, Flek' and I nod off.

DAY 117

26th April – Deu Coch Abersoch to Ty-Newydd Site, Aberdaron – 18 miles

Audrey Winteringham boils me up an egg with tea and toast while her husband Norman talks about his lifetime work as a haulage contractor. He is passionate about lorries and their history. It's a reluctant goodbye to a family whose support has been outstanding.

In overcast weather I head down the road to LLanegan village and join the Llyn Coastal Path on to the firm sand of a lovely beach. After three miles the tide comes in and I am forced to escape, scrambling up a detritus-strewn gully and into a field. Now off any public footpath, I feel exposed and hurry across the fields taking tracks leading to a minor road. Seeing an upturned stranded ewe, I let the farmer know when passing the farmhouse,

Now on the B4413 I come to Rhiw and the longest and steepest road ascent so far. Half way up I'm joined by four cyclists, Simon, Rachel, Jackie and Ray, and we battle our way on foot to the top. From here they can virtually freewheel down to the three miles into Aberdaron.

Eventually I join them in a café and we lunch together. They are from Sandbach in Cheshire. Rachel tells me she drives past CLIMB's office in Crewe every working day. They leave for their long cycle ride back to the Deudoch site, and I find out that they've paid for my lunch. They were a lively ebullient bunch and it was a delight to be with them.

I still have a way to go. En route I come across a couple renovating an ex-Methodist Church into a home, a sort of 'Grand Design' project. A hundred yards away in this tiny hamlet stands another abandoned church for Baptists. Both were built within three years of each other.

As I trundle along I think about the 'baptism of fire' that erupted here in Wales in the 19th century as congregations rallied to the ideals of the Baptist, Calvinists, Methodists, Presbyterians, Congregationalists, Welsh Independents, Zionists and so on.

I trudge uphill on a slow and tiring last couple of miles to Ty-Newydd, the penultimate camping site before the tip of the Lleyn Peninsula. Shirley, the owner, opens her little café for me and produces tea and cake. The site is deserted. I pitch the tent and with my iPod off the run I slumber in no time.

DAY 118

27th April – Ty-Newyad Campsite, Aberdaron to Graeanfryn Camp, Morfa Nefyn site – 13 miles

It's a Sunday. I slink out of the sleepy site early to return the two miles down to a junction, turning briskly north. I shall be following miles of back lanes, adopting a leisurely pace over the flat topography.

The day is not without incident. I come to an isolated stretch of road which has recently received tar macadam treatment. It appears to be a one-off. After all, this is the time of the year when councils often find that they have a budget surplus.

Instead of a sub-committee frittering away cash on a continental exchange trip, have they had actually spent the surplus for the benefit of ratepayers? But this is right out in the sticks. My thoughts race: is this a laundered job gone wrong and the money hurriedly spent doing up the road? Has it anything to do with what happens next?

I have halted at a crossroads for a comfort stop, drink and yet another adjustment to the blasted rucksack. Suddenly, out of nowhere, a man tears up on his bike, slides off it a few yards away, looks furtively in either direction (he must have seen me) and starts to climb up a steep roadside ditch to a telegraph pole. Just seconds later he slides back down the bank to the verge, utters some indiscernible small talk in my direction and speeds off.

My mind wildly speculates. Can the purpose of this daring daylight mission be to retrieve the rain-sodden envelope, perhaps from a cache, which I could see clearly in his back pocket as he raced away? Was this the clandestine cash transfer for the road job?

It is difficult to think of an innocent explanation but I try. Finally I content myself that this go-between picked up Harold's latest covert communiqué from Marina!

I get some lunch at the Red Lion, Tudweilog, part sponsored by the proprietor.

After a long day in the lanes I arrive at Graenfryn, and owner Janice Harrison points out a delightful field adjacent. I pitch the tent in lovely late afternoon sunshine and then wander down to the local shop to supplement my provisions, as it's a rest day tomorrow.

28th April – Rest day – Graenfryn

Oh the joys of lying-in, even if it is in a tent. Always present, though, is the almost paralysing stiffness from yesterday's effort. It takes an age for the mental message from the brain to reach the muscles, and even longer for them to respond. It's a monumental task to lever myself out of the sleeping bag and then upright.

This morning I spoil myself and consume two sachets of banana flavoured porridge followed by cheese biscuits and a brew of coffee. I get some emails and blogs away and make phone calls to family. I also phone in my progress to Lesley at CLIMB and then make another visit to the shop for a newspaper.

I return to the site to find mayhem. A caravan being towed into the next field site has got stuck in the gate because it's too wide. A traffic jam has built up – well, four cars and a couple lorries to be precise. I join the 'sizable' crowd gathered to witness the outcome. Janice's husband just takes the gates off: simple!

I leave this chaos and stroll down to the excellent Bryncynan Inn at the next crossroads for lunch, consuming the best coronation chicken baguette I have ordered so far. The experience is somewhat spoiled by an ever squawking Whitney Houston. It doesn't seem to annoy anyone else, so it is all down to my jaundiced Victor Meldrew outlook.

Undaunted, I return in the evening to a huge plate of sausage and mash. The busy dining room is full of Welsh speakers.

'What the hell are they talking about,' whispers Flek.

'You obviously haven't heard, chum, that the Welsh are bilingual.'

'What does that mean?'

'They speak with forked tongue.'

'What, like Red Indians?'

'We had better shut up Flek or we'll get thrown out of here.'

I get back to the tent and – more by luck than technical expertise – solve the 'pause' problem on the iPod. The Evening Concert's line-up, chosen at random, includes excerpts from Miles Davis' iconic album 'Kind of Blue', Oscar Peterson's Hymn to Freedom' andPurcell's 'Dido & Aenaes'. My Wish List track is 'One of These Nights' by the Eagles.

DAY 120

29th April – Morfa Nefyn to Pontllynfi – 15 miles

A cold wind blows as I passed through Nefyn. I resist the tea shops as another long day beckons.

Walkers always score over the motorist because there is ample time to notice what is around you. There is always something of interest: believe me, I've had lots of practice. Sometimes it hits you straight in the eye or, in my case this morning, the ears. Instinctively sheep always do follow a lone figure carrying a pack. When I didn't deliver the grub pellets they gave me a right bleating. The noise was deafening.

Here are some other examples just today:

A tourist sign states that the granite quarried at nearby Yr Eifl is some of the hardest in the world. Apparently the mine provided the material for the Curling Event at the 2006 Winter Olympic Games. Not a lot of people know this!

One chapel I passed had the bust of a past man of God over its entrance door. No offence, but he resembled Lenin.

A mountain to my left is scooped out at the top l like a boiled egg!

It seems a must that every community gets itself twinned with some foreign place. I pass a hamlet this morning that has found asylum for this purpose in Argentina! To be fair, I do seem to remember that there is a Welsh community down there somewhere.

The B4417 elevates and eventually a pass breaks through the line of Snowdonia's foot mountains, which presents an impressive backdrop to the road. I get my first glimpse of Anglesey, a near-future destination. A slight diversion to LLanaelhaeran finds me at the Rivals pub for lunch.

The landlord, Dave, is an amiable fellow from Bolton, Lancs. The place is deserted, and I am soon to find out why: he is having cross words with his wife, who never appears. I am served up a lamb dish with roast potatoes. Left over from yesterday, he says, and very tasty. What he really means is the day before yesterday – it's just palatable. He then offers me a jam sponge for sweet. It's dry as old bones, with little sign of any jam. We chat on about Bolton Wanderers and Fred Dibner, the town's famous son. The only consolation is that he doesn't charge for this gastronomic incompetence.

I break back to the A499, where I am going to have to take care. The reason is five miles of intermittent roadworks as a massive scheme to reline the road is in progress. I have to watch it as the traffic is in pulses. I dodge it between traffic light halts and the road gangs are chatty as I skip through. They obviously haven't seen an idiot playing musical chairs with traffic for some time.

I get provisions from a Londis at Clynnog and tramp up the three miles of boringly straight road to Pontllynfi.

My timing is perfect, as it starts to rain. I get the tent up, brew up some tea and, starving, scoff the provisions.

The usual notebook recording and electronic communication are completed and phone calls made.

'Use what you've got' is an unwritten rule in camping. I have solved my pillow dilemma at last by stuffing two kitchen rolls and my 'Patagonia' top into the mattress sleeve. The proof of this improvised comfort is that despite the pounding of rain on the tent I sleep soundly.

DAY 121

30th April – Pontlyfni Camp Site to Caernarfon – 9 miles

I go up the A487 to pick up Sustrans Route 8 through a wood to Dinas Station on the Welsh West Highland Railway. At Bontnewydd platform station stands an ingeniously designed bench made up from rail sleepers and lines. I take a shot.

It starts to rain steadily. I will never get used to putting on wet-weather gear and enduring the perspiration that follows, but sometimes one has to. I admire the locomotive steamed up at the Terminus Station and proceed into town. It's becoming a miserable day. I find an ATM and then dump myself into the Bakery Café. I have a meal and read the *Telegraph* for an hour, my concentration constantly interrupted by the high-pitched bantering of the female staff in their own language.

'Dont they go on!' bleats Flek, but then adds that the cakes look scrumptious.

Surprisingly the Cwm Cadnant Valley campsite is only a short walk from the town centre. I pass the fire station and call in for a chat with the duty crew. The area is a Welsh-speaking stronghold, this station the only one in Wales that takes emergency calls (shouts) in both languages.

Jean Bird and her son welcome me to the campsite. By now the ground is sodden, and I have to pitch on a semi-mud surface which is sloping! In the gloomy atmosphere I am comforted to find that the shower room is warm and fit for purpose: so many are not. Later I wander down to the chippie nearby and return to the site's warm laundry room to consume my supper. Why? Well. apart from the warmth it has the luxury of a chair to sit on.

Despite deteriorating weather and camping out on a wet and muddy sloping ground surface, I place my head on my newly improvised pillow and sleep soundly.

Mavis

'One day her prince will come'
– Snow White

In late spring there came a time when I was obliged to widen my accommodation experience, i.e. actually having to pitch the tent. CLIMB had spoilt me, keeping me under cover at night continually for the first three months.

So towards the end of a day in April I found myself slumped on a coastal park bench wondering where on earth to pitch for the night.

Suddenly I heard a call – 'Yoo Hoo!' It came from a large caravan site to my left. A middle aged woman was beckoning me over. Seems promising, I thought.

'I hope you don't mind. I can see you're tired. Would you like a cup of tea?'

She led me into her van, where a man sat intently watching the TV – horse racing from Wincanton. He had a 'form' page on his lap.

'I'm Joan and this is my husband, Norman,' she said.

Without as much as a glance he nodded, eyes firmly affixed on the nags that had been emptying his pocket all the afternoon.

'Him and the gee-gees,' Joan scolded, and fussed away preparing the tea.

A woman in her thirties entered the van. Well proportioned, she had a faded beauty.

'This is my daughter Mavis' said Joan.

We shook hands and entered into small talk. I could see that Joan was building up to a big announcement, and she finally blurted it out.

'Mavis was once second in the Miss Bridlington Fancy Dress Competition 1990. She was Snow White. Oh how she flowered that day – all the boys were after you, weren't they, Mave?'

Mavis smiled awkwardly. She had heard all this before.

'That Sylvia Wilmshurst won the competition because her Dad played golf with one of the Judges,' Joan continued, still harbouring bitterness.

It was apparent that in horticultural terms Joan's precious bloom had now gone-over. Sadly poor Mavis was still stuck with Mum and Dad on their early-season holiday trips in the van.

Joan, now in full control, insisted that I stayed the night.:

'We have a lean-to extension. Mavis sleeps out there. It's got a divider – you could sleep in the other half.'

I panicked a little, uneasy thoughts raced through my mind.

Flek came through: 'Do you think that Mavis or Joan see you as their last chance saloon, Col? ' he questioned and then fantasy got the better of him. 'What happens if Mavis appears in your half of the lean-to scantily dressed like the temptresses in the Fry's Turkish Delight ads.'

Blimey, he was going back a bit! He might be joking, but real panic set in. I dived into my division, pulled the sleeping bag over my head and froze.

I needn't have worried. Minutes later I heard Mavis crash on to her camp bed, and soon she was snoring away like a drunken sailor.

Eventually woken by her loud snorts, I came to – and found myself still sitting on the bench. I had had one of those one-minute dreams, or was it five or ten minutes? No one has ever come up with a satisfactory explanation of how long these involuntary sensations last.

I hauled myself up and moved on, later finding a pitch for the night. Before passing into oblivion I remember thinking of Mavis and wishing that for this Snow White one day her Prince would come.

DAY 122

1st May – Caernarfon to Fron Caravan Park Camp , Anglesey – 16 miles

I pick up the A487 and its flanking Sustrans Path 8, but I am thwarted as long stretches of it are hurriedly being resurfaced in time for the coming Bank Holiday. Being forced to use the road, with no pavement, brings difficulties with traffic. Later this situation is resolved. and I am able to use sidewalks all the way to the Menai Bridge. I find an amusing group of stone sculptured molluscs on permanent display as I pass a long a diversionary path

'These are unusual,' says Flek. 'Tucked away on the path away from the main road they don't bare any graffiti, which makes a welcome change.'

I have a standard fare lunch in the Antelope pub which overlooks the Menai Bridge, and get a female pedestrian to take my photo crossing it just before she jumps on a bus. This is one of Thomas Telford's masterpieces. Modern buses have to gingerly negotiate the pillars at each end with inches to spare.

Now on Anglesey, I make my way into Llanfair Pwlgwyngyll the Welsh village which bears a fifty eight letter tongue twisting name. I take a shot of its full designation emblazoned over the local car-dealers showroom.

I turn off on A4080 for a five mile slog to Fron, which is a four-star caravan and camping park. I'm greeted fondly by the owner family, Mrs Geldard, her husband George and son Mark. It's midweek in early season so I have this spotless place to myself. This caring affable family have promised to chase up some sponsorship from the host of caravan folk who will descend on the site during the coming weekend.

From the field I look out over Anglesey, which by and large is flat. But the real view is the other way across the Menai Straight to the mountains, with Snowdon towering above.

DAY 123
2nd May – Fron Camping Site to Penybont Campsite, Malltreath
Anglesey – 12 miles

Still savouring the wonderful view across the Menai Straight, I join up with the Isle of Anglesey Coast Path for the first time. Walking down to the shoreline, I find Foel Farm Animal Park, have tea and and walk the stony shore. The pathway then zig-zags inland. I go over some marsh land, carefully negotiating huge stepping stones that cross the River Braint at Gatehouses Ford. A café at Pen-Lon donates a tea and apple crumble. I have to take in a lot of calories, you understand!

Push on down to skirt the Newborough Forest, passing a modern sculpture which depicts the past use of Marram Grass for making baskets in this area. The intensive commercial use of the grass caused serious shifting of the sand. There has been talk of lost villages!

Marram grass sculpture, Anglesey.

Flek is impressed by the sculpture

'I like it when past industries are commemorated,' he remarks, 'It's a reminder of how people had to struggle making a living from natural sources and then had to endure the dire consequences.'

Pressing on, I follow the edge of the Newborough Forest to the dazzling white sand beach area. This two mile-square forest was planted to arrest the erosion of the dunes, once the largest area of their kind in Europe. This is a wonderful walk, with Anglesey living up to its reputation.

A long hot walk through the forest roads takes me towards my next camp site five miles away, where I receive welcoming hospitality from my hosts, farming folk Katy and Jeff Hughs.

DAY 124

3rd May – Peny-y-Bont Farm Malltreath to Rhosneigr Camp Site – 12 miles

I am woken at 5 o'clock by the dawn chorus. What a wonderful sound – haven't heard it for years.

Flek awakes, rubbing his eyes in bewilderment and mumbling 'Go on then, shout about it to the world. Wake everyone up. Tell them they don't know what they're missing.'

He has got it just about right. Apart from farmers and milkmen out on their floats most people are oblivious to this early morning natural phenomenon.

'Listen to it, Flek! This is real 'tweeting' – none of your social networking nonsense here.'

It is my first warm morning start. I say good bye to the Hughs and strike out for Malltreath just up the road. I get a bacon and egg bap at the village store; it's just passable as food. *Flek is appalled.*

'Do these people actually eat like this?' he exclaims.

Outside the shop I have an odd encounter. The village is deserted but suddenly out of an alley steps a wild man. He is a tall individual who from the neck up looks like Billy Connolly, but scruffier. The clothes on his torso are torn, filthy and completely dishevelled. Ben Gunn must have looked like this when Jim Hawkins found him on Treasure Island. Was he a recluse or the victim of village inbreeding? Who knows! I scrambled to get the camera out, but too late – he slithered into another ally and like a Fagan he was gone.

Following the coastal path, I arrive at Aberffraw. It is a Sunday and the place is comatose. The Heritage Centre and tea room has attracted handsome investment, but it's closed save for a TIO lady on duty. Out of sympathy she lets me use her computer to check on the CLIMB donation current total. Disappointing news: after the initial surge of cash back in the spring, donations are now just trickling in.

I'm getting hungry,

'You could try the pub,' the TIO advises, 'but it doesn't open till one.'

Of course, it's a Sunday and we are on Anglesey, which might as well be Wales. I have to kill valuable time. When it does open I am told it is not doing food today! Well, it's only Bank Holiday Sunday, I tell myself once again. I am getting niggled.

'Here we go again, Col, they must know it is a Bank Holiday. Surely the landlord has anticipated some passing trade?,' says Flek. 'Look, you've waited for some time for this place to open, I can sense your frustration – now go over to the bar and make a noise!'

This time I take his advice.

'Look, I'm a long distance walker. This is Day 124 for me and I'm starving,' I plead.

I hear a muffled staff consultation behind the bar and they relent. Scampi and chips arrive, served up by a rotund giggling girl. She is turned out in a complete Arsenal kit, socks and all. Proudly I tell her

Lonely at Rhosneigr, Anglesey.

about Portsmouth being in the FA Cup Final, but she doesn't seem to know who they are!

I am now late, and speed the last three miles to the campsite at Rhosneigr. It's a Bank Holiday weekend and the site is buzzing.

My Helliberg tent is tiny compared with the Bedouin type structures that are going up all around me. Then there are the conservatories tacked to the sides of countless caravans or 4 x 4s. Huge Hummer-type vehicles are pouring in, pulling large, impressive speed boats, each arrival outdoing the others. In the centre of this lot is a large recreational green space with one isolated tent on it – mine! God I feel so out of place; it is so lonely out here in no- man's land. I have the overwhelming feeling of being a poor relation.

'I'll remind you what kind of relation you are, Col,' says Flek, his voice quiverying with anger, 'You are a grandad. If this consumer-besotted bunch ever realised that you were socially marooned out here they would wince with embarrassment.'

'Thanks Flek for trying to bolster my confidence. Thing is, the visitors here are doing their own thing, and that's the way it is.'

I saunter around the huge site with its access to a fine beach. Everyone appears to be having fun. I find an alfresco seat in a café out of the breeze and enjoy an unhealthy snack. I treat myself to a beanie hat with the Welsh emblem on it; it seems appropriate.

A blustery wind pummels the tent and the resonance keeps me awake for long periods. In the early hours I look out and am reminded that I am surrounded by luxury. I remember pining!

4th May – Rhosneigr Caravan Site to Rhoscolyn (Nr Hollyhead) – 10 miles

I leave the site and follow the sand dunes around Valley RAF Station. It's a Sunday so there is no flying activity today. I disturb an adder basking in the early morning sun. A lady takes my photo on the beach.

Flek chips in with some early morning sarcasm,

'Your mugshots seem to be coming thick and fast, Col. Missing a mirror in the mornings, are you?

'Listen you, these are a record of my presence. How on earth can I prove I've actually been here?'

It was a weak answer and he knew, brushing it aside.

The Island Coastal Path cuts inland and I am now on the Holy Island part of Anglesey. Suddenly I am caught in a heavy downpour, which persists. To make things worse I search in vain on the map for my B & B's location in Holyhead. I trudge on down the long main road, passing the huge aluminium works. I stop in a Mace shop and get a sausage roll some chocolate and a large beaker of tea out of a vending machine.

Cold, miserable and uncertain, I consume these sitting in a bus shelter. At a roundabout on the outskirts of Holyhead I enter the Prince of Wales pub. Here I get lucky. It is quiet, and Judy the barmaid listens to my problem and confirms that I am some way from my intended B & B. She tells me she lives close to it and, seeing me wet and fed up (some days this malaise kicks in early), gets another staff member to stand in for her and offers me a lift.

The reason for her kind assistance soon becomes apparent when she tells me about her loss of two children to cystic fibrosis. Like all metabolic diseases, this is a genetic condition, and she is a carrier of the defective gene. Fortunately her other two children are unaffected.

Stupidly I had allowed myself to be misled by the postal address, so I was four miles adrift in my direction for the day!

'Don't make that mistake again, Col. Chop-chop, get with it son,' advises know-all Flek .

Thanking Judy profusely, I enter Glan Towyn B & B, Rhoscolyn (01407 860380), where Dave and Carol Goth offer me most welcome and comfortable quarters.

DAY 126

5th May – Rhoscolyn to Penryhyn Camp, Llanwrog – 11 miles

Assessing my progress I realise that I should have planned another two days to cover Anglesey – it's four times the area of the Isle of Wight!

Early morning mist suggests a hot day. I zigzag around the coastal path in reverse of the route I should have taken yesterday. For some way I squelch along a marshy permissive path running parallel with the main road. Slopping out of it, I cross the Four Mile Bridge and enter the village of Valley – and there is the Mace shop I visited yesterday. I get some bananas and chocolate, of course, and trek up the long straight road to Llanynghenedl.

The Gwesty Pub on the main road doesn't open until 3pm. Why didn't I plan for this? Of course, it's another Bank Holiday! The bucket of fag ends at the front door offers some hint of the clientele. Opposite, though, is a shop operated by an enterprising Indian proprietor. It's full of provisions. I get a sandwich and Stella and defiantly consume them sitting in the Gwesty's garden as the traffic roars by.

Back at the Coastal Path the views are glorious. I cover the last three miles to the campsite, but find little benevolence here. It costs me £10 to book in and and the same to obtain an ablutions block key. Lesley Greene at CLIMB usually persuades site owners to waive their charges, but this time her wiles have not worked.

'There are three kinds of men,' said Will Rogers.'There are those who learn by reading. Then there are the few who learn by observation. The rest will have to pee on an electric fence for themselves.' Here at Llanfdwrog I opt to follow his observational prophesy.

Why? Well I'm an outsider again permanently in boots and belonging to another tribe. A scruffy tramp of a bloke who is quite out of place in the affluence I find all around me. I wander around to observe, gawping at each pitch in turn. The campers have stoically endured miles of traffic jams to lug all their little luxuries of life here.

I can't even get any gas here: I draw a blank in both site shops. They don't get many long distance hikers calling in!

I force a distraction and glance out to sea to watch a ferry pulling out of Holyhead on its way to Ireland. I expect the Aussie girl I met at the B & B last night is on it. I wave, but I don't expect she's seen me.

As consolation in my disenchantment I discover a bar on the site which dishes up splendid liver and bacon.

Today has been hot, and I must get a hat. Soon it will be time to be donning some summer kit.

I retreat to my modest little tent and arrange a concert. Mood music is required, so I settle for a mournful blues by B.B. King – appropriately entitled 'Help the Poor' – and then give up for the day.

DAY 127

*6th May – Twyn Campsite Lllanwrog to Llanbadrig Winery
at Cemaes – 12 miles*

It's going to be hot again. I can hardly be thought of as a revolutionary on the march but cannot resist buying a Che Guevara peak cap while a café lady makes me some tea and toast. I leave to walk up the rest of Anglesey's west coast.

Wonderful beaches. I note oystercatchers zooming,while the flora provides thrift, gorse, bladder campion and bluebells. The going gets tough as I approach the northwest corner of the island at Carmel Head. Discovering a pill box, I sit in the sun on its steps to eat my lunch. There are a couple of steep descents/ascents before I round the head. The terrain becomes so much easier, giving up to a gradual grass slope down to the cliff edge. Two structures come into view – an abandoned brick-works' chimney and beyond, in the far distance, my second nuclear power station at Wylfa.

Approaching Cemaes, I enter a farmyard where the young farmer is showing off his new monstrous tractor to his friends. We have a congenial chat and they get me some water.

In town I purchase an excellent gammon steak lunch and some provisions. I ring my next host, Tom Barlow, and warn of a late arrival. The walk out to Llanbadrig is a delight: the road twists and turns, continually dissecting hillocks.

'It's like walking through Teletubbies Land' observes Flek.

'Didn't know you were a fan?'

'Oh yes, I know all about them. Tinky Winky is purple, Dipsy is green, Laa-Laa is yellow and Po is red. I used to watch it with my sister.'

'How old were you at the time?

'Nineteen' he says sheepishly.

'You'are a late developer, then?'

'Yes, but then I went onto watch the Boobah show when I was twenty-three.'

He must be having me on.

At Llanbadrig Tom and his wife Lisa welcome me to their vineyard (01407 710416), and soon we are swigging a bottle of their vintage wine. He heard of my project through the local Lions Club. The winery produces for local outlets and visitors.

Mine hosts kindly offer me one of their static caravans for the night. The hot weather plus the ambience of the place made it feel like central France: I won't want to leave!

DAY 128

7th May – Llanbadrig Vineyard Cemes to St Davids Bay – 12 miles

With reluctance I have to leave Tom's vineyard and amble down the lanes through more hillocks, scouting for Teletubbies. I can hear Flek chuckling to himself.

I break onto the coastal path and enjoy a pleasant passage along the clifftops before moving inland from Bull Bay to Amlwch for a 'greasy spoon' breakfast. I search around at a local retail park and find a sports retailer, but they don't have what I want – a new rucksack for instance!

I now gain height via a series of lanes back to the coastal path and get to Dulas Bay, where I find a pub for lunch. The plan is that my next host, Andrew Owen, will drive from Benllech to pick me up.

Andrew and Karen Owen are a CLIMB family, their eldest son Chris having a metabolic generic condition. Like all parents of disabled children, they have had a long and difficult time but have now secured for him a place in a nearby community care establishment. He is now 21 years old and has settled happily in his new environment. Their other son Gareth is a local apprentice.

Andrew has an interesting occupation, travelling off the Island into Snowdonia each day to work at an underground pump storage system which hydraulically uses 'header lakes' to produce 1800MW of electricity.

This is then transmitted eight miles underground into the grid. The clever bit is that the current is used at night to pump the water back up to the lakes.

DAY 129

8th May – St David's Bay Camp Site to Red Wharf Bay – 12 miles

Due to Andrew and Karen's work commitments it has to be a 7 o'clock start. He runs me down to Lligwy Beach. On a lovely morning I enjoy a 'free' day relaxing. A two-hour walk following the cliffs passes patches of wood anemones and bluebells.

I find a nice little café at Traeth Bychan and tuck into tea and toasted sandwiches. At Benllech I mix with a scattering of early holiday makers enjoying a perfect day on the beach. I get a fish and chip lunch plus a dessert for only a fiver! What a bargain!

I visit another Spar shop for provisions (camping tonight) and finish off the last two miles to the campsite. Andrew arrives, delivering my rucksack on his journey home; we have a nice chat.

I pitch and cook up a dehydrated meal, which is palatable. I usually finish up with a bar of chocolate (nearly always Cadburys Fruit and Nut or occasionally a Snickers Bar) and now I settle down to a night of rain and strong winds.

I am going to change my rucksack as soon as I can and a boot replacement is becoming due.

There is too much noise from tent-flapping to enjoy any music.

DAY 130

9th May - St Davids, Whaft Bay to Treborth Hall Farm – Menai Bridge
– 12 miles

The schedule doesn't allow me to finish the coastal path via Perch Rock, the most easterly mainland of Anglesey: I needed another two days on the island. So I take the road to Pentraeth, purchase some goodies from a super bakery and turn left towards Beaumaris for a memorable last day on Anglesey. I stop and to talk to a Welsh-speaking farmer, who with his brothers runs his father's farm. After a chat about life on the island he recommends the Bull at Beaumaris for lunch.

I follow his advice and get a delicious bowl of chowder in the Bull. This is a nice place, with a quality dining room, but because of my appearance I fall victim once again to feeling out of place. This low esteem is enhanced by the presence of a party of well-heeled elderly ladies having their 'weekly luncheon'. They probably meet while their husbands are on the golf course. If they do notice a scruffy tramp, or hear him slurping his soup, they don't let on. They are, as you would expect, skilled in measured humour and good manners.

I phone Steve Hannigan, the executive director of CLIMB, and talk about things which need to be addressed. I will be staying with him soon, so early communication gives him a chance to consider the following:

- The blog photograph, which needs to be changed regularly
- Chances to meet metabolically disabled children
- A new rucksack cover to announce who I am
- A polo shirt with more project information on it

Administratively it is easier to offset some 'agreed' accommodation expenses using donations received on the road.

The last leg to the Menai Bridge is up a hot hill. I am forced into a pub loo to dry my shirt out under their gents' dryer. This is life on the road for you!

I am sorry to leave Anglesey, but so pleased to have included it in the Itinerary. Back across the Menai Bridge I find my intended campsite deserted. It is 6pm and I pitch the tent with a tired body. I waive all my usual procedures, i.e. cooked meal, showering, making notes and phone calls/blogs etc – I can't be bothered!

My adversary, Flek, spells out an admonishment.

'You are beginning to wane, my friend. Listen, my calculation tells me that you have only covered a third of the ground so far. The trouble is that you get distracted by people too often. Stick to the scenery a little more, there's plenty of it. Got it, chum?'

He's right, but when one is filthy, irritable and alone normal social protocols can so easily be abandoned. I must show more discipline.

Coping with a call of nature is for me a monumental effort during the night. Getting out of a sleeping bag is always a struggle, e.g. aching limbs and the possibility of cramp come to mind – not to mention those blasted zips that always seem to jam.

I have just enough strength to pull down the tent's outer zip and pass out.

Re-crossing the Menai Bridge.

DAY 131

10th May – Menai Bridge to Penmaenmawr (Noddfa Hostel) – 13 miles

A passer-by snaps me leaving the bridge. With no breakfast in my stomach, I hurry two miles into Bangor and come across a dream café for students. Never have I seen so many menu choices chalked up at such reasonable prices. I tend to settle for a 'cowboys breakfast' i.e. bacon and beans, but this time I hog it by adding two eggs, toast and a huge mug of tea.

Bangor looks delightful to explore, but I have to march on down the A5. I escape into a pretty country lane lined with spring flowers which runs for several miles in sight of the A55 (T) to Conway. I meet yet another farmer, who gives me a pound for a drink. Soon I am walking the Sustrans Route 5 flanking the main trunk road into Llanfairfechan. Two indifferent pubs drive me onto a café on the seafront for a snack. No sea view today, as it is misty.

The landscape transforms dramatically, dominated by the Llwyther Mountain (849m), which towers above the dual carriageway. The road splits, one lane disappearing into a tunnel. I follow the other lane, skirting the rock face. Here the railway just hugs the coast. A pedestrian bridge allows a walk into Penmaenmawr. I locate the Old Conway Road and find my next hosts (the contact unknown to me) at Noddfa.

The name means in Welsh 'haven or refuge; place of peace and welcome', and is run by the Sisters of the Sacred Heart of Mary – and a great welcome I get. Sisters Mary, Jo and Judith fuss around me. Later, after a meal, I get an opportunity to speak to the elderly guests/students. Thirty of them gather in the lounge to listen sympathetically to the plight of metabolic diseased kids and then raise £40.

Afterwards I look out of my guest room window and ponder how circumstances change overnight. This lovely old Victorian house set in its extensive grounds is worlds apart from my lonely tent setting of the previous night.

'Nos da' everyone!

The First Charity for All Rare Metabolic Diseases

As is often the case, the charity CLIMB (Children Living with inherited Metabolic Diseases) was inspired following the birth of a child, in this case Jennifer Greene. Her parents. Peter and Lesley, discovered in 1980 that their 14-month-old daughter had a 'rare, incurable, genetic metabolic disease' called Cystinosis, for which at that time, there was no treatment or cure. They set about finding as much information, and as many experts and contacts, as they could in order to establish a charity then known as the Research Trust for Metabolic Diseases in Children, or RTMDC.

Jenny's parents decided it should be a charity that encompassed all rare metabolic diseases, because this umbrella concept, the first of its kind in the world, would give more impact. Today CLIMB represents over 700 rare metabolic diseases, and there are similar umbrella groups in Europe, America, Canada and Australia.

As part of their research, and with the help of another patient organisation, the Greenes discovered an expert in Birmingham and enrolled Jenny in a clinical trial. She began her treatment with cysteamine, which later became phosphocysteamine and ultimately the current marketed 'orphan' drug Cystagon. Orphan drugs are those which have been developed with the support of special legislation for rare diseases with a small market, since companies are otherwise unable to see any return on their investment and therefore would not consider the development of these drugs worthwhile.

The experience of searching for information, researchers, contacts, experts and related patient groups became a major influence for the structure and primary objectives of the charity. Furthermore, the experience of discovering a clinical trial for an orphan drug with the support of another patient organisation led CLIMB to ensure that it continued to discover, track and support the research and development of many orphan treatments, including Lorenzo's Oil (page 49).

CLIMB (www.climb.org.uk) supports young people, adults, families and professionals with current and accurate information, gives grants for research and put those affected with a metabolic disease in touch with others in a similar situation for mutual support – just as happened in 1981. The difference is in the speed and method of contact because of the internet and world wide web, together with better awareness of rare and metabolic diseases, not least because of CLIMB'S efforts (since it was established in 2001) to embrace new technologies.

Having established RTMDCin 1981, Peter Greene acted as chair and vice-president, being awarded OBE for this work in 1994. Lesley Greene continued to work as a volunteer and then a CLIMB staff member for 28 years, retiring in April 2009. Steve Hannigan, the current executive director, took the charity forward as CLIMB following the registration and name change to 'Children Living with Inherited Metabolic Diseases', and has implemented many new services to improve the lot of families affected, especially in the area of information technology.

CLIMB was a founder member of EURODIS, an umbrella alliance for rare disease organisations throughout Europe. As CLIMB's representative, Lesley went on to become director and president of EURODIS. In July 2009 she was appointed as the EURODIS and CLIMB patient representative on the Committee for Orphan Medicinal Products (COMP) at the European Medicines Agency which assesses applications for companies developing drugs for all kinds of rare diseases throughout Europe.

CLIMB has remained closely involved in research into rare metabolic diseases and the monitoring of fair and equitable access of orphan drugs. Jennifer Greene, who benefitted from several orphan drugs during her lifetime, died aged 28 in March 2007. The need for safe and effective drugs for rare diseases remains urgent and acute, while the need for motivating individuals, companies and groups to continue raising funds in inventive, ambitious and attractive ways remains more critical than ever in these challenging times.

11th May – Noddfa Penmaenkmawr to Colwyn Bay – 6 miles

A short day which includes an exhausting haul through the Sychnant Pass. I bid fond farewell to the lovely Sisters and go into the Pass, which dissects two 800ft hills. The road's gradient ever increases as I toil to the top. Tiny figures appear on the ridge to my left. It is a hot day, and getting to the spur is a mighty relief.

Now, with plenty of time, I have an easy, relaxed and steady drop down the three miles through Mount Pleasant to Conwyn Bay to join my hosts Julian and Janet Beadle.

In May 2007, following my emotional experience of witnessing a teenager in the terminal stages of a metabolic condition, I joined the Battens Disease Family Association's sponsored walk. The event was their Peak District Challenge through the lovely Dovedale Valley.

At a refreshment gathering afterwards I found myself talking to Julian and Janet Beadle, who were supporting a friend whose child was

affected by Battens. My story and plan for a GB walk came out, and they immediately volunteered to host me.

Eventually two hundred and fifty family hosts surfaced to assist me, but Julian and Janet were the very first to do so.

They pick me up, and at their home we discuss my progress. I hear about their musically talented son who has just won a place to study in the USA.

I retire to bed relaxed: tomorrow is another of my fortnightly rest days.

Julian and Janet Beadle.

DAY 133

12th May – Rest day – Colwyn Bay

Janet takes me to Llandudno. I am very impressed with this famous Welsh seaside landmark and its Great Orme headland. Old fashioned it may be, with its Victorian shops and covered pedestrian ways, but I can see the attraction of visiting the place.

I find a Black's outdoor gear shop and buy a top, shorts and at last a 'Berghaus' replacement rucksack. I have never settled with the American 'Gregory' sack. I feel sure that this change is the right decision and I can now launch the new rucksack's debut, together with my change to summer kit.

We return to Conwy and on its promenade I consume a wholesome beef bap. Wandering around the town later, I must say that I'm very taken with the whole area. Picturesque, with its historical bridge, castle, wide promenade and boosted with a host of independent shops and cafés, it's deservedly a tourist hot spot.

Back at the Beadles house I sit in the sunny garden and write up my notes. Most importantly my hosts charge up my iPod and offer to send my winter kit home, kindly finding a box for this purpose. I have to make some tough decisions on what to discard, but many items will be heading home.

DAY 134

13th May – Colywyn Bay to Prestatyn – 16 miles

On a nice morning Janet drops me off on the Sustrans Route 5 which will lead me all the way along a promenade to Prestatyn. I say farewell to my good friends. There is no map work today.

Out to sea I observe a fifty tower wind farm and a huge floating crane erecting another one. I get to a beach café run by Simon and Marina and have just *got* to have a mug of tea. (I am getting addicted to the stuff.) Marina takes photo of me having my 'fix'.

A couple miles further on I catch up with an elderly lady. Her name is Macia Winterbottom and she is Polish. Being curious, I ask her how she came by her surname.

'I must start at the beginning,' she says in a sorrowing tone.

Addicted, Colwyn Bay.

At the beginning of World War 11 her family was living just inside the Polish border from Russia. The Russians took her father to fight in their army. Her mother and five daughters were transported to a camp in Siberia. They suffered untold hardships with little food and no medicine.

Her father was lost, but because he had served the Russians the family was released after two years. Long train journeys across Europe were necessary trying to find sanctuary in camp after camp until in 1949 mother and daughters turn up in London. Her mother passed away after several years, and Macia married a Winterbottom, now deceased. She still has a surviving sister.

It is a harrowing story from one of so many displaced persons in Europe after the conflict. What can one say? I give her a peck on the cheek, we shake hands and she leaves the path.

Approaching Rhyl, a tea urge has to be attended to and another beach cafe looms ahead just in time. With it I order my favourite, an eccles cake, which turns out to be the biggest I have ever tackled. The pastry is as large as a discus: I don't know whether to eat it or throw it!

I'm not impressed with Rhyl, the Blackpool of north Wales. How may I be stunned by any seaside resort? Most provide the same amusements and tat shops for the visitors.

In the town I find Millets to get a map, withdraw some money and have a good lunch of fish pie.

I have been following miles of glorious sandy beaches. Like this endless promenade, nearly all are deserted on such a beautiful sunny day. The railway line rejoins the prom, its trains interrupting the monotony of the route.

I have been to Prestatyn before: my good friend Brian Coote and I walked half of the Offa`s Dyke Path from Knighton to here many years ago. Memories of the trip flood back, such as walking across Telford's Pontcysyllte aqueduct. Now a world heritage site, it's up there with the Taj Mahal and the Great Wall of China. It took ten years to build and cost £47.000. What a bargain!

In Prestatyn I see an umbrella in a service station going for three quid. It is a bargain: I might need one.

'What do you think you are you doing?' shouts Flek. 'Walkers don't use umbrellas. It's cheating – not the right image to portray, old man.'

He is tieing himself up in knots with indignation.

'You don't wear glasses, do you Flek? If you did, you'd soon find out why an umbrella is a godsend. Anyway, I need another friend. I'm going to call it Sarah after the alcoholic nurse Sarah Gamp in Dickens' Martin Chuzzlewit. You had better get used to her. She may be more use to me than you.'

'Oh that's nice! I have to put up with a troublesome woman now, do I?'

He does go on. Acting wounded by my 'treachery' is a ploy; his tone will soon change when precipitation prevails.

Mrs Rowley's Nantmill campsite is a nice field once you get use to the busy road on one side and the railway on the other.

'Why is it that those in nearby tents always seem to be self-contained?' I mutter.

'Because they just are,' says Flek getting his own back after the earlier banter.

Despite the noise, I have a sound sleep on a warm night.

DAY 135

14th May – Prestatyn to Castle Wood Leisure, Halkyn (A55T) – 15 miles

The coastal path ceases and I gradually move across the hinterland for miles using a myriad of country lanes. For lunch I enter a village pub where Louise is the only member of staff on duty: it's the chef's day off so there's no food and the Stella has run out. It's quiet and we have a chat out on the elevated front lawn which has expansive views cross country. It's a frustrating day for her, and I commiserate. How could the landlord leave her in such a position, on a Sunday too?

Several miles on I make a very hungry call into the Misty Waters bar, devouring a large plate of chilli. Fortified, I press on and after a very long day arrive at Castle Wood leisure site. Peter Cook, the owner, invites me into his on-site bungalow and, over a drink, pledges £50 on behalf of the local masonic lodge.

Once again I pitch alone. I have only tea and half a packet of chocolate hobnobs tonight, so make the best of it. I select the Shostakovich 'Waltz' from his Jazz Suite and a Round the Horne to cheer me up, and I turn in early.

DAY 136

15th May – Castle Wood Halkyn (A55) to Neston – 15 miles

The dawn of another day arrives – only a couple of biscuits and coffee to march on. I brave the verge of a very busy road for half a mile to reach a pedestrian bridge which luckily gives me access to a lane going two miles north to Flint on the River Dee estuary.

In the main thoroughfare of this last town in Wales the facade of the Ritz Kaf doesn't proffer confidence but, as so often with seedy looking oases of nourishment, it's the food and service that counts. I am not to be disappointed. The one thing I notice in these working men's 'restaurants' is that it's cool to read the *Daily Mirror*.

I visit the train station. As you might expect, I am now fluent in Welsh. Fortunately for any none-linguistic passenger, notices are printed in both languages – handy for spotting any possible errors in interpretation!

The straight road has pavements all the way, a novelty. I pass through Connors Quay to Shotton; it seems endless. Finally I can turn north-east and cross the Queensferry Bridge.

I am out of Wales at last and on the Wirral. It's taken me sixty-one days to get round the principality. With only two flurries of snow and several wet half days, the weather had been exceptionally kind.

I note that the Merseyside twang cuts in before I get to Flint. I visit a service station for a drink and chocolate and walk up to an intersection where I manage to break through some foliage and pick up a path cross a field into a lane.

I meet Margaret and Elizabeth, who waste no time in claiming that their rambling club is the second largest in the country.

Flek can't help himself and blurts out, 'Somebody always has a record to flout, so today we should say jolly walking sticks to Mags and Liz!'

This is not the first burst of local pride I have encountered. Everywhere I go I hear constant claims of the highest, shortest, longest, heaviest, oldest, newest, greatest (herring catches in fishing ports), busiest, most concentrated or used – and so it goes on, endlessly. Ramblers Marge and Liz are only perpetuating regional pride. After all, it come natural to us Brits!

I have made a phone arrangement to meet Steve Hannigan, chief executive of CLIMB, at Neston railway station. He duly arrives. We drive onto his home at Heswell; I realise what a lengthy commute he has each day to his office at Crewe.

After a meal with Steve's wife Barbara and daughter Louise we discuss the points that I brought up earlier and seek solutions for them. I asked him to forward my appreciation to Lesley Greene, Chris and Pam back at the office in Crewe for working very hard to seek out hosts for me. Their diligence will have to intensify in the months to come.

DAY 137
16th May – Neston to New Brighton – 14 miles

We leave early as Steve needs to drop me back to Neston before going on to Crewe. The Dee Estuary panorama from Neston is of an enormous marsh area which was man-made to overcome silting problems.

It's fresh and overcast. I shake hands with Steve the exec. He wishes me good luck on behalf of the CLIMB staff. At the end of the front road I turn in to pick up the Wirral Way, utilised from an old railway line.

Although an almost straight five miles to West Kirby, the Way is full of interest. I see for the first time late spring arches of dog rose bending out of the hedgerows. This wild and supposedly 'mother' of the species is a survivor from medieval Europe. Unlike most roses, the flowers are not profuse, just single cream blooms with a blush of pink evenly spaced. I personally think its appearance represents the pinnacle of England's natural flora activity: the blooms announce summer. A strong view perhaps, but for me it is the outstanding hedgerow sight and represents so much.

At West Kirby an early lunch is taken of bacon and scrambled eggs served up by café staff member Giles, who states his desire to do the Lands End/John o' Groats Walk. He cheekily slips me a fruit slice as a treat. That's my boy!

The path ends at Royal Liverpool Golf Course, Hoylake. which is the second oldest (here we go again) links golf course in England. It was the scene of the English Open in 2006, won by Tiger Woods.

I notice an old boy leaning on a gate enjoying the view. His name is Bob Williams and he lives just down the road, his

In shorts at last: on the Wirral Way.

home overlooking the golf course. He takes me in for a cuppa. I meet his wife Ruth in their comfortable lounge overlooking the golf course, and notice that she has enough wool stocks to knit for England. Before reaching seventy he was a volunteer driver on Llangolan Railway in Wales, but has now reverted to being a station master. I tell him that my grandkids would love to meet a real life 'fat controller', which makes him laugh. They are a great couple, who will donate. It had been a charming interlude.

I cannot emphasise enough that the experiences of meeting people is the equal of the stunning environments I frequently find myself in.

I complete a seven-mile plod through Hoylake via the seaside Sustrans Route 56. I often find that the National Cycle Path numbering system seems to have no logic. Perhaps, when the plan is finally completed it will all make sense.

On the way I jump on a wall and get a member of the public to photograph my legs.

'Blimey, Col,' says Flek. 'What's that all about?'

Lesley Greene has found me some digs at New Brighton. The door is opened by an old retainer. If the borough has an annual 'Mr Completely Indifferent' contest then he would be the outright winner. For £35 quid I get an adequate but dingy room at the rear overlooking the windows of similar cubicles. The basin light and TV remote are not working. No biscuits or bath here, not even a soap tablet to take on my travels!

I pop out to explore New Brighton's attractions. Clearly there has been some investment in landscaping, and the old amusement park has been retained. Steve Hannigan a Liverpudlian (and Everton supporter) tells me that when he was a kid this was the cheap 'daytrip' across the Mersey Ferry for thousands.

Tomorrow is a big day for me. At present I'm a Pompey fan in exile, so during the evening I frantically coerce the TV to yield up its review of tomorrow's big game, but with limited success.

Getting to sleep is a struggle. I keep thinking of tomorrow's contest, last undertaken by Portsmouth in 1939 when I was three years old. Mind you, an even greater epic started on the 1st of September that year!

DAY 138

17th May – New Brighton to Blundellsands – 8 miles

I am now on the Sefton Coastal Path. It's going to be a momentous day but it begins with a disappointment. I am told the Mersey Head Ferry is out of service because of damage to the Pier. It's galling because of all the ferries this one has always captured my imagination. Gutted, I have to cancel Gerry and the Pacemakers! I had so looked forward to the trip across, but it is not going to be.

Steve Hannigan suggests I start the day with a train ride from New Brighton to James Street Station, Liverpool. This glitch in my route arrangements is fortuitous, as I need to make rapid progress to my next host.

Today is the FA Cup Final at Wembley, where Pompey take on Cardiff. I emerge from the James Street subway with my team shirt on, blazing away verbally from both barrels, deliberately flaunting my allegiance. I soon come under fire from snipers as disillusioned supporters of both Liverpool and Everton in the city centre shout abuse. Worse still, they purport to support Cardiff. Ducking and diving I make my way to Black's sports shop for a much needed lightweight raincoat, and then quickly make off past the Royal Liver Building and up the Crosby Road.

I think I am the only Pompey supporter around, but not quite. I am now trudging along a city highway towards Crosby, adjacent to a dock area now in decline and lined with commercial buildings and pubs boarded up. Halfway along I find an oasis in the form of a carpet warehouse. Standing outside having a fag is the proprietor. Seeing me, his face lights up with a welcoming smile and he beckons me over.

At first our conversation becomes incoherent as he chats away in his native tongue, i.e. Scouse. I simply cannot understand a bloody word he is saying. I persevere and glean that, for some reason he does not explain, he has placed good money, getting long odds, on a Pompey victory. How could he possibly have known that on the very morning of the match a genuine Pompey supporter with shirt would stroll past his premises? To him it is an amazing coincidence and must be a good omen. Beaming, he pats me on my back and we part with a vigorous handshake.

I press on to Blundellsands noticing signage pointing to its seafront with the words 'Another Place'. On the long beach here Anthony Gormley, probably Britain's most celebrated modern sculptor and the creator of The Angel of the North, has installed his Iron Men. These are a hundred life- size figures permanently displayed intermittently at various levels along a couple of miles of beach. They look out to sea 'Easter Island' like, and are covered and revealed by the tides. I get a local to take my photo posing next to one of them which has many rings on its fingers. Apparentlyvisitors dress them up for photo shoots! This is an expression of modern art that definitely works.

I ring my hosts, Sue and Peter Salmon. Their lodger Dani answers and pops down to the beach to fetch me. Sue has been informed of my TV viewing request for this afternoon. Her son Colin kindly prepares some lunch for me and I quickly settle down in the lounge to watch 'The Match' on TV.

It is history now. Portsmouth pulled off a 1 – 0 victory over Cardiff City. The elation of the architects of their victory – Harry Redknapp, the manager and Kanu scorer of the winning goal – manifests themselves on the screen. I also happen to know of a Scouser who will be jumping up and down on his carpets with glee a couple of miles down the Crosby road. I only wish my Dad could have been here.

The Salmon's are a CLIMB family, their two daughters, Ruth and Jane, have the metabolic condition Hyper-oxacuria. Now in their twenties, with medication and care they have so far come through.

Peter commutes into Liverpool each day from the train station at the bottom of their attractive garden and is a lecturer at the university. I spend a relaxing time in this comfortable, rambling house.

With Gormley's 'Iron Man', Blundellsands.

Day 139

18th May – Blundellsands to Southport – 15 miles (Map dump)

Sue and Colin walk back down to the Beach with me. The Iron Men stretch as far as one can see. I am told that when the beach is busy they 'dissolve' into the crowds; its Gormley's great trick.

I am walking the Sefton Coastal Footpath. Shortly it crosses sand dunes on decking for easy access. This has allowed the two ladies in front of me to push an invalid wheelchair. They ask me where I am off to. One of them tells me that the young girl (she is 20 years old) in the chair is her daughter Natalie and that she has cerebral palsy.

'Her twin sister gets married next month,' she says, and anticipating my reply goes on stoically, 'It's the lottery called life. They were born a few minutes apart – but we get on with it.'

Not for the first time I am choked by the gross unfairness of such a situation. The mood lightens as we talk about the Iron Men.

'I suppose you noticed that they're all equipped with their genitalia', she says with a smile. 'Rumour has it that when a party of old ladies came down the beach to observe, one of them could not resist and grasped the lucky iron man's protrusion, saying aloud to the multitude "I haven't done this for years"!'

We all have a belly laugh. I offer my best wishes for the wedding and they turn back.

The sandy path is hard going for a while but thankfully turns a little way inland to follow a railway line. A couple of twists and I find myself in a well-heeled area of Formby. I get back on the beach, which has firm sand. A couple of miles on I scramble over the dunes into the Ainsdale National Nature Reserve.

Virtually every week on TV naturalists like Chris Packham or Simon King visually transport us effortlessly into the countryside to observe the diverse wild life of this country. It all seems so easy, the programme schedule observations of the fauna always on cue. For the rest of us any similar viewing success is just a matter of chance. I say this because this reserve harbours red squirrels and the natterjack toad, but it's going to be very unlikely that I shall spot these creatures! I keep a sharp eye out but have to console myself that I have only ever had one red squirrel sighting, which happened several years ago on the Isle of Wight.

Breaking out of the reserve I have tea and cake in a holiday centre's pub, then take the two-mile straight into Southport. I glance out over its beach and yes, it's true – when the tide is out here the sea is over the horizon.

My next host, Lindsay Sutton, picks me up at the pier and takes me to her impressive house. I meet husband Derek, whose ancestor William was one of the founders of the town.

DAY 140
19th May – Rest day – Southport

I sleep until 8.30am. Lindsay has, unknown to me, arranged for the local newspaper to photograph me in bed with my boots hanging around my neck while she serves me tea. What a laugh!

I wander into Southport and am impressed with the shops and parks layout, the town has some class about it. I find the public library seeking information about its famous inhabitant (*see facing page*).

I buy a summer-weather jacket and trousers: that's another £220. Lindsay picks me up and we collect her children from school.

The local lollipop man in summer mufti is the smartest of his ilk I have ever seen.

'Well turned out, sir!'

226

The Eagle Comic

When I was growing up in the post war years comics offered us kids escapism from our parents, school and all the problems of puberty. There was a host of these publications, the most memorable being the *Beano, Dandy, Rover, Hotspur, Radio Fun* and the *Wizard* – which featured my all-time hero, Wilson the Wonder Athlete.

Then in 1951 a comic appeared which was well written and dazzlingly illustrated in full colour on gloss paper – it was the best ever.

Frank Hampson, who lived in Southport for thirty years, was the brilliant illustrator of the glossy *Eagle*, which set new standards both in comic art and science fiction with its main characters of Dan Dare ('pilot of the future'), Digby his faithfull crew member and their arch enemies the Mekons.

Its first edition sold nearly a million copies and it ran to **987** issues until its withdrawal in 1969, still selling half a million to the end.

In Southport I visited Hampson's house from which the illustrations emanated. In my opinion it should be made a shrine to the memory of the pleasure he gave us kids every week living in austerity following the Second World War.

DAY 141
20th May – Southport to Eccleston – 10 miles

Lodging with the Suttons has been a treat. The contact came through a friend of a friend of my daughter Suzanne.

I notice that the tide still hasn't come in; I stroll along the Prom around Crossens Marsh. Bob Mortimer rings to discuss my schedule and informs me that today I will be involved in a 'live' interview with Radio Lancashire. They ring warning me to stand by for a phone call at 3.15, and when it comes I'm forced to liberate myself from the noisy main road into the quieter yard of a market garden.

The interview goes well and now Lancastrians for miles around know that an eccentric from 'daarn sarth' is tramping around on their patch.

I arrange a rendezvous with Bob, who roars up on a 1000cc BMW motorbike. Attached to it is one of those classic streamlined, flamboyant, flashy post-war sidecars. He has been saving its annual spin for me.

There is a set procedure on how to get into the sidecar, so I receive roadside instruction, much to the puzzlement of passing drivers. It is now Wallace and Gromit time as the 'beast' takes off on a quick tour of central Lancashire. My head is right next to the engine and the noise is deafening. The suspension is noticeable by its absence. What a bone shaker!

'The wife won't come out on it anymore!' yells Bob as he as he leans over to shift weight when taking a roundabout.

'I'm not bloody surprised,' screams Flek as he is bounced about like a cork on a water spout, 'I would rather be blasted into space. Oh, my bum hurts – he could have brought some cushions.'

After what seems a lifetime we pull into Bob's forecourt drifting up to the back door. He takes off his massive gloves, smiles and extricates

me. A bag of bones (mine) tumbles out. I notice yet another classic bike, an Ariel 'Leader', up on its stand in the yard. Wife Margaret opens the back door; with a knowing smile she enquires dryly how our ride went and puts the kettle on.

During the evening we have a great chat, mostly about the vintage vehicle rallies over the years with Ray Pratt in Hampshire, who had arranged the Mortimers to be my hosts.

Aboard Bob Mortimer's 'beast'.

Day 142
21st May – Eccleston to Lytham St Annes Fire Station – 16 miles

In the car this time, Bob proudly takes me on a tour of the area. I can't get over how much he looks like another Bob (Dunn) I know back in West Sussex.

It's a long old walk on the main drag past the Lancashire Police HQ at Hutton and into Preston. I go over the Ribble and drop down into Riversway Docklands Marina development for tea and a 'wad' in the spanking new Boathouse café.

A combination of the A583 and A584 brings me to Wharton, home of BAC and the European fighter aircraft. I call into the Pickwick Pub and sit outside to have a chat with two ex-BAC employees. Suddenly our conversation is stifled by the deafening roar of a Typhoon taking off on test.

On the second long stretch into Lytham I am stopped by a man who had heard yesterday's broadcast.

'Fame at last, Col,' utters Flek on a sarcastic charge. 'Fancy – you've been talking to their only listener.'

Lytham St Anne's fire station.

What can I say about Lytham St Anne's fire station? Well rather a lot actually. I'm welcomed with open arms by the on-duty watch of Steve, Dan , Ray and Tony. It's my first overnight stay at a fire station on the Walk, and it's long overdue. First tea, then a shower, and they do my washing.

There follows a half hour massage administered by qualified masseur firefighter Tony Barlow. Without mercy he pummels me into submission – just the sort of pick-me-up I need. I join the crew for a lasagne meal and we watch the European Cup Final (Manchester United v Chelsea on an enormous screen. It is a quiet night for the men, without a 'shout'

Tony Barlow is a larger than life character. A veteran of the Falklands war, he is preparing to abseil down Blackpool Tower in front of the Queen on 27th July and will appear in a documentary 'Above and Beyond' the same day.

DAY 143
22nd May – Lytham St Anne's Fire Station to Bispham – 9 miles

The oncoming Green Watch and admin staff assemble outside to bid me farewell. I had been looked after in the best traditions of the fire service: many more such stop-overs will follow.

I spend this comparatively short day wandering up the coast road and prom to Blackpool. I was last here in 1941. Entering the Golden Mile I come across a bloke slumped up against a wall, replete with the *Sun*, a bottle of vodka and a pack of six.

'He looks happy and set up for the day. Can¿t we do the same?' pleads Flek.

'No we can't. We're clean and keen outdoor types who do not and will not stoop to such temptations. Anyway he's a Blackburn FC supporter – what can you expect? '

'Oh, hark at him!' is his reply.

I press the lounging fellow as to whether he is on a family day out, and he replies in a triumphant tone, 'No way! I've escaped from the missus. With any luck she'll jump off the Tower up the road.'

I somehow feel it would be futile to refer him to Relate.

The famous, enormous big dipper looms over me. At its base is a parade of retail shops, most of them fish & chip outlets.

'There seem to be more 'chippies' in Blackpool than soldiers in the Terracotta Army,' observes Flek, licking his lips.

Hearing screams from above, I can only hope that the two facilities had been used in the right order. I find what I am looking for, i.e. a 'Kiss Me Quick' hat vendor. I put one on and get the proprietor to take a snap.

Obligatory in Blackpool.

I pop into Primark and get a pair of shorts for seven quid which will last me for the whole trip. What a bargain!

I note that the council are already checking the one million light bulbs which make up the illuminations.

'You know, Col, I think the council must be in a bit of a quandary,' says Flek. 'By using these low energy bulbs the economic savings will be enormous. However, when they get a really important celebrity to switch them on, like Eddie the Eagle, the crowds are going to have to wait ten minutes for them to warm up. Sort of knocks the spontaneity on the head, don't it.'

I have to agree, although I expect technology will solve the problem.

My hosts at Bispham are Alan and Lesley Bennett, the contact being Doug Murgatroyd of the Chichester High School Old Boys – Lesley is his cousin. This is Doug second favour to me and there are more to come.

Alan picks me up on the seafront. He is a passionate biologist and has spent much time in Costa Rica studying the red-eyed frog. I still have the picture of it he gave me. His garden is full of plant and insect specimens.

Later that evening they take me out to a pub for a curry meal which is a nice change from my normal fare. Lesley is deputy head of a large primary school and is a delight to talk to on a variety of subjects.

DAY 144

23rd May – Bispham to Lancaster Fire Station – 17 miles

Alan Bennett drops me on the road to Cockerham. I am exposed today, walking into a stiff breeze. It's a long slog along the Lancashire Coastal Path with its twists and turns. At Glasson it turns into the Sustrans Route 6; with the River Lune on my left I get to Lancaster.

Lancaster Fire Station is quite a large complex surrounded by a busy road. Watch manager Alan Priestley welcomes me, and a female fire fighter, Suzanne, shows great interest in my project. It seems only yesterday that the controversial policy of recruiting females to do what had previously been deemed a male dominated career had been sanctioned, but Suzanne is now in her twelfth year of service. The Watch find me a room of my own. A standby fire fighter from Lytham St Anne's kindly goes out to get me a curry.

I have come via Lancaster for another reason. During the Second World War my mother, brother Alan and I came to live here. Tomorrow I shall attempt to walk down memory lane.

During the night the on-duty Watch attend a serious house fire and two people have to be rescued. I hear the crews turn out. Ah, the memories, the uncertainty and the excitement!

DAY 145

24th May – Lancaster Fire Station to Bolton le Sands – 9 miles

I have deliberately arranged a short day so that I can revisit my family's war time refuge. Leaving my rucksack, I ascend the steady hill to the Bowerham district to find York Road.

Memories come flooding back as I locate the very house. Here lived my Dad's Uncle Ern and Aunt Charlotte. At that time my Dad, a chief petty officer, was in the North Atlantic on *HMS Vanessa* hunting U-Boats. Having twice survived the enemy bombing of Portsmouth he thought we should move right out of the area.

My Mum and Aunt Charlotte didn't see eye to eye, but we stuck it out for a year. My indelible memory of Charlotte was that she was nosey and always sniffing. To our amusement, every time she emerged from the lavatory her skirt was still up and it took the whole walk down the long corridor before she had adjusted her wartime utility bloomers. Uncle Earn was a lovely gentleman who worked on the railway. One memorable day he took my brother and me down to the goods yard and lifted us up onto the footplate of a loco for a shunt up the line. I vividly remember the heat from the fire and the frantic shovelling of the fireman.

Olive, their daughter and Dad's cousin, was rather like her namesake in TV's On the Buses. A career spinster, she worked in the Co-op all her life. The family hardly knew the war was on up here.

One other memory stands out. There was no need for alarm clocks in most Lancashire towns. Factory workers still wore clogs, and the first one down the road in the early hours woke everyone up, including my Mum who, to make ends meet, had got herself a job sewing buttons on the jackets for aircrew in a mill by the River Lune.

I return to the fire station for my rucksack, and take the straight walk down the old railway line to Morecombe. Here at last, in the seafront indoor market, I get myself a pair of crocks for just £2.50. Not only cheap, they are as light as a feather to carry and very comfortable at the end of each day.

I pose for a photo by the impressive Eric Morcambe memorial on the seafront. It records the guest artists that appeared on the Eric and Ernie Shows: the list is amazing.

I have lunch at a café recommended by Suzanne the Lancaster firefighter. The food is excellent but, as so often, the service is poor.

It's an easy walk to the Holmes Farm Holiday Park and as it's a Bank Holiday it's pretty full. At last I get some tent folk for company on a site, and I have a surprise visitor, too. Relaxing in the tent, I hear my name called, and I crawl out to find that Suzanne and her children Sam and Amy have come out to see me. It's so thoughtful of them to visit an old man who, once again against all odds. will be pitching himself against the elements tonight. Hark! Can I hear Flek playing the violin?

When the family has left I notice a camper squatting outside his tent dipping three shortbreads into his mug of tea.

'That's a poor effort; he would never dunk for England,' says Flek. 'I once got seven garibaldis into a mug.'

'Perpetuating a working class habit, Flek. That's my boy.'

In Morcambe today I catch a newspaper headline which reminds everyone that it's the final of the Eurovision Song Contest this evening.

Flek sums it up: 'How lucky can we get, Colin?' he smirks. 'Being continuously on the move offers us little opportunity to scrutinise this annual bonanza of banality. What a shame! Terry Wogan's scathing commentary will be sadly missed, though.'

I couldn't have agreed with him more.

Who else?

DAY 146

25th May – Bolton le Sands to Arnside – 10 miles

I break camp and push north along the Lancs Coastal Path to Carnforth. The town gathered fame as the location of an iconic post war cinema romantic drama. I find myself standing on a platform of the famous railway junction where scenes from David Lean's production of Brief Encounter were shot – although the film crews were based here for only two weeks.

THE BUFFET ON THIS STATION WAS THE SETTING FOR THE 1946 FILM "BRIEF ENCOUNTER"

Apparently female lead Celia Johnson, an established West End actress, was paid ten times more than Trevor Howard, who was virtually unknown at the time.

Even in daylight I find the combination of the station's refreshment room (under track connecting subways with express trains roaring over) and the original platform dial clock (also a star of the film) give the place a distinct atmosphere. Part of a platform has been taken over to provide a permanent museum from which emanates the haunting Rachmaninov Piano Concerto theme used in the film. I sit down to watch the film for a while. God. it is so terribly, terribly middle upper class and correct with its depiction of stifled romantic emotions, but it will always be in my top ten films. National Movie statistics still rate it as the no.2 of all time.

I press on into Silverdale and find the home of my next host – Keith Stephenson, the Arnside fire station Watch manager. He and his wife, another Suzanne, ply me with tea and cake. She is into care home management, and with my own knowledge of this type of care we have an interesting debate. Keith's station gets a shout, and he disappears to deal with an unusual gas leak and jet flame issuing from a private house.

I find the Ye Olde Fighting Cocks pub facing the estuary, where the Stephensons have called in a favour to provide me with accommodation. Later I meet up and have drink with local councillor Dave Wallicy, who pledges a cheque to CLIMB from the local Authority.

I hear and read about a charity walk on tomorrow, which crosses the treacherous Morecambe Sands. In the meantime I savour the comfort so generously donated.

Managing to get a *Telegraph*, I glean the devastating news that the UK has failed to impress at the European Song Contest in Belgrade. Russia has stitched up the other Eastern European nations to win, and one of the two newcomers, San Marino (the other being Azerbaijan), has awarded us six points, so bringing the UK total up to a plucky 14.

'Oh, the humiliation of it all!' sneers Flek, 'Time for Sandy Shaw to make a come-back methinks – or Bucks Fizz – or anyone!'

DAY 147

26th May – Arnside to Grange-over-Sands – 6 miles

It looks as if another coincidence has brought me to here on the very day there is to be a charity walk (Schools in Nigeria) across Morcambe Bay's treacherous sands. This is an opportunity to good to miss. What's more, it is going to chop probably six miles off my intended journey. I walk down to the pier, and at first there is just a trickle of entrants, but the crowd soon swells to three hundred.

The gathering is being led across by an expert on the Sands, Queen's Guide Cedric Robinson MBE. It is sunny, without a cloud in the sky. At first the headland offers shelter from a very strong wind. Eric warns the crowd to stick with him. His route means wading through some deep channels, which prompts me to hang my boots around my neck and wear the crocks. With my rucksack I stand out and have to answer enquiries from puzzled entrants. Unlike them, I'm not going back to Arnside. It's worth pointing out that only a few months ago many Chinese cockle pickers were cut off by the tide and drowned just a few miles down the coast.

The party breaks cover into this vast area of sand. The wind is horrendous, and participants shout to each other trying to catch their breath. One-and-a-half miles out Eric stops to relate dour tales of people and tractors gobbled up by the quicksand. The wind howls on. A half-tracked vehicle arrives to transport the exhausted kids, and the adults move onto a long sand bar to finish on terra firma at Kent Banks railway station on the north side of the estuary.

We all pick up our certificates, and most slump down on the station's tiny platform; it is completely covered with bodies. After all this effort the train will drop them back to their transport at Arnside in just fifteen minutes. I stay to watch the two-coach train pull in and the ten-minute Tokyo subway-like scrum that follows to get everyone aboard. I am now alone. As it pulls out I exercise a Queen Mum-type parting wave and get some quite diverse hand gestures in return!

It has been a memorable morning adventure – now for a pleasant walk out of the wind into Grange-over-Sands for a café brunch. I meet Bernard Keeley, the fire station manager, who has thoughtfully brought in an air bed for me. This is a retained (part-time) station and doesn't have sleeping facilities. Fire stations are like home from home to me. I have a shower to get the salt off my body and use the station's hot drink facilities.

Guided crossing, Morecambe Bay.

I complete my blog to CLIMB and phone my next hosts, Jack and Liz Rice (my third Doug Murgatroyd contact), who advise me not take the map path across the Cartmel Sands. This unfortunately means going an awfully long way round.

'Oh well, we've had to do it all before,' Flek retorts.

I like the 'we'!

'After spending much of the day paddling, your legs must be honed for a route march. If it's good enough for race horses then it's good enough for you, mate.'

His voice fades away as I flop down onto the airbed.

DAY 148

27th May – Grange over Sands to Ulverston – 17 miles

I chalk up a short explanation of Walk GB 4 Climb on the station's training board, expressing my thanks for the hospitality, then lock up and post the keys into the letter box.

It's going to be a long detour today up to the River Leven into the Lake District National Park to Backbarrow. Turning west, I follow the banks of a beautiful fishing river for some way and then it is back to reality – I join the A590 heading for Ulverston.

As I approach the town the road is dominated by the 100ft-high Sir John Barrow monument standing on the top of the 400ft Hoad Hill. A local boy, he became the 2nd Secretary at the Admiralty. Barrow promoted explorations to find the North West Passage, including the ill-fated one led by Sir John Franklin. Barrow was a founder member of the Royal Geographical Society and an explorer. For those who love true adventure stories, Fergus Fleming's book *Barrow Boys* is a exhilarating read of the hardships he subjected ships' companies to in an effort to find a new route across the top of the world.

The Cumbria Coastal Way Path protects me from the main road for a mile. The pavement runs out with no verge. Without protection from the heavy traffic, except a map case held at arm's length for recognition, I proceed as quickly as possible. This dodgy passage into Ulverston brings me to Tesco's store on the outskirts of the town where my next host, Jack Rice (my fourth contact via Doug Murgatroyd), turns up.

Jack and his wife Liz were born in the area. After service in the Royal Navy and a position at the Sellafield nuclear power station, he returned and is now a local councillor. We talk about Ulverston's famous son Stan Laurel, who emigrated to America in his teens, becoming an understudy to Charlie Chaplin – and the rest is history. Jack tells me that at long last a statue of the great man has been sculpted, but the council can't agree where to erect it.

He has arranged for a Radio Cumbria outside broadcast car to call in the morning.

Liz draws my attention to an *Evening Mail* news item of a two-year-old boy, Taylor Smith from Barrow, who has developed the metabolic condition Niemann-Pick. I will become involved with this story during the next couple of days.

DAY 149
28th May – Ulverston to Barrow-In-Furness – 15 miles

Intermittent precipitation and murk are going to be the order of the morning. Radio Cumbria turns up outside the Rice residence and, in the rain, I explain my presence in Ulverston.

Jack drives me down to Priory Point and I begin the long shore walk. This turns out to be as pleasant as it can be in the gloom, but when the rocks get too big I come off at Baycliff for an indifferent pub lunch.

In the meantime the Taylor Smith story is still running. The interest level has been heightened following a local press headline "Two Year Old Boy Has Alzheimer's". This symptom is often associated with the Niemann Pick metabolic condition inherited by young Taylor.

Press interest is mounting, as my arrival has added a third dimension to this saga. Newspaper reporter Sam Walker rings and drives out to the pub for an interview. He explains that a touching story is unfolding concerning a young boy of eight, also called Taylor, who has – on hearing of Taylor Smith's plight – rallied local traders to donate a large toy for his namesake. He's done this because his own grandmother has the Alzheimer's condition. Clearly the use of this condition's title in the press has stirred up added interest. Also by sheer coincidence I have arrived in town promoting awareness and family support for metabolic conditions during my stop off in Barrow. I agree to meet young Taylor Smith and his mum at the newspaper offices tomorrow. By yet another coincidence, tomorrow is my rest day, so everything is set in motion.

I cut inland to Leece, bypassing the Walney Island headland, and pick up the main road into Barrow, walking through to stay at the large modern fire station, where I receive a warm welcome.

I have entered shipping weather forecast area Malin.

DAY 150
29th May – Rest day – Barrow

After breakfast with the duty crew I stroll into Barrow, mail my second log book home, get some provisions (I'm back in the tent tomorrow) and make for the local newspaper office.

Young Taylor Smith arrives with his mum, Stephanie. She has another child, is extremely shy and looks no more than a schoolgirl. With a reporter we go over Taylor's story again. She tells me that he is improving but this may well turn out to be wishful thinking. Outwardly he is very noisy and boisterous like any other little boy. I explain to her why I happen to be in Barrow and emphasise to her the support that CLIMB can provide if and when she needs it. I give her the details and stress that the first contact must come from her. Later I am heartened to hear from CLIMB that she has called them.

We have our picture taken on the pavement outside the offices. Taylor is still very restless.

'He's certainly a bit of a handful – it's a shame his future is going to be so uncertain,' ponders Flek. 'What a lottery these metabolic conditions are.'

I enjoy a walk through the town centre. Geographically Barrow suffers from being in a backwater, but its importance is announced by the huge BAC structure which dominates the town. This is where Britain's nuclear submarines are built. I'm impressed by a sculpture depicting the local engineering skills which stands at an intersection of the main shopping malls.

I return to the fire station and indulge in individual discussions with fire fighters on the day and night watches. There are no 'shouts' tonight.

Day 151
30th May – Barrow-in-Furness to The Green, Millom – 15 miles

I have another deep estuary to get round. I go up to the A 590 (T) and cross to the beach at Sowerby Lodge where I find a 2nd World War pillbox. Nothing unusual in that – there are thousands of them still standing – but this one has been dragged off its footings and is now lying on its side. These things must weigh fifty tons, what is the point?

I visit an owl farm, then, get on the cycle lane of the A595 to Askham in Furness where I wolf a super tuna mayo baguette in a café by the level crossing. I return to the beach. Ahead. at the top of the estuary. I can see Coniston Old Man in the distance. I find a superb pub/brewery under restoration at Foxfield. Pressing on right up to Duddon Bridge to get round the Sands estuary, I now strike back south, avoiding the main road by taking the very long and quiet Lady Hall Lane.

I find my next hosts, the Wilsons, at Dunningwell Farm. They are mum and dad, Alan and Lorraine, with family Chris, Elizabeth, Harry and Thomas. They are a CLIMB family having lost their son Jack to the metabolic condition Progeria Type C Debrsey Syndrome. This is the early aging condition and extremely rare.

Lorraine outlines the harrowing time they went though, receiving a nonchalant response from the medical practitioners until Jack's early death.

They are a lovely, happy family unit, and I have enjoyed being with them.

The strangely tipped-up Zee Pill Box. (See following page.)

Zee Pill Box

I feel sure that this is how the Goon Show would have dreamed up a likely battle scenario played out here long ago:

The wave of German Army Corps commanded by Haupmann Klaus von Iddlebugger hits the beach. He scours the sand dunes for targets with his Rommel Mk II bins and spots a pill box exclaiming, 'Gotten himmel, I don't believe my eyes Fritz, the 'Tommies' ze cunning swinehounds, haf turned zee pill box target zideways. Curses ve vill now haf to train our Howitzers at zee right angles!'

Anxious to add another Iron Cross to his CV, he barks the order to Oberleutnant Fritz Gross-Villi recently promoted under the Bundes-besoldungsordnung (it's a Wehrmacht German Army regulation:: honest, I am not making this up) who screams the obligatory, 'Schnell, schnell, blast zee Tommies right up the long way to Tipperary.'

The 'Wehrmacht' gunners now open fire with their Howitzers tilted on their sides, a typical sneaky Teutonic counter manoeuvre.

Meanwhile the tough Warmington-on-Sea fighting unit are lying in a big heap at the bottom of the pill box which had been formerly upright. Captain Mainwaring's grammar school rancour rains down on Sgt Wilson, still entrenched in his blasé public school demeanour, for allowing it to tip over. Fraser insists, 'We are doomed'; Jones is yelling 'Don't Panic' and 'Those Jerry's don't like it up em',;Godfrey wants to be excused! In battle Pike has lost his scarf and Walker calmly lights up a fag.

Remarkably Pike's wind-up HMV turntable with the new needle his mum told him to bring along for recreational breaks is still revolving and from it Vera Lynn is squawking 'There'll be Blue Birds over . . .' etc, causing massive interference on Jerry's Enigma machine!

'It's Not Only his Socks that Hums!'
– Rambling Syd Rumpole

I've been carrying about my person one of those new fangled iPod things! Amazingly spirited away in this tiny 'silver bar' are three hundred of my favourite musical tracks. However, I am somewhat short of a catchy jingle, an air that I can hum as I stroll along – something that announces or indeed enforces my growing stature as a lone and blissful minstrel meandering carefree along footpath and tarmac.

So as a new-age vagabond I couldn't do better then seek the advice and musical guidance from that doyen of 'folk verse' Rambling Syd Rumpole. I had caught up with him at the ancient Lummock and Bogle Twisters gathering in Chipping Sodbury.

While he rummaged in his gander bag, he had this to say: 'Well me deario, I know that prior to you frolicking about on the highways and byways malarkey you caught a dose of the nadgers, but undeterred you left them to ruminate and now your moolies swing unfettered in the dust and on tarmac thoroughfares as they should.'

'What an artist, this man is so perceptive,' says an enthralled Flek. 'He will go down, some say buried, as a national treasure.'

Syd is now in full artistic flight and urges, 'Now please feel free to sing this terse ditty to any refrain but not, with respect, the National Anthem. We don't want to scupper our chances in the New Year's Honours List, do we? Clear your throat, me deario, and sing up, perhaps to the jingle of 'The Lincolnshire Poacher'. Sing it with a soupcon of anguish: this should be a goer, so take it away!'

'When I was one and twenty boys. my bogle did I plight
And many lummocks I did scrote beneath the pale moon light.
Now haul away me potted Meg
There's limpets on me dando.

Now all you jolly sailor men who listen to my song,
Come plight ye bogles while ye may, they don't stay fresh for long
So hurry up me potted Meg
There's an octopus up me dando!

'Bravo, bravo Syd, I am captivated by your musical pedigree and artistic acumen. I venture that no one will ever have the faintest idea what it all means! All I can say is that I feel sure your lyrics will go down in the annals of folk song history for – well, at least a couple of weeks.'

'Isn't he bold', exclaims the irreplaceable Syd as he scurries off.

DAY 152

31st May – The Green Millom to Banks Spring Brewery, Kirsanton – 9 miles

I get a free day as Alan and Lorraine volunteer to take my rucksack onto my next hosts. A country lane leads me back to the Cumbria Coastal Way and I follow a long moat to pass through Millom. It is a short day, so I take advantage of sticking to the Path's true route and eventually swing around Hodbarrow Lake, a huge man-made barrage. I talk to a birder and we watch colonies of sandwich and artic terns settling down on the islands created within.

At the hamlet of Haverigg I get a fix of tea. Later, discretion is called for as I tip-toe past a naturalists' encampment.

'Now, why are you so coy, Colin? Flek asks. 'It's because you're in England, isn't it? Go on admit it. After all, if this was the South of France you would have walked between the skinny dippers without any qualms. I bet you would have even joined the ladies gymnastics team. What a load of prudes we English are!'

'Steady on Flek, where's your decorum? We're British, by the way'

'Not me, mate – I'm from the Smoke,' he brags.

Suitably admonished, I choose to 'admire' a group of power wind-mills. When objectors at planning appeals use noise levels to back up their claims I can understand why. These leviathans do make a nervy swishing noise. Heath Robinson would have put musical boxes in them – a brilliant solution.

I have to come off this lovely coastal path, turning inland to find my next hosts, Michael and Julie Wills, who live in a tastefully converted old brewery. Julie is the sister of Lorraine Wilson back at Dunningwell Farm. Michael is a full time fire fighter stationed in Whitehaven.

DAY 153

1st June – Kirkstanton to Ravenglass – 9 miles

Another reluctant departure as the Cumbria Coast Way beckons. Stones and soft sand impede my progress, so it will be the parallel A595 for the whole way today.

I go through the village of Silecroft and trudge another five miles to Bootle (Cumbria) in persistent rain. The village does not look promising for lunch. In the village store I get chocolate and bananas. A nice old gent comes in and we get talking. It is a useful encounter because he makes a donation and, perhaps more importantly, informs me of a first-rate restaurant called the Byrne, which is just up the road.

The Byrne is popular and soon fills up. I go for a roast followed by rhubarb crumble, which the owner donates.

'Never judge a place because it is raining,' says the prophet Flek.

After a pint in the Brown Cow at Waberthwaite I reach Muncaster Bridge, where the road turns sharp left and takes me right down to a great welcome at the Ravenglass campsite. The tent is pitched; I brew up. This tiny village has two railway stations, the main line and the Eskdale Mountain Railway.

In the Ratty Arms I talk to a man from Sevenoaks in Kent who has found peace at last travelling around in a camper van. Back at the tent I feel the temper of midges (all females of course) – they really are irritating little swine. Time to trowel on some lotion.

'If there is such a thing as natural order, then why can't the males sort the females out?' Flek chuckles.

It's another example of his simplistic solutions to life's problems.

A tummy scare calls for an uncomfortable walk in the night, but it has passed by morning.

I wake up to a drizzle. It's the old faithful packet porridge for breakfast, with coffee to follow. The midges hurry me along as go over the main line railway to join the Coastal Way and across some fields to the beautifully preserved stone arched Holme Bridge. I cross another field strewn with orchids and mauve/white clover to Drigg Church and then straight down the B5344 into Seascale. Eager for sustenance, I find a café.

This town generates nostalgia for me. Where have all the years gone? Fifty-seven years ago, together with my brother Alan, several adults and a small group of teenagers, led by a senior boy Rodney Bowen (I stayed with him at Shaldon on Day 22), I waited here at Seascale station for a train to continue our walking tour of the Lake District. The place was fog-bound and we were cold, hungry and homesick. It seemed to us like the end of the world. Today is sunny, and I find that the station has been demolished and replaced with two modern, but open, platforms.

Memories come flooding back.

My trail-worn appearance and the rucksack attract the interest of a woman waiting for a train, and on hearing my story she needs to confide that her family is riddled with arthritis. I sympathise, the train pulls in and she is gone.

'Another person affected by a life-changing illness – is it going to be depressing like this all the time, Col?'

'Flek, you can't sweep these things under the carpet, my friend. If we could I might not be standing here.'

From the station car park I pick up the Cumbria Coastal Path again. This is a delightful ramble, the way flanked by endless clumps of *Rosa rugosa*, Birdsfoot trefoil and the ground-hugging cream-coloured Burnett rose. The fragrance is overpowering.

I approach the Sellafield nuclear power station site, my third. It was formerly known as Windscale and before that Calder Hall. (Confused?) It's now a centre for nuclear waste reprocessing operations. In rail sidings the low-base wagons carrying huge flasks testify to this.

A small footbridge crosses a stream that dissects the site.

As we pass over Flek delivers another of his provocative theses: 'Got your Geiger counter with you Col? We could be showing a high reading. Look at your watch, man – the dials should be turning bright red,' he says glowing himself with mischief.

I proceed inland to Beckermet and visit a pub before tackling the last five miles to St Bees. It is hot and hard going for two reasons. Apart from the gradient, there are no escape verges, and a convoy carrying the station's afternoon shift is homeward bound.

St Bees is a delightful place. I have rung my next host, David Dunglinson, a cousin to Maurice Hall my colleague on the Old Cicestrians committee. David sees me in the main street. He has come a long way to pick me up from his home at Tallentire three miles outside Cockermouth.

I am to stay with David and his wife Jill for three nights and he will be with me me each day. My walking companions are few, unfortunately: that's the way things have worked out, so I am rejuvenated when somebody joins me.

DAY 155

3rd June – St Bees to Workington – 14 miles

Jill drops us off at St Bees. The village is best known for two reasons – first, the 400-hundred-year-old co-educational public school here and, secondly, because it also marks the start of Alfred Wainwrights 'Coast to Coast' walk which stretches 190 miles across the land from here to Robin Hood's Bay.

It is a 'free' day, and on a cool morning and into a fresh wind David and I take off around St Bees Head. Sure enough we meet a Dutch couple who are just about to begin the 'Coast to Coast'.

After Saltom Bay we turn up at Whitehaven. David and I sit on a harbour wall and tackle the corn beef sandwiches prepared by Jill. Then a saunter across to Tesco's for a cup of char. These stores are likened to perennial weeds: this one has sprouted within the harbour precinct!

The place is swarming with police security officers lifting manhole covers – the Queen is to pay a visit in a few days time. Whitehaven Harbour, once a major fishing port, has been transformed mainly to support the tourist industry.

Once every year a peculiar ceremony takes place here. An American Naval vessel arrives to celebrate the raid on the town from the sea by John Paul Jones, United States adventurer, in 1778. The circumstances and purpose of the raid are still hotly debated. What is not in doubt is that it was a bungled failure, not least because of the mutinous nature of the landing party. It must have been the noisiest drunken run ashore ever. However, the raid seems to woken the nation up to the dangers of invasion. The United States Navy takes the annual anniversary very seriously.

Refreshed, we punch on through Parton and Lowca, the latter being unbelievably deserted. At Harrington an old boy, Dave, is sweeping his front path. It turns out that he worked as a gardener for Lady Egremont at her nearby Egrement estate. I point out the family's connection with Petworth House, West Sussex, which he is familiar with.

Yet another connection surfaces, this time with my own family. He tells us that his late wife spent the last months of her life in Royal Free Hospital at Hampstead. This is where my brother Alan was an engineering technician for so many years.

We enter Workington, which I am somewhat embarrassed to say has until now only figured as a Football League result to me. As with so many northern industrial towns, decline has set in, with pit closures and the departure of the steel giant Corus, which had a railway line production plant here.

Although now retired, David is a gas engineer through and through. He likes to talk about pipes and distribution. I recall one of his gas leak scares. While investigating a serious gas escape close to a permanent way, his attention was drawn to a loco coming down the line. It was pulling loaded ammunition trucks! Here was his opportunity to get on the after-dinner talk circuit for years, the subject 'How I prevented Workington from being blown apart.'

Gill picks us up, and soon we are cruising through the countryside in her open-top VW limo back to their splendid home. It has been a wonderful day out, gas distribution pipes and all that!

DAY 156
4th June – Workington to Silloth – 17 miles

Today's stage will be a bit of a marathon. David has gallantly elected to join me again on a jaunt up to the Solway Firth, still following the Cumbria Coastal Way.

On the way he resurrects a local tale which could only have come out of Dad's Army. Apparently during the war a Home Guard exercise was set up whereby the nearby coastal town of Maryport's platoon would attack their neighbouring outfit down the coast at Flimby. Probably on a moonlit night, the Flimby defenders fanned themselves out in a defensive line on either side of the railway line to await the offensive. Maryport's lot came up with a cunning plan. They simply caught a train which clattered through Flimby's unwitting line and later ambushed them from behind. Simple! Mainwaring's face must have been a picture.

Our first major stop will be Maryport. After hunting for the OL4 Map we retreat to a nice tea shop. My phone goes and it's Lesley Greene from the CLIMB office to tell me that Lorenzo Odone (*page 49*) has died at the age of thirty.

Striding continually past patches of Burnet rose, we arrive at Allenby which has a store locally famous for its stock of provisions. On the spacious green we enjoy Gill's picnic lunch, supplementing it with chocolate, fruit and an ice cream.

It's a long but utterly enjoyable yomp onto Silloth. On arrival David and I are pretty exhausted. He has done extraordinary well. With little training, he has kept up with me for over thirty miles in two days.

Gill arrives, lowers the canopy on the VW and, with a sigh of relief from our legs, we motor the long trip back to Tallentire.

In the evening David takes me down to his beloved cricket club at practice. I ask him to take me to the youth hostel in Cockermouth which I last visited on my 1950s walking trip around the Lakes. I have vivid memories of the older boys on the trip, Rodney and Maurice, rousing us from our beds and 'encouraging' us to jump into the shallow River Cocker. A knock on the door summons the young woman in charge. We enter, and I try to recognise the interior without too much success. Well, it was over fifty years ago!

David has been my constant PR man, and not for the first time mentions to the lady warden the charitable reason for my trip. To my surprise she informs us that her husband has long suffered from the metabolic condition Mitochondrial Encephalomyopathy Lactic Acidsus and is now blind.

Her pronouncement stops me in my tracks. Once again I am abruptly reminded of the distressing randomness of neurodegenerative disorders.

Another reminder awaits me when at our final rendezvous, David's local pub the Bush, its landlady informs me that her friend has a metabolic condition.

'These are the reason you are here,' mutters Flek.

It has been another thought-provoking day.

DAY 157

5th June – Silloth to Oulton – 15 miles

Although it is overcast I am finding the days are really hot and energy sapping.

For the last time David delivers me the long way back to the trail. Silloth is a nicely laid out town with wide avenues. It's a port where Carr's Flower Mill is serviced by regular shipments.

I am so sorry to see David drive off – another of those wistful goodbyes.

This is to be a straight forward day, using quiet country lanes. I venture inland through a gently undulating terrain.

'Looking for a day of reflection, Col?' Flek enquires.

'Spose so', I sigh.

However the day is not going to be completely devoid of distraction. I find myself wandering along a narrow lane right out in the sticks. I cross a bridge and glance over, expecting to observe weed swaying mesmerisingly in a gurgling stream. What I see is a dumped settee, its cushions having drifted downstream to randomly arrange themselves like paisley patterned stepping stones. There is also a tyre with aquatic plants growing through. Across the lane in a hedge lies a burnt out car.

'Oh what exquisite rural scenery,' says Flek, 'It must have cost some to dump this right out here.' He pauses and then goes on, 'Ere, I've been thinking,'

'Steady as you go, Flek, is my immediate thought.

He goes on, 'It seems to me that these manifestations of consumer waste could be seen as splashes of modern art – you know, like graffiti. A trend like this could add new words and phrases to the dictionary, perhaps. I tell you what, some of these abandoned piles are better than that Turner Prize rubbish. What do you think?

Responding positively to him for a change, I have to think quickly and come up with a couple off the top of my head,

'How about, "a littery of error" or "rubbishesque"?

'You've got my gist. Not bad, Col, not bad at all.'

It's praise indeed.

Further down the lane is a rare sight – an immaculate and clean farm yard. In it a farmer is pressure washing a tractor off. I lean over the gate and enquire who might be the culprits of the abandoned waste up the lane.

'Bloody litter louts, they should have their hands cut off,' he replies uncompromisingly.

I nod as if in approval, but can't help wondering whether such an action might contravene many a health and safety directive.

Later I view another rarity in the form of a lone wooden bench on the verge of a long stretch of isolated road. There are wild flowers growing up through the slats. Who put it here and why? It seems strangely out of place.

'It's fate,' proffers Flek, 'which as you know is the ultimate agency predetermining the course of events. At this moment in time you badly want a rest and this amenity has popped up out of the blue.'

How on earth he drums up this street philosophy I will never know. Nevertheless I drop the rucksack to take advantage, park my bum and have forty winks.

A cow mooing in the distance disturbs my slumber. Times were when every rural village council provided public seating, usually at road junctions. I can remember as a kid seeing old folk gathering to rest on summer evenings for a natter; taking interest in all things passing. Not any longer: this is yet another rural service that has disappeared, like village stores, pubs, bus stops and red cast-iron phone boxes.

I move on and arrive early at Peak House in Oulton, the home of my next hosts, Nick and Rita Ditchburn. They are a CLIMB family, their granddaughter Jessica having Multiple Acyl CoA Dehydrongenase Deficiency (MCAD)

Nick arrives, and after a pot of tea I am being shown over their substantial house and developing garden.

DAY 158

6th June – Oulton to Carlisle – 16 miles

I wake still recovering from the Cumberland sausage that Rita served up last evening – the best yet.

My route today is initially again on the road, up a straight lane for the first five miles to Kirkbride. I then join the Cumbria Coastal Way to Bowness-on-Solway. The view from here is significant. because across the channel of the River Eden (a natural extension of the Solway Firth) is Ayrshire, Scotland. The Hope and Anchor at Port Carlisle provides a wholesome lunch; I chat to the interested locals.

The Coastal Way merges with the Hadrian's Walk Path. It is also the Sustrans Route 72, and all follow a dismantled railway line.

On rough grass land near to the foreshore close to Drumbugh (site of a Roman fort on Hadrian's Way), I deliberately lie down and sunbathe for the first time during the Walk.

In need of a fresh photo shot for my blog records. I ask a couple of birders, who duly oblige. They are on the way south after a week's stay on the Isle of Mull, where they have observed a white-tailed eagle, golden eagle and osprey.

The day is cut short as Nick is coming home early; it is convenient for him to pick me up at Monkhill some three miles this side of Carlisle. It is quite a way back to Oulton for a second night with the Ditchburns.

DAY 159

7th June – Carlisle to Longtown – 11 miles

Nick and Rita and their friend are going to join me for the first half of my free journey today. The plan is to motor into Carlisle, park up and then enter the city to cross the Eden Bridge.

We immediately drop down some steps into a superb cricket ground. The late Colin Cowdray said of it: 'In my long career this is one of the most delightful cricket grounds I have ever seen'.

At a spot nestled in a bend of the River Eden behind trees, it's hard to imagine that the bustle of the city is so near. We walk reverently around the boundary line.

We break out onto the banks of the River Eden, which is aptly named. Men are fishing, and the river has cut out deep banks into which sand martins are darting to and from their nests holes. After another four miles, using a lane to cut off an oxbow (Sustrans Route 7), we arrive at the Crown and Thistle in Rockcliffe.

After a refreshing drink my hosts decide to catch a bus back to the city. Ruth is obviously tired. I carry on another five miles, following Route 7 partly on an old railway line.

Nick comes a very long way to pick me up at Longton and once again I return to Oulton.

Tomorrow I shall be in Bonny Scotland.

DAY 160

8th June – Gretna to Powfoot Golf Club – 11 miles

Nick and Rita Ditchburn have seen to my welfare, been involved with considerable transportation requirements and joined me on a walk for half a day. What more can one expect from hosts? Marvellous support!

Nick drives me to Gretna. We stop by the SCOTLAND road sign and I get out. The town of Gretna/Gretna Green became famous because of the liberal matrimonial laws around here and was a Mecca for runaway marriages. More than five thousand ceremonies are still performed here each year.

Traditionally marriage vows were exchanged in two blacksmiths' shops, one of which is just yards inside the border where I am standing. However, it is the Greta Hall Hotel which has become the centre of these ceremonies. Nick points it out to me and then, sadly, we have to say goodbye.

I walk across the lawn and up the hotel steps on the permanently laid red carpet. The paraphernalia of wedding ceremonies is everywhere.

A hundred days to go round.

A number of coaches arrive, their passengers anxious to raid the large gift shop and café, so I push my way in to have a look. It's packed.

'You haven't planned to do anything silly here, have you?' asks Flek nervously.

'Certainly not. I bet things have not always gone smoothly here,' I say, hoping to assure him.

I can just imagine, though, the Beyond Our Ken's accident-prone roving reporter Cecil Snaith coming unstuck here. In his inevitable whispering tone he takes us through another of his dramas . . .

This is Cecil Snaith reporting . . .

'This is Cecil Snaith reporting from Gretna Green. I am here to scotch (*pauses for hollow laughter*) the ridiculous notion that it is only necessary to turn up here to make a match. To test this out I have won a bid on eBay for a delightful young lady to help me rubbish the idea. I am told that Sandra works in an engineering workshop at Ormskirk as a spindle polisher. She looks an awfully nice girl on the Net and will be arriving at any moment.'

In a hushed voice he goes on: 'Ah! I can see her car now. She is getting out. Good lord, I have been fooled! She is not the model-like creature shown on the download. She looks more like a shot-putter from Barnsley. Goodness, she has spotted me.'

'Hello big boy, I hear you wanna get hitched?, she drawls, and pouting triumphantly adds, 'Well, let's get on with it then.'

Cecil yells in a panic

'Oh dear she's got hold of my arm. What strength –she really *is* a shot putter.'

'This is your roving reporter Cecil Snaith returning you to the studio.'

His protests fade way as he is yanked screaming into the register office!

Many areas of the country have to rely on tourism for employment and financial return, and Scotland is no exception. However, I always find the scramble to procure souvenirs, mostly now made in China, as a little tasteless – especially as most of the visitors seem to be stocking up for Christmas already. I know we've all done it and it's harsh of me to criticise. but I wince at some of the tat they are snapping up.

The place is stocked up to the gunwales. Disappearing by the minute is the obligatory pile of shortbread. I have to smile, though, at a mechanical presentation of a Wee Jock with sporran. Every time someone tugs his badger hair attachment he broadcasts a saucy phrase. I hear one bloke say, presumably to his missus, 'Tug mine and see what you get!'

I arrive at Eastriggs and at the end of the village sit down in the Millennium Garden. A nearby café opens up for business. Well, not quite – John and his Italian wife run it as a 'hobby', mainly for the local youth. I quaff two cups of tea with them, a wonderful old-fashioned couple. Their daughter joins in a chat with me on the phone.

I am stuck with the B721 Sustrans route 7 for most of the day.

It is wonderful to be in Dumfries and Galloway with its gentle rolling hills and billowing cumulous. I keep plodding on up the main drag, which is very busy with lorries making for the ferry terminals of Stranraer and Cairnryan.

Waiting at the church.

At a bungalow I stop to admire a long front garden. A couple are putting out their bedding plants in straight rows, all *Begonia semperfloras*. This is an old-fashioned planting scheme and would raise eyebrows at the RHS. Jokingly I ask the husband whether he has been in the Army and he has to admit it. We all have a laugh when, from my position on the pavement, I am able to help him fall in his flowers like 'troops' into rank and file lines. For a 'consultancy fee' they gave me a fiver!

A few miles on, at Annan, I spot an old boy standing at his front door facing the main street. I nod and he walks down his path for a word. He is George, aged 95 years, who spent 35 years in the Royal Air Force. I ask him if he had ever been stationed at Rheindahlen, then in West Germany, and he said he had, in the mid-Fifties. It turns out we were both there at the same time. He was a warrant officer in charge of the motor pool and I a lowly corporal pushing a pen. Another co-incidence: there will be many more in the coming months.

At last I turn off the road and make down an entrance lane to the Powfoot Golf Hotel which overlooks the Solway Firth. Newly built, it is an impressive facility. I am given a nice welcome. My stay is being sponsored by Annan Rotary. A couple of its officials David Hodge (its president) and David Gillies (secretary) come out to see me, and we socialise over a drink. Their small branch's present charity priority is in supporting the victims of flooding in Burma. They have answered an appeal from David Garforth, Bognor Rotary made on my behalf.

I look out of my room's window and see scores of golfers happily hacking away on a lovely course laid out in a sublime spot on the Solway Firth. Tomorrow I'm bound to Rabbie Burns country around Dumfries.

My Evening Concert: Bill Evans' 'Waltz for Debbie' and Erroll Garner's 'Red Top/April in Paris'. An appropriate Wish track is called for. I settle for Andy Stewart's 'Donald, Where's Yur Troosers?'

DAY 161

9th June – Powfoot Golf Hotel to Dumfries – 12 miles

I'm missing a map for this stretch, so scour the hotel's copy for directions. After long stretches of main road I come to the A764 and turn left into the tiny village of Ruthwell. It is here, in a single-storey cottage, that in 1810 the Rev Henry Duncan launched the savings bank movement which spread to ninety-two countries. The building is now a museum, but it's closed for the day. His pioneering scheme was the first to encourage the poorest to save whatever they could in a bank account attracting interest.

Further up the road is the Brow Well, a roadside memorial to Robbie Burn's last-ditch attempt to find a cure for TB when close to death's door. His doctor advised him to come here, ten miles from Dumfries, and take the foul-tasting waters of the well. He was also prescribed wading into the Solway Firth up to his neck. The details of his fatal illness are a mystery but the doctor's perscription can't have helped!

Looking down to the muddy bottom of the Well, I see that it is the colour of iron ore. No wonder he passed on two weeks later.

Beneath the flag of St Andrew is an engraved tablet which outlines his last days. It also links him with the Rev Duncan's family at Ruthwell; he is buried at Dumfries Cathedral.

I soldier onto Bankhead, asking a couple for directions and water. They give me five pounds. On the way to Dumfries I visit the tea room

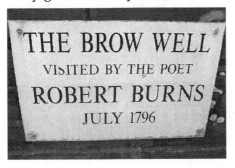

at Caerlaveroch Castle. It's unusual, a triangular shaped pile. There follows the long estuary road eight miles into Dumfries.

I'm picked up by my next host, Alan Franks, a cousin of Ken Franks, one of my Southern Trails walkers.

CLIMB
'Children Living with Inherited Metabolic Diseases'

CLIMB is a charitable organisation offering free, confidential and impartial support to both families and professionals worldwide. The charity holds information on over 700 different inherited metabolic disorders, many of them very rare, all of which cover a wide spectrum of symptoms and individual needs.

However, the problem that all families face is the sense of isolation that comes with being affected with a rare metabolic disease. Many GPs and medical professionals may not encounter the vast majority of them in their entire career, so specialist help, support and information may be difficult for the families to access. CLIMB promotes awareness of metabolic diseases among medical professionals, therefore enhancing the services that are currently available.

CLIMB, based in Crewe, Cheshire, is the only organisation to support all of the inherited metabolic diseases. The information the charity provides is backed and approved by medical specialists and is recognised as a unique specialist service. It provides long-term support from diagnosis to care and bereavement counselling for all those affected. It is important that all information, support and advice is tailored to individual needs. It also supports all the young people affected from paediatric to adult care services.

A freephone helpline is available as often as needed for affected families. This vital service links contact networks to put families in touch with each other, gives disease specific information, and advises on disability living allowance (DLA) and holiday insurance.

CLIMB is very active in the metabolic disease world and keeps in touch with a large range of specialists and pharmaceutical companies. It is also included in the National Screening Committee and has links with many national bodies and European networks. CLIMB has funded hundreds of research programmes into metabolic conditions and commissioned a Black and Ethnic Minority Information Service.

Freephone – 0800 652 3181
Make a Donation – Just Giving
www.climb.org.uk

I have had a fine stay with Alan and Margaret Franks. He takes me into the city to visit a super wet fish shop: cool!

After a meal last evening, we talked about his cousin Ken Franks down in West Sussex and also about the local Scottish Football League team, which he tells me is Queen of the South. I am pleasantly surprised – so *this* is where it is! He proudly relates that last month the team only just lost to Rangers 3-2 in the final of the Scottish Cup. Their ground only holds six-and-a-half-thousand spectators.

Alan runs me out to the city's outskirts. I take the Military Road running parallel to the A75 for ten miles. The long and twisting route is a delightful passage through the rolling hills of Galloway on a traffic-free road.

I retreat half a mile to retrieve a dropped hat. A lady bus driver offers me a lift to make up for my lost time. I arrive at the awkwardly named village of Haugh of Orr!

'Clear your throat, Col, cough and you've cracked itm' suggests Flek.

The store is open for some chocolate. I find a bench on which to enjoy it.

David Duncan, my next host, says he will walk out from Castle Douglas to meet me. During another long haul I see his smiling face and his labrador Polly's wagging tail coming towards me. It is a short drive to his charming cottage at Twynholm. His wife greets me with a splendid tray of tea and cake. Interestingly the place was once owned by Sir Frank Whittle's chief engineer.

In the evening David, a doctor and Rotarian, takes me over to Kirkcupbright to a branch meeting – a high-powered get together attended by thirty or so local professionals. Rotary offers support with ideas and financial assistance in many fields of life. After dinner several speakers present long reports on projects delegated to them. As the business of evening finally ends the members are rallied yet again by the chairman of a neighbouring branch who delivers what I can only describe as 'evangelistical' entreaty to do even better. Phew! It has been a long evening.

'It almost seems as if they are trying to organise the whole world,' says a fascinated Flek.

The gathering arranges a whip round for CLIMB which raises £130.

I fall asleep both physically and mentally battered.

Day 163
11th June – Castle Douglas to Gate House of Fleet – 16 miles

David runs me back to Castle Douglas. As I am walking back past Twynholm, I agree to meet him at the Pit Stop Museum for lunch. There's no pavement down the busy A75, so I seek some sort of safety by walking on the roadside no-parking verge. My weatherproof jacket comes on (it keeps a chilly wind at bay) and I get to Twynholm, make a few phone calls and meet David at the museum for lunch in its café .

We view the exhibits. Formula 1 driver David Coulthard was brought up in the village and has an exhibition hall here housing several of his cars and all his trophies and awards. His whole career is all here: his racing go-karts, three Formula 1 cars, all of his trophies and his career statistics (thirteen grand prix wins, upteen podiums and most FI points gained by a British driver).

We sit in and admire the village Millennium Garden and then I say farewell to David. It's another nine miles to the Auchenlarie holiday park, and I'm stumbling along the uneven grass verge now to keep clear of a constant stream of lorries making for the ports of Stranraer and Cairnryan on their way to Ireland.

I have to keep my wits about me, and the roadside Tea Pot Café is a welcome sight. I eventually arrive at a large campsite, but can't get the tent pegs to go in for some reason –

'Perhaps you should move off this caravan's hard standing for starters,' sniggers Flek.

Fool, I am standing on one of those current 'green' ideas – concrete under grass. We share the joke for a change!

I cook up a meal, pondering over the high mileage tomorrow. CLIMB confirms that I shall be occupying a static caravan: great!

'Hoo-jolly-ray!' shouts Flek. 'No nasty tent with condensation on the inside and midges on the outside.'

Some music is called for. Flek asks me what I have selected and I mention Walton's 'Spitfire Fugue.'

'My uncle was in the RAF. He said it was cushy. Come to think of it, you must be old enough to have done National Service?'

'Yes Flek, it's true – I joined millions called up to serve my country. I did my duty mostly loafing about in Navy Army & Air Force Institute's (NAFFI) cafés in Rheindahlen in what was then West Germany. Unfortunately we had to endure an irksome procedure once a week. Let me bore you.

'You see Flek, life for the RAF "erk" (lowest airman rank) was infinitely better than your Army 'squaddy' (an even lower soldier rank). Soldiers marched everywhere all the time. Life in the RAF life was taken at a more relaxed pace. This blasé attitude to discipline was never more evidently displayed than in our unit's weekly parade.

'At the request of the commanding officer, shored up by the enthusiastic disciplinary station warrant officer (SWOMAN), we boys in blue were summoned to the parade ground. Hundreds of us took part in a march-past, the CO took the salute and at the conclusion everyone was ordered to a "halt". Being a bit rusty, the airmen usually made a hash of it. Instead of one sharp crack of a thousand boots hitting the concrete simultaneously it sounded, as the SWOMAN succinctly put it, like the noise of "skeletons, having an orgy on a corrugated roof".

'After a chat with the adjutant the CO suggested, Sgt Wilson-like in Dad's Army,"that the chaps should have another go round". The result was exactly the same. By now fed up, the CO congratulated us and we were dismissed.

'I sauntered back to my billet usually with my friend Bernard Taylor, like me posted in from Credenhill, Hereford. We had to flop down on our pits (beds) to get over it.

'Pragmatically the C.O. relied on the Hunter jet fighters at the nearby RAF Bruggen base to stave off any Eastern Pact invasion, not on airmen having the ability to march.

'There Flek – you can go to sleep now.'

But he has already dropped off.

So the music tonight is: Abba's 'Thank You ForThe Music', Art Blakey's 'Jazz Messengers Moanin', Bud Powell's 'Un Poco Loco' and William Walton's 'Spitfire Prelude & Fugue'. My wish track is Gilbert & Sullivans Three Little Maids from the 'Mikado', which I think is typical of the tempestuous duo's light opera numbers.

DAY 164

12th June – Gatehouse of Fleet to Drumroamin Farm Camp Site – 16 miles

I break camp for an early start yet again, because there's another long way to go. I have another estuary to get round today – Wigtown Bay.

The lorries stream to Stranraer and Cairnryan on the A75 and I persist in my efforts to avoid them. It's not easy on a rough, uneven grass verge. I get to recognise the many different carriers, but oddly Eddie Stobbart never shows up. Two miles on, a friendly couple operating a lay-by outlet donate a scrumptious bacon sandwich and tea.

I am heading north now the six miles to Newton Stewart. Approaching the town centre I meet James Risedale, a gallant old boy who is partially sighted and using a zimmer. We have a great chat and I take a photo.

'Keep your legs going, that's what I keep telling myself,' he says. What an inspiration!

At an outdoor shop the owner rewards my walking effort with a map case at cost, with a £5 donation, a box of insect repellent wipes and a new mobile case thrown in. Such generosity!

Now I can turn south and head for Wigtown, designated Scotland's premier 'book town', with over twenty dealers/shops in residence. I catch a café just as it is to close. The proprietor Sally offers me tea and tells the harrowing story of her family's battle with genetic blood groups, causing the deaths of five of her siblings: only she and a sister survived.

I stride on somewhat in shock but recover and remark to Flek, 'Pretentious as it might sound, Flek, I know that I am doing the right thing'.

I take his silence as an endorsement.

I forge on the last few miles to Kirkinner. My host, Lesley Shell, picks me up and we motor to Drumroamin, a lovely static van park near the Baldoon Sands in Wigtown Bay. She, husband Ralph and family have relocated to operate this lovely site: they live in a superb bungalow. I get a static van to myself, am invited to the family evening meal and Lesley does my washing. As we sit on their patio Ralph, a nice man, draws my attention to parent Ospreys delivering food from Wigtown Bay to three newly hatched chicks in a tree just half a mile away.

Contented, I enjoy a very comfortable night in a static van all to myself.

DAY 165

13th June – Drumroamin Farm to Kings Green Caravan Park,
Port William – 13 miles

Lesley provides a substantial breakfast and the hospitality just goes on as she offers to run my rucksack onto Port William. First, though, she elects to guide me through the maze of paths in the extensive Forestry Commission woodland en route.

We are well into the forest and she suddenly stops and produces £100 as a donation to CLIMB. I have been stunned by the Shell's warmth, kindness and generosity, and now this. I ask her to forward via the 'Just Giving' website. (*See page 260.*) We hit the road to Port William, and it's good bye to a wonderful family.

After an eight-mile hike I reach the coast. The campsite is next to the beach, and in a strong wind there follows a pathetic struggle to get the tent up. I just hope that no-one is watching.

I walk into the town square and enter the Monreith Arms Hotel. In a large bar are three men. The campsite proprietor, Diana Higgins, has forwarded my publicity 'blurb' from CLIMB to the hotel, and landlord John Kay has pinned it on the wall. One of the men removes it and says in a Gaelic timbre, 'Is this yuu pal? Wherrd yu cum fae.' I tell him Chichester, but the name fails to ring his bell.

His mate overhearing the conversation pipes up, 'Didnae see you trampin on the big road a couple of days back? Ah'm tellin ye, ah know this road like a backside furrit. Yu sholdnae be on it, pal, yu have to watch where ye're gaun awright. Yurr rucksack was nae on right eether!'

I smile. Many days I have been so tired I haven't cared whether my rucksack has been upside down at the end of the day. However, as 'Jimmy' has recognised me on the Stranraer Road I acknowledge that I'd been shabbily dressed on a main highway and feel I have to accept his pint to atone for my slumminess.

In the meantime a crowd of noisy Jocks are gathering at the other end of the bar, laughing and joking. I just wish I could understand their heavy patter. What *are* they talking about? Their conversation sounds something like the following:

'Ah tell ye tae go afore but naw ye never bothered your shirt.'
'Ya cheeky peasant your're cruising for bruising.'

'Three heavies an a Mick Jagger.'

'All Ah say wis "Eindy gaumny len us a pearl diver?" and they aw like snaw alla dyke.'

'You're gauny end up in your soap bubble, pal.'

I am not going to interpret these communication. I couldn't possibly understand them, so why should you! It was like listening to an episode of Rab C. Nesbitt.

Landlord John Kay comes in with a bar menu.

'Am urny goin to give ye 'ay meal on the hoose.'

I select liver and bacon and thank him.

'Nae bother,' he replies. 'Good choice Ah'm havin the same myself.'

All the time my 'blurb 'is being passed around the gathered Clan, and in no time a pile of fourteen fivers arrives like an expensive serviette next to my plate. All this is happening while I am trying to concentrate on a giant screen showing the Dutch thrashing the French in the European Cup.

What an evening! I stumble down to the site and, despite the wind hammering on the tent all night, I fall fast asleep.

Glasgow patter

The Glaswegian Patter is a dialect spoken in and around Scotland's big city and its development has been influenced by Highland talk and perhaps more extensively by Hiberno (Irish) speech. Its full flavour can be captured in TV comedies such as Rab C. Nesbitt, Chewin the Fat and Still Game. Glaswegian Stanley Baxter has parodied the patter on TV spoofs many times and there has also been the Russ Abbot character C.U. Jimmy.

I was exposed the Glasga Patter in Port William (locals) and Durness (visitors) both of which are remote from Glasgow. I also endured a mouthful of Central Scots dialect east of Inverness.

It's not just the pattern of words but the fact that it's spoken with a fast guttural intonation that renders it almost impossible to interpret. Try – 'whaursyercludgieweefulla' (where is your toilet, small person?) You might need just this patter when you're next in Glasga!

14th June – Port William to Glenluce Caravan Park – 13 miles

I cook up porridge laced with honey and tea, then call into the Monreith Arms once again for something substantial. John Kay the Landlord is still around, and he directs a staff member to give this man what he wants. I go for coffee and toast.

I set out along seven miles of a lovely coastline. Galloway is so scenic; it's called the forgotten coast. The cars tear along this road, one every five minutes. The Isle of Man is still in view. I get some lunch at Auchenmaig where the road turns inland. The roadside is a continuous trail of purple wild foxgloves. This flora persists all the way up the west coast of Scotland.

I take a parallel lane to the main road which lasts for five miles over the hills and walk into a one-horse town called Glenluce.

I stagger up its main drag like Clint looking for trouble. The landlord of the Kings Arms is standing in the doorway having a fag and utters, 'Where yu awf pal'

He verbally drags me in for a pint. It is a shabby old-fashioned pub which seems to be run as hobby. Anyone is at liberty to serve behind the bar and a group of 'seedy' locals are hard at dominoes, swapping noisy expletives. All seem oblivious to any customer who cares to wander in.

The van park is a model run by a Mrs Rankin, a lovely lady. I find it to be an oasis of calm away from the town. The only other campers are Den and Sally (with children), who donate £10 to CLIMB. Den asks me if I will be visiting Glen Coe on my Walk, which I confirm. He is a MacDonald and knows every infinite detail about the infamous massacre. I am quite taken aback when he ends the conversation with, 'I never have a tin of Cambell's soup in the house' – and he means it.

'How long do people carry on with their feuds?' puzzles Flek. 'Our friend has been wrapped up in the history for so long he obviously can't let go. It's a shame – he seems a nice bloke.

I find myself rendered speechless by Den's statement.

The town isn't open for food and I make the best with what I have got. During the evening I wander back to the Kings Arms and the domino game is still going on. Outside in the street the local laddies are exchanging insults with the local lassies in the middle of the road at a couple of hundred paces. It is a sort of 'stand-off'. If they can only wait for a couple of years they'll be able to do it in the comfort of their home on Twitter.

I pitch, batten down and close up the tent's zips: the midges are about.

My concert artists are Jelly Roll Morton, Arty Shaw, B.B King, Saint-Saens and Bill Evans. On my wish list is Gustav Holst's St Paul's Suite. Round the Horne provides a giggle before I turn in.

'Got any heavy metal? I faintly hear Flek say as I nod off.

DAY 167
15th June – Glenluce Caravan Park to Stranraer – 10 miles

I am starving when I spot a bill board on the A75 which announces that the Wigtownshire Golf Club do snacks. I wander in and get breakfast in the comfort of the club house.

As it's Sunday the traffic is light, and after a long and uneventful five-mile straight hike, I arrive early at my B & B opposite Morrisons in Stranraer. Jimmy and Wilma McMillan of Ivy House welcome me to a nice room on the top floor.

'A steep climb carrying your rucksack up a narrow dog-legged staircase will do your legs the world of good,' advises Flek, tongue in cheek.

I wander down through the town and in a large touristy restaurant on the sea front I order up a steak dinner, because I really fancy it.

In a car park by the Ferry Dock (to Belfast) I observe, not for the first time, how the youth of today expend surplus testosterone. In the fifties we hung around on street corners or (in my case, as I lived by the sea), the pier. Then I bought a Lambretta – as did my brother, though he soon got himself a 500cc Velocette motor bike.

Now the trend is for souped-up Astras with noisy exhausts. Any town, if it's not careful, becomes an unofficial racing circuit. So here are a dozen or so boisterous lads whose parents have coughed up for the insurance and now are just about to use some townsfolk homesteads as one continuous chicane.

Jimmy runs me out to one of the town's roadside signs and I have a photo taken. Why? Well, using the pin-point accuracy I was famed for in my Southern Trails days, I calculate that I've travelled 2,000 miles – about half way. I'm prepared to concede that the exact spot could be a hundred miles in either direction, but I'm sticking to my hunch!

It's odd that this bench mark still leaves me nowhere near the top of Great Britain. The large peninsulas of the West Country and Wales have so far gobbled up the miles, that's why.

In the European Nations football tournament I watch Turkey's shock late win over the Czechs, then listen to the sound of missed gear changes from the Astras as I get into bed.

Half way?

Jimmy and Wilma have waived their fee, and with a warm handshake I'm off. I still haven't shaken the lorries off though, as many motor on around Ryan Bay to the other ferry terminal (to Larne) at Cairnryan. Loch Ryan is a most impressive inlet.

The A77 eventually swings inland. A massive road-building programme is going on; they are adding another lane to upgrade the road. I chat to the road crews and one them takes off his helmet and takes out a midge net.

'You might need this,' he says. 'The company issue them all the time.'

I slog on up the never ending incline of Glen App, a beautiful wooded passage through the hills. In an opening a buzzard lands on a tree close by and then swoops off across a field; some dozy rabbit is about to cop it.

On the spur at the top I am spotted by a 'Jimmy' from a further road gang who jumps over the crash barrier to take my photo. My fame must be spreading. I have experienced two other instances of this behaviour in the last few months. I am beginning to realise what the Beatles had to go through!

'You've been recognised as many time as that, have you?' queries Flek, adding sarcastically, 'Hardly a paparazzi pandemic, is it? You need some media hype mate. There's this bloke, I think his name is Max Clifford, who could fix you up.'

Sometimes his ideas make sense, but I have to tell him that this time he is definitely flying a kite.

The two- mile flat terrain along the top is a relief, and it's now a long twisting drop down to Ballantrae on the coast. The town became best known as the fictional setting for Robert Louis Stevenson's novel *The Master of Ballantrae*, a story of a family torn apart by the Jacobite uprising.

My next host, Gordon Baird (Rotary), motors down from Girvan to pick me up. We return along this dramatic coast road to his home and wife Ann. Gordon is a retired ship's master and has many interesting tales to tell. Ann goes out to the last night of her art class while Gordon and I settle down to the European Cup.

I have a great kip in this lovely, comfortable house.

DAY 169

17th June - Ballantrae to Girvan 13 miles

Gordon runs me back to Ballantrae. This will be a free day, a jaunt along the quiet coast road. The sea view is dominated by the giant Ailsa Craig rock. Ten miles out it rises to over 1110ft. Once inhabited, it is now a bird colony. Its geology is made up of micros granite; until recently 70 per cent of curling stones were made of it.

Gordon will tell me later of a family who once lived in this coast's Sawney Beans cave and whose menu included many a traveller!

I arrive at the impressive Russian memorial to the cruiser *Varyag* at Lendalfoot. This vessel is iconic in their naval history and was sunk off the coast here in 1920 whilst being towed for scrap. The memorial was erected in 2007 and attended by high ranking officials from Russia. Very gothic, it is a typical sculpture from that country.

At the Woodland Garden Centre I get lunch. Staff looking at the CLIMB logo on my shirt quiz me about it.

As I leave, it starts to rain. After a mile a car suddenly screeches to halt in a lay-bye up ahead. One of the Centre's staff jumps out and offers me a fleece with the compliments of the manager. I find myself hurriedly trying out two sizes in the rain. It is such a thoughtful and spontaneous gesture.

I rejoin my hosts and Gordon invites me to his Rotary branch meeting in a local pub. This isn't to be the organisational bonanza that I sat through at Kirkcudbright Rotary. Each official states that he has little to report and we soon sit down to an excellent meal. Gordon is the current club president, and he presents me with £50 for CLIMB.

It's back to the Lairds to watch Italy's win over France. It has been a wonderful day.

DAY 170
18th June – Girvan to Culzean Castle campsite – 10 miles

It's a fond goodbye to Gordon and Ann. The coastal road continues. Ailsa Craig dominates the coastline, jutting out of a deep blue sea. Until recently the name only meant a variety of tomato to me.

Just before Turnberry I find a superb café – in layout, menu and standard of food plus a friendly staff, it ticks all the boxes. For the record I have a couple of eggs on toast followed by rhubarb crumble with ice cream.

As I consume my meal a woman at a nearby table accidently drops her knife on the floor.

'Oh dear Colin, she's not going to pick it up, is she?' Flek whispers. He goes on, 'My mother harboured superstition and always insisted that this brought bad luck; someone else had to pick knives up. Also we kids were scolded if caught rotating knives on the table – it was a sign of impatience while waiting for our meal to arrive. As for bringing green foliage into the house to pep up a vase of flowers, this was never tolerated. Does any of this jog your memory, Col?'

'Not half! In my home dropped scissors could lie on the floor for days until a neutral retrieved them. You've got to remember that our parents were born at the beginning of the twentieth century when old wives' false notions were still widespread. These fears are now gone – I mean, people walk under ladders with impunity these days!'

I pass the British Open Golf Championship course at Turnberry. The Open was last held here in 1994 and won by Nick Price. Unlike other Open courses I have passed, this one cuts the mustard: it's smart, has impressive hotel facilities and is very professional looking. The British Amateur Championships are in progress and I observe players practising their putting on immaculate lawns in front of the clubhouse.

At a second café I fancy a change and have fish and chips, devouring an excellent plate full. I buy a *Telegraph* and take it easy for the last three miles.

Pitching on this excellent site I make tea, then don Martin's headlamp. I check the *Telegraph*'s Court Circular, I'm not listed in there, or in the society weddings, and in hope flick through the Obituaries. No, not buried in their either. I get a laugh as always out of Matt's cartoon.

Carry on Camping

'Don't get into a fret about having to carry your home,
think of the snail who is stuck with it!'

– Old proverb

On arrival at caravan and camp sites I am often the only backpacker in temporary residence. My insignificance is enhanced further when I erect the smallest tent – grounds for an inferiority complex you might think?

Well, not really. I know my place, and from it I can observe without hindrance the extraordinary rituals going on around me.

From mid-afternoon a steady stream of caravans and camper vans sporting adventurous names such as Clubman, Commodore, Sprite, Swift and Sterling start arriving. They are parked up with care, a manoeuvre completed only after heated debate. Finally an electrical umbilical cord is produced and a 'hook-up' is made, as they say in Camp Speak. This is the defining moment when any semblance that owners are going to adopt an out-door life goes pear-shaped!

Once the vans are anchored, large plastic containers on trolleys are wheeled away to scout for water. (Come the morning, a similar procedure is repeated – only this time the aim is to dispose of nasties accumulated over night. All life is here!) The arrivals are now busy erecting plastic lean-to extensions, attaching them to the sides of their pride and joy, all of this without planning permission. Translucent designer living spaces evolve, and there's a lot of one-up-man-ship going on. All that remains now is to hoist the satellite dish and drive in the bird feeding pole (I kid you not). and before you can say Jeremy Clarkson everyone is installed.

Caravan people in smart casual wear (no Primark clobber here) begin to circulate, the old ones walking their dogs while peaceful corrals are bombarded with crashing footballs from 'that lot on the next plot'.

With amused fascination I watch this 'other world' from my segregated encampment. I zip myself up in my temporary hovel and escape to my iPod comfortable in the thought that I am treading a true path.

You know, Flek, there's nothing quite like lying on the hard ground in an inadequate-rated sleeping bag wearing four pair of socks and multiple clothing layers nourished by a dehydrated meal and a warm cup of coffee. Now this is the real outdoor life!'

'You must be bloody joking.' he replies in disbelief.

19th June – Culzean Castle to Ayr – 10 miles

Early rain makes for a messy start, but I get going eventually and move down the main road flanked by woodland. A sharp left on to the A719 follows a long ridge overlooking the village of Dunure on the coast.

This is Sustrans Route 7, and after several miles it gradually descends past the impressive Ayr Farm Park. I am now in the Alloway suburb of Ayr and pass close by to Burns Cottage. I find a superb little café staffed by pretty girls and take lunch. I ring my next host, Liz Hamilton, who knows the place well, and she comes down to pick me up. We have a long conversation about metabolic conditions.

Liz and her husband Bill are a committed CLIMB family. They lost both sons Christopher and Philip, at five days and eighteen months respectively, both suffering from the genetic metabolic condition Hyperammonaemia Ornithine Transcarbamylase Deficiency (OTC). We return to their home at Prestwick for a meal. The couple take great interest in my progress around the land, organising donations which go on to the Just Giving website.

The Hamiltons show a resilience in the face of their double tragedy, and I find them inspirational.

Liz and Bill Hamilton.

DAY 172
20th June – Ayr to Irvine – 16 miles

I look back on my stay with the Hamiltons with immense nostalgia. It's another day free of the backpack, and first I have to call into an O2 shop in Ayr to sort out an email dilemma on my mobile. The trouble is only partially solved: the staff tell me to call into their shop in Irvine where one of their whiz kids (probably only fourteen) will put it right.

I follow the long straight road out of Ayr and find amongst the shops at Prestwick a smart restaurant bar called Elliots. I order tea and scones. In my appearance I look totally out of place, but I brush aside my embarrassment despite inquisitive patrons.

The main road passes Prestwick Airport which in the post war years was a famous hop for transatlantic flights, not least when Sgt Elvis Aaron Presley stopped over here for an hour on 3d March in 1960. He was on his way from Germany to a discharge from the US Army. It was to be his only visit to the UK.

'I can't see any screaming girls waiting for YOU, Col. Your publicity machine is failing you. I've told you about if before.'

'You should have seen me in 1960 Flek,' I boast. 'They'd have been here then!'

I turn down Sustrans Route 7 and pass the British Open Golf Course at Royal Troon, the championship last won here by Todd Hamilton, USA, in 2004 when he won a play-off against Ernie Els.

It starts to rain heavily, and the course doesn't look at its best. I retreat to a café in the town of Troon. Donning my full water proof gear, I get out of town and on to the A78. I find a parallel B road for some way and then cross the River Irvine using the impressive Shopping Mall Bridge into Irvine town centre. There's no joy at the O2 shop, but I'm advised to call in tomorrow morning when their 'whiz kid' is on shift.

The rain abates and I stroll out to the Ship Pub at the harbour entrance. I ring my next host, Eddie Peatson (friend of a friend), who collects me, and we go back to Prestwick. By coincidence CLIMB have booked hosts who live just a couple of roads away from each other in Prestwick. Bill Hamilton pops round from a couple of streets away to return my rucksack, and we say goodbye again.

Eddie is a widower and kindly takes me out to the Golf Pub for a meal.

Eddie runs me back to Irvine. After a call from the O_2 shop to Steve Hannigan at CLIMB their 'whiz kid' Stuart gets my Sony Ericsson email settings back in sync. Well, it *is* a job for a young person – he understands these things! Amusingly the shop has a South Sea Island theme promotion going on, and all the staff's young girls are in grass skirts.

'It's time for the lawn mower jokes,' suggests Flek. 'I don't suppose they've heard them before.'

'Yes they have – from the first bloke who came into the shop this morning carrying a pair of shears. Don't be so obvious, Flek,' I retort. 'And you talk to me about image!'

I find a B road going north visiting the Garnock Floods wildlife reserve, and talk to a chap who tells me that in retirement bird-watching has changed his life. A weasel scampers across an entrance track.

The McMenemy CLIMB family, Ardrossan.

Two miles further on the trunk road leads me to a Morrisons for lunch. I turn off onto the B780 and walk through the three small towns of Stevenston, Saltcoats and Ardrossan, which curiously have five railway stations between them!

I arrive at my next hosts, Jim and Ann McMenemy, with their children Kirsten and Cameron. They are a CLIMB family. Young Cameron has the genetic metabolic condition Medium Chain Acyl Coa Dehydrogenase Deficiency. Despite having almost fatal seizures as an infant, with the help of a strict diet and medication he is developing into a boisterous seven year old.

I find that lots of mail has arrived for me, plus a parcel from CLIMB containing a new style T-shirt and rucksack cover to enhance the publicity of my venture. I put them on and have a photo shoot.

Once again I'm with a super family, and looking forward to having a rest day tomorrow.

DAY 174
22th June – Rest day – Ardrossan

I enjoy a rest day, and sometimes wish they would come round more often. After breakfast with the family I stroll down to the ferry office and get my tickets for Arran tomorrow. I walk along the seafront, but it rains. Jim and I go down to the local for a pint.

In the evening we settle down to attack a haggis. For the uninitiated this is a Scottish dish made from offal mixed with suet, oats, onions and seasonings. It is traditionally cooked in a cleaned sheep's stomach, but artificial casings are now frequently used. Made even more famous by a Burn's ode, it's served up with neaps (turnips) and potatoes. The family tuck in and I follow at a respectful pace. The jury is still out for me! I remember having the same thoughts when tackling tripe and onions in Lancashire during the war.

In the evening I keep up with the European Cup watching Spain go through on penalties against Italy. It has been a quiet, tranquil day, a chance to really take things easy with a caring family – just what I need!

I've now entered the shipping weather forecast area Hebrides.

DAY 175

23nd June – Ardrossan to Campbelton, Kintre Peninsular – 15 miles

I have a long way to trudge today, so catching an early ferry is a must. Jim carries my rucksack down to catch the Caledonian MacBrayne ferry which takes an hour to reach Brodick on the Isle of Arran.

On the island I find a bakery, stock up and set off on a 15-mile walk up the eastern side of Arran cutting across the Sennox Pass to catch another ferry at Lochranza on the north-west tip. I ring my next host, Ian Teesdale, with an ETA at Claonaig on the Kintyre peninsula.

Crossing the pass I am conscious of buzzards circling above looking for carrion.

'I hope it won't be you Colin? chirps up Flek.

'So do I. My first aid kit isn't up to such an assault.'

It's a long, hard, strenuous plod up the pass, but I am rewarded with great scenery. Finally a long, gentle descent brings me down to the Isle of Arran Distillery. This is set in a modern and purposeful building and I get a snack in the café upstairs. Here I make friends with some farmers on a break, who make a donation.

I wander down to the ferry for Claonaig – a look-alike tugboat. Aboard I befriend James and Katie from New Zealand. He currently has a vet's practice in Campbeltown. They invite me into their camper van for coffee while I await Ian's arrival. We are in a barren car park which surprisingly has an elevated digital read-out screen.

A motor cyclist shows up. He approaches and in heavy Glaswegian asks what is going on. Apparently the read-out now says THIS SERVICE IS SUSPENDED UNTIL FURTHER NOTICE. We can all see the ferry boat chugging its way back to Lochranza.

Quoting a local poem hinting at the dominance of the ferry company seems appropriate:

All the Earth belongs unto the Lord
And all that it contains,
Except the Kyles and Western Isles –
And they're all Macbrayne's.

Later we discover that the ferry crews took industrial action as soon as we disembarked. How lucky can you get? If they'd decided to strike

278

any earlier Ian would have motored the 25 miles from Campbeltown for nothing, and I would have been stranded in Lochranza.

We motor down to Campbeltown on the quiet east side of this picturesque peninsula. Ian and Jean Teesdale live in 'Ardbeg', a substantial residence (originally built for distillery managers) overlooking the harbour. My room on the first floor gives super views.

While Jean is cooking up a splendid meal I assist Ian with garden maintenance. It's mid-summer, and the evening light will be panning out for hours. We are finally driven indoors by the midges.

I am to spend three of the most memorable days of my journey with this charming couple. Their daughter lost a son, three-year-old Tom, to the genetic metabolic condition Rhizomelic Chondrodysplasia Punctacta.

Off to the Isle of Arran.

Day 176
24th June –To Carradale, Kintyre and return to Campbeltown – 13 miles

Our long-term plan is that Ian will join me later in the week for the first three days on the West Highland Way. He is certainly no stranger to walking but needs a 'work-out', so he suggests we get a bus to Carradale half way up the peninsula, then walk back.

This is an entirely on-the-road day. Ian is a keen amateur botanist and our steady progress is brought to a standstill every time he spots a specimen. He points out mollis, cotton grass (everywhere in the Highands), Northern marsh orchid and many others. His enthusiasm spills over. There's going to be some amusing banter on botany matters during the week ahead as this good humoured man badgers away at my attention span. (It doesn't end here. On finishing the Walk in December one of his long letters is waiting for me which begins 'Dear Trainee Botanist!')

Jean has made up a scrumptious picnic lunch which we enjoy when stopping at Saddell Abbey. During the afternoon a 4 x 4 screeches to a

Ian and Jean Teesdale.

halt: it's the farmers' group I met at the distillery yesterday, stopping to say hello.

Ian finds today's walking particularly difficult but he soldiers on bravely over the last few miles. Once back, I step outside and find that Jean's vegetable garden is kept in grand order and is absolutely weed-free. This garden husbandry is all the more remarkable because time has not been kind to her physically. Despite this, she stoically gets on with life and still manages to drive the car.

In the evening, after tea, Ian takes me down to the part-time Campbeltown fire station and I meet Ronnie and Paul Souden plus the fire crew. They explain their local responsibilities and we meet a young lad in the fire service cadet scheme. The station manager hands me a £50 donation for CLIMB.

Today I reach the half way stage in days of Walk GB 4 Climb and I feel very good about it.

DAY 177

25rd June – Rest day – Campbeltown

After Jean's splendid breakfast I wander into Campbeltown and draw enough money to see me along the seven days of the West Highland Way (WHW). I get postcards for home and have a coffee. It rains as I return to the Teesdales' house.

After lunch the three of us have a planning meeting for tomorrow's journey to north Glasgow. The rain stops and I help Ian in the garden with the awkward chore of netting his raspberry canes.

'You amaze me, Col,' says Flek. 'I never thought you would have the strength left to take part in Gardeners World. I have to agree with you, Jeans vegetable patch is as neat as a pin.'

I make quite a few mobile phone calls as contact might be patchy during the coming week. Meals here are invariably on time, and we sit down to a table with our places laid up to perfection. Jean prepares herrings followed by raspberries from the garden.

I have to say that the care and consideration I receive from this charming couple, steeped in the mannerisms of yesteryear, are a testament to wonderful hospitality.

DAY 178

26th June – Campbeltown to Milngavie, Glasgow – Car trip of 140 miles.
The West Highland Way (WHW) – Milngavie to Drymen 13 miles

Leaving at 7am, our aim is to arrive at Milngavie at 11.00 in time to complete the opening stage of the West Highland Way. In the south, completing a 140-mile road trip in this time span would be a tall order, but this is western Scotland. This time we take the west coast A83 main road to get off Kintyre at Tarbert and proceed on up to Loch Fyne and Inverary.

We meet the A82 and follow Loch Lomand down to North Glasgow to arrive at Milngavie at 10.00. It's been a wonderful early morning journey through glen after glen and following loch after loch, and we made it in good time.

Today Ian and I will walk to Drymen, the first stage of the WHW, where CLIMB has secured me B & B, the Teesdales making their own arrangement. A plinth marks the start of this eight- day 96-mile walk to Fort William. Jean, who is to be our back-up, takes our photo, and we are off at 11.00 sharp.

With Ian at the start of the West Highland Way.

The WHW has been described as Scotland's walking gem. The route takes us past individual mountains, through long stretches of woodland and past a couple of small lochs. A rogue shower interrupts, but from then on it is fine all day. We consume Jean's yummy picnic lunch and later call into a pub for some tea. Ian's botany lesson for the day includes meadowsweet, mimulous and tufted vetch, with continuous displays of dog roses, which keeps him and me happy. Jean is waiting for us at Drymen and we agree to meet at the village pub later for an evening meal before retiring to our B & Bs.

I'm staying with Frances and David Lander. She is listening to my story when the phone rings. I am about to experience another sort of coincidence. A friend has called, and during their conversation Frances says, 'I have a man here who is walking around Great Britain.'

Her friend replies, 'My ex-husband did that in 1978. His name is John Merrill.'

I gulp in astonishment. This is the man whose feat of 6,824 miles around GB got him into the *Guinness Book of Records*. He later wrote the book *Turn Right at Lands End*, one of the several walking 'bibles' I read before embarking on this Walk. Completing marathon walks all over the world, Merrill is a walking machine and his name will crop up again during my journey.

A Japanese couple are also staying, and in their mannered way they show an interest in my goal. In his country the man is a department store manager and, beaming a smile, he kindly presents a trinket to all he meets.

It has been a most satisfying day and is completed with the Teesdales sharing a fine meal with me.

Along the WHW several outfits provide a 'porterage' service, lugging walkers' rucksacks from venue to venue each day. I go with 'Travelite,' who charge twenty seven quid for the eight days – well worth every penny.

DAY 179

27th June – Drymen to Rowardennan – 15 miles

The initial task is to ascend and walk round Conic Hill, savouring the Central Highlands for the first time. We get caught in a high wind at the top with misty rain. The rapid descent is slippery. Tearing along, our Japanese couple pass us and lose their footing, taking a tumble – fortunately without any injury. Relieved to survive our first weather assault on the Way, we descend to a visitors' car park at Balmaha on the shores of Loch Lomond. Jean arrives to administer her usual substantial picnic.

We are faced with a seven-mile trek along the shores of the Loch Lomond, a marvellous experience. This is the longest stretch of inland water in the UK. The going is flat, but the condition of the path deteriorates, slowing our progress considerably. Rain persists for a while, but eventually ceases to give us expansive views across the loch when gaps in the trees allow.

Ian's botany lesson goes on, and he points out monkshood (the only clump we ever see), ragged robin and common cow wheat.

'The latter's Latin name is Melampyrum pratense, did you know that Colin?' says Flek, seeking to impress.

'You've you been talking to Ian behind my back – that's a sneaky thing to do,' I reply. He beams.

Seb Green

Steve Hannigan at CLIMB has alerted me to the news that 18-year-old Seb Green set out from the south coast a few days after me with a similar charitable objective. South Today TV has featured his story.

Apparently in order to right a recent misdemeanour, he and his dog are walking round the country in an anti-clockwise direction, supporting a couple of charities on the way. On completion of his marathon he intends to join the armed services. There will be more about Seb later.

CLIMB have booked me into the YHA at Rowardennan Lodge. We arrive under leaden skies, and midges still smoke the air. Jean appears to pick Ian up, and I escape inside. My rucksack has been delivered; the transfer system is working well and continues to do so.

I have an en-suite room to myself, but there are no edibles on sale so it's a dehydrated meal. Some youths on a field craft trip hog the kitchen. Their party leader, Mark, tells me of his recent meeting with Seb Green (*facing page*) on the northern shore.

I endure a fitful sleep, because the duvet is too thick. This is always a problem at YHAs.

DAY 180

28th June – Rowardennan Lodge to Inverarnan – 14 miles

After a mile Ian and I take the optional High Route. Three ladies we met yesterday show up and we have a photo shoot. Originally from Scotland, they now live in Michigan USA, their husbands being in the car industry. Although participants make their own accommodation arrangements, individual WHW parties inevitably merge on the Way each day. The ladies are great company. One of them informs me that her cousin has a metabolic condition. On their return to the States they will forward a healthy donation to the Just Giving website.

We make out Ben Lomond to our right. A ben is a Munro, i.e. a hill over 3,000ft. People actually seek out the 249 of them and climb the lot. These afflicted souls are mockingly called 'baggers'. I have met some of them: they are obsessed.

We pass by Rob Roy's Cave/Prison, which he frequented a lot when on the run. Rob Roy MacGregor was a Jacobite outlaw whose life was punctuated by misfortune. Imprisoned, he was finally freed. He is buried at Balqueder, a spot that I visited on another trip up here.

We rejoin the shore-line, crossing streams and observing waterfalls to reach the imposing Inversnaid Hotel. A constant flow of walkers with welcomed disposable income considerably pull off their boots and are directed into the ballroom.

The staff cope with the inflow admirably, plying refreshment, and soon the place resembles a reception centre for damp refugees.

Flek ponders: 'Just shut your eyes, Col, and imagine the grand balls held here during the last century'. He then gets flippant, 'Of course if it were a Monty Python sketch you could imagine the content of the small talk among the dancers waltzing around the floor.

'"Oh, Berty darling, you dance divinely in your boots. Are they hand made?"

' "Not exactly, Fiona dearest. These booties are manufactured with a heel and hydroguard membrane supporting a hermoplastic urethane midsole plate with lateral flex and having a dual density plate. They are also well cushioned with foam flow and, golly gosh, I'm told they are fully Gortexed."

' "Oh darling I adore it when you get technical." exclaims Fiona in ecstasy.

'As the orchestra strikes up, the terribly, terribly happy couple swirl off to the next number. Charles is desperate to maintain some decorum but, alas, he crashes on to the sprung floor. He has forgotten to tie up his boot laces!'

I get a tray of tea and we munch away at Jean's excellent picnic lunch. I make a phone call to my dear friends Brian and Beryl Coote with daughter Deborah, and also say hello to our Japanese friends again.

We press on, negotiating several miles of difficult rocky pathway. Clear of Loch Lomond at last, we enter a beautiful glen at the top of the smaller Geal Loch. Here Ian finds bog myrtle and the rare lesser-butterfly orchid.

A further three miles on and we rendezvous with Jean in the famous Drovers Inn at Inveraman – said to have been one of Rob Roy's 'locals'. This ancient grubby little inn dates back to 1703 and has been furnished from clearance sales in the Highlands Displays of fierce stuffed animals greet you in the entrance hall and there's little evidence of any house cleaning. No namby-pamby health and safety rules here.

The motto over the door reads IF IT WAS GOOD ENOUGH FOR ROB ROY . . . and another announces VOTED PUB OF THE YEAR 1705. The place is teeming with tourists who sense that they are dining in a significant boozer in Scottish history, but are perhaps unaware that the staff in kilts are from Eastern Europe and Australia! A burst of Burns 'Scots Wha Hae' wouldn't go amiss.

Jean shunts me up to my B & B at Lodge House (01830 300 276) Crianlarich, run by Kath Orr and June Cassidy. I have a lovely room looking out to Ben Lomond, and my hosts are first class. Ian and Jean return to collect me for a meal at the Ben More Restaurant.

DAY 181

29th June – Inverarnan to Tyndrum – 13 miles

Jean collects me, and on bright morning we set off. Ian has brought along his friend Jonathan. The three ladies are with us once again. We veer north-east and enter Glen Fallochm, which offers a long but open passage. For the first time it's possible to glance backwards and forwards and see all the acquaintances we have made along the Way – just dots in this vast landscape.

The tumbling river takes its name from the glen, its bridges 'landscaped' with rowan and birch trees underpinned with ferns and pink foxgloves, a grouping I am to see again and again in the Highlands.

Ian spots lousewort and bedstraw, but this is to be my final botany tutorial. At the top of the Glen, as the Way suddenly turns west, I sadly say a final goodbye to him as he peels off to rendezvous with Jean at nearby Crianlarich.

For six days this delightful couple have fussed and cared for me as if I were family. Waving to him as he disappears with Jonathan is a tearful experience. A compassionate Flek moves to console me.

Wiping my eyes, I rejoin the ladies and later share a hasty lunch, thanks to the midges. They fly in waves, peeling off in squadrons to attack individual targets.

Flek, immune from this threat, offers a viewpoint: 'Do you know, Col, why the Scots used bagpipes to repel invaders mystifies me. All they had to do was to manoeuvre their opponents into an encampment close to water and let these little buggers finish them off!'

Elated but tired, we all file into the busy stop-over village of Tyndrum. I find the modern 'By the Way' hostel booked for me by CLIMB, and settle in. In the evening I enter Paddy's Bar – for two reasons. First, I need some grub, though the chilli is an indifferent meal. Never mind, the Japanese couple appear again and I'm pleased to buy them a drink. With a lovely smile she presents me with a necklace for a loved one – a typical gesture from this respectful couple.

My second reason is to watch Spain take on Germany in the final of the European Cup. The Germans are in the game for just fifteen minutes and then, much to everyone's delight, the Spaniards outplay them, taking the title with a fine goal from Fernando Torres.

30th June – Tyndrum to Bridge of Orchy – 8 miles

God my legs are tired, but do I care? This breath-taking daily trek through the central highlands is a marvellous experience and, guess what, Travel Lite keep doing what it says on their tin – returning my kit! I venture down to the Tyndrum Lodge Hotel for a full-monty breakfast. I am not exactly alone. Looking down at me from a large poster on the wall are Charlie Parker and Miles Davis, blowing their brains out at Mintons Nightclub on New York's 52nd Street.

This is a welcome short day, accompanied by the ladies. The Way mostly follows the railway line along a glen that skirts Meall Buidhe (651m) and Beinn Dorain (1072 m).

I arrive at the Bridge of Orchy Hotel early and secure a room. To make some calls I haul myself up a slope to the railway station to get a signal.

'Are those bagpipes I can hear, Flek?' He grunts a reluctant answer.

Nothing unusual, you might think, in the Highlands – except that this piper is droning out Elvis's hit, Wooden Heart.

I investigate, following the sound to behind the hotel. I question the perpetrator, who is standing in the middle of the Bridge of Orchy blowing into his bag. He has a rough-and-ready face and a full set of beard – the sort who rides a Harley Davidson. I am right, he confirms later.

'I am a German pipe major and my name is Guinness,' he reports proudly.

He notices my surprise and goes on: 'Oh yes, I have changed my name. It is on my passport. I am from Bochum in Germany and we are the German champion pipe band.'

'What are you doing here?' I enquire.

'I am on holiday and I have motored ahead of my good friend David Johnson from Northern Island, a former world champion piper. Today he is walking the West Highland Way and he will be here soon. Come with me to meet him.'

We wander off to the railway station forecourt and Guinness pipes in the world champ, his German wife and Willie Park, a pipe tutor at a Glasgow College, as they finish their walk.

All off this racket has attracted the hotel staff – mostly Eastern Europeans who have abandoned their duties and emerged from the hotel, cameras flashing. We all retreat to the bar lounge, where one of the staff requests an encore.

Flek gasps in horror: 'If you can hear these things two mountains away what is the decibel count going to be in here?

'In understandable vernacular, through the bloody roof,' I shout.

Everybody's inner cochleas are stretched to bursting before Guinness runs out of breath. Never has the sound of a bagpipe dying been so gratefully received.

Eric Hutchinson and his family from Glasgow, whom I had met earlier in week, arrive and joins us in the bar. All the talk is about piping. Willie Park tells us that he once dragged his pipes screaming to the base camp of Everest.

'Really,' I say, and frown.

'You must remember his story,' says Flek trying to stifle a cackle. 'A Reuters communiqué confirmed that terrified Yetis were reported to be fleeing the Himalayas in all directions.' He can't stop laughing.

Guinness and his fellow pipers, Bridge of Orchy.

Desperately trying to appear technical, I ask Guinness about the air reservoir. Is it really a sheep's bladder? Are there no difficulties in cleaning it?

'No problem,' he says, and he unzips the outer bag to reveal the new technology.

'The reservoir is made of Gortex,' he proclaims. 'Very little cleaning is necessary.'

The afternoon's drinking bout has left me a little short on funds, so for an evening meal I resort to my dehydrated provisions. Glen Coe will loom up tomorrow.

DAY 183

1st July – Bridge of Orchy to Kingshouse Hotel, Glen Coe – 13 miles

The WHW walkers are now well known to each other and group together as we plod up through the forest and then out in the open heading for the Inveroran Hotel. We go Past Loch Tulla and press on for several miles, crossing bridges with their burns in an endless rush, searching for open water and peace.

The desolate Rannoch Moor is ahead of us. We can cross it only because of Telford's Parliamentary Road. What an amazing construction record this man had! For the military, he constructed 929 miles of road in Scotland alone. (I have had the pleasure of crossing his masterpiece. the Pontcysylte Aqueduct.) In the pouring rain we are very glad of his engineering skills. I snack with an American family, and we chat away in adverse weather conditions.

There is now a long descent to the Kingshouse Hotel at the head of Glen Coe. The place has an 'interesting' history, once being a barracks for the Duke of Cumberland's troops carrying out their murderous pursuit of the Jacobites. Dorothy Wordsworth visited in the late 18th century and described it as a 'miserable and wretched place'. A hundred years later it was reported to have improved!

It is a busy and popular stop-over, but it still gives the impression of being run down. The standard of my room could only be described as 'concessionary'. Despite this, I am glad to get accommodation in one of the oldest coaching inns in Scotland.

There is a great view from my room of the brooding Glen Coe. Daylight persists well into the night. Outside in the dusk deer venture on to the front lawn right up the windows, and house martins are still busy returning to and fro.

Judy, one of my three Scottish-American ladies, confirms that she has made on online donation from the hotel to CLIMB, bless her! My good friend Eric Hutchison, with his family Billy and William, also arrive. Young Stuart, also with them, is partially disabled and finds the going difficult. Eric is the only plasterer I meet on my travels – strange that, isn't it?

Flek, impatient with my late dallying, pleads: 'Come on, Col, you must have soaked up the ambience by now. I'm sure you must be knackered, so do go to bed, old chap.'

Good advice!

Day 184
2st July – Kingshouse Hotel, Glen Coe to Kinlocklevan – 8 miles

After some showers we set out down Glen Coe, following the A82 for two miles to Altnafeadb. The WHW turns north up the Devils Staircase, a series of torturous chicanes, to arrive on a rocky plateau.

From here there is splendid view of the Three Sister Peaks of Glen Coe, the rock strata apparently the oldest in the world. (Another one of those claims!) They have an overpowering presence and epitomise the foreboding of this Glen: the infamous massacre of thirty-eight MacDonalds is always in the back of the mind.

The WHW peels away from the scene, descending gently into a depression until we reach another steep glen. A breathtaking, near vertical, view of Kinlocklevan opens up. Nearby, rushing water from a small feeder lock flows into huge hydraulic supply pipes that plummet down to Kinlocklevan – originally to generate power for a now de-commissioned aluminium works. (In 1907 the village became the first in the world to have every home connected to electricity.) It's a dramatic drop. Fortunately the Way takes the gentler descent, following a zigzag access road.

At the campsite there's bad news. I can't obtain a room and will have to pitch the tent. Even worse news is that this place is notorious as a strategic air command base for midges. The fact that you can blame their maddening quest for human victims on the females of the species is no consolation.

I talk to some older campers who know all about John Merrill of *Turn Left at Lands End* fame.

In the village the water rushing down those pipes now torrents into a tailrace around the old aluminium works, tumbling into the River Levan. The old building is now a leisure complex called The Ice Factor, its main attraction being a rock-climbing wall.

Entering Glen Coe.

In its café I meet Phil, who is walking from Lands End to John o Groats for Cancer Research in memory of his mum. Joining us is a computer geek from Utrecht in Holland. He tries to explain the IT ideas now coming off the drawing board. Phil and I are dubious, but our Dutchman just smiles. He well knows the plethora of technology about to hit us.

I can't help remembering that when I was a kid there was a comic with a cartoon detective called Dick Tracey who had a famous two-way wrist watch radio. We thought it was pure fantasy: it's not now!

Over at the Blackwater Hostel I double check that the Bunkhouse is fully booked. It is. Disconsolate, I pitch my tent and cowardly spend the whole evening in the Tailrace pub, with the only Scottish plasterer I know.

The insect wipes given to me back in Newton Stewart are priceless. I think of the dear old 'enry Cooper advert and 'splash 'em all over.'

'Why don't you let music take your mind off the imminent danger?' Flek suggests. *'Remember, the orchestra was playing as the* Titanic *sank!'*

For once his is a good idea. So what's on the menu this evening?

For the First Course I select 'Savoy Blues' by the Saints Jazz Band. It reminds me one of my first exposures to British Trad in the 1950s.

The Main Course presents a classical gem. I am touched by Pergolesi's setting of the Stabat Mata. This 13th century sorrowful hymn is usually sung by the male countertenor and alto.

For Dessert I will settle for Nat King Cole's 'Let There Be Love'. 'King' Cole had arguably one of the finest voices ever, but he started as a brilliant jazz pianist. Ironically on this release he is outshone by the blind jazz pianist, Battersea born George Shearing, whose accompaniment is sensational. This number is still used on countless intros and adverts.

If I am going for Cheese & Biscuits, then it has got to be Round the Horne.

From my 'wish list' I'd like to hear the Sibelius Violin Concerto in D. Nigel Kennedy will do.

DAY 185

3rd July – Kinlochlevan to Fort William – 14 miles

I zip open the tent: the little 'darlings' are still swarming around. I waste no time in breaking camp, heave up the rucksack and walk down to the Tailrace pub to meet Eric and his gang for coffee and toast. Bidding them farewell, I walk out of the village, gradually gaining height for five miles. I'm joined by three ladies from Edinburgh who set the pace. We all puff like mad, swinging north along another glen for a further three miles, and overtaking a string of walkers now well known to us.

Lunch is taken with stunning views. High above us trees are being 'harvested'. A huge machine fells, bark strips and cuts to size the trunks in one continuous action. It's so sudden – these trees have grown for decades, but they are a yield, like everything else on the land.

We trek on through dark and spooky forest areas punctuated by open areas of the native foxglove. The western massive of Ben Nevis now looms above us.

My next host, John Hutchison, suddenly appears, having walked out several miles to meet me. We stride back towards the huge Glen Nevis holiday park busy with mid-summer campers.

Now on the road, we take the final strides of the WHW west into Fort William. John has gathered a reception committee at the visitors' centre. Present are the provost of Fort William, Allan Henderson (all kilted up), local Rotary president John Goodall and fire chief Gilbert Gallie. It's a wonderful gesture. I thank the provost, and congratulate those responsible for providing the Way, a visionary outdoor challenge.

Temporary friends made on the Walk keep arriving; there are many reflective farewells. John whisks me off to his home, which is on the northern shore of Loch Eil, a couple miles out of town. It's a splendid elevated property, and his wife Margaret makes me feel so much at home, preparing a splendid meal.

John is an experienced walk leader, and during the evening he and I pore over maps and discuss my route over the next week.

From my bedroom I overlook the town, with a backdrop of Ben Nevis towering above it: the scene at lighting-up time is quite magical.

'Flek, I have to tell you that tomorrow, providing the weather is OK, we are going to scale that mountain.'

'What the hell are you thinking of man?' he shouts. 'I was looking forward to a rest day. Do I have to go?'

'Fraid so, mate. Let me explain. When I was fourteen I got up Scarfell Pike; when I was eighteen I got up Snowdon; and tomorrow this septuagenarian finally gets a chance to bag the third of GB's highest mountains – and I'm going take it. I know I've left it late, but I'm going – so there!'

I hear him grumbling under his breath. He isn't happy, but I have to be firm on occasions, and this is one of them.

DAY 186
4th July – Rest day – Fort William – Scale Ben Nevis

It's estimated that a hundred thousand people ascend Ben Nevis every year. John and I swell this number by triggering a digital counter on the Pony Trail starting point leading up the mountain outside Fort William.

The going is easy at first. We follow the ant-like procession, but soon the trail is strewn with boulders and large stones. This surface is essential to prevent excessive wear and tear from constant use, but it makes progress difficult. Half way up there's a respite as an easier path traverses the slopes. Now for a series of seven zigzags over more stones and boulders until a small snow field has to be crossed just below the summit.

Ben Nevis isn't a traditional looking mountain. Frankly it is disappointing – no peak to speak of, and a small cairn represents the ultimate goal of the climb. As I stand on it for a photo a snow bunting perches on a pole just above my head, showing no fear of human presence. I have never seen

John Hutchinson on the summit of Ben Nevis.

one before – not surprising, as their habitat is normally high up. It starts to rain and visibility gets poor. With so many climbers it is all a very chaotic. John is a warden of the mountain and has been up so many times. One annoying aspect is that sponsored groups leave behind tokens of their feats, which have to be removed.

Due to the man-made terrain I find going down very tiring, but John is very patient. He makes a flurry of phone calls to ascertain the present location of Seb Green the other 'Round GB' guy. Hurried car trips try to intercept him at two lock ferry terminals, without success.

We return for Christine's evening meal. Some further phone calls inform us where Seb will be tomorrow.

As I get into bed Flek anxious to make his point utters, 'Happy now, are you?'

It's a flippant remark which I am too tired to answer.

Snow field, Ben Nevis.

DAY 187
5th July – Second rest day – Fort William

I catch up with Seb Green, the teenager from Weymouth who is also walking round GB. He arrives at the Glen Nevis campsite with his dog and support team. He's a nice lad, very self assured, and seems to be on schedule despite some recent food poisoning and a bout of 'trench foot'.

'Blimey,' says Flek, 'I thought you could only get that on the Somme!'

We chat about our different projects. He is supporting two charities, one for an air ambulance. Our photograph taken, we wish each other luck. He then disappears with his friends to shin up Ben Nevis.

John and Christine are away for the weekend, so transfer me to another host couple, Duncan and Patizia Gillies. He has just retired as the towns fire chief. He jokes that he has received the ultimate retirement gift – no, not a gold watch, but a serious outbreak of fire down the High Street a few days before he hung up his helmet for good.

With Seb Green, Fort William.

I settle in and go into town for some serious shopping. I shall enter Knoydart, a very remote part of the Highlands, in a few days. Have I got everything? As it's the summer I fool myself that I can swap my bulky -10° sleeping bag for a lower tog value one. I am mistaken.

I also have to purchase Statin tablets for ongoing cholesterol control: my prescription is out of date.

'Comes as a blow does it, Col, being an OAP and having to buy your own tablets?' provokes Flek. 'Do you know that, although I am on the dole, I have to fork out as well. A bit much – I don't know what the NHS is coming to!'

I get provisions for four days, pay visits to an ATM and a post box and treat myself to a heavy lunch in a smart restaurant on Loch side.

At the Gillies' home I talk endlessly with my stand-in hosts over an excellent meal. All day I've kept thinking about crossing Knoydart during the next few days. It's regarded as the remotest part of the Highlands.

As I turn in Flek comes to the point: 'It's going to get pretty lonely, Col. Finding your way through it could get dicey. Do you think you're up to it?

'To be frank with you, Flek, I've always regarded this stage with some apprehension. What's in my favour is that I have walked across parts of this land-locked peninsula before.'

DAY 188
6th July – Fort William to Glenfillan Memorial Centre – 10 miles

For a week I have enjoyed wonderful company on the WHW, been the recipient of perfect hosting in Port William, but now I brace myself for the complete loneliness of Knoydart tomorrow.

First, a hike to Glenfinnan. John's thinking is that I keep away from the busy A 830, crossing Loch Linnhe to reach the head of Loch Eil on a 'quieter' road to do so. To achieve this Duncan Gillies has called up help from the Fort William Yacht Club. He runs me down to the club jetty, from where brothers Robbie and David Robertson are in a skiff ready to ferry me across. There is a strong wind blowing up the Loch, and the water is exceedingly choppy. I have to don all the safety gear, and with trepidation I clamber in. Lugging a 35-pound rucksack also presents stability problems, but at last they cast off.

Battling into the wind, David tells me he swam across last week – it's an annual race he explains. In the freezing water with no wetsuit he finished down the line in 38 minutes. He is sixty two!

'Who won?' I shout?

'Oh, our local dentist triumphed. After coming ashore he took off on his bike for twenty miles. He's one those triathlon freaks who just has to rub it in to us mortals.'

I detect some resentment. I disembark and, with a little help from the brothers Robertson, I struggle out of the safety kit.

'Good God, Col, that was a little hairy, says Flek fearfully, 'I've read Three Men in a Boat. *There was no mention of being tossed around like a cork!'*

The first five miles of the day lead me past the occasional dwellings and, surprisingly, a primary school: where on earth do the children come from? I find it difficult to grasp the need to adapt by a lesser density population.

I reach the main A830 – it's still another five miles to go. The road is being used today for unofficial TT time trials! As I approach Glenfinnan my legs virtually seize up, a new experience. I deduce the extra weight in the rucksack is tipping the balance from my being a well oiled machine to a clapped out old banger!

I literally fall into the Glenfinnan visitors' centre cafe, downing three mugs of tea and copious lumps of fruitcake. I spend some time despising the hard-done-by visitors as they struggle the few yards from their cars to obtain refreshment.

Flek, with a sudden spark of loyalty utters, 'Colin, why don't you stand up for yourself and yell out, "Look everyone, it may be a holiday for you, but I've walked two and half thousand miles to get here this afternoon!" '

It seems an appropriate rallying cry, but I decline on the grounds that that I may have to ask one of them to help me hoist my rucksack on!'

After an hour with my legs up I summon up enough energy to walk across the road to view the 18m Glenfinnan Monument, erected in 1815 to mark the place where Bonnie Prince Charlie raised his standard and gathered 1,500 followers for the ill- fated Jacobite uprising.

CLIMB tell me that the Glenfinnan Estate manager has granted permission for me to camp nearby. By chance he turns up in his Land Rover. He is Alistair Gibson, and interestingly started his career on the Cowdray Estate at Midhurst. He points to a spot at the foot of the famous Glenfinnan railway viaduct. This curves around the top of Lock Sheil, being part of the West Highland Railway from Fort William to Mallaig – regarded as one of the great railway journeys of the world.

The viaduct is notable for three reasons. It was the first reinforced concrete structure in the world built by Robert McAlpine, who became known as 'concrete Bob'. Next there are its twenty-one arches, which raise the structure to a hundred feet. Even more special to some, its fame rocketed when the location was used in two Harry Potter films.

Later I rest in my tent listening to the steam loco on its way to Mallaig thundering above my head. Oh, how my grandchildren would love to be here. I lie back thinking about Knoydart tomorrow. My legs fall asleep first, and I follow!

DAY 189
7th July – Glenfinnan to Strathan (Rough camping) – 9 miles

I am awoken very early by the sound of excited chatter. I zip open the tent and am amazed to see a group of Japanese teenagers running up the access road to the viaduct, cameras at the ready. Such is the craze for anything 'Harry Potter'.

Flek wakes up, rubbing his eyes.

'What the hell is going on,' he mutters. 'It's only 7am for God's sake!'

I explain but he is unimpressed and resumes his slumbers.

I break camp and go down to the Glenfinnan cafe for the last civilised breakfast for some time. Shortly I enter Knoydart: there are not going to be any defined paths for some days. A little intensive map reading is going to be necessary, and I hope the weather holds fair. After a mile I come across my first bothy, which is provided by the Estate.

Unusually it not only has a power point and kettle, but a discarded two-day-old *Daily Telegraph*. I sit down amongst the detritus of walkers past and pause for a read.

'I see our tennis hopefuls have become no hopers again at Wimbledon, Flek. To think that the last time we took the men's title was during the year I was born!'

'When was that then?' he asks.

'Well, it was before the war, my friend.'

'Which war?' he laughs, and goes on, 'I've heard that the ground staff don't have to water Henman Hill any more – there's so much crying going on up there that it is not necessary.'

'Oh, very funny. Now, we're entering the unknown. so let's concentrate on the going, shall we?'

'Want me to hold your hand?' he chortles.

I shake my head and take a track which sucks me further into the wilderness. It turns into a rough path which disappears, and then I continue on uneven ground for five miles up Glen Curianaan – a strenuous morning. I meet Kevin from Wigan, who warns me of the hazards up ahead. This cheers me up no end. He tells me he is off to catch the train back to home comforts. Thanks, Kevin!

It's now over a spur to take a lengthy uneven traipse down to the coniferous forest ahead at Strathan. It is late afternoon. I take some time finding a dry patch on boggy ground to pitch. I cook up a dehydrated meal and enjoy the couple of cakes I bought at the café.

It is still light at midnight, with very few stars about. Settling down to sleep, I realise the folly of swapping my sleeping bag. From now on I will have to enhance my warmth protection by putting on extra

---

Bothies

These are rough stone shelters, usually unlocked, and free of charge, which provide basic accommodation that is normally windproof and watertight. Sleeping areas are on hard, raised platforms to avoid draughts. No bedding is provided and access is by foot, cycle or boat. They are mainly found in Scotland and Wales, and they get inspected by volunteers – sometimes!

garments. I curse because I find this manoeuvre particularly difficult in the confines of the tent – I'm not elastic enough.

'How naive, Col. You should have listened to the bloke in the Outdoor Shop,' says Flek ruthlessly pointing out my error.

'Yes, all right,' I fend off his criticism. 'Now tell me, my supposed confidant, why you didn't open your mouth and offer advise at the time of the purchase. Call yourself a mentor?'

It must be 2.30am when I awake desperately needing a pee. What follows is a farce which wouldn't be out of place in a Carry On film.

First I have to carry out all the necessary adjustments to the extra clothes, then slither out of my sleeping bag and the tent. It's pitch black, and without warning two personal disasters occur spontaneously – I experience a massive attack of cramp in a leg, while my head is simultaneously covered by hordes of midges.

I holler naughty words into the dark abyss. No offence will be taken: I'm miles from anyone. It seems an age before the cramp diminishes, and I still haven't been able to relieve myself. The situation is eventually resolved, and I crawl back into the sleeping bag exhausted, the midges having left their marks – hundreds of them!

'You should have taken a salt tablet' advises Flek

'It's too bloody late now, you know-all!' I cry out in great discomfort.

This is to be only time during the whole year that I regret being where I am. I feel very alone. My pride and skin have been attacked and I feel rather stupid. However, I manage to drop off sporadically during the rest of the night without further disturbance.

DAY 190

8th July – Strathan (rough camp) – Sourlies Bothy – 10 miles

I'm up early. It's porridge and biscuits again. I pack up and cross a very boggy enclosure to round the edge of the forest. A gentle climb up a glen track takes me to isolated and deserted gamekeeper cottages at Upper Glendessarry. Further on, to my left, I see my next bearing the almost hidden and lengthy Lochan Mhaim. It starts to rain and I have to put my full gear on. I always hate this adjustment.

'There's no drying room tonight, mate,' Flek reminds me.

Towering up to my right is Sgurr na Ciche at 1040m. At the end of the hour glass-shaped Lochan I pass the 'crystal clear pool' where I spoke to the Highlander in 1995. (*I cover this event in the 'Knoydart' chapter, page 305.*)

An amazing meteorological phenomenon occurs as I come out of the glen. As the rain stops a window appears in the heavy black cumulous. The sun bursts through, forming sharply defined beams over a wide area at the head of the loch. It's as if a giant spot lamp has been suddenly switched on, the very dark background exaggerating the phenomenon. It lasts only a few minutes, but the effect is remarkable.

I have a reference manual, *North to the Cape*. It describes the drop down to the head of Loch Nevis as 'uninspiring', which is a bit of an understatement. I find coming down the seemingly endless zigzag path in the rain, strewn as it is with boulders, precarious and an enormous strain on the legs.

I eventually emerge on to a small plain at the head of Loch Nevis and there, a mile away, is the Sourlies bothy.

It has taken me eleven strenuous hours to reach it. My original plan today was to carry on to Barisdale, but this is now impossible – a miscalculation which will have ramifications later.

The bothy is already occupied by a young couple, Steve and his Dutch girl friend Freare. They kindly make me some tea, decamping to their tent nearby. In the meantime Tom and his noisy family turn up with their dog. It's a jolly and friendly atmosphere. We sit outside in the evening to soak up the scenery down the loch.

This is my first ever stop over in a bothy, and when we have all settled down, a peaceful sleep is had by all – including the dog.

DAY 191

9th July – Sourlies Bothy to Rough Camp – 9 miles

I begin the day scrambling over a headland. In 1995 I did the same, only in the other direction. I venture warily across a marshy area to reach a bridge that crosses the River Carnach. This structure is dilapidated and on an old board swinging in the wind the words DANGER – DO NOT CROSS are just discernible. Anxious not to get my feet wet so early in the day I take a chance and gingerly pick my way across the swinging heap of metal to the other side.

Close by is Camustror, the abandoned croft from the 'clearances' where the Tornadoes screamed over my head in 1995. As last time I stop, and in the deafening silence wonder just how anyone could have survived in such a forlorn place, beautiful as it is. The roofless dwelling still has an enclosure in which I assume the hardy folk grew crops: it was very much subsistence living. I still have a small piece of granite from here which I picked up in 1995 and use as a paper weight.

I strike out along the banks of the Carnach. It is a lovely day. To my right rises Squrr na Clche (1040m) which I climbed in 1995 and is a proper pointy mountain. I follow the river, its course constantly meandering. After a couple of miles it turns north, but the path is often blocked with undergrowth or trees and I have to force my way through. When its direction swings back to north-east again I am in another glen. It's midday: time for a snack and a think.

For some reason I decide to battle up through the ferns on the northern side in an effort to locate a high path out to Barisdale. Beaten. I return to the river, sit down and do some proper map reading. I find that I should have followed the river bank for another mile before heading north. It's late afternoon so I camp for the night.

This is an idyllic place. The river picks up pace and plunges over three waterfalls. On one side it's flanked by a hundred feet of sheer rock and mature trees jut out from fissures at right angles. I manage to find a level spot to pitch. I'm aware that I am behind schedule. Unknown to me, the tracker device isn't working: getting a mobile signal is technically impossible. Tomorrow I must find a way out of here.

No evening concert tonight. Introducing any form of modern culture into such a remote and beautiful location seems a gross intrusion.

Knoydart
'The Last Wilderness'

Following a chance meeting with an ex-fire brigade colleague I received an invitation in June 1995 to join a party who regularly visited Knoydart for a walking holiday break. The leader, Tim Boon, and I motored the seven hundred miles to Fort William to greet the rest of his friends. After obtaining provisions for a week we all took off for Mallaig in a fleet of cars and then caught the ferry across to Invarie.

Knoydart is a landlocked peninsula, and because of its harsh terrain and remoteness it's known as 'Britain's last Wilderness'. The Forge Inn at Inverie is the remotest pub in Great Britain. Knoydart is only accessible either by ferry or by taking a 26km walk over a rough terrain: its one tarred road of 11km isn't connected to the UK road system.

For some reason I was left out of the male group on the day they decided to climb Sgurr na Ciche, a 1040m Munro. Somewhat miffed, I decided to have a go on my own later in the week – much to the concern of the leader. The weather was perfect, and armed with a borrowed compass, I was dropped off by the Brocket Monument at 4am On a beautiful morning I took the long ascent up Gleann Meadail over a spur and down a long zigzag path to a croft by the River Carnoch abandoned during the 'clearances'. To my left was Sgurr na Ciche, a distinctive 'pointy' mountain easily recognisable from the umpteen peaks in the Highlands.

It was now 6am and I was hoping the weather would hold. The surface of the nearby Lock Nevis resembled a mirror. To my surprise I came across a tent with all its backpacking detritus strewn around. A fit, weathered man man emerged, introducing himself as Richard Hunt, a dentist from Tunbridge Wells. He called out to his wife, Shally, 'We have a visitor!'

She crawled out to offer me a cup of tea, apologising that she only had Earl Grey.

Richard explained that they were on a year's walk around GB raising funds to build a hospice at Tunbridge Wells. Looking back, it was this remark that triggered my quest in 2008. As we were chatting away about the local flora, Richard suddenly said, 'Can you see what I can?'

He pointed over, and to our amazement emerging out of the Sourlies bothy a few hundred metres away was a fully dressed Highlander. Only a claymore was missing. – he cut it as the classic Scottish stereotype, with a forward curved white beard as you might observe on a Camp Coffee bottle. A traditionally dressed gillie trundled along behind him.

They marched by us offering only a curt salutation.

'It's like a scene from Brigadoon,' said Richard. 'The Americans would love this'.

Oh, if only I had remembered to bring my camera!

We chatted on for a few minutes longer, then I wished the Hunts the best of luck, and hurriedly moved on to follow the Highlander and his friend. I caught up with them sitting by a crystal clear pool of an undeterminable depth on the edge of the beautiful and still Lochan a Mhaim.

'Where are yous off to laddie,' he asked, sounding like Findlay Currie.

I told him, and he gave me some sound path directions.

'By the way, laddie' he explained, 'we've been coming here for over twenty years. If anyone asks you about this place, tell 'em the natives are hostile, the midges are man-eaters and there are wild animals around – got it?'

It was his way of telling me that they regarded the location as their secret.

The Highlander was right about the path, which first led me through a bewitching culvert with its own micro- climate, then on to two small snow fields and a couple of rock piles and finally to the summit. To my bitter disappointment it was clouded over. On the way up I found myself above a couple of Tornadoes roaring through the valley below on their low flying operations.

It was late. Tim had advised me to turn back if I hadn't reached the summit by noon, and it was now 2pm. I scratched my name on a rock, placed it on the cairn, had a pee and once again followed the Highlander's instructions to exit abruptly off the mountain on the River Carnoch valley side. One painful memory still exists. On the way down I had to virtually tumble down a very steep tussocky grassland slope, and my thighs were burning with pain by the time I had reach the river valley.

By late afternoon I had returned to the abandoned croft and elevated my legs to drain blood back up my legs. Any walker will tell you what a sensation that produces. Suddenly the silence was shattered by the arrival of two more Tornado aircraft. I was below them this time and, with pressure waves emitting from the wings, they screamed overhead their sound gone in seconds.

I still had to drag myself back up the zigzag, but once over the spur it was downhill all the way through Gleann Meadail. At the bottom Tim arrived to meet me in the 4x4. It was 8.00pm, and he was mightily relieved – I had been out for sixteen hours. In that time I had covered eighteen miles and ascended three thousand feet.

This was the most memorable day's walking I was ever going to complete. When I got back to Inverie the group were in the Old Forge pub. There were congratulations, but I had just a feeling that some of them didn't believe that I had done it. I look back at that day with pride, hardly believing I was ever that fit. What an adventure I'd had!

DAY 192

10th July – Rough Camp to Barisdale – 10 miles

I wake to the thunderous sound of rushing water nearby. Thank goodness it's another fine day. I double-check the guide book for my route further along the River Carnoch. This passage is delightful, the river building up momentum to plunge over the series of waterfalls.

I reach the spot where the written word confirms that I can no longer progress along the river. It advises ascending north up a very steep fern-covered bank. I find a faint semblance of a path and take a fix north as advised – I should pick up a path higher up. It's a very steep climb while trying to balance the rucksack. I have no intention of repeating the farce of yesterday, keeping clear of shoulder height ferns.

I must admit that I'm getting a little worried, but suddenly there is the 'defined' path. On it is a puddle with a recent boot print in its mud. Oh, the relief! This is how Robinson Crusoe must have felt when coming upon Friday's imprint.

The way is now west. The peace is soon shattered by a couple of Tornadoes using the twisting valley for low-flying training, and later a Hercules also turns up. It is some time before I reach the spur which will lead me down a very long glen to Barisdale.

Passing through the spur I slip and settle on my bottom. The rucksack has settled in a backrest position, so I decide to sit and take in the ambience of the place. Ahead, looking deceptively near, is Loch Hourn, its blue surface forming a V between the descending mountains. A spur is normally a turbulent place, but today complete silence reigns. Necessity eventually moves me on, but as I'm in good time I take two hours to pick my way down the long easy descent to the loch. For the last three days I have hardly seen anyone during the day. Nourishment for the soul, perhaps? I expect to be asked whether I have ever felt lonely. My answer will always be that I was often alone but never lonely.

To the south is Ladhar Bheinn, the most westerly Munro, which I also climbed in 1995. Barrisdale comprises just three dwellings and, unexpectedly, one of them is classed as a bothy. The normally efficient CLIMB accommodation communiqué didn't show this.

A friendly man emerges and tells me about the benefits of the place. It has a flush loo, 13 amp power points and bunk beds, so it's more of a 'bunkhouse' really. Before I settle in I have to pay my dues. A huge padlocked metal box with £3 written on it confronts me. It is grossly out of all proportion to the cash it is expected to hold. My new acquaintance looks at me and we laugh. It takes a full second before my three pound coins hit the bottom with an almighty crash!

A father and his two sons are also present, and despite the amenities they are determined to camp out. I notice they are building a fire, presumably to ward off the murderous midges. I learn that those present today have already 'bagged' two hundred Munroes between them! That evening we all dine together. I charge up my Sony Ericsson.

The ever prying Flek spots a Visitors' Log Book, and I make a comprehensive entry. Little do I realise how important this information is going to be during the next twenty-four hours.

With no mattress the bunk is hard but it is good to be inside.

My schedule is in disarray. If the tracker unit isn't functioning correctly then, at this stage, nobody knows where I am. But I should be able to phone CLIMB and my family from the B & B at Kinlock Hourn Farmhouse tomorrow.

11th July – Barrisdale to Kinloch Hourn Farm – 9 miles

The five of us prepare our own breakfasts and then we all sit down together – a most civilised way to start a day. I bid my farewells and take the track past the working farm. As Knoydart is a landlocked peninsula, the farm vehicles have to be brought in by sea down the loch. Loch Hourn is fourteen miles long and is said to be the most fyord-like of them all.

It's nine miles to Kinloch Hourn Farm at the head of the Loch. The path is laborious and winds, climbs and descends over rocky ground. I stop to have a drink, and an elderly couple; Hugh and Elizabeth, turn up. Hugh tells me he helped to build the bothy forty years ago and hasn't been back. I note that they are not wearing the appropriate gear and query whether will they have enough daylight to return. They brush aside my concerns and move on.

It turns out to be ironic that I should be concerned for them, because I get to within a mile of my destination when I hear the chopping sound of a helicopter approaching. For what happened next, see 'What's Your Name?' on page 311 . . .

When I reach the farmhouse Joe Williams, who is in charge of the accommodation outlet for the estate, is standing at the door.

'The police have been looking for you,' he says. 'You'd better give them a ring.'

I make the call. I'm a missing person! A policewoman says that they will carry out formal identification, although in the end they never show up.

Joe seems reluctant for me to use the phone and allocates me just two calls. First I ring to explain the situation to Steve Hannigan, the chief executive at CLIMB, and thank him for 'pressing the red button' – he had little option, the Walk being under the banner of the charity. I assure him that I will reappraise my schedule and will get back to him ASAP.

The reception from my daughters is mixed. Suzanne heaves a sigh of relief and pesters me as to my welfare. She later informs my sons. Sonya, still wracked with worry, says she will 'kill' me if I go missing again. The tension broken, we both laugh at her futile ultimatum.

Staying at this farmhouse is an uneasy experience. Joe is a small timid man, who I sense has escaped to this lonely backwater for six months of the year to get away from the outside world. He seems to run the place as if it is an irritating chore. He tells me the sparse use of the telephone is necessary because calls are routed through the estate's lodge half a mile away. His mindset seems a little feudal to me. My offer to pay for the calls doesn't relieve his anxiety.

'There is a payphone over at the estate house half a mile away,' he says, trying to get off the hook.

My room is satisfactory, but the evening meal, which I share with a Munro bagger, is poor repast.

I study the map and plot my route for tomorrow. The instructions in the *To the Cape* book are not clear. Walking routes throughout the Highlands are not 'way posted', so navigation is key. Joe tells me that walkers have remarked on the book's inaccuracies.

'So how do you think the day went?' It is both a nonchalant but barbed remark from Flek. 'Got the bottle to carry on, Colin? Don't worry, my friend, I'll be right behind you as always.'

Bully for him!

It has been an extraordinary day, to say the least. A sense of uncertainty comes over me, and I spend an uneasy night.

'What's Your Name?'

'Keep Calm and Carry On'
– Government propaganda poster, 1939

It's Day 193 and I'm coming to the end of a hard days trek. I proceed with haste towards the Kinloch Hourn Farm B & B and its landline, anxious to confirm my whereabouts, having been out of touch for three days. I'm within half a mile of my destination when suddenly the normal tranquilly of the loch  is interrupted by the unmistakeable sound of an approaching helicopter.

Around a rock promontory appears an RAF 'Sea King' search-and-rescue helicopter. It is progressing low and slowly up Loch Hourn, its crew member air marshall's legs dangling out of the side. I raise my poles in salute and it starts to reverse towards me.

'They're looking for someone!' yells Flek over the din. 'Hang on. they're coming back for another butchers at us.' Then with great excitement he shouts: "Yes, it's you they're after!"

The chopper hovers down to a sand bar at the side of the loch a few hundred metres away. The air marshall jumps out, then strolls purposely through some scrub towards me: 'What's your name?' he barks.

In reply I flippantly give him my RAF number, name, rank and posting. I can't resist it. It's more than fifty years since I last blurted out this information, and it pours out of me as if it were yesterday. What a memory!

'Oh, yeah' he says,. 'We've been looking for you.'

I confirm my identity with a debit card, and tell him that I'm OK and will shortly be ringing my charity.

He radios back to his skipper, whose message to base stops the mountain rescue teams and police from further searching. The police inform CLIMB.

I apologise for any trouble my 'disappearance' has caused.

His name is Bruce and he tells me not to worry.

'We've had a pleasant trip out from Lossiemouth,' he says casually, as if it were a day out rather than an emergency.

'How did you know where I was?'

'Well, you left a message in the Barisdale bothy logbook and we got to know about it,' he smiled knowingly. 'We surmised you were going to trek up the loch, and we were right.'

We chat about the RAF for couple of minutes and then, wishing me luck, he saunters back to his chopper, which flies off.

'It's reassuring, Col, that they come looking for people as part of their job without a charge,' ponders Flek. 'Goodness knows what the cost would be.'

. Apparently my exploits make the *Oban Times*. Such is fame. Little did I know that a "Sea King" would be landing close to me again in five weeks time!

DAY 194
12th July – Kinloch Hourn to YHA Shiel Bridge – 10 miles (Aborted)

After breakfast I cross a river, pass the estate lodge and gradually ascend a hill, following some pylons. The guide mentions an estate shelter, which I find: it's derelict. I am now in a vast amphitheatre, and then the path runs out. I am to ascend the mountain pass to the Forcan Ridge. I find the going hard and the terrain difficult underfoot, with continuous tussocks and water sinks. It's difficult to keep a grip, and I fall over many times. I look at my watch. I'm not getting anywhere. I stop to have a hard think.

Flek makes my mind up for me with his most profound statement to date: 'Colin it might have been a good idea in the original planning to take the North to Cape route, but I think it's too much for you. Just think: your remit is to get round GB in your own allotted time, i.e. three hundred and forty seven days. Now, I suggest that you concentrate on that schedule. Remember that dozens of host families' dates are already booked, and any delay will throw the whole plan into jeopardy My advice, mate, is to return to Kinloch Hourn, take a day off to rest and then hit the highway.'

Sitting down, and soaked, I figure that this is my first 'bite the bullet' situation of the Walk. This may seem an easy way out, but Flek is being pragmatic – he's trying to help.

Decision made, and any uncertainty dissipated, I retrace my steps, literally slithering down the endless slope and falling on many occasions. Later I stumble flat on my face into a stream. My glasses become detached, but miraculously they aren't damaged.

It takes me four hours to get back to Joe's place. He is in his usual spot just outside the front door, having another cigarette and typically takes his time offering me my room back.

I have a bath, cook up a dehydrated meal of chilli and rice and finish with some chocolate hobnobs I have left. *What do I do now?*

Trying to unlock Joe isn't that easy. There is a tension about him. His constant smoking at the door indicates that he's longing for something to happen – or, has he escaped from something and is frightful of being found out? My rationed phone calls emphasise his insecurity.

I spend the day plotting a road programme. I've rung Steve at CLIMB to tell him that I have decided to walk the Highlands route by road. He is relieved to hear this: we can't risk another emergency.

It's so quiet here that only the hum of the farmhouse generator breaks the silence. There are no provision outlets. Everything has to be brought in from Inverness (forty miles) or Dundee (even further).

Kinloch Hourn is at the end of what has been described as 'the most beautiful and longest cul-d-sac' in Britain. Glen Garry runs for twenty-two miles and, save for a few homesteads, it is deserted. It was formerly home territory to five thousand men, women and children before the clearances. The narrow road (really a lane) terminates on the A87 main Invergarry-to-Kyle of Lochalsh road.

It's a two-stage walk to the main road. I am already two days adrift and have to ask the indifferent Joe for advice. At first he tells me that if I stand outside I just might just get a lift from someone returning from fishing on the loch. He then casually adds, 'My wife and baby with her friend will arrive this evening. I know they're going to Inverness tomorrow to shop. Perhaps she might give you a lift to the main road.'

'So suddenly its good old Joe now is it? ' Flek tantalises. 'Great, but I still don't think he realises how cooperative he's being. Beautiful as Glen Garry is. I am not walking all that way down to a main road, get my gist?'

I go to bed very reassured.

'It's time for a Concert to celebrate, eh Flek?.'

'Got any Punk?' he says.

'Funnily enough, I'm right out of that 70s genre of hard-edged music which eschews the perceived excesses of mainstream with short songs, stripped down instrumentalism and often with political and anti-establishment lyrics.'

My reply shuts him up and mystifies me.

I start with pianist Brad Mehldau playing 'No Moon At All' and finish with Grieg's 'Holberg Suite'. Round the Horne is always a laugh.

Day 196
14th July – Kinloch Hourn to Shiel Bridge (via Invergarry) – 25 miles by road

I have to spend some time waiting for the ladies to get the child ready, but finally at mid-morning they kindly find space for me and the rucksack in their car and we're off.

It's a wonderful drive through the isolated glen. Two sights en route I remember. The first is a Highland bull, standing on a hummock, surveying his harem – a real picture postcard shot. The other is a long wire fence in front of one of the few homesteads on the 22-mile run. Mounted on it is a magnificent collection of car and lorry wheel embellishers. It seems rather pointless though: who is going to admire them out here?

Arriving at the A87, I am driven on down to the Invergarry Hotel, where the ladies drop me off. The idea is that I catch the service bus to Shiel Bridge and walk up to the YHA there. With a two-hour service, I order some lunch. When the bus arrives I hail it, but it doesn't stop. Fuming, I go back into the hotel where the barmaid tells me this is not uncommon. She advises me to go out and hitch a ride. It is the busy holiday season and the traffic is continuous – I might get lucky.

I stand at the side of the road for about an hour being totally ignored by the stream of 4x4s until a small grubby little Japanese car with a couple inside pulls up. Miles ahead, this road splits, so it's important to me that they are travelling the Kyle of Lochalsh route. I'm in luck – they are. The car is packed with their luggage, but somehow they make room for me. Both are in their thirties and in education: her name is Chrissie and he is French. This is evident from his driving, which is approaching maniacal. The wonderful Highland scenery flashes by.

Flek, hanging on for dear life, bellows into my ear, 'He thinks he's Popeye in The French Connection.'

At Shiel Bridge we miss my turning by a mile. He scheeches into a U-turn and delivers me to the front door of the Ratagan YHA. I can't thank them enough. I am now back-on-track: in the space of four hours I have been given two lifts in excess of forty miles.

'Boy, you've been so lucky, Col,' says Flek, still recovering from our break-neck journey.

The first words from the warden when I enter the YHA are, 'Where the hell have you been? You should have been here two days ago. The police rang here looking for you.'

I tell him my story.

Standing in reception, waiting to be processed, I am joined by a German couple and their two metre-tall son. Seeing my rucksack. they ask the usual questions and listen to my story intently. I find a bed and return to the kitchen-dining room packed with hostellers. This is a well-run outfit and has wonderful views down Loch Duich. It 's difficult to express my feeling of relief at being on schedule again.

The German couple, Olaf and Helli, ask me over to their table. She explains that they've caught some pollack at Gairlock and they invite me to supper. The fish with sauté potatoes and salad makes a delicious meal.

We have a great chat. Olaf is in the truck industry and Heldi in education. Their son Nickolas wants to be a fighter pilot, but his height will stand against him.

My fortunes have changed dramatically. I attempt to share my positive outlook with Flek but, tired, he is snoring his head off. I go to sleep a much relieved man.

DAY 197

15th July – Ratagan YHA Sheil Bridge to Strathcarron Hotel – 18 miles

I say goodbye to my generous German friends and Steve the under-standing warden. I am fresh despite the trials of yesterday. It's a new start, and nothing better matches my mood than what I am about to witness. In a field off the lane leading to the main road I witness a jet black mare giving birth to a jet black foal. After a while the new-born struggles to its feet. The owner has comes out reassure the animals. It is a wonderful, gentle moment – an apt start to the day, symbolising rejuvenation.

'Makes you want to boogie along with glee. Why don't you have a go?' encourages Flek. 'Go on, skip along. Nobody's looking.'

'All right then, but you'll have to shoulder my rucksack, though.'

'Well, I was only offering advice, Col,' he stutters.
When it comes to hard graft he really is a lazy sod.

I reach the A87 and set off round the head of the loch with its marvellous views. Like Jack Kerouac, I am On the Road. In truth my only affinity with his novel is the penchant for jazz. The reference is tenuous, but just enough to grasp the spirit of Sal Paradise and his friend Dean Moriarty on their wild dashes across the States.

Wanting a cup of tea, I knock on the door of a B & B at Inverinate to enquire about a café. Mrs Fraser invites me in for tea and toast. A lovely lady, she chats on proudly about her grandchildren who go to school in the village. There are wonderful views across the loch from her lounge.

It's another five miles to my next significant stop. On the way I have to stand well back as two huge transporter vehicles carrying wind farm blades go by with their warning escorts.

I arrive at one of the most popular tourist attractions in the Highlands, namely Eilean Donan Castle. Ravaged over the centuries and rebuilt, it's a magnet for visitors. Of course it comes with a tourist

Eilean Donan Castle.

centre, café and gift shop (yet more short bread), and there are clean toilets. The place is packed, and I join the multi-national crowd on the standard tour.

'The castle must look magnificent when it is floodlit at night time' says Flek. 'I've seen it on postcards in the shop.'

In the café I join some Canadians at a table. An old gent tells me he was born on the same day and year as Margaret Thatcher. I commiserate, we laugh and he hands me a fiver. A young lad smartly turned out in highland dress and playing the bagpipes entertains the tourists in the car park. I have a word and he tells me he is supplementing his education grant. He's a pleasing lad, and I give him the old boy's fiver, requesting the lament Flowers of the Forest, which he plays beautifully.

I hit the road again and turn off onto the A890 which winds around an energy sapping gradient for about a mile.

'That's made you puff a bit, Col. Sitting on your shoulder, I admire your grit, fortitude and sheer determination on these road ascents,' rallies Flek with disguised sarcasm. 'I'm sure there are going to be many more.'

I haven't got a map for this area. It starts to rain. Steve Hannigan, anxious that I make up time, rings with some suggestions on future stages. I've covered thirteen miles, much of it uphill. With another eight miles to go I'm getting a little despondent. Once again I fall in luck. A car stops and a chap invites me to hop in. He's Paul Sloan, an ex-RAF type. I'm wacked, so his assistance is most helpful.

He replies, 'Our meeting was to be.'

A surveyor, he works in the Highlands and lives in Inverness. He delivers me to the Strathcarron Hotel, waiting until I've confirmed that a room is available, then gives me a £5 donation and his mobile phone number should I need further assistance.

'Anything I can do to help, just give me a buzz,' he says and drives off into rain.

The hotel is comfortable and I relish a good meal while chatting to the locals. This is a remote place but has a railway stop on the Kyle of Lochalsh line.

'Another adventure tomorrow, Colin,' says Flek.

Neither of us has any idea how spot-on his prophecy will turn out to be.

DAY 198
16th July – Strathcarron Hotel to Gerry's Hostel, Craig Achnashellach
– 7 miles

I set out from the Strathcarron Hotel on a seven-mile jaunt to Gerry's Hostel at Achnashellack – the oldest independent hostel in Scotland. The man himself has been running it for nearly four decades. It's well publicised at several road junctions.

To my surprise, in the early afternoon I meet Gerry coming up the deserted Achanshellach Road on foot.

'You must be Colin,' he says. 'Your charity has been on to me.'

He gives me a key to the premises and offers instructions on how to settle in. He's off to play golf, and hurries away to catch a train. The hostel is well appointed, with ample dormitories, and its large, comfortable common/dining room comes with a log fire. Importantly there is no TV. This is a sanctuary to revive aching bodies and recharge the brain cells, with a good book from the extensive library or to talk over mountain conquests.

The hostel is central for many activities in this part of Wester Ross. With twenty peaks over 2500ft (known as Corbetts) and many of them Munroes (peaks over 3000ft), it's not surprising that the obsessed 'Munro baggers' make for this place.

(There's a plethora of other mountain classifications, such as 'Grahams',' 'Hewitts', 'Wainwrights', 'Nuttalls' and even 'Marylyns'. These are categorised according to the size of the drops each side, as challenging hills or as just ascents of ascetic beauty.)

The place appears remote, but Scotland is full of surprises. Behind the strip of trees running parallel to the road is the railway line to the Kyle of Lochalsh.

After letting myself in, I make a drink and place my damp walking gear in the ample drying room. So far, so good . . .

Gerry

'The way of the transgressor is not so hard'
— Errol Flynn

Later in the afternoon of my arrival at Gerry's Hostel a couple of ladies return from their days mountain walking, and we're all settling in when a door slams and Gerry appears. He is extremely irate and very different from the man I met on the road.

Pointing at me like a headmaster, he says 'You come with me,' and he leads me to the drying room.

'What are all your damp clothes doing laid out over my clean laundry? Didn't you see the notice?'

He points to a notice behind the door. To be fair to me, its position is obscured by the door, and to be fair to him it's in large writing.

'Remove your garments without delay,' he insists.

He 'invites' all three of us to follow him again into the dormitory.

'Why are your walking poles in here? They're to be left outside.'

He ticks me off again saying, 'You should know better than to bring gas canisters inside.'

Lesley at CLIMB, who secured my booking, has obviously mentioned that I am an ex-fire officer.

'They are to be wrapped up in plastic bags and placed in a bucket outside the back door. Don't forget them when you leave,' he says – and storms off.

I haven't had such a ticking off since being at school. We all hung our heads in shame.

'We have broken his rules, transgressed,' says one of the ladies. 'He has hundreds of them, so I've heard – issues admonishments as the mood takes him. He is well known as an eccentric that way.'

'Who's been a naughty boy then?' taunts Flek, sounding as if he is talking to a parrot.

'All right Flek, I'm not in the mood, so shut it.'

Later in the evening we all meet up in the comfortable dining room to prepare our food. The atmosphere is subdued. Gerry comes in and, without any greeting, lights the fire. The fireplace is laid out to perfection with all the kindling placed to produce an instant ignition. This is his well rehearsed daily ritual. Then, to our surprise, he places a candelabrum on our table. Without a word, but forcing a grin – more of a grimace, really – he lights the candles.

'He's beginning to thaw out,' whispers one of the ladies, 'He doesn't appear to be harbouring a grudge any more, does he?'

Gerry isn't finished yet. Fetching an LP from a drawer, he puts on some Beethoven. The player is an ancient Pye 'Black Box', the epitome of amplification in the 1950s: we could not afford one at home. With the atmosphere improving I feel brave enough to ask him if he has any 'Jazz'. He instantly throws his arms up in uninhibited excitement, returning to the old chest of drawers to pull out another LP. This time it features Jelly Roll Morton and his Red Hot Peppers.

Gerry's eyes light up again as I tell him that I have a dozen tracks from the very same LP on my iPod. Under the onslaught of Jelly Roll, the ladies and a Munro bagger who has come in for a quiet read, make a retreat, leaving Gerry and me to chat away about the music. He really opens up, going on to reminisce about a girl he had taken a fancy to at the Darlington Jazz Club decades ago. We enthusiastically natter away for some time.

He retires for a while, returning in his dressing gown looking like a house-master in a boarding school.

'I'm off to bed now Colin,' he barks. 'Please put the fire guard over before retiring. Have a word with me about your route in the the morning.'

'Crikey,' says Flek, 'he's left the fire safety of the place to you, so in his eyes you have gone from being a villain to being vigilant. What a turn-around! I have to say your Jazz intervention was a master stroke and saved the day.'

Admonishment has turned to atonement. Having completed my late night fire instructions, I climb into my bunk cleansed of guilt.

Jelly Roll Morton

For the uninitiated, Ferdinand Joseph Lamothe, a Creole and known professionally as 'Jelly Roll Morton', was born in New Orleans in 1890 and became a pivotal figure in early Jazz. Morton was one of the first great ragtime pianists and, controversially, he claimed to have invented the genre. He directed two groups, The New Orleans Rhythm Kings and, more famously, The Red Hot Peppers, with whom he produced some outstanding recordings in 1928. These are what we had been listening to.

Towards the end of his life the American folklorist Alan Lomax recorded him in an extensive series of interviews and performances for the American Library of Congress – an invaluable oral history of the early days in New Orleans. Morton was awarded two 'Grammy's and died in Los Angeles aged 55 in 1941. Oh, and if you're asking. the term 'Jelly Roll' has a sexual connotation!

DAY 199

17th July – Gerry's, Achnashellach to Kinlochewe – 10 miles

After breakfast Gerry appears still in his dressing gown. He tends to my preparations.

'Now don't forget all your gear, Colin.'

Finding out that I intend to take the road down to the Achnasheen junction then back up the Gairloch Road he says, 'Look, if you turn left outside, walk back up the way you came for a mile to a way-post. This will take you into a wood and out on to a steep bank of ferns. Its' quite a long push up, but keep going until you come to an estate track, turn right and you'll be OK for the rest of the day.'

In a final show of reconciliation he places my booking fee on the table as a donation to CLIMB. I am humbled and rendered utterly speechless. Clearly Gerry blows hot and cold, but I'm convinced that he rose early to look after my welfare.

Going up the road, Flek summed up the experience, 'I know he flew for you about the drying room, perhaps with some justification, but prejudice, Col, is often a premature reaction. You need a code of practice for these moments – a code of honour even a motto. What about "Judge not but be judged" (anon).'

That seemed to fit the bill, and I thanked him for his advice. Now for that steep bank.

It's a bit of a struggle, but I find the estate track leading into a long shallow valley with a splendid river tumbling though it. Crossing a bridge along the way, I satisfy a whim and take a personal mugshot. Taking the camera out I prepare to 'put one in the can'. Surely a Sony Eriksson can smooth out a few wrinkles.

'Resist it, Col,' panics Flek. 'You won't like the image. We outside your head have to view you all the time– it's not a pretty sight.'

Of course I ignored his advice and took the shot.

'God, do I look this old Flek?'

'Fraid so. You should have smiled, it has the same effect as a lick of paint on rotting wood. You've still got some hair, though most of it's on your face, mind you.'

'You say the nicest things, Flek, and are a great comfort. Cretin!'

I continue at an easy pace, passing by several exclusive pads and then finally get out onto the Kinlochewe Road. It drops down four miles towards the village. Cromasaig, my B & B, is the very first house on the right, which makes for a nice change. So often I have to go looking.

Proprietor Liz Forest offers me a pot of tea and a splendid plate of cakes and biscuits. I unashamedly scoff the lot. I have arrived early (it's only 2pm), so I take a walk down to Kinlochewe, have more tea and an eccles cake, and, wandering back, get a *Daily Telegraph* to read from end to end. What a luxury!

This village has held at times the unenviable record of having the lowest total of sun hours per year. Bournemouth, Hastings and Eastbourne all squabble over who has the highest. One year Bognor easily beat the lot of them, but somehow it just hasn't the same pull for tourists as the others!

Liz and her husband Tom are forceful characters and are advocates of Highland life. He's ex–Royal Military Police and recalls his service at the Rousillon Barracks at Chichester; he was eventually invalided out the Army.

Tom tells me that pine martens, tawny owls, buzzards and siskins all frequent the property and its grounds. Our evening meal with another guest includes mushrooms gathered on the road bank opposite. It's a nice house and I have a very pleasant and interesting stay.

DAY 200
18h July – Kinlochewe to Gairloch – 10 miles

I walk back down to the village in the rain, turning left on to the A832. Now for a five-mile hike to the Bridge of Grudie, where my next hosts Ian and Phil Robin are going to motor out to and pick me up. The road passes through forest on one side and Loch Maree on the other. When I get to the bridge I dodge into a wood for a comfort stop and, of course, the Robins motor past. They are soon back, and we speed on to Loch Bad an Sgalaig, where Phil and I get out.

She and I take an easy but muddy four-mile walk on an old track through what I am told is Macpherson clan country. Ian picks us up. Phil has arranged an interview with Alex Grey, the manager of Two Lochs

Radio. The station building is a corrugated roofed stone structure and has the smallest listener base in the UK – some 1,691, he boasts.

When it's over, Alex says, 'You should have been here yesterday. A pod of dolphins came into the bay and performed a prolonged "Disney" display. Pity you missed it.'

It *was*, because I never saw a dolphin on the whole trip.

I settle in with the Robins. Contact here was made by my good friend Maurice Hall of the Old Cicestrians of Chichester High School, where Ian was a teacher for four years in the Sixties. They help me with a revised schedule received from the CLIMB Office. I can now have a rest day at Ullapool.

In the evening I am upstairs preparing my blog for CLIMB, listening to Ian practising his bagpipes in his den along the corridor while Phil is downstairs strumming on the harp. It's another world up here: sheep-dog trials tomorrow!

The smallest UK radio station, at Gairloch.

DAY 201

19th July – Rest day – Gairloch

After breakfast I make some phone calls and pass on my schedule adjustments to Lesley Greene at CLIMB.

We all go out to the bank and shops. In a garden nursery and hardware store I purchase a pair of thick woollen socks for twelve quid. Not only do they last me for the rest of the trip, but I still frequently wear them four years later – quite a bargain. Every time I put them on I think of Gairloch. Two pairs of thin inner socks that I wore on the entire trip (bought from Millets and classed as 'Thousand Mile Socks') have now clocked up over five thousand miles and still have no holes!

We have a pub lunch and go on to the sheepdog trials. It's a great little gathering in a field on a hill overlooking Strath Bay. A heavy shower drives us into the only big tent, allowing an excuse for tea and home-made cake.

In the evening the Robins invite a dozen of their friends around for snacks, allowing me a chance to explain CLIMB's work. This leads to a donation. Sadly the town is in shock following two fatal vehicle accidents at difference locations involving the same Gairloch family.

The Robins impress me. Phil is a great organiser, and Ian such good company.

As I fall into bed Fleks chirps up, 'Could we just have rest days and cut out the walking?'

Seems a wonderful but completely impracticable idea!

I pull out my Ipod and play just one track, Ralph Vaughan Williams' 'Fantasia on a Theme by Thomas Tallis'. It's sixteen minutes of sheer joy. Like much of his work, it's so English.

DAY 202
20th July – Gairloch to Ullapool – 12 miles

Master planner Phil is trying to help me catch up on my schedule. Together with Bob, their friend, we motor along the A832 to Corrie Hallie and walk on from there.

The Robins have recce'd a walk across to the Strathmore Valley, but our efforts to get across are thwarted by swollen burns impossible to negotiate. We return to the car, where the thoughtful Phil produces a picnic lunch.

Disappointed, we settle for a visit to the Corrieshalloch Gorge, which is 1.5km long and 60m deep. There is an access bridge to a platform set in the side of a cliff to view the 46m Falls of Measach. It is quite a sight.

Phil dilutes the disappointment by driving into the Strathmore Valley, and the party walks for two miles down a track which runs parallel with the main A835 to Ullapool, with coffee and cake at the finish. Bob then runs me to an Ullapool Road lay-by and it's time to

Ian, Phil and Bob, Corriechalloch Gorge.

leave my good friends. I am a little envious: they are shortly off to Inverness to hear the Scottish National Youth Jazz Orchestra.

I have six miles to march into Ullapool. Three miles out, on a remote stretch of road, I am astounded to see a frail little old lady, standing in a lay-by on the opposite side of this isolated road. She is watching me intently. I cross the road and speak to her. In a soft, child-like and well-mannered voice she says, 'My name is Alexandrina McCleod and I was born in that house over there' – pointing across the road.

'Queen Victoria's daughter-in-law was sometimes called Alexandrina she proudly announces. My garden is just here. Would you like to have a look?'

I regret to this day that I didn't take up her offer. It wasn't as if I was in a hurry.

This diminutive lady has long straight hair and is wearing a dated paisley frock and knitted shawl. However, it's her buttoned-up shoes with ankle socks that indelibly links her to a long-gone era. I have the feeling that she has been left behind: time has passed her by. I ask her if

I can take her photograph and she agrees. She waits patiently and, when the shot is taken, without a word this 'frail' old lady marches briskly across the road up some steps into the house and slams the door.

All the way into Ullapool I wonder if I have witnessed an apparition, the occurrence being so unusual.

The road now converges with the head of Loch Broom, and I saunter into Ullapool.

I find that the Scottish YHA is delightfully positioned, looking down the Loch and run by an enthusiastic young couple. I book in for two nights.

Alexandrina McCleod.

DAY 203
21st July – Rest day – Ullapool

When committed to a continuous daily schedule it is difficult to describe the sense of liberation that a rest day releases. It has nothing to do with not having to walk. An overwhelming sense of freedom prevails. In simplistic terms it's having the time to put worry aside, relax and read a national daily from cover to cover over a coffee or pint.

Ullapool, somewhat remote and beautifully place, is an industrious fishing port. Every couple of hours a huge lorry passes the YHA carrying tons of crustaceans for consumption all over Europe.

The town is now also famous for its 'chippie'. Recently a Radio 4 journalist went into the Seafort takeaway down on the quay and came away so impressed that he wrote up his 'find' in a national Sunday supplement – the ultimate accolade. Always the Doubting Thomas, I go down to the Seaforth and sample their haddock and chips – the experience is a joy, but I am to hear many similar claims along my route.

During the evening the town's junior pipe band (most Scottish towns have one) marches up and down to the delight of a large crowd, including curious continental tourists.

The hostel is well appointed. Last night I shared a bunk room with seven other blokes. Trust me to get next to the one who snored all night. He is French and banging on his headboard had little effect. There seems little chance of entente cordiale.

Later in the day I manage to grab the prestigious single bunk, but I now have another problem. The latest bunkroom guest confides that he's had rows both with his boss at work and his girlfriend. He has withdrawn all his money and is 'running away' until it's all spent. The trouble is, he wants a shoulder to cry on – and doesn't he go on! It's all right being a Samaritan, but I can't get a word in edgeways.

Flek is quick off the mark: 'Remember, Col, someone once said "It's a bitter pill swallowing one's own medicine," or something like that!'

'Flek, you get so personal sometimes – it could affect our relationship.'

A door opens. Oh, no! The Frenchman is back!'

My secret weapon to counteract all annoyances is the iPod. Let me see: some Oscar Peterson, Beethoven, J.S Bach and Gerry Mulligan should do it.

DAY 204
22nd July – Second rest day – SYHA Ullapool

I have a late breakfast and loaf about all day. First I follow the loch-side path around the harbour. In the town I go into the North West Outdoors outfit: they sell bandanas. Competitively priced, these head-bands are the ideal alternative to wearing a hat, but I've already 'misplaced' two of them. Although it's not intended to be waterproof this headwear is warm and can be folded into many useful wearing shapes. What's more it provides an identity – some might call it posing! From today I am to wear one of these for the rest of the Walk. In fact I believe that I'm still on the *bandanashop .com* website wearing their paisley Kauai Buff design.

'*Oh very continental I'm sure, ducky,' jests a jealous Flek.*

'*Flek, that is a typical view of the Brits, whose millions of years in isolation on this off shore island make it difficult for them to express themselves sartorially.'*

After a pub lunch I watch the ferry casting off for Stornaway: wish I were going. Back at the hostel a couple of Harley Davison riders have moved in. Dutch, they maintain the image of Vikings and ride vintage bikes on which they bestow constant attention. I'm intrigued as one of them unreels an oil-stained roll, selects a tool and, like a surgeon, carries out the daily ritual of setting the tension on the extended suspension forks.

Threatening as they like to appear, I don't think they could muster a pillage between them!

It's brightening up, so I sit outside with a *Telegraph* and soak up the view for the last time. I must be away very early in the morning, as the next stage is over twenty miles. Keeping a close watch on my diet I've purchased a hermetically sealed cheese sandwich plus plenty of bananas, and chocolate bars/biscuits for the journey!

Rest day relaxation, SYHA Ullapool.

DAY 205

23rd July – Ullapool to Inchnadamph – 18 miles

I creep out of the hostel at 7am: not even the wardens have turned up yet. The A835 rises gently out of the town and I stroll along, the early morning vista glorious with verges drenched in summer flowers. The morning soon becomes a never-ending slog as I pass through the hamlets of Ardmair, Strathcanaird, Knockanrock and Elphin.

I don't suppose I meet more than three lone walkers on isolated roads during the months away.

'Hang on, Col, here comes one now,' spots Flek.

Tanking along is a German girl looking hot and very flustered in full kit. Maintaining her march, she yells, 'Ullapool?'

I yell back, 'Another eleven miles!' I haven't got the heart to tell her in k's. She sweeps by without so much as an 'auf wiedershen'.

After a gruelling fifteen miles a couple of blokes renovating a cottage instantly stand down for a tea break and include me. Sandy, the old boy, is a plumber and has come thirty miles from the East Coast to do some pipe strangling (plumber's expression) for James. The latter has met a local girl and moved up from Somerset to get married and settle here. We sit in the sun and chew the fat.

Shortly I enter Sutherland. Its mountains ahead are beginning to impress. It's often described as a wilderness, but within a short distance a café appears. At the foot of a sheer rock wall, it's run by a couple who sold up everything in Lancashire to set it up. Good for them. I enjoy a nice snack and a cup of tea – for a change!

On the road it's the hottest day so far. I have now covered eighteen miles and am under continuous attack from horse flies. In military aviation terms, if we regard the midges as Folland Gnats then the horse flies are the B52s, with same amount of strike power.

The heat beats down and I'm in a delirium, but salvation is at hand. A car pulls up and I'm told to get in. Christine and Margaret, who work at the Inchnadamph Lodge hostel ahead, have been asked to look out for me, and I'm whisked along the last four miles for an early shower. They will turn out to be the most helpful staff yet.

This substantial lodge was once a manse: how the clergy lived long ago! Surrounded by spectacular mountain scenery of the Assynt, it provides low-cost accommodation for up to thirty-six people and is regarded the best of its kind in the north-west Highlands.

Now here is a first for me. The lodge has a unisex bunkroom policy. I share my room with two lovely young things, but I haven't got any jim-jams to preserve my modesty Like Baldrick, I dream up a cunning plan, which is to wear all my all-weather gear for protection in bed in case I get ravished.

Flek burst into fits of laughter: 'You ravished! Listen to me, Grandad – you wouldn't understand what they were getting up to. It's too late for you, mate, so dream on, pal!'

There are times when he works wonders for my self esteem!

At meals I make friends with a charming couple, Ian and Gill from Leeds, who listen intently to my CLIMB commitment. What great company they are. Ian works for the homeless and Gill for a cancer charity.

Later, after a precautionary knock on my dormitory door, I slip into a bottom bunk and dream on.

DAY 206
24th July – The Lodge, Inchnadamph Hostel to Scourie – 15 miles

I make my way to the drying room and search in vain for my expensive 'no-odour' underpants. The lodge is full, so the room is choc-a-bloc with everyone else's clobber. Oh well, one pair now has to last me for the final 1,500 miles!

I say goodbye to staff Christine and Margaret and head off up the A837 Lockinver Road. Two miles out I fork right onto the A884 road to Kylesku, which follows a tumbling burn.

I'm not the only singleton about today.

'Hey up, Col – who's this character trundling along?' exclaims Flek. 'He looks a bit odd.'

Approaching is a man in wet-weather gear and long wellingtons. Around him, like a bandolier, is what seems to be a piano accordion. As he draws near I can see that it's a large metal-leafed filing-fact recording system. He is also carrying a catch net in each hand.

'Hello, what you up to?' I enquire.

'I am ze here to make ze vole count,' he answers in a thick accent.

'You sound a long way from home for such research,' I remark. 'Are there many voles up here then?

'I am from Norway and studying at Edinburgh University. Voles? Zere are bloody hundreds of them!'

It's comforting to hear that his English is improving.

Struggling to share his ecological interest, I ask him if the mink have arrived from the south. He shudders at the thought.

'No, zey are not hear yet, thank Got.'

Then he trolls on down the road – well, he is Norwegian!

After visiting a welcome café I stroll into Kylesku and across the magnificent curved bridge which straddles the junction of the sea loch Chairn Bhain and two other lochs, Grendhu and Glencoul. Opened by the Queen, it's a masterpiece of simple design but dramatic effect.

On the other side, a lone car is parked up. Its passengers have opened a bottle of red, and they kindly offer me a glass. At the top of a long and laborious ascent I reach a viewpoint. Some Polish bikers are taking a break. I stop to admire their Honda Redwing machines, one of them having rare white fairings.

The road undulates and is endless, and I'm getting short of water. Suddenly my two friends from the Lodge hostel, Ian and Gill, turn up in their car. They're returning to the hostel and immediately offer their water, also volunteering to take my rucksack back many miles to Scouries campsite from whence they've just come. It's a wonderful gesture.

I can now turn on the gas. A couple of miles on they arrive back from their good deed. To my utter surprise Gill has brought me back a dark chocolate Magnum ice cream, my favourite. What a couple of pals! I take their photo.

The Scouries camping site is well appointed, with great views across the bay of the same name. The weathered elderly owner directs me on to a nice flat patch to pitch on and waives the charge. An excellent restaurant on site provides a substantial meal.

25th July – Scourie to Richonich Hotel – 10 miles

I have a fitful sleep due to a strong wind blowing up the bay, causing the tent to flap noisily. Up early, I prepare my normal simple breakfast of porridge and biscuits and take to the road.

The geographical mass at the top of Scotland now leans to the north-east. This is a well-built road with steady holiday traffic, much of it camper vans from the Continent. I stop by a lochen to take in some lunch, chatting to a Belgium couple.

The sun beats down, so I have to take the severe inclines at a very steady pace. The road is modern and wide with little traffic, and it seems to stretch into the distance like the yellow brick road. Bikers roar by and usually acknowledge me: in this landscape their speed is deceptive. They appear to be just cruising along but must be passing at over a ton.

'They get an exhilerating ride out here,' says Flek, obviously envious of the freedom.

I agree. but have to remind him that despite the long, straight, clear roads (or perhaps because of them) there are still many fatal motor cycle accidents.

Eventually the Rhiconich Hotel appears. It looks oddly out of place. I am warmly welcomed by two lads in their twenties who are running the business for their mother. Eamon and Liam fix me up with a room at a reduced rate.

In the bar an old boy, local journalist Andrew Marshall, buys me a pint. It seems odd that such a sparsely populated area sustains his occupation. He is well known, having recorded much local history.

To capture the stunning views. the dining room is located upstairs. As I wander in for a meal a lady at the next table introduces herself as Phillipa Goodall, confiding that she is taking short break with her dog from everyday life. She has had her troubles with a divorce and four children, one of whom has sadly passed away.

Noticing my charity T-shirt, she asks me whether I am representing CLIMB at Crewe, founded by Peter and Lesley Greene. I confirm that I am, and she tells me that Peter was her French teacher at school. The world is getting inexorably smaller.

Settled in bed, I resort to my iPod for entertainment. The Evening Concert comprises 'Requiem', Lennie Tristano's tribute to Charlie Parker; 'One Note Samba' with Dizzy Gillespie; 'Pick Up The Pieces' by The Average White Band; and Fool If You Think It's Over' by Chris Rea. My Wish Track is 'I'm Alright' by Free.

Highland fishing bailiff.

This is going to be special day as I will be arriving at the top north-west corner of Great Britain – or almost! As I didn't arrive at Cape Wrath as planned, I intend to put that right tomorrow.

After an initial climb, the terrain flattens out into a shallow valley, and expansive views open up. This road has changed to 'narrow with passing places', a classification often used in the Highlands. Road signs are placed to advise traffic where to pass, and there are poles which give an indication during the winter of how deep the snow is drifting.

There are just a few signs of life. Landmarks include Gualin House, which has the only trees for miles planted around it as a windbreak. The odd remote farmhouse is just visible, and at the Drochaid Mhor Bridge stands what must be the remotest red telephone box in the country.

Flek makes a point which confirms he is not into technology.

'How can that be connected to anything?' he demands. 'I mean, you're going to need a very long wire!'

The valley terminates as I approach the head of the Kyle of Durness. Not far to go now. I pass the turning to the ferry I will catch tomorrow for Cape Wrath.

I finally walk into Durness over 800 miles from home. The Lazy Crofter Bunkhouse will be my home for two nights. This is Clan Mackay country, and in the adjoining hotel I find Fiona Mackay, who books me in without charge. One of her South African waiters takes a photo outside, and then I enter the detached but noisy bunkhouse block. It's going to be an interesting couple of days.

A dozen Jocks are staying for the weekend. They come from a town called Auckinleck, which is between Ayr and Kilmarnock, and arrived packed in three cars for a fishing and walking break. Some hopes of that! This lot are mostly ex-miners. Among them is a landlord (John, who does all the cooking) and, believe it or not, one of them has a ladies' hairdressing salon.

It soon becomes obvious that their true purpose is to get away from the 'hens' indoors and get p.....d! They are amiable, likeable and generous. feeding me with an evening meal on both nights. They even have a whip-round and collect £30 for CLIMB. Forced to sit around waiting for the one pub here to open, they congregate on the veranda decking and volunteer their 'Glasga' patter. I nod, acknowledge and laugh at their constant jokes and argument but, as with my previous experience at Port William a few weeks ago, I am unable to decipher their meaning. The patter has beaten me again.

I quote the following exchanges. (Well, I *think* this is what they said):
'No work til Mundae. We're away from the hens, ya beauty.'
'Big eat-ath-breid's snaffled the last yum-yum.'
'Ah tell ye tae go afore but naw ye never bothered your shirt.'
'Crash us a fag, will yer' or geis another daub a yer pie.'
'Got you'er arse in parsley?'

Of course, reading it is one thing, but listening and interpretating are a wee more baffling. My advice is to use the same acumen as the Bletchley Park decoders, i.e. imagine you are completing a crossword puzzle!

Soon it's opening time, and with 'Ah'll see youz after' they all tramp down to the pub for 'A reit bucket the noo!'

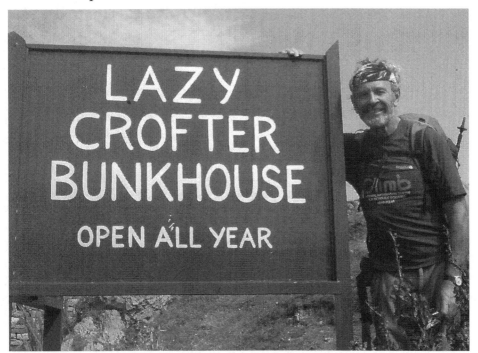

Durness – 800 miles from home.

DAY 209
27th July – Durness to Cape Wrath return to Durness – 24 miles

I have breakfast with my guttural friends, then walk the two miles down to the ferry that crosses the Kyle of Durness for Cape Wrath. I meet Graham from Warrington, and we strike up a friendship. The ferry chugs across to pick us up. The ferryman jokes – will he have enough fuel to return us? – which draws faint laughter from the waiting passengers. This stops when he asks them to part with a fiver. On the other side a people-carrier awaits: we cough up another nine pounds.

It's ten miles to the Cape. The driver is full of merry quips as we speed along. The bumpy track was first laid down for the Stephensons when they were building the lighthouse in 1828. Four generations of this amazing engineering family built eighteen lighthouses. Robert Louis Stephenson was a scion of the third generation.

Someone asks what the high chequed poles at intervals along the route are for. The joking driver tells us that this is a NATO Bombing Range and *thinks* there are no red flags flying today! The poles, he says, are well marked to ensure that the Yankie pilots reach the target, which is an island down the coast. The faint laughs expand to chuckles.

'Oh, don't worry about our speed, we don't get traffic cops over here very often,' he chatters on, hurling the battered vehicle across a narrow bridge. Anguish replaces laughter.

Flek is not impressed, and with a naivety that stretches one's patience to the limits he sputters, 'I don't think that joking about the American pilot's competence helps the "special relationship" which is supposed to bond us together. So if they miss their targets, who is going to notice it up here?'

Our driver stops at a clearance where the local school once stood: it closed in 1947. It's hard to imagine the crofters' children battling across this wild plain in all weathers. At last we reach the Cape.

Now, I always imagined that this was a place where wearing full oil-skins and a southwester were obligatory. What a let-down: there's hardly any wind and the noise of breakers below the massive cliffs is just perceptible. No roar today– the Cape is purring like a pussycat.

Cape Wrath is the most north-westerly point in Great Britain. The name is Norse for 'turning point', and the Vikings veered north for home here.

We have only an hour to explore the coastline. There is a lighthouse (now automatic), a sort of museum and abandoned Coastguard cottages. The cliffs just south of here are the highest on the Brtitish mainland. On our return we note numerous seals basking on sand bars in the Kyle

Graham gives me a lift back to Durness. where the Jocks are 'sponsoring' the pub to record takings for the year. We talk over a pint – he's another bloke escaping domestic problems at home. Bored teenagers are hanging around outside as we leave. They have all the open and rugged terrain to explore, but they are an awful long way from anywhere up here

Graham departs, and I walk a mile to view a local oddity – the large Smoo Cave often seen on Google as a UK must-visit. I get provisions from the Spar shop and later walk out to the Baknakeil Craft Village forged out of an old army camp. With little or no passing tourist traffic I wonder how the traders ever make a living – except, that is,for the chocolate making workshop and café.

I settle down with a book I have found and listen to some music. Mendelssohn's 'Fingal's Cave' is appropriate, followed my Miles Davis leading into 'Freddie Freeloader' on his Kind of Blue album.

I turn in, waiting for the inevitable boisterous return of the Jocks. They joke away in the kitchen down the corridor for an hour or so. The most inebriated of them has, of course, got the top bunk next to me. He enters, muttering a wide selection of profanities, hauls him self up with great difficulty, grunting and expelling air, gives us a song, has a talk to himself and finally passes out – much to the relief of myself and a mysterious woman huddling in silence on another top bunk in the corner.

It's 3.30 am.

At Cape Wrath.

DAY 210

28th July – Durness to SYHA Tongue – 29 miles

It's early and the Jocks are already up. Despite their heavy evening at the pub they are having their eggs and bacon by 7.30am. With military precision they are all packed up and in the cars by eight, and I wave them off.

I step off as I have a long day, though little do I realise how long it is going to be. The weather deceives with its mist, the warning of a very hot day to come.

This is the start of my journey across the top of Scotland, which will take only six days to complete. This is surprising when you think that it took nearly fifty days for me to walk the south coast.

By 9.30 the mist abates and Loch Eriboll appears. This massive sea loch penetrates inland for six miles, which means it will take five hours to complete the twelve-mile round trip. The loch was the scene of a mass surrender of German U-Boats at the end of the Second World War.

The sun is really beginning to burn. To my utter surprise and delight I find a café. At first is looks closed, but I go round the back to find the proprietor sitting down reading a newspaper. He is immaculately dressed in full whites, including a baker's trilby: it is all a little unreal. Is he expecting a health inspector out here? I buy some lunch and chat to a group of cyclists. Moving on down the loch, I'm under continuous attack from horseflies. It's a good mile round the causeway at the end of the loch which leads back up the other side.

At the top of a rise I come to a viewpoint car park. In a lone camper van are Paul, Joan and Melissa a family from Hatton in Derbyshire: he reminds me of Rab C. Nesbitt. With the heat, my water supply is getting low.

'Can you help me? I'm short of water,' I plead.

'Fancy a Stella?' says Paul, who can just fit behind the steering wheel. He hands me a cold can of the nectar. Seeing that it didn't touch the sides he utters the immortal words, 'Fancy another one?'

This happy-go-lucky family are enjoying a great getaway in their chaotically furnished van. I am not with them long but it's been a joyous encounter.

As I move off Flek says, 'Blimey, mate, you fell on your feet there. A couple of chilled Stellas – what luck! The nearest pub must be at least fifteen miles away.'

The road undulates with alarming regularity and eventually swings away from the loch, bringing me to the hamlet of Hope Lodge. I have planned to rough camp here, but there's no suitable place to pitch. I knock on a door for a water supply. The lady is a gamekeeper's wife and we discuss the idea of carrying on to Tongue. She tells me that it's another nine miles to go, and adds that the first three miles are uphill! The road sign confirms the mileage. It's 6pm on a gorgeous sunny evening.

Flek speaks out: 'Colin, you've done twenty miles – so what? You're always spouting on about the prowess of those legs of yours. It's another nine miles. Now give them a good walk out, and the best of luck!'

I ring the warden at the Tongue YHA. He confirms a bed for the night, so I set out on the lengthy initial incline.

Joan, Paul and Melissa, Loch Eriboll.

Barring any injury, limbs can be made to persevere, but I have to call upon old-fashioned 'fortitude' to will my way to the top. The road levels out at last and proceeds across a barren moor. The setting sun's rays are impinging on the tips of the Sutherland Mountains away to my right, producing a magical pink hue – a wondrous sight which keeps me going.

A solitary car goes by. This moor goes on and on. but at last I begin the graudual two-mile descent towards Tongue. I finish my last water and struggle across the causeway to the SYHA. It's July, but I haven't seen a soul for hours.

I stagger in at 9.30pm and am cordially greeted by John, the warden and his wife. She bakes and sells cakes. I help myself to three and go into the kitchen and slurp several mugs of tea. Collapsing on my bed after a shower, the realisation sinks in that I have completed twenty nine miles in thirteen hours, not to mention the elevations, on a boiling hot day carrying thirty pounds. It turns out to be the longest trudge of the year.

'Col, you did it and I'm proud of you.' Flek is magnanimous with his praise, but adds, 'Now promise me there'll be no repeat act.

'By the way, you've won yourself a rest day tomorrow. You deserve it – and so do I.'

I sleep for ten hours.

I have now entered the shipping weather forecast area Fair Isle.

On the Road

*'The fight is won or lost far away from witnesses out there on the road,
long before I dance under the lights'*
— Muhammad Ali

Half of my journey in 2008 was spent 'On the Road'. I can't pretend that the experience bore any resemblance to that of Jack Kerouac's adventures portrayed in the book which influenced the so called post war 'beat' generation.

His agenda of 'seizing the day,' living life free from the constraints of a higher belief, or any notion of ideology, while capitulating at the same time to the joys of sex, drugs and jazz were way-out in the 1950s, even if only that they threatened the end of the American dream.'

That's all very well, but for me any spiritual deliverance means that I shall only salvage 'jazz' from his philosophy.

Walking the highways is, of course, not a satisfactory alternative to following national tracks or footways around the land. Long distance walkers have to weigh up the pros and cons of their strategy. The major principle for me was to keep to the schedule. I did some reading, but in no way was I an expert on what to expect when trudging the highways. I soon became one!

The main advantages of 'being on the road' I found were:
• I could keep to time and honour the schedule for the host family dates
• Navigation exercises were seldom necessary
• Sustenance was usually readily available.

The disadvantages:
• Loss of freedom, abstaining from the lure of the countryside and thereby bypassing some stretches of the coastal routes
• It's tough on the feet, especially when on concrete or asphalt with a camber
• The hazards of treading along uneven grass verges with hidden drainage gullies and discarded bottles etc cannot be avoided
• Last, but not least, is the threat of traffic and associated human man error.

I developed my own Highway Code. The golden rule is to always place yourself in a position where you can be seen by traffic at the earliest opportunity. Pause and think – never be in a hurry to expedite a decision. With this in mind I adopted another practice familiar to my Southern Trail walkers and proceeded 'in a single file with no talking', not even to Flek.

I often failed to notice hard pavement refuges on the other side of roads because the local authority hadn't t cut the grass.

I recall Ken Dodd's old Music Hall joke: 'I had a sheltered upbringing, Mrs –,you know, mainly in bus shelters.'

These little havens of protection from the elements were often of great comfort to me. (Sad, isn't it?)

I did take some chances and got away with it, but I must have got something right because I was rarely harassed by motorists and only occasionally beeped by lorry drivers.

I was helped by the introduction of the Sustrans National Cycle Route, mainly incorporated in conjunction with new road schemes – just as well, as there are road routes across the country which are a no-go for pedestrians. On one occasion I did find myself on a motorway, but that's another story!

Despite their development, I found little use was made of Sustran routes even at weekends. In a country which has sold its soul to motor transport they are much needed avenues of safety for walkers and cyclists alike. It's a concept I became truly grateful for.

Finally there are the 'unacceptable' habits of pedestrians. Call me a prude, but I take a dim view or people eating or drinking while walking in the street.

This attitude irritated Flek who often asked, 'What's the harm? Just how prejudiced can you get?'

What I'm referring to is discarded rubbish – my biggest beef when walking the roads of this country. The problem goes mainly unnoticed when motoring, but on foot you see incredible amounts of it. I've heard it said that our nation is developing into 'a rubbish society living in rubbish'.

And another thing: when approaching urban areas I always came across red rubber bands strewn, not only on the pavements, but also in people's driveways. Why do 'posties' do this? Unfortunately the general attitude of so many is clearly reflected in their actions. Their employers seem impotent to act.

Flek was very patient but occasionally couldn't stand any more of my carping.

'Col, I'm going to have to call you Victor from now on if you keep going on like this!'

I can't blame him for his reaction but, when the circumstances demand it, having a good moan is great therapy!

'Yeah, just as long as you keep it to yourself,' he retorts. 'Got it?'

DAY 211

29th July – Rest day – SYHA Tongue

I wake up and cannot move. Enormous effort is required to manoeuvre into a position where I can fall out bed and on all fours, manhandling my body into a sitting position on the bed. This may sound like a long explanation for a simple exercise. Well, I can tell you, it took a long time to complete.

After some stretching I go downstairs. The dining room is empty – I am the last one up. After breakfast I, oh so slowly, walk the mile into Tongue village to get some money and provisions, then go into the renowned Tongue Hotel.

In the very early days this was the most famous hotel in the northern Highlands. It still has an old fashioned air about it. I heard that some acting celebrities were here recently on location and were not impressed with the service. I order tea and toast in the lounge, and the busy staff do keep me waiting. In the meantime I pick up a book which describes Scotland's dark period during the 'clearances', the Duke of Sutherland, who owned the top half of Scotland, being one of the main protagonists.

Two young lads are flopped down at the side of the road. Tony and Greig are on a sponsored cycle ride from Skye to John o' Groats: good for them.

At the hostel I replace lost calories with more cake, take another nap, sort out phone calls, email and do my blog. I am sharing my room with a seasoned visitor and walker from Germany, and we have some informative chat. I then sit in the garden and read the *Telegraph*.

'How on earth do they get the daily papers up to here each day?' Flek ponders. *'It's eight hundred miles from London and the railway never reached here.'*

'That's a good point, my thinking friend. Sorry but I can't help you out on that one.'

I'm forced to escape inside: the midges have been scrambled for a mass attack.

That's my rest day, folks.

DAY 212
30st July – Tongue SYHA to Bettyhill Camp Site – 14 miles

Down to Tongue again – first to the post office to send back maps, and then into the hotel again for tea and toast. Two miles on I come across another tea room. Splendid in its layout, with a gift shop. What a shame the proprietor was so miserable – not a smile.

Flek gets annoyed, 'What an image! The café was deserted. This is a long way from anywhere – he can't afford to offend customers like this'. I agree.

With tea now sloshing around in my ballast tank I settle down to what will be largely an uneventful day. At midday I sit in sun at Borgue Bridge for lunch. Occasional motorbike and camper van traffic drums past me. It's a peaceful spot with a wonderful scenic backdrop.

Relentless Highland roads.

A large roadside information sign appears two miles out of Bettyhill expounding the attractions of the place. We shall see!

I reach this coastal village and pass a pub, getting a raucous reception from those sitting out on the front terrace.

'Do you know, Flek, I have a good mind to throw up a 'reverse Churchill.'

'I know how you feel, Col, but they might be back here tonight and buy you a pint. I'd desist if I were you.'

'Good thinking Flek.'

I settle for a Queen Mum waive. This results in an even louder rumpus.

The village store is a construction of ship lack and corrugated iron. This dilapidation is deceiving" an Aladdin's cave of goodies are piled up within. CLIMB has given me an address, and I seek out the owner of the Craigdhu campsite. She returns from a shopping expedition with her grown up, unresponsive son. Unlike him, I give her a hand to unload. Parting with a fiver, I cross the road descending an access track into a field: a few camper vans have already arrived. It is difficult to find a flat area to pitch. I inspect the toilet/shower block which is in an atrocious condition. How the place has got official approval I do not know.

In the evening I walk down to the pub for a meal which is OK. They say one can always judge a venue by the state of its toilets. That this place is crying out for renovation is a gross understatement.

Standing at the bar I watch the unresponsive son spending his mum's money.

A genial chap called Steve approaches. After finding out what I'm trying to achieve, he tells me he can get me contacts for kit sponsorship. I sound him out and find that he is married with kids. He keeps spouting on about his 'impressive' record in rock climbing achievements. Interestingly his day job is changing the gear box oil at the top of wind farm towers. He leaves the bar, possibly with intent to follow up on his sponsorship proposal, and then disappears. So much for bar talk! I haven't seen the last of him yet, though.

Back at the site the wind gets up, but despite the noise I finally get adequate rest.

Due to the lousy facilities I have opted out of having a shower this morning and elect to remain filthy. After all, this is a state of mind little boys dream about and old men put up with. Anyway, hiking for a considerable period in a semi wilderness seems an ideal opportunity to ditch social responsibilities. I have a complete set of 'no odour' under-garments as a first line of defence. As a back -up I have also developed a four-rule strategy.

On meeting and conversing with anyone I first manoeuvre around them to a downwind position. Secondly, I take up a hands-off stance of at least three metres. Next I keep them talking so that they don't sense the state I am in, and finally give them only two minutes' exposure for questions and then break off the encounter. It all seems to work very well.

Despite the attractions of Bettyhills' white sandy beaches, I'm glad to leave. Into a stiff headwind I strike out on a steady climb for three miles up the winding road. Half way up I spot a modest monument, the

memorial to two separate fishing disasters of 1890 and 1912 that occurred in the local bay. A total of nine men drowned, and eight of them were Mackays.

When I get to the top it is moorland as far as I can see. Caithness is going to be very different from Sutherland; I pass from Mackay Clan territory to the Sinclairs.

I'm resting on the roadside Arco when a car pulls up. It is Steve my erstwhile benefactor from the pub the night before, and he has a young woman with him: she clearly is not the wife he spoke about.

Paul's Enfield: made in India.

'We are on our way to a challenging days rock climbing' he says purposively. After some further chat he wishes me good luck and drives off.

A sceptical Flek chips in: 'Challenging climb? I know what he'll be clambering over later.'

'Now, now Flek, you heard what he said,' I replied naively, concealing any mirth.

A Dutch couple stop their camper van and offer me a lift. I decline and they graciously accept my decision.

I stop to talk to Paul, his Enfield motor cycle on its rest. He tells me the name Royal ceased when they began their manufacture in India.

I've made good progress and reach Melvich by 4pm. The campsite has an excellent shower house and it adjoins a pub, where the locals buy me a pint. The landord is huge and very friendly, in a Herman Munster kind of way, and he drives home to get me a towel! It's one item you never carry on a journey like this. All this bonhomie is topped when the Dutch couple who had offered me a lift earlier turn up. They are Maria and Jan Bussel, and we agree to meet for a meal later. Maria speaks excellent English and is very interested in what I am doing. I share a most pleasant evening with them. .

Tonight only two camper vans, a cyclist with his tent and I share the site. I try to settle down but, God, the ground is hard! I have never got used to the experience. My mind wanders back to an incident of yesteryear and I start to smile.

Several decades ago I was a member of a small group who travelled to Nottingham to take part in the Fire Service National Athletics Championships. Nearly everyone had to sleep on floors of a fire station. Finding myself in the snooker room, I grabbed the only camp bed provided.

Later a small party entered, including John Walker – 'JC' to all his brigade friends. They slid into their sleeping bags and reluctantly settled down on the room's hard tiled floor. The lights were extinguished and after much entertaining banter the room fell silent. Some time had elapsed when suddenly a stoical voice came out of the dark and exclaimed,

'I don't know – this floor has got a little give in it!'

It was JC, and everyone in the packed room burst into laughter.

Of course one had to be there to appreciate the ambience. Perhaps I should explain that hidden behind his sardonic comment, thinly veiled, lay a forbearing British acceptance, e.g. of POW's banged up in Colditz having to put up with a cold shower once a week, or, an end-of-the-pier cast carping in their digs about the poor houses at their shows.

'JC's' tone was vintage Tony Hancock! I fell asleep laughing!

DAY 214
1st August – Melvich to Thurso Campsite – 16 miles

I'm out of provisions but I don't have to worry. Maria and Jan kindly invite me into their van for a continental breakfast. What a lovely couple they are. I give them my card and later I find they have made a donation on the Just Giving Website. I take their photo and get going.

Maria and Jan Bussel from Holland.

I am now at 2,500 miles and still going strong. The early rain stops as I enter the village of Reay. At the store I obtain a welcome big beaker of tea. The village gives its name to the Dounreay nuclear power station that I will be passing shortly. Built in 1951, it was the first enterprise of its kind built in the UK. It's now being decommissioned. The process will take decades, and the site is being revamped as an enterprise development.

The trek across the top of Scotland involves long stretches of straight roads through the featureless coastal plain of Caithness. A wind farm breaks up the monotony. A French couple stop by and offer me a lift. They stare in disbelief as this crazy Englishman, dripping wet, declines their kind offer.

Entering Thurso I pass 'Pennyland House', birthplace of the town's famous son William Smith, founder of the Boys' Brigade. I remember in the fifties on their way to summer camp the Brigade's boys used to pile off the train at Bognor dressed in their makeshift uniforms, i.e. Pillbox hat and body crossband. Their bugle band would form up and blast its way through the town.

This prompted one local to remark, 'Just listen to that racket,' to which his mate replied, 'Well, I suppose it keeps the kids off the streets!'

The movement is still quite active in Scotland.

I book in to the seafront campsite. The lady owner sympathises with my purpose: she has a grandson suffering from a metabolic condition. I seek out Mike Potts, a Rotarian who takes me for a meal and then to his home for tea. His interesting life includes having been a tea plantation manager in Africa.

I return to the site. It's now a beautiful warm evening. Living on the south coast in my early life, it was France directly south that always beckoned sixty miles across the English Channel. Now, eight hundred and fifty miles away, I am looking directly north to the Hoy part of the Orkney Islands just few miles away across the Pentland Firth. To me it poses an amazing contrast, and I fool myself that it's not all that different – but of course it is.

DAY 215
2st August – Rest day – Thurso

After an all day breakfast in the town, I go to get my glasses repaired. Moving on, I sort out a niggling financial problem at the Halifax, which handily is nearby. The town is particularly known for its flagstone industry. Divided by a river, much of it is laid out on a grid system with wide avenues.

Back at the site I meet Barry Slaven from Kirkcaldy, whose tent is nearby. He is a tall lad, a student, and he tells me he terminates his tour tomorrow having become unsure of its purpose. I gather that things at home are not too clever, and he mentions Rachael. There lurks a girl interest, then. Where have I heard all this before?

Anyway, it's gala night, with a procession parading around the town. We pal up for the evening and watch the local boys' pipe band march around the streets, leading a procession of floats on to which everyone hurls their loose change for local charities.

We retreat to a pub crammed with locals and then treat ourselves to haddock and chips. It's been a big night for this town. The local youths, pumped up with testosterone, are generally making a nuisance of themselves. Ah, I remember it well!

Barry is a nice lad, and I do hope he can sort things out at home.

DAY 216
3nd August – Second rest day – Thurso

I get up early and find that Barry has gone. Today I am off to the Orkneys. Unfortunately it's a Sunday schedule for the ferry, so my visit will be short, but I'm going all the same – I might not have the chance again.

Zipping up the tent, I take a brisk two mile walk down to the ferry port at Scrabster. The vessel is immaculately appointed, with all the tourist facilities, and I treat myself to a steak pie dinner aboard followed by coffee in the lounge.

Star attractions on the 90-minute voyage include the incredible stack known as the Old Man of Hoy, standing at 137m. It was first climbed in 1966 by Chris Bonnington, Rustie Ballie and Tom Patey over three days. Further along are the massive cliffs at St John's Head, the highest vertical drop into the sea in Britain.

The boat docks in Stromness harbour. I only have three and half hours to explore the town. As it's a Sunday, the place is very quiet. I wander over paving slabs and cobbles of the streets, and visit the interesting museum. These Islands haven't always been as tranquil as today. Naval history dominates, recording the significant and often tragic consequences of warfare. Four instances stand out.

• The sinking of *HMS Hampshire* in the First World War by a mine laid by a German U-Boat in which Lord Kitchener perished.

• The explosion of a gun battery aboard the battleship *Vanguard*, the force of which propelled a 400-ton gun turret over a mile into a field. Nearly all aboard perished.

• The scuttling of the German Fleet at Scapa Flow in 1918. following conflicting orders given to the German admiral.

• The sinking of the battleship *Royal Oak* at Scapa Flow by U-boat 47 in 1940. which was probably the first major propaganda coup of the Germans in the Second World War.

I wander back to the ferry quay and enjoy a pub lunch watching a young lad in an Astra circling the square hoping to impress girls – who just laugh at him.

On the trip back to Scrabster I am fascinated by the antics of a boisterous stag party. The only lady present is, I presume, the bride-to-be. She gets scant attention: this is unmistakably a noisy boys' party which packs out the bar during the crossing. Participants only emerge on deck for fresh air and to view the scenery . . . No, I don't think so. A fag seems to be their priority.

Back on the mainland I take a last walk around the town and stop to talk to man having a ciggie outside the British Legion. He goes on about the role of the TA. He worked at Dounreay for 35 years and explained that it was an experimental station, with only one turbine putting 127Mw into the Grid – all very interesting.

Just then three men emerge from the Legion's bar. Two are quite chatty: it appears that they have all returned from a Sunday army parade at Wick. The third individual, a Mackay in a kilt, has a pink face and stares directly ahead with unblinking eyes, saying nothing. He can't because he is blotto, only sheer will power keeping him upright.

Flek cuts in, 'It's a good job he did the parade first. Now I know what they mean by being in an alcoholic haze. His "hen" will cut up when he gets home. She's probably downed half a bottle of sherry in readiness for a showdown.'

Finally, before I leave the town, I must mention Thurso's amusing theological incident. In 1860 the Rev Duncan's sermon at a church in the parish went on for so long that all 600 of the congregation were reported to have fallen asleep! Has his 'fire and brimstone' warning garnered repentance? It appeared not.

I am now going to embrace the legacy of his parishioners: goodnight!

Stromness, Orkneys.

DAY 217

4st August – Thurso Camp Site to Dunnet Camp Site – 8 miles

A short day. I can relax and consume an all-day breakfast. I soon return to the relentless straights of the Caithness main roads. In Castletown I slurp some excellent soup in a hotel and spoil myself reading the *The Scotsman* before moving on. At last the road starts to curve for several miles, skirting behind the sand dunes of Dunnet Bay.

The campsite is of a high standard. The manager's wife was born in Chiswick (I lived there for some time), and she is a long way from her mum, who lives in Hunston near to my home at Chichester. The couple kindly lend me a towel.

It's very windy and I have a difficult time in getting the tent up. I settle for a 'first course' of dehydrated beef with rice and, for my 'sweet', Cadbury's fruit and nut. Tent flapping nullifies a selection of music: I am in for a disturbed night.

DAY 218

5th August – Dunnet Bay campsite to John O' Groats campsite – 14 miles

It's overcast but warm, just right for trudging some more straight roads! I have come to the conclusion that no one knows better than me how dispiriting it is to follow straight highways, through a barren landscape, that constantly disappear over the horizon.

I take a diversionary walk out to Dunnet Head. Why? Because, it happens to be the most northerly point in Great Britain.

Returning to the main road, I stop at the Mey Hotel, which is quaint and old fashioned. Cosy and warm, it's an ideal place to get a sandwich and a pot of tea.

Just up the road is the entrance to the Castle of Mey, the Queen Mum's favourite holiday home.

Passing a ferry terminal to the Orkney's, I plod onto Canisbay and enter the church where the Queen Mum worshipped. She loved its simplicity, and it certainly had that. T-shaped, with a two-tier pulpit and almost completely void of any adornments, it's stark and to the point.

Finally, after seven months, I reach John o' Groats, which is thought by many to the most north-easterly point of Great Britain, but isn't quite. Opposite a lock up garage (it must be the smallest fire station in the UK), a man services his Rover car. His sense of purpose demands a salutation.

'That's a nice old wagon, a reminder of the car industry we used to have,' I cheerfully articulate.

'That may be,' he says, 'but it is a bloody long way to go and get spare parts.'

'Never come between a man and his car,' pontificates Flek. 'He's from the old school and probably still sets the points and plugs. That lot are completely dismissive of the modern electronic and digital rubbish that make up car engines today. They're in a time warp and you know what. . . .'

'Yes, yes all right, Flek, don't go on old chap. By the way, haven't you grasped the significance yet of where we are?'

He falls silent – in awe, I think!

John o' Groats is named after a Dutchman who obtained a dispensation to run a ferry from the Orkneys in 1496.

The first task is to get photo shot done in the official compound and its famous marker post. Apart from the detail it's the same set-up as at Land's End. Both 'corners' of the Land, 874 miles apart, are served up by the same photography outfit. The chosen shots will be mailed on. This is the most popular test of sponsorship in GB and undertaken by countless individuals each year.

Now on to the campsite, which is across the large visitors' car park. The elderly owners are so friendly. I pitch my tent with great views out to Duncansby Head, the *true* north-east corner of GB. I go in search of a meal. Before me, around the carpark, is a string of cafe's and tat shops. There is no covered way here as in Land's End. The 'Disney' turreted hotel is shut, and efforts to renovate it have never materialised. In short the place is functional, but featureless.

It has got cold, and I curse my sleeping bag decision back at Fort William. So it's on with all my spare cloths to keep warm.

'Serves you right, Col, what were you thinking of?'

'What do they say about hindsight, Flek?'

At John o' Groats.

DAY 219

*6th August – Rest day – John O' Groats to Duncansby Head
and return – 6 miles*

Lesley Greene of CLIMB calls and asks me to abandon the second Rest day. An alternative strategy is required to get me back to the hosts' schedule.

I heat up some porridge. I'm hungry and cold, so to complete my breakfast I devour a breakfast at the better of the cafés. Today I will walk the three miles along coastal path to Duncansby Head. There are white sandy beaches here, washed by a chrystal clear tide. To the north are the turbulent Pentland Firth, the Island of Stroma, the Orkneys and the Skerries.

Built by David Stevenson, the lighthouse at the Head is unusual. as it is square and is only 11m in height.

Duncansby Head, the real north-east corner of Great Britain.

Walking on past a bungalow I can see to the south the dramatic pointed 'Stacks of Duncansby'.

'Fancy living right at most north-easterly point, Col,' says Flek. 'Don't rush it today – take it all in now. Ask that bloke over there to take your photograph.'

I did.

Karol Eager has been in touch. She's contacted Jonathan Manning, the editor of *Country Walking*, who is interested in placing an article re Walk GB 4 Climb. (Details were to go through Lesley at CLIMB, but nothing was finalised in the end: pity.)

On my return to camp I cook up a bacon-and-lentil dehydrated meal which is quite tasty. In the late afternoon I stroll up the road to the Seaview pub for a pint. While I'm in in there a Tornado screams across the rooftop. People get used to calls from the RAF up here.

After the noise abates Flek remarks, 'I couldn't see them putting up with that in Tunbridge Wells, could you, Col?'

On my return to camp I am still hungry, so I opt for you know what!

'What kind of diet do you call this?' worries Flek.

'Well Flek, it's a gastronomic advance on the Romans.' (Trying to fend off his direct comment.) 'They started their day with porridge – no sugar as it hadn't been invented yet – and sour wine. Apparently Caesar had the same. Later in the day it was bread with anything they could lay their hands on. Don't worry, I'm walking all these calories off every day, am I not?'

'You do talk a load of cods wallop, Colin. Just like a politician, you've laid a smoke screen – that is, you never answered my question. With talent like that I can see you getting on Dimbleby's Question Time. By the way, you're always talking about using a Wish List, so how's this for my panellists: Germaine Greer, Kelvin McKenzie, George Galloway, Boris Johnson and the BNP's Nick Griffin (Arthur Scargill can't make these days). Stand by for fireworks, eh?'

I have a warmer night thanks to the milder weather.

Those Tattoos

'If the body is a temple, then tattoos
are its stained glass windows.'
—Vince Hemingson

I was sitting in a pub one day when a couple of lads walked in, their arms covered with the latest designer tattoos.

'What do you think of those?' said Flek, deliberately seeking out a discriminatory answer. I didn't disappoint him.

'What I can say, Flek, is that I accept being tattooed is certainly traditional. My Dad 'inherited' a couple of modest designs on his arms after going ashore in the Royal Navy. However, my view is that tattooing has got out of hand. They are now just pathetic fashion symbols of non-conformity sported around with monotonous regularity. Anyway, the daring ones are nearly always out of sight. Fifty percent of those so marked eventually want them removed. Did you know that?'

I had caught Flek on the back foot. Spluttering, he said he didn't.

'I mean, the skin eventually wrinkles, distorting the designs, and, of course, circumstances change. For instance, in time the ink-stained term of affection for 'Doris' may have to be changed in favour of 'Sandra'— painful! The common thread is that tattoos often become the marks of regret. There again, I could be a tad prejudiced!'

'What a flipping understatement, Col. You're just being a killjoy, completely out of touch,' Flek argued, trying to recover from my pious onslaught. 'This body art form was developed as an icon of tribal identity, like an army cap badge, so what's your beef? I think if anyone is unsure of spoiling their skin then the use of temporary transfers would be a much cheaper option. Any long term problem could be completely erased.'

'What an excellent solution, Flek — you have the potential for gaining a City and Guilds in Body Design. You hit the nail right on the head, though, classifying tattooing as a way of maintaining tribes, like bikers, power lifters or train spotters!'

'Fortunately, my friend, humour lurks within this human frailty. I remember the popular cartoons of Popeye the Sailor Man. In one episode he is about to beat off his sworn enemy Bluto who is giving his girl friend Olive Oyl to much attention. His usual ploy is to produce from nowhere a tin of spinach which he swallows in one gulp. The vegetable has magic qualities; the effect is that his muscles swell up to Mr Universe proportions to deter his opponent. The spinach dramatically changed the butterfly tattoo on his chest into an air force bomber with the propellers on it four engines clearly revving up. Now that's what I call a tattoo!'

'Oh that's just fantasy. Col. Anyway, be practical: the idea wouldn't work today,. The pods of jet engines couldn't demonstrate the same effect'.

He had fallen for that one. Now somewhat flummoxed by our discourse he admitted that his father had never been in the navy.

I finished my pint and we called it a day, leaving the lads still trying to impress some giggling girls. I had to press on.

7th August – John o' Groats to Skirza – 5 miles

Giving up my second rest day, I'm to walk the five miles down the A99 to Skirza. Here I shall tent in Ronnie and Lynn Ball's garden at their home on the coast. Lynn has insisted that I first pay a visit to Patchwork Pleasures, Caithness, a regular quilting class she holds in the Old School Hall at Skirza before I walk onto their house.

I book out of the site, the owners refunding their original charge, and then the moment I have been waiting for! At the road leading from the complex I look at the compass. It has swung round ninety degrees and is now pointing south: I am on my way home. I still have over a thousand miles to go, BUT it's in the right direction and at last I shall have the sun in my face.

For the umpteenth time I hoist on the rucksack and move forward with purpose.

I get a hundred yards up the road and a cyclist careers towards me. He is on the last knockings of his sponsored ride from Land's End. Seeing me he assumes that I have just started the same project in the other direction and stops, presumably to wish me luck.

'Just started?' he enquires, a little triumphant.

'Well, not quite' I reply.

'In case you've forgotten, it's 874 miles to Lands End,' he says smugly. 'Thought I would cheer you up,' he ventures with a smile.

'Well, since you asked, I've still got another thousand miles to go. I've already covered three thousand miles – I'm walking round Great Britain.'

He blinks and rides off without saying another word.

Flek scolds me: 'What a poser you are, Colin. That was a bit over the top, for God's sake.'

'Well, he started it,' I blurt out, sounding like a schoolboy who has just been pulled out of a playground fight by the duty master. 'Frankly I couldn't resist it.'

I go up the road chuckling to myself, much to the Flek's disgust.

Today's mileage is soon eaten up. Skirza is a community over a mile from the A99, scattered on a gentle slope towards the sea – a wonderful peaceful location in stunning scenery. I find the Old School Hall and am met by Lynn, who introduces me to the lady students attending her Patchwork Pleasure class. Many of them have come a long way to absorb her skills.

They prepare a lunch and Lynn has included me. We sit down to carrot and feta cheese soup with fresh rolls, followed by white chocolate cheesecake. Lynn kindly gives me a chance to explain my adventure and we have photos taken. It's a memorable lunch hour.

I walk down to Skirza House, a former pilot boat skipper's house which has its own stone jetty: the waves are crashing in from a deep blue sea. Lynn's husband Ronnie is having a sleep in the sun but wakes to welcome me. He is a lean man with a weathered face. He talks with a heavy brogue and is a Caithness man through and through with, by inference, little time for the English.

He makes me a cup of tea and shows me his vegetable garden created out of nothing between the house and the sea wall. Also he proudly points out an extensive dry-stone wall which took him several years to complete, the stones selected from the foreshore. With its setting so near to the sea wall, its stone jetty and the backdrop of the rugged Caithness

Lynn Ball's patchwork class at Skirza.

coastline I have little hesitation in stating that this is probably the most stunning residential location I encountered on the whole walk.

Ronnie, a former policeman in the Caithness force, carved out a second career as a security officer at the Dounreay Power Station. We talk a lot and he tells me about the pilots who rowed out from the Jetty to catch the ships. Some, he tells me, were unable to disembark after their duties were done and were fated to complete the whole voyage! He is scathing about the English habit of using prohibition road signs anywhere or everywhere. At first his dialect is difficult to understand (I hear the Norse influence), but once I'm on board I find him a very interesting to converse with.

Lynn returns from her class and we finish off the remnants of the Old School Hall lunch.

I make several phone calls. one in particular to John Hutchinson (my host at Fort William), who is setting up a meeting with the Highlands fire master at Inverness

I retire to my tent in the garden a contented man, and play some music.

The Evening Concert includes more of Dag Wiren's 'Serenade for Strings', Dave Brubeck's 'Balcony Rock' and Oscar Peterson's 'Hymn to Freedom'. For my Wish track I go for Jimmy Shand and his White Heather Club Band. Lots of reeling inside my sleeping bag would get my feet warm – at the moment they are freezing.

DAY 221

8th August – Skirza to Wick Caravan and Camping Site – 12 miles

Ronnie runs me up to the A99. He needs to get his newspaper from a tiny shop on the Wick road Its proprietor is a diminutive, smiling, silver-haired man who must be in his eighties. In retail terms the shop is as basic as it gets. Shelves hold small quantities of tin food, tea and sugar etc. He still uses the old-fashioned cash draw, its coin compartments worn down and shiny with decades of use. Nevertheless, this courteous old boy provides a vital service to this much scattered community, and nothing emphasises his role more than the recent installation of two stainless steel petrol pumps standing out in the open with just a fire extinguisher for company. This is the bleakest gas station you are ever likely to pull into, but you get a wonderful view of the rolling Caithness terrain while filling up here!

I shake hands with Ronnie and begin a long association with at first the A99 and then the improved A9. On the seaward side in the distance I notice several castles. Without previous knowledge it is often difficult to differentiate between the ancient ones and Victorian 'pseudo' fortifications.

At Keiss I find a public toilet. I've never really been able to shake off the early morning 'running nose' syndrome, and so this is the umpteenth time I go in and help myself to lavatory (I use this word deliberately, it sounds so British and effortlessly 'rolls' off the tongue) paper.

I pass a farm and observe farmhands using a dozen vehicles frantically reaping in the harvest – they've heard that dire weather is forecast for tomorrow.

In Wick I pop into Tesco's for lunch, and on my way out I pick up a couple of apples. Courageously I select one of the self-help 'fast lane' outlet machines. They are all right if you have a bar code on your purchase, but I hadn't. Unknown to me, fruit has to be weighed separately. Soon I find myself floundering as the machine relentlessly barks orders at me.

'You had better press the panic button, Col – a restless queue has built up behind you,' beams Flek.

Staff member Zoe appears on the scene to rescue the situation. To shrug off embarrassment I tell her she has made an old man very happy. The smirks in the queue now change to raised eyebrows, and I beat a hasty retreat.

'The trouble is, Col, you appeared in the store kitted out like Bear Grylls only to be defeated by nothing more than a slot machine.'

I thought I had got used to his barbed criticisms, but they still hurt.

I press on through the town, get on to the campsite, book on and locate a communal washroom. I chat to a man who enquires whether I have ever walked round the Isle of Wight.

'Yes, on many occasions actually,' I reply.

He isn't impressed, so I ask him, 'Do you live there then?'

'Yes, at Whippingham near Cowes. Why?' he says.

'I've got a cousin who lives there,' I explain. 'His name is Terry Lashley. Do you know him?'

'Well, I never – he lives just a couple of doors away from us,'he gasps.

Flek interjects, 'Blimey, Col, that's yet another coincidence – they just keep occurring. It's all slightly spooky, man.'

The camper goes on, 'I'm Ian McDonald. When you get a chance come across to look over the van and meet Linda, my wife.'

He has got his priorities right. I agreed to it, later.

A cyclist pitches his tent close by. He is very disciplined and self-contained. Why can't I be like that?

Even more interesting is a group of young things who fall out of a car and erect a tent for six. Their next move is so predictable.

Flek sums it up: 'Oh dear, they're going to have a barbeque. I bet they've just got it "on offer" at the local B & Q. Let's watch as they smoke their sausages to death instead of cooking them. The British can never crack this outdoor ritual – it's pathetic.'

We watch as the men poke and prod the bangers to little avail. After a couple hours enough smoke had been produced to facilitate an Apache email plus attachment!

Most of them give up and move off, presumably to get a burger in the town, leaving a lonely sentry who keeps raking the embers while reading a book. His eyes seemed transfixed upon its text.

'Bet he's reading The Meaning of Life,' *I proffer idly. 'Flek, it makes sense to know about the purpose and significance of existence.'*

'Get you with the philosophy', he retorts. 'I know all about it anyway, cos I saw the film. The Python team were brilliant.'

Another chance for reflective discussion has been snuffed out.

This is one of the better equipped sites. It has pub tables, making it easier to prepare meals. I have a good night without having to get up. Such triumphs now govern my life!

I have entered the shipping weather forecast area Cromarty.

DAY 222

9th August – Wick Camp Site to Acarsaid B & B Lyster – 10 miles

Before moving off I seek out Ian McDonald and his wife Linda. He shows me round his van, which runs on TLC. He has the undying enthusiasm to keep it going. Beaming with pride, his face says it all.

The weather forecast is bang-on: it always is the further north you go. The day turns out to be one of the most miserable yet. I endure ten miles of the A9 in steady rain and driving wind. There are no shops or pubs out here.

Just before Lybster a white van spooks me and I take a tumble, a nasty moment. There is no indicating sign, so I walk past my B & B ('Arcasaid' 01593 721 275) and enter Lyster village. An old boy stands on a corner. His face is puce and he has a bottle in each pocket.

With Ian McDonald, Wick.

Anxious for directions I foolishly ask him if he lives here.

'Of course I f...... do. Now sod off!' he shouts, and staggers off into what is the 'downtown' area.

My fatigue is worse than I thought. I can't believe that I ask him such an obvious question. I improve when popping into a hotel for directions.

A few minutes later Sheena Millington opens her door to see a sodden individual shuffling down her drive. She diligently tends to me. I can't get into the hot bath quick enough. This is a going to be a huge chalet bungalow – when her husband Norman finishes his lifelong DIY plan.

Over a meal Sheena explains that as they are not trading yet, so I can stay two nights without charge. They will also transport me to and from my route. I am overwhelmed by their generosity: Norman is a big man with a heart to match.

Now for a concert. Lying in a luxury bed, I click onto the first movement of Beethoven's Fifth Symphony, ABBA's 'Thank You for the Music' and Gerry Mulligan's 'Bernie's Tune'.

For my Wish Track I hark back to when I was fifteen. My mother ran a guest house in Bognor Regis and used auction rooms to furnish the letting rooms. One day a job lot arrived that included a wind-up gramophone. I was soon off to get the No.1 Bakelite 78 of its day – Les Paul and Mary Ford's 'How High the Moon'. Remember. in those days it was necessary to fit a new needle in the pick-up for every record. I look back with pride at being around during the birth of technology!

Les Paul was arguably the father of the electric guitar and multi recording. In 1979 'How High the Moon' was entered into the Grammy Hall of Fame.

DAY 223
10th August – Lybster to Berriedale – 11 miles

I have a free day, without the pack. I'm hardly out the village when an old boy stops me, listens to my story, then thrusts a fiver in my hand.

An exited Flek pops up, 'It's a great start, Col. Let's tell people that we are on a pilgrimage, like flogging The Big Issue.

'You're being silly. Anyway, we haven't got a dog!'

Four miles on a café manned by attentive 'dinner lady' volunteers serves up a pot of tea and a cake with a smile.

I come to Dunbeath, which has been spoilt by a necessary flyover. The tiny museum devotes itself to the author Neil Gunn, who was born here. The curator tells me I am today's only visitor.

The village found itself in the national news in 1941 when a Sunderland flying boat crashed into a local hill, killing all the crew including the Duke of Kent.

Plodding on, I descend the steep road, zig-zagging into Berriedale; dodging the lorries becomes critical. I eat my sandwiches at the foot of the impressive war memorial. A McGonagall is listed in the fallen. Whenever I hear this name I see Spike Milligan with a big hat on.

Only a steep hill ascent to go now, finishing at a car park where Norman collects me. I get a call from daughter Sonya, to tell me that her partner Simon Hill has run a golf tournament in memory of his brother and raised £500 for CLIMB. This sum eventually reaches £1000, the highest donation of the year.

In the evening the Millingtons take me out for a sight-seeing tour, first to view Grey Cairns of Camster and then through Lybster village down the widest street in the land (another of those claims) to the harbour. It hosts the World Championships of Knotty – whatever that is.

What a great day. Sheena and Norman are marvellous hosts.

DAY 224

11th August – Berriedale to Helmsdale YHA – 10 miles

I am so reluctant to leave the Millingtons. Sheena had a career in the justice system sorting other people's problems out and finally has had enough. The experience has left her well versed in the politics of Scotland. With Norman, she is changing direction. Having purchased the land and built what will eventually be a substantial chalet bungalow they are now well advanced with their B & B plan. In the meantime he holds down a rep job with the double-glazing firm Everest. They are a very understanding couple and have been so good to me.

She runs me the considerable distance back to Berriedale, and on a fine morning I begin the ten-mile march down the A9 to Helmsdale. An undulating highway, it allows expansive elevated views across the North Sea. I pause at a road side car park to admire the view, when Norman turns up in his company van: he is also going south. From a parked car a man introduces himself to Norman as a former employee of Everest – he was one of the original staff of the fledgling company. The two engage in a mutual natter about its operational history. Norman is having his very own coincidence.

Cheekily Norman offers me a lift, but I desist. I can see Helmsdale and it is all downhill on the vastly improved highway. The hostel, run by Irene Drummond, has excellent facilities. However, there remains the constant problem with most hostels – regardless of the time of year they always issue duvets with a high Tog value, so I use my sleeping bag. I meet some nice people and enjoy my stay.

I am out of Caithness and back in Sutherland.

DAY 225
12th August – Helmsdale Hostel to Dalchalm Caravan Site – Brora
– 11 miles

My iPod is playing up, so I wait until 10am when the local library opens. It's fixed it with the help of the librarian's computer terminal.

This is another ten-mile stint down the A9. I have followed the deep pink foxglove trail up the west coast of Scotland. Now, down the east coast, the same colour prevails, only here it is continuous swaths of rosebay willowherb that provides a calming effect on the relentless highway.

I arrive at the excellent Dalchalm site and I find they are out of milk The warden senses my plight, kindly gifting me half a bottle.

I pick my way through the avenues of posh caravans to the camping area which is on the periphery of the site. It is exposed to the wind out here, and I am to spend a cold night.

No music tonight: I'm just trying to keep warm. After all, it is August!

Rosebay Willowherb.

DAY 226

13th August – Brora Caravan Site to Dornoch Caravan Site – 16 miles

I get breakfast in Brora and follow the A9. Soon the turrets of Dunrobin Castle come into view peaking above its surrounding forest. It is said that these 'fairy tale' structures were the inspiration for the Disney theme parks. The castle is the seat of the Dukes of Sutherland. With 189 rooms, it is the largest house in the northern Highlands.

The next town is Golspie, where I first get some soup and a sandwich, then further up the road some tea and cake.

Flek, bemused by my gluttony, has his say: 'You should write a pamphlet, mate, about the ingestion indulgencies of long distance walkers. This fascinating read could include a whole chapter analysing that age old excuse, "Well what of it – I'm walking off the calories, aren't I?" '

Walking through the town I spot a van with a company trade name BONK displayed in large letters on its bodywork. Despite my sheltered upbringing it attracts my interest.

'You might like to know that my granddad had a similar upbringing Col, so to speak' states Flek. I fear a tirade of trivia is about to follow.

He goes on, 'After the war eight of his family lived in an air raid shelter. Then they got on the council list and were eventually awarded digs in a large bus shelter on the 36A route. It was somewhat cramped, but allowed him to watch the typists queuing up for the bus in the morning going to work. That's how he became a man of the world,' he said.

'Is that it? All very interesting my friend but I must get on.'

At last I filter off the A9 into a lane running alongside Loch Fleet. Here I observe a dozen seals basking on a sand bar and a pair of buzzards hunting for rabbits.

At a campsite I purchase an awful meal, then suddenly realise I am in the wrong place. Curses, I must be losing some marbles. As dusk sets in I trek on a further three miles to the Dornoch caravan site. The error is all I need at the end of an exhausting day.

Once again I have to pick myself through the lines of caravans to pitch on an exposed spot. Rough campers seem to be regarded as the poor relations, generally allocated out-of-sight areas to pitch, a mighty long trek from the toilets.

I am spending another cold night with spasmodic sleep.

It's a comparatively short day. CLIMB's announcement to the Highlands and Islands fire service has got around, so the district fire manager William Scott picks me up and takes me to his home. His wife cooks me breakfast, and with his kids and a dog there is a nice family atmosphere. Until recently William was a district fire officer based at Benbecula and responsible for seven small part time fire stations throughout the Outer Hedbrides. What a posting! All good things come to an end.

He runs me back to Dornoch. It's a nice country town and I wander into the imposing cathedral, which dates back to 1239. Burnt down during some clan wars, it was largely restored in 1616. In December 2000 it was besieged by the world's press and paparazzi, when the eyes of the world descended on this spiritual place to cover Madonna's wedding to Guy Richie. This small community did not know what had hit it!

Darren and Steve, Fornoch Firth Bridge.

On the advice of William, I take a most pleasant short cut from the A9 to arrive at the sleek Dornoch Firth Bridge. When completed in 1991, at 900m in length it was the longest bridge in Europe. Opened by the Queen, it drastically shortens the journey around the Dornoch Firth on the A9.

'We've picked a lovely day to walk across here, Col. I must say the scenery and skyscape are truly spectacular. Eh up! There are a couple of bikers relieving themselves in the Firth. Don't get too agitated, mate – somebody has got to top it up,' says a smiling Flek.

Chatting to them, I find out that Darren and Steve are from Newcastle and we inevitably get onto football. They bemoan United's lack of success and ask me about my affiliations. I'm almost apologetic when mentioning Pompey's triumph at Wembley, but they are most complimentary. I take their photo in honour of the many bikers who have tooted me along the highways.

A call comes in from my kit sponsor. My third pair of boots will be available shortly. However, I get a little peeved when I am being pressed how I am going to pay for them!

'Do they think you are going to leave the country?' sounds out Flek in exasperation. 'They haven't even enquired how you are!'

I pass the site of Tain's Highland Games. Great big hairy men are trying to toss telegraph poles. The sport is very impressive, but entrants do take salt in their porridge. Over the fence can be heard a lone piper who has detached himself to a corner of the field to get tuned up.

Flek winces: 'God almighty, Col, what a racket! It sounds as if he's got his chanter jammed in a gate.'

It's a long, steady climb into Tain. Dave McLeod opens up the fire station for me and explains that they can provide a portable bed. His crew are training this evening and are looking forward to meeting me.

They muster and listen to my story. Later I hop into female fire fighter Karaine Smith's 4x4, and she drops me at the best restaurant in town. She explains that the crew have had a whip-round, hands me twenty quid and tells me to order a meal direct from her friend the proprietor. I do, and have two superb courses.

I wander back to the station. They've all gone. I fall gratefully on to the futon provided. A super, if not exciting, day.

DAY 228

15th August – Tain Fire Station to Fortrose Campsite – 12 miles

I leave in steady rain. It's a short trip down the A9, then turn I off. I'm on my way to catch the unique Nigg Ferry. The 'smallest ferry' vessel in the UK, carrying only two cars and fifty passengers, it chugs across to Cromarty.

This next hurdle to cross gets me reminiscing. In the days after the Second World War, long before ordinary folk could afford a TV set, sound radio was all we had. The Light and Home programmes were so dreary: countless times I sat through the shipping forecast and it became inevitable that weather area designations became etched in my memory for ever. Now, here I am crossing one of them, the Cromarty Firth.

The *Cromarty Rose* ferryboat has a chequered history. There are plans to replace her with another vessel which will carry four cars. It's not often that a transport ferry increases its capacity one hundred per cent overnight!

In Cromarty village I enter the hotel for a pint and some soup. I move on and stumble upon a superb cake shop where the bubbly owner treats me to tea and cake,

This area down to Inverness is for some reason called the Black Isle: maybe it has something to do with the colour of the soil. Now full up, I stagger along the long stretches of straight road, the boredom broken only by stretches of forest and a call of nature!

At the village of Balmungie I see a man sweeping his forecourt. I have been told this is red squirrel country, and I ask him whether he sees any. His answer is 'Quite often'. He told me of a unique encounter when a female carrying a baby (pup, kit or kitten – take your choice) froze in front of him for some time. He said he marvelled that, although tiny, the baby was fully recognisable as an adult.

I try to get a B & B as I near the end of the day, but with no luck. I walk on to the Fortrose campsite on the Morey Firth. The owner waives the fee. I pitch, and will benefit from a good sleep.

DAY 229

16th August – Rest day - Fortrose campsite

I wake up to lovely weather, fix myself some porridge then walk into Fortrose for the rest of my breakfast. I get a *Telegraph* and read up on the GB successes in the Olympic Games. My lazy morning reaches lunch time, and then it's time for a pint.

Close to my tent a woman lives in an old unkempt caravan. She has an agreement with the site owners, doing some tasks for them. The trouble is that she has a noisy and wayward German Shepherd dog. On my way back from the town I take the shoreline path. It's twisty and a little overgrown. As I push my way through the dog appears and goes for me, stopping just short of biting. So close is its aggressive behaviour that I feel its saliva on my arm. The woman appeared within seconds and calls it off. She can see that I'm shaken and apologises, explaining by way of mitigation that it's a 'rescue dog'.

Disguising my anguish in order to pacify the animal, I tell her that she should keep it on a lead, especially here with children on the site. She slips away in embarrassment.

Flek is taken aback: 'Blimey, Colin, that was a near thing. I hope you've had your jab.'

'Yes, I had one following a dog bite on a Southern Trails reconnoitre stage. Do you know what really annoyed me?'

He shakes his head.

'Having to spend four hours in A & E at St Richards Hospital, Chichester, that's what. There are dog owners and there are dog owners, mate.'

Calmed down, I later returned to the town and get a take-away haddock and chips. It's a lovely warm evening. I sit on a bench and look across the Moray Firth to far away Inverness lit up in the twilight, and I enjoy my supper. From simple experiences often comes sublime contentment.

17th August – Fortrose Camp Site to Inverness – 12 miles

I pass through the hamlet of Avoch and stock up with chocolate bars. I press onto Murlocky passing the Black Isle Country Park. A gymkhana is in progress, and every other vehicle entering is a 4x4 – lots of daddies taking lots of daughters to show off their ponies. The paddock scene reminds me of the Thelwell's Riding Academy cartoons.

I come to the A9. How am I going to cross it? I can see a footpath on the other side of the dual carriageway. I fume. Time and time again I find major new road systems in GB take no account of pedestrians. I am going to have to run the gauntlet again, i.e. waiting for gaps in the racing traffic to hastily cross both carriageways, hopping over the arco on the central reservation on the way. It's dangerous, but I have learned to be very patient on these occasions.

Relieved to be over, I walk up the footpath to the car park and café just north of the Kessel Bridge and ring my next host, Roderick Beaton. He has to come quite a way from Beauly so, parched, I get a much needed pot of tea.

Roderick picks me up and we go over the bridge, which is yet another of Scotland's superb structures, stretching 1000m over the junction of the Moray and Beauly firths (long narrow estuaries, especially in Scotland). It has one of those dramatically 'high' designs to allow navigation.

Roderick is my host by reason of his cousin Arthur Wells being an old boy of Chichester High School. He is the village postman. I meet his wife Katrina: they have a lovely home.

Over a meal he explains the difficulty of getting planning permission to build on the land, which is still registered for crofting. There is an intensive process of 'due diligence' before permission can be granted – the land isn't given up easily. I share a sense of humour with them.

Roderick takes me to Inverness. He has arranged for me to meet Brian Murray, the chief firemaster of the Highlands and Islands Fire Brigade. He meets me first thing Monday morning and is very generous with his time. We have a great chat, and I am most pleased to tell him about the hospitality I have received on his fire stations.

There are nearly fifty separate fire and rescue services in Britain. What is interesting about this one is that it provides fire cover for forty per cent of GB's total landmass, leaving all the other brigades to share the remainder.

Inverness is the only full-time station, and there are in excess of ninety part-time stations throughout the Highlands. An interesting man, Brian hints that on retirement he may move back south.

Rodney drops me off on the Nairn Road. It's not too long before I arrive at the Culloden battlefield site. I wander up to the brand new visitor centre and get a bite to eat in the well-appointed restaurant. There is, of course, the ubiquitous gift shop.

I go outside. The battlefield covers a large area and is flat – probably moorland at the time of the last pitched battle on British soil. It's marked up as a walk around tour to spots where e.g. the Macdonalds were slain (if only), Big McDuff was brought down, the Campbells were routed and where the Duke of Cumberland's government troops overran the Jacobites. It was all over in an hour.

While the centre and shop was packed with coach parties of tourists, I counted just half a dozen interested souls walking the hallowed ground. It seems to me that the only reason most visitors are here is because of the restaurant, gift shop and comfort stop.

Ann Wilson, my next host, picks me up at Cawdor, and we have a pub drink. She and her husband John are both artists and have a splendid home. He unfortunately had a stroke in his forties. Ann was a student with John Byrne, the playwright and artist who is probably best known for writing the TV series Tutti Frutti starring Robbie Coltrane. He's married to the Oscar-winning actress Tilda Swinton, who personally stages a Festival at Nairn which is showing this week. Unfortuneatly I just miss out on a ticket.

After a meal, and while Ann goes off to the show, I sit and have a long and interesting conversation with John. It has been another day full of interest. My legs are now well run-in, and I allow them to sleep well!

Evening Concert (in a bed): Randy Crawford's 'Street Life', The Who's 'Pinball Wizard'. Wish track: Phillip Glass's score for the film The Hours.

Ann Wilson with CLIMB donation.

Dentures

'I'll never forget that terrible sound, of a set of false teeth hitting the inside of a bucket. Perhaps you would like to hear it again?
—Neddie Seagoon

I am progressing up the B9006 from the Culloden Battlefield towards Geddes near Nairn. Passing a rural detached house with large grounds, I spot an elderly man on the other side of a front five-barred gate. In military parade ground terms he is standing at ease, holding a large spring wire rake out-stretched at his side and looking straight ahead over the road as if on sentry duty. Pausing to let a biker race pass (he's probably doing a ton), I cross the road for a chat.

I observe that the man has just completed mowing a very large area and is about to scarify the surface. The stripes of mowing lines lead for some way up a sharp slope to the front of a substantial property. For a man of his age this seems a monumental task. No wonder he's seeking a pause in his labours.

All this effort calls for some recognition. and I duly congratulate him. Bolstered by my interest, he stands down from the 'at ease' stance and the conversation goes something like this:

'Hello sir, I see you're taking a rest.'

'Aye, ah could sleep on the edge ae a razir. Ma nave been Pat and Dick do ya ken' I'm awright naw but another clean shirt and that'l be me!'

Somewhat puzzled by his reply, I press him further.

'That's an awful big area to mow,' I continue.

'Och Aye, it's an ongoing jobby. Didnae you see aw ma lorn lines up to the hoose. Isnae a greet seet? Am urny goin finish soon, there's gauny be a plump. Huznae youse got any grass?

'Well not at the moment' I reply, guessing his gist. 'You'll be pushing a wheel-barrow of cuttings all day.'

'When you are gaun, I'll haunbaw aw myself . . .' and so he goes undecipherably on.

I can't help noticing that the effect of his prolonged replies has loosened his dentures, and he is starting to foam at the mouth.

Flek has also noticed the phenomenon: 'Blimey Col, if he goes on like this then both sets will get launched. I should keep your head down if I were you.'

Acknowledging the old boy's replies. I raise my map case to ward off any pre emptive strike. My only hope is that he his vocabulary doesn't run to machine gunning bursts of four syllable words.

Surrealistic thoughts surface. One can imagine the headlines in the local rag, possibly the nationals, reporting that Britain's oldest walking circumnavigator has been found lying at the side of a road In Scotland with two sets of false teeth embedded in his throat. The editorial reads:

Eye witnesses saw a burly traffic police officer leaning over the victim and heard him castigating the culprit, 'Ya awright, pal? Listen, ye didnae fix yir wallies [false teeth] the day. I'm telling ylr too keep them in yur heid or the procurator fiscal will hear aboot this!'

The dejected culprit has not yet been name named but is now being referred to in the press as 'Gummy', as he looks a prime contender for the national Gurning Championships.

Tributes have come pouring in nationwide for the septuagenarian walker so cruelly struck down. Ironically a confidante let slip recently that, despite appearances, the seventy-year-old was apparently fed up to his teeth walking around GB and was about to settle for a bus pass.

'Who can control his fate' – 'Othello'

DAY 232
19st August – Geddes to RAF Kinloss – 14 miles

Mary Wilson drops me into Geddes. With husband John she has given me a memorable stay. I start with a jaunt along the B8101, bypassing Nairn. I experience some driving drizzle (we don't get much of this these days).

I am really wet by the time a smart roadside restaurant appears. Entering this establishment is going to be an uncomfortable experience. Heads turn as, in full gear and rucksack, I order a sweet of apple pie and custard followed by a pot of tea.

My embarrassment triggers Flek to comment, 'I admire your panache, Colin. To hell with them all I say. Your fellow diners have all arrived in air conditioned limousines – they know nothing about a septuagenarian tramp's suffering, walking the highways and byways through all weathers. First impressions can be deceiving. For all they know you could be a nuclear scientist who is down on his luck and wants to get away from it all. After all . . .'

'Dont make it sound like a Hollywood script. Let's get out of here now!'

Four miles further on I have another bit of luck as a substantial road side 'chippy' café appears out of the mist. Run by Chinese, it's a life saver on a day like this.

I turn off the Forres bypass and head for RAF Kinloss as the weather clears up. Tripping along, it strikes me that history of a sort is manifesting itself today. Let me explain.

Back in the Fifties, good-looking strapping lads like me were 'politely' invited to join the armed services – it was called National Service. Joining the Royal Air Force entailed being taken as part of an intake to RAF Cardington, where nasty 'strange' men (drill instructors) shouted at us. Having been equipped with itchy clothes (battledress) and a big pair of boots (didn't fit), followed by a distressing tonsorial experience (hair cut) we were all shunted onto a troop train to Wilmslow in Cheshire, where even nastier strange men shouted at us again. More drill instructors, they insisted that we march up and down a parade ground for two whole months.

After some leave, another train took me with another intake onto Credden Hill, Hereford (now home of the SAS) for trade training. One wet morning two months later we paraded outside the guard room to hear our final postings, grimacing as they were read out. What nobody wanted to hear was RAF Kinloss! Taunting us, our instructors let out that this air base was hundreds of miles north in deepest Scotland. It turned out to be geographically the furthest RAF posting in the UK at that time.

Just think what it meant – how would anybody get home at the weekends to enjoy Mummy's cooking? It was with a sigh of relief that I heard my fate, allotted to 2nd Tactical Air Force, West Germany!

Tramping along endless lanes, my twisted thinking tells me that the RAF has long a long memory and doesn't give up. Here I am fifty-three years later approaching a host 'posting' to – guess where? At the invitation of its commanding officer, I am invited to billet at RAF Kinloss. Those crafty swine at the Air Ministry have finally triumphed!

Warrant Officer Carl Morgan spots me in the village shop, takes my rucksack on to the base and I finish the last half mile. I get a great welcome in the guard room, and an enormous aviation fire truck takes me to the sergeants' mess. The newly built barracks will be my home for the next two days. I eat in the mess with the NCOs: I must say the grub has improved.

Flight Sergeant Jack Ashworth in charge of the fire section has hinted that he has arranged some events for me tomorrow, so I fall asleep in anticipation.

DAY 233
20th August – Rest day – RAF Kinloss

Fire fighter Kenny McGhee picks me up in a huge fire truck and Flight Sergeant Jack Ashworth introduces me to the duty crew.

He has organised a training exercise. The mock up fuselage of a Nimrod aircraft is ignited using an accelerant, and the crew tackles the spectacular blaze with two appliances projecting foam and water spray. The station photographer takes shots of the incident, and a group photograph is arranged.

I get shown over a Nimrod. These aircraft have seen decades of service in reconnaissance and search-rescue roles, but their future is uncertain. The station extends over a large area: Jack tells me that it's a seven-mile walk around the perimeter fence.

After lunch I take it easy, sending emails, writing my blog and watching the Olympics. Usian Bolt gallops around the 200m in a world record time. Lesley at CLIMB rings to tell that even more hosts are volunteering to look after me.

Nimrod, RAF Kinloss.

DAY 234

21nd August – RAF Kinloss to Lossiemouth – 12 miles

It's raining hard as I leave. Jack and his crew turn up at the guard room to see me off with gifts of maps, an RAF beanie hat and a photo disc.

Weather wise this is going to be a lousy and difficult day. After eight miles trudging through country lanes in pouring rain, the landing lights of RAF Lossiemouth shine through the gloom, their paths disappearing into the distance. A lone Tornado glides over me and touches down.

While I am sloshing up the road parallel to the runway. a yellow search-and-rescue helicopter lands on an airfield pad close to me. *Deja vu!*

The rain finally stops as I arrive in Lossiemouth and find my hosts, Ken and Ann Owens. The connection here is that Ann's sister works with my daughter Suzanne at Warwick University. I'm fixed up with a bath and refreshments.

Later we all go to their daughter/son-in-law's farm south of Elgin, where a substantial family meal has been prepared. I sleep there overnight.

DAY 235

22rd August – Lossiemouth to Buckie Fire Station – 16 miles

Kennie gets me back to my route. Four miles of country lanes makes for pleasant walking. When I get to Garmouth it's time for a late breakfast. On entering the Garmouth Hotel's dining room I'm met with friendliness and consideration.

Now, call me old-fashioned but I'm a stickler for the way a table is laid out and the food offered. My order is modest tea and toast and the hotel's presentation is the best of the year. I congratulate the manager and would have awarded her ten out of ten *but* have to dock half a mark because the serviette is missing. For a moment this stranger in his walking kit and rucksack must seem to her the most convincingly disguised tourist inspector she has ever encountered!

Just up the road I follow a dismantled railway line to cross the River Spey Viaduct. People often ask me for my greatest memories of the year, and this has to be one of them. I chart these transient joys at the back of the book, and will just say now that, following the inch of rainfall yesterday, this mighty Spey River is in full spate (no pun intended), roaring down to the sea half a mile away.

After crossing the Bridge I reach a road and turn to my left. For a while I am distracted by actions of pigs fighting over a wallowing hole in the adjacent field At Nether Dallachy I suddenly find myself ambling on to the abandoned aircraft assembly apron and perimeter track of a Second World War airfield. I had been given a clue by the approach road, its designation being 'Beaufighter Way'.

I suppose it is inevitable that post war aviation analysis often leads to compare the performances of similar combat aircraft. The best known example has been the soaring reputation of the Spitfire as against the Hurricane, which was equally as successful operationally or even better. The domination of the Lancaster bomber over its cousin

River Spey rushing to the sea.

the Halifax comes to mind, and the reputations of the fighter bombers, i.e. the very fast all-wood Mosquito performance as against the Beaufighter night fighter.

In the last year of the war four squadrons of the Beaufighters, with GB, Australian, New Zealand and Canadian aircrews flew from this place to attack enemy shipping in the Norwegian fjords, suffering heavy losses.

It is very still. l pause here for a moment and, not for the first time, try to imagine the frenzied activity taking place here in 1945. I experience an empathy with the opening scene of the film 'Twelve O'Clock High', starring Gregory Pack, when in the newly won peace Dean Jagger takes a nostalgic cycle ride out to an abandoned English airfield and the action flashes back to 1942. (Jagger won a Best Supporting Actor Oscar for his role.)

A few miles on, at Buckie, I am met by a cheerful station fire manager, Dougie Annand. He buys me lunch and has sympathy with my quest, telling me about the disability of his two children, who have spinal problems.

Later I chat to some of the crew, and the sub officer makes a donation of £100 to CLIMB. They find me a mattress for the night. This station has been impressively refurbished and has a unique fire appliance which is designed to carry a crew of ten. Opening a few lockers, I can see that there's been no stinting on equipment – it is the best.

DAY 236
23th August – Buckie Fire Station to Banff fire station – 16 miles

Dougie turns up to wave me goodbye as I start another long day of walking, mostly along the A98. In perfect weather I stride out down the Moray Coast. I keep coming across National Cycle Network mileposts. Sponsored by the Royal Bank of Scotland to celebrate the formation of the network, a thousand have been sited along national and regional footways There are four types, but I find it difficult to work out what their designs and shapes are supposed to designate.

I pass through Findochty and Portknockie and go on to walk the old railway line track which follows the cliffs. From these heights I can look down on the spectacular Cullen golf links sandwiched between the cliff base and the Cullen Sands.

Six miles on, at Portsroy, I get some lunch in a café. Still to come is another strength-sapping six miles to Banff, where I am met by Kevin Dingwall, the fire station manager, and his wife Margaret. They fetch me some fish and chips. Brian, a member of the fire crew, brings in a lilo for me to sleep on at the Station.

The only problem with any floor mattress is I still find that, due to my physical state (that is, stiff as a board), it is virtually impossible to rise naturally in the morning. I still have to roll over, crawl to a solid object chair or table etc and, with great difficulty, pull myself up! However, I am grateful for the station personnel's care and attention and I sleep well.

DAY 237

*24th August – Banff Fire Station to The Palace (near Gardenstown)
– 12 miles*

Kevin apologises in advance that he can't see me off, because he is competing in a triathlon today. Locking the station door, I walk across Banff Bridge and around the bay to the town of McDuff for some breakfast, then take on a further six miles through rolling hills, passing isolated farms. My accommodation tonight is uncertain. I decide to come off the main B9031 and walk into Gardenstown. I should have looked more closely at the map because it's a hell of a descent down to this village on the coastline.

This is an extraordinary place which has evolved from a pretty 18th century fishing village founded by Alexander Gardenstown. It now merges seamlessly into a distinct line of modern properties up the hill.

Although I am late, the landlady of the Garden Arms Hotel finds me some gorgeous soup. There's no B & B available in the village, but she rings Pat who has accommodation at a place called 'The Palace' back up the hill on the other side of the B9031. Just when I am thinking of having the severe climb back up the hill. Pat's husband Robbie comes in for a drink and, thankfully, I have my lift. While I am in the pub I have a most interesting discussion with an elderly American who has sort of 'migrated' to this place!

'The Palace' tries to live up to its name with a crown on the gate, and has other pseudo palatial outside ornaments in place to impress. Behind the pretention it is a very comfortable farmhouse. and Pat and Robbie make me very welcome.

DAY 238

25th August – Gardenstown to Fraserburgh – 16 miles

An elderly guest, Paul. gives me a lift back to the main road another marathon hike today. After two miles I pass close by to Pennan Harbour. Much of the filming for Bill Forsyth's popular film Local Heroes, starring Burt Lancaster among others, was shot there. This film was particularly memorable for its wonderful sound-track music. Although Lancaster is a Hollywood hero of mine. I think the real star of the film was Fulton Mackay of Porridge fame.

I get caught in heavy rain approaching New Abadour. It's a dreary place. The pub closed two years ago and the post office is doomed, but mercifully still has chocolate bars.

The weather has cleared by the time I get to Rosehearty. I call into a pub which appears to be more than it is. This is explained when the landlord tells me that it used to be a night club. An impresario of the old entertainment school, he speaks in expletives. English being his second language.

'We had 'em all here,' he says. 'Freddie and the Dreamers, the Batchelors and Terry Lighfoot – they all came through that door.'

Some common ground is found when he gets on to talking about his time in the RAF's whose motto is 'Per Ardua ad Astra' – meaning 'Through Adversity to the Stars'. Our friend left me with an impression that, when serving his country, he operated according too the revised rank-and-file interpretation, viz 'Through Other Buggers' Efforts to the Stars'.

I arrive in Fraserburgh. My next hosts are John Anderson and his wife Margaret. John has just retired as the fire station manager after thirty-seven years, well earning his Queens Fire Service Medal. His office at home is strewn with fire service memorabilia, a fine collection. The town is still reeling from a recent fire incident aboard a moored trawler in the harbour, which claimed the lives of two of its crew.

We find a lot to talk about. As nearly always, mine hosts are of great help to me.

DAY 239

26th August – Fraserburgh to Peterhead – 16 miles

I am conscious of continually mentioning the weather, but the amazing thing is that I rarely have put my waterproofs on. As for my route, I still have to use mainly roads. Yes, there are lovely beach walks but, time-wise, soft sand and river inlets will cause unacceptable delays. The situation is completely different on established National Paths. At this stage I think it worth repeating that though my schedule of 347 days will allow me to walk round Britain, I would need another three months to walk all around the edges.

I take the old railway line path going south and soon come to a station now beautifully converted to a charming cottage. An old lady appears and tells me that a local lord and wealthy landowner had the station built, possibly as a status symbol. Well, I suppose it made a change from a boring folly. She remembers catching the train from here to school. However there was one stipulation: if his lordship was board-ing the train, nobody else was allowed on! Fortunately, she says, this didn't happen very often.

On reaching the A90 (T) I turn left to head for the coast again. Several miles on, the massive onshore St Fergus North Sea gas terminal looms up ahead. Initially drawing the gas from the Frigg Field. it now receives gas from another twenty fields, supplying up to a third of the UK's supply. So this is what lights up my gas boiler at home!

I get to Peterhead and call my next hosts, Peter and Anne Herridge.

They have come on the scene as a result of the appeal by BognorRegis Rotarian David Garforth. Peter has not long left the Navy and now runs a model shop, Peterhead Puffers. He recently became a Rotarian and has jumped at the chance to help me out.

This area is well known for its locally quarried granite which has mica deposits, making it sparkle. It also comes in several hues. The Herridges' substantial property is pinkish in colour.

Mine hosts are going to put up with me for two days, which will involve ferrying trips to and from my route. Many hosts have appealing backgrounds, and the Herridges are no different.

DAY 240

27TH August – Peterhead to Bullers O' Buchan – 6 miles

It is about time that I had a leisurely day.

As always Flek has something to say: 'We deserve an easy day sometimes – can't keep the foot-slogging-and-fortitude ethos up all the time, Col.'

I like the 'we' inference!

It is therefore a day free of the backpack, and I amble down the A90, passing such beauty spots as Peterhead Prison – used for sex offenders and Category A prisoners. Built in 1888, is has been described by inspectors as the worst prison in the UK. Next up is an oil and gas unit power station which is, as usual, unsightly but essential. Finally RAF Buchan, formerly the site of an Air Defence radar post, and now used as industrial units.

The scenery changes dramatically when I turn off onto the A975 and arrive at Bullers O'Buchan village. This coastal spot is known for its natural arches and cliff stacks. It's a charming spot.

David turns up for a return to Peterhead. A handsome young lady drives up to her nearby cottage home and chats to us about her job as a meteorologist.

A short but interesting day.

Flek moans. He says he's clapped out! I haven't heard much from him today. My guess is that he has a touch of lockjaw. Hallelujah!

Into the Abyss

'Have no fear of moving into the unknown'
– Pope John Paul II

It is August 2008 and most of the nation are at home riveted to their TV screens as the excitement of the Beijing Olympics is brought direct into living their rooms. Paramount viewing are the gymnastics disciplines, producing 'shock and awe' performances on the arena mat.

Little known, in contrast, are the covert ground displays carried out by the UK Septuagenarian Backpackers Guild. Unlike their Olympic counterpart, these are held on anonymous campsites throughout the Land. The commencement of their performances isn't announced with a competition arena 'start beep', but with the 'rasping' sound of a zip in a remote field.

The veterans have long lost any elasticity in their limbs and begin their performances by agonisingly dropping onto their knees, producing from their rusty joints cranking sounds reminiscent of the Tin Man in the 'Wizard of Oz' They enter their tents by flopping onto ground sheets on an 'arena' of only six feet by three.

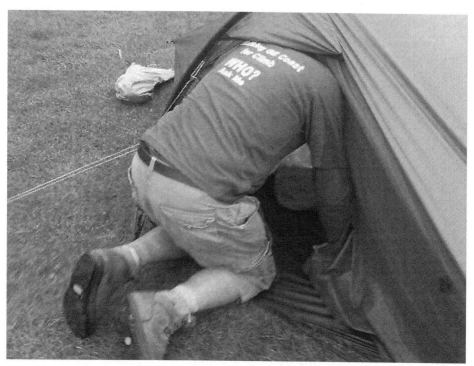

However long it takes, their purpose is to remove garments, then lever the body into a sleeping bag using gymnastic disciplines such as stretching, ground pommel, arching and grunting, egged on by a liberal use of expletives.

A sudden spasm of cramp accelerates their gyrations with involuntary tumbling flip-flops and the famous Japanese 'Tsukahara' discipline, not easily achieved within the confines of a tent. Unlike the Olympics, there are no spectator gasps or arena applause here – just a triumphant 'Yes!' coming out of the campsite darkness from those who have finally trussed themselves up for the night. Others whose performances have failed lie sobbing in a heap of despair.

There are no gold medals to be won here either. The points system for this event (known to the unfortunates taking part as the 'nocturnal nightmare'), was abandoned years ago as unworkable. But does it matter? Some crusty old baron uttered a hundred years ago that 'The important thing in the Olympic Games is not winning but taking part'.

Not winning!!! The man was a buffoon.

The Night Soilers

Tent gyrations on an Olympic scale have to be repeated all over again during the early hours when a need to relieve oneself occurs.

I refer, of course, to 'night soiling.' Rough camping usually means being beyond any artificial light and, in Scotland particularly, the coal blackness of the night gives up a spectacular sky.

I like to think that it was not beyond the night soilers of old, while relieving themselves on the compost heap, to develop the knack of reading the night sky. Can't you just hear the pronouncements of a star-gazing Somerset peasant at his morning breakfast of grouts and mead: 'Ahrrr, I saw The Plow in the noight. Twas in loin with the Pole Starrrrr; not a lot of those ere super novas abowt mine yu.'

From such deliberations 'The Sky at Night' emerged!

28 August – Bullers O' Buchan to Newburgh – 14 miles

David returns me to the car park at Buller's. I have just got going when I notice the spooky towers of a castle and take a muddy track down to investigate. A young man on a training run comes towards me and stops. His sweatshirt shows his affiliations to a rugby team, and we talk sport.

I ask about the ruins and, being local, he informs me that they are the ruins of Staines Castle, once owned by the Erroll family. They were big around here, he states. To explain further, he draws my attention to the film 'White Mischief', the true story of the Earl of Erroll, who was mysteriously murdered in Happy Valley, Kenya in 1941. He can't remember the name of the film's leading lady. When I tell him that it was Greta Scacchi he applauds my knowledge as a film buff. I brush his plaudits aside to tell him that I have recently met her cousin in a Welsh pub. 'What goes around then come around', as they say!

The 'castle' is one of these pseudo structures which apparently gave so many Victorians a grandeur they weren't entitled to, and it has long been abandoned.

The A975 takes me through Cruden Bay. After lunch in a hotel I find a road skirts the Forvie National Nature Reserve and crosses the River Ythan at the Waterloo Bridge. It's a pleasant last couple of miles, the road hugging the River.

I am being sponsored at the Ythan Hotel by a local, Ruth Milne. She and her parents, Ronald and Jessie Milne, are a CLIMB family. Ruth's daughter Eilidh has the metabolic condition Propionic Acidaemia..

The proprietor, Lorna Summers, ensures that I have a comfortable stay. Ruth has contacted the local press, and a photographer turns up to interview me.

DAY 242

29th August – Newburgh to Aberdeen – 15 miles

I leave the first-rate Ythan Hotel and continue walking the A975. I manage to keep off the trunk roads for most of the day by using parallel quiet lanes. I have had a blitz on my rucksack, so it is a little lighter.

This is a different Scotland – undulating fields of ripening cereals as far as one can see. The ploughs are out. inviting huge flocks of seagulls. There are also crows, many of them perched on fences. (Shades of Hitchcock!) It is also a delight to see herds of healthy cattle after the horrors of Foot and Mouth in 2002.

Looking about me today, I notice for the first time this year a fully laden apple tree. I am a little taken aback. Why? Well, the sighting announces that I have been away for three seasons. It's an odd feeling.

At the village of Potterton I see a menu on an A-board outside the sports club, and I have an excellent lunch. Eventually I have to rejoin the A90 and take the long urban walk into Aberdeen, a city transformed by the off-shore oil fields and infamous for its coastal fogs. I'm in luck – it's fine and clear.

My next hosts are Howard and Pat Scholey, a CLIMB family. I ring Pat and she drives the fifteen miles in from Crathes to pick me up outside the Beach Ballroom on Aberdeen's seafront.

Howard and Pat's son Ben was diagnosed at two years with the neurodegenerative metabolic condition Alexander's Leucodystrophy (a very rare disease). Despite experiencing other traumas in his life, with the love and care of his parents he lived until his 18th year, passing away in 2000.

I will be staying for two days. Howard is a geophysicist and works in the oil industry.

I am returned to Aberdeen and as it is a Free day I get a move on through the Aberdeen suburbs. The A90 has a cycle track, which nearly always means unhindered progress.

I find myself having a conversation with a man pushing a bicycle. A bit of an oddball, he advises me how to avoid encounters with travellers. He says they are usually a pain in the arse and goes on alarmingly about the confrontations he has had. The fact that his open eccentricity has drawn public interest has eluded him. Suddenly he takes off – possibly because he isn't practising what he is preaching. So why did he pick on me?

This triggers an outburst from Flek ,who I thought had disappeared for the day.

'You're just the sort of person he was going on about. You talk to anyone whether they want to or not. He's obviously a cycling evangelist and saw you as a prime example of his philosophy. That's what I think.'

'Well, you can think again. I like to socialise, Flek. Remember Shakespeare's Julius Caesar speech: "Friends, Romans, Countrymen, lend me your ears." '

'Yes, and look what happened to him. Don't get intellectual with me, mate. I studied at the University of Life. I see it as I see it,' he shouts back.

It is impossible to talk to him when he this kind of mood, so I ignore his protestations.

There are no hold-ups, and I march into the hustle and bustle of Stonehaven. Enjoying holiday spending sprees are crowds of early autumn visitors. It's lunchtime, and they crowd in to sample the eating spots. I join in. I've developed into a bit of a sweet tooth and I am not letting up – it's traditional apple pie and ice cream for me. I ring Howard and he picks me up.

As I have finished early, Howard has had an idea. He lends me his National Trust card and drops me off at Crathes Castle. Home of the Burnett of Leys family, it's the best example of baronial architecture in Scotland you are ever likely to see.

These structures are built with options, i.e. live in style at one end and retreat into the safety of the other when threatened. This sort of strategy was often required in Scotland. Interestingly, the horse trainer

Sir Henry Cecil has family connections. A guide inside tells me he has visited the aviation musuem at Tangmere near to where I live. The remark reminds me of warm autumn days walking the lanes surrounding that famous Second World War RAF airfield, plucking blackberries and sloes from the hedgerows. I am returning home to bottles of maturing sloe gin.

'Not a lot of people know that,' says Flek trying to get back in favour – or, in this case, flavour!

This evening Pat has invited numerous friends around for a cheese and wine party. It's a fundraiser for CLIMB which raises £150

'All this activity in one day, Flek. I don't know how I'm going to keep the pace up. Some days it's pure hell out here.'

'Your Mother would have been proud of you' he replies.

For once I think he means it.

I have had a wonderful stay and am settling into the east coast passage nicely!

DAY 244
31 August –Stonehaven to Johnshaven – 11 miles

Howard drives me down to Stonehaven. I struggle up a steep hill to an entrance leading to Dunnottar Castle. Tourists are taking the long path down to see this ruined medieval fortress on a rocky headland. Some filming of the Shakespeare's 'Scottish Play' starring Mel Gibson was shot here. I took the same path a few years ago.

The day is going to be messy, in the order of play rain – muggy – fine rain – finally heavy rain. I get lunch at the Cree Inn, an award winning pub in Catterline, then call into the village store for chocolate. It's another post office under threat, says the post mistress, who has lived on site for decades.

On to Inverbervie. It's raining hard now. Taking shelter under a tree I wait my next host, Dave Clark. He drives me on to pick up his wife Micchi at Montrose, and then it's back home to Laurenskirk , a rambling house full of interesting artefacts. Dave, a Scot through and through, is an oil platform engineer and Michi, of Canadian-Japanese descent, is an artist.

The eye-catcher here is the 50ft sailing ketch *Anntoo* which is chocked up outside. Dave explains how he came by her. He was being treated for a knee injury by a Dr Shiers, who had her up for sale, and he bought it. Built at Gosport in 1947, it later became the centre of a huge drug busting operation. Dave is now refitting her with the idea of sailing (where else?) around the world.

I am here because the Clark's are friends of my previous hosts. The clan territory is now Barclay, and on the way down to Dundee I shall enter Duncan terrain.

I have entered shipping weather forecast area Forth.

DAY 245
1st September – Johnshaven to Montrose – 10 miles

The weather has settled when I get up. Dave has already left for Aberdeen. Michi gets me some breakfast and then I climb up on to the *Anntoo* to have a look round. Dave has certainly got a lot of work on his hands.

Michi donates £20 for CLIMB and takes me on a tour of Johnshaven which is sandwiched down the slope between the shore and the higher main road. She drops me at the village of St Cyris. After a few miles I get coffee, soup and some chocolate bars in Spar.

The roadwork is OK but laborious. These must be very words of every boxer taking early morning training.

My next host, in Montrose, is Derick Strutton – the ex-partner of my host tomorrow at Arbroath. Derick is a loner and understandably obsessed with his lovely King Charles spaniel. He likes to fly model aircraft and is a member of the local club, although he doesn't get on with its members. He tells me about his disagreements about how the club should be run, and it's clear that they don't listen to him. I think that it's this bickering that keeps him going!

I get egg and chips, have a nice bath and turn in early.

'How about an Evening Concert?' says Flek 'Got any Grunge?'

'Ah, you're trying to catch me out again, old boy,' I reply, responding to another of his musical tastes. 'I know you mean – the alternative Rock which

emerged in the Eighties. It was inspired by hardcore punk and heavy metal and characterised by distorted electric guitars. It's played by musicians noted for their unkempt appearance and a rejection of theatrics.

'Now for the short answer to your question – no. I haven't got any Grunge.'

DAY 246
2nd September – Montrose to Arbroath – 10 miles

Derick doesn't do breakfast so I file into Tesco's down the road for the early day's sustenance. The morning mist belies the hot weather to come. I latch onto a National Cycling Route and later sit on the Lunan Bridge for a rest – a charming spot. An elderly cyclist, John, passes and returns, having read my shirt.

There's a gust of wind and my map blows off the bridge into the thick balsam that edges the river. I drop down from the bridge and, with help of John and another passer-by, retrieve it. The three of us have a chat about the decline of society etc, as old boys do!

A few miles on I deviate from the route to Inverkeilor for a pint. Approaching Arbroath I meet Martin coming along the road. He is Danish and, seeing my shirt, seems to know about CLIMB. He explains that his partner's child Megan Anita Crompton has a metabolic condition. I check this out with the charity later.

It has been such an easy day's walk to my next host, Loretta Dean. She is the cousin of Barbara Holt, a gentle lady who has walked extensively with me on the Southern Trails excursions.

The Arbroath area is renowned for its 'smokies'. This way of preparing fish originated in the village of Authmithie a few miles north of here. The folk are of Scandinavian descent, and they smoke haddock in a special way.

In the evening Loretta takes me out to dinner, and I select a smokie. It covers a very large plate and is delicious. In 2004 the European Commission designated the Arbroath areas as the definitive geographical location for this fish dish. The same sort of protection is given to Melton Mowbray pork pies.

Loretta is determined to make a fuss of me and I do not resist.

DAY 247

3rd September – Arbroath to Carnoustie – 8 miles

I shall be with Loretta for two nights, so it is a Free day. I walk into Arbroath and stroll along the seafront. I pass across the head of a steep bank of seeding wild plants which attracts large flocks of goldfinches.

A large stand structure dominates the front – Arbroath Football Club. The gate is open and I wander in and stand on the pitch. The club secretary appears and I tell him that as a southerner I have always regarded the town as a Pools' football result.

He is very tolerant of my utter ignorance and explains that being on the seafront renders the club unique. It is rarely affected by frost, so avoiding match postponements – and thus nearly always providing a valid Home result for the Pools coupons. The one problem they cannot avoid is that flocks of seagulls land on the pitch, leaving their feathers everywhere. Win some, lose some!

The club operates in Scottish Division 11 and has average gates of eight hundred.

'How on earth do they survive?' butts in Flek. 'I suppose they have part-time players on expenses.'

Once again it is easy walking, and there is always a pub in which to imbibe. Approaching Carnoustie I pass the sports injury academy of the Scottish long distance runner Liz MacColgan. (Remember her?)

I need to get a train back to Arbroath for the second night's stay at Loretta's. Sitting on the Carnoustie platform I see a huge board announcing that Mark Beaumont, a local boy from Dundee, has just cycled around the world in 195 days. The feat is mind-boggling and, for me, humbling.

I'm glad when the train glides in and distracts my thoughts.

DAY 248

4th September – Carnoustie to Dundee – 9 miles

Loretta has looked after me diligently, and it's time to make a heartfelt confession. I have never been able to shrug off the feeling of guilt I get from the fact that, despite my hosts' steadfast hospitality, I am no sooner with them than I am gone.

I have developed a head cold today – remarkably my first ailment of the trip – so to make an easy start to the day I get a taxi down to Arbroath railway station and catch a train back to Carnoustie.

Almost immediately I come into contact with a challenging character. In the ticket hall is a short, austere looking man who is in a state of confusion. He looks to me for help and starts to converse in broad Glaswegian through the thinnest of closed lips. Clearly he wants to purchase a ticket and isn't sure of the procedure – he wants me to do it for him. To bolster his request, he shows me a 'prisoner -on-release' certificate' from the Barlinnie HM Prison at Glasgow. His brogue begins to get through to me and I distinctly hear the words, 'I have got away from those murdering bastards for a few days.'

I get him a ticket, but this saga has not yet run its full course. We board the train and a lady pushing a refreshment trolley appears. He fancies a coffee and offers up a £20 note. She has just started her shift and hasn't got enough change. This man, after possibly years of imprisonment, is finding himself in an alien world. He's confused and extremely nervous, and the rocking train is spilling his coffee all over the place. As the train pulls into Carnoustie, I pay her the exact money, wish him luck and swiftly alight. It pulls away, and his still expressionless face disappears from my life.

It is fortunate that this has all happened over one stop, but the incident had moved me and I felt really sorry for him.

I start a pleasant stroll in early autumn sunshine. At Monifieth I sit on a wall and have a coffee. It is now a matter of following the River Tay with its dockside heavy industry all the way up to Dundee.

Prompted by CLIMB, the *Dundee Courier* rings and arranges for me to meet their photographer on my way in. Ron gets his shots and copy, then takes me on a brief tour around the city.

I ask about the cake, sweet and marmalade products for which the city is renowned.

'They're all gone' he says, 'but we still make rope. Sit tight and I'll show you something really interesting.'

He pulls down a side road and two large football stadia come into view.

'There you are. One is Dundee and the other is Dundee United. The grounds are only sixty yards apart – I know because I've paced it,' he says with pride.

Apparently when either of these teams hosts a European side, visiting supporters can't believe their eyes!

Ron runs me to my hosts Kenneth (a maths teacher) and Jennifer Head to stay for two days. They are my third contact via my good friend Doug Murgatroyd. It's a lovely day and we have tea in the garden with their daughter and grandchild.

DAY 249
5th September – Rest day – Dundee

Kenneth takes me on a tour, the highlight being a trip up to the war memorial on top of Law Hill which overlooks the city. At over 550ft, there are splendid views to the River Tay and its two bridges. At the waterline under the rail bridge are the stumps of the original structure, which collapsed disastrously on the 28th December 1879 taking a train and seventy-five people to their deaths. The incident spawned possibly William McGonigal's best known poem which finishes,

> *That your central girders would not given away*
> *At least many sensible men would say*
> *Had they been supported on each side with buttresses*
> *At least many sensible men confesses*
> *For the stronger we our houses do build*
> *The less chance we have of being killed/*

While on the hill I get a surprise phone call. It's from Judith McLeod, daughter of Chris Hyde an ex-fire brigade colleague of mine in West Sussex. She motors up and we chat about old times. Judith drops me in the city, and I have a leisurely afternoon, at first discovering the large statues in the square of Desperate Dan and Keyhole Kate. The *Beano* comic was printed here. I then tour Captain Scott's ship *Discovery*, which was built here in 1901.

Finally, I'm not the only 'famous' person in town today, sharing columns in the *Dundee Courier* with ex-world heavyweight boxing champion 'Smokin' Joe Frazier.

Flek asks me what hell he is doing here. I don't know. Probably strapped for cash so is on tour, is my guess.

Fiona Bruce is also in town, hosting the Antiques Road Show.

I spend a most congenial second evening with the Heads.

Desperate Dan, Dundee.

DAY 250
6th September – Dundee to St Andrews – 17 miles

On a fine day with a cold wind. I set out on a seventeen-mile journey to St Andrews. Kenneth has put his boots on today and joins me for part of the way. The plan is to drop me at the Tay Bridge, with him taking my rucksack on to Tayport. The bridge, with forty-two low spans, is 1.4 miles in length. With the head wind, it seems to take an age to cross.

Kenneth does his own walk and I meet him at the appropriately named Snook Head on the Fife Coastal Path, which runs for 150km. Surprisingly we find a village café open at Tayport and get hot drinks. Our walk terminates at the Lunin Bridge, where it is farewell.

The Fife Path takes me through the Tentsmuir Forest to pass RAF Leuchars. It's the weekend, so the Tornadoes aren't airborne today.

Crossing the Tay Bridge.

'I do hope they're on standby,' says Flek 'You never know – the balloon might go up today. We mustn't get caught out with our pants down!'

Aptly put, my friend. His bags curled around his lower extremities would place him in a ludicrous position – so encumbered, how is he going to run to the nearest nuclear bunker in that state?

By late lunchtime I am belting along, making good progress in the rain, but it's still another four miles on to St Andrews.

The large complex of the Royal and Ancient, comprising seven courses, comes into view. Nobody is hacking around today: the weather has put a stop to that. The last British Open winner here was, yes – who else? – Tiger Woods, in 2004.

The following is an extract from my Blog of the Day.

'Dear Readers, I address you from the ultimate digs, the police station at St Andrews.

This is the only 'nick' in the UK which lets out accommodation, mainly to police officers who come here for the golf. I have secured a bed for the night by courtesy of my walking friend Doug Cheal an ex- copper back in Hove who has arranged it with a retired policeman Tony Crozier of the local force.

The duty sergeant gives me a key and I stagger up four flights of stone stairs to join four Irishmen from Tipperary (a nice change from the Jocks) who are on a golfing break. The apartment is very comfortable with TV lounge and kitchen.

We all hope to get bail in the morning!

Colin

Going out to view the town I get a super meal in a local pub on the main street. St Andrews is a rather swish town, all golf shops, estate agents, pubs and, of course, university students.

I talk constantly to the jovial Irish party, and then we all flop down for a hard-earned rest.

7th September – St Andrews Police Station to Crail – 13 miles

The weather is rough so I decide against the Fife Path and take to the road. At Kingbarn I fancy a pub roast dinner and get one. On entering Crail the first camp is a no-no (closed). but the second on the coast says yes, so I talk to them nicely and secured a free night's pitch.

It's overcast, with a strong wind,and I struggle to get the tent up. Food today is dehydrated nosh, 'cooked' beef stew with noodles, followed by cinnamon rice and then a couple of chocolate hobknobs plus a bar of fruit and nut. Bursting at the seams. I send my daily blog to CLIMB, make some phone calls and settled down to an Evening Concert.

In my early twenties I first embraced a Classics culture in an unlikely location. I must explain. My first posting in the London Fire Brigade was to Lambeth on the Albert Embankment. This station was the largest in the country, with seven bays of appliances. The building was also the brigade's headquarters, which occupied the six upper floors. This meant that a large number of station operational staff were joined on duty by many specialist HQ bods and a fire boat crew – totalling nearly forty. During the long stand-down hours there was a choice of TV rooms.

Fire stations are not generally known for being bastions of culture, so most of the personnel opted for the large ITV lounge. There was a tiny room for viewing BBC (black and white screen), and on a Sunday night about eight of us would squeeze in to watch Hugh Weldon's 'Monitor', regarded as TV's first documentary series.

I have always loved the soundtrack music used for this ground-breaking programme – Dag Wiren's 'Serenade for Strings' – and it's on my iPod. My second choice tonight is 'Ruby my Dear' by Theolonius Monk. He wrote this lovely tune as a tribute to his wife.

My Round the Horne edition includes an hilarious sketch where, during the programme's Armpit Theatre production, an enraged Kenneth Williams, frustrated by the script, rants on: 'I am not appreciated, my talent isn't recognised. I have never been serviced. Am I not a sacred cow? I am a myth in my own time," to which Betty Marsden retorts, "What you do in your own time, Kenneth, is *your* business.'"

Thunderous audience laughter was allowed to run on in those days. It gave listeners the feeling that they were in the studio. Today audience reactions are manipulated, i.e. switched 'on' and 'off.' This is such a pity because much comedy spontaneity has disappeared. Thankfully it survives in 'I'm Sorry I haven't a Clue', now in its fortieth year.

DAY 252
8th September – Crail to Earlsferry – 14 miles

I break camp and, on a sunny September day, follow the Fife Coastal Path. The sea is calm and the going flat. The Path is easy to follow, allowing a delightful passage.

At Cellardyke I venture up inviting stairs to the Haven Bar for some lunch and hit the jackpot. I start with a bowl of delicious haddock chowder (a favourite of mine) and finish with plum tart and ice cream washed down with a Stella. Coming out of the bar speakers is Miles Davis's 'Kind of Blue', one of the greatest albums in recorded jazz history. To cap it all, Wendy behind the bar deducts a fiver from the bill for CLIMB. In a weird way it has been a surreal experience. I know one thing for sure – I am so fortunate to be here!

Cellardyke is immediately to the east of Anstruther Easter and Wester, all three effectively joined. Originally fishing villages, they have now succumbed to tourism and are delightful places. In Anstruther I come across yet another 'award winning' fish and chip shop. What a shame I've just eaten!

Further along I meet Ann and Richard, a delightful couple. She has just returned from nursing in Africa and he has a background in care. Almost immediately I am stopped by Geoff and Stefanie, who on hearing my story relate a tragic family medical history. Cystic Fibrosis (also a metabolic condition) has claimed five members of their family! They make a donation. .

I am now fully at ease wandering along this attractive coastline. I pass through Pittenweem, another tiny hidden' fishing village and then onto St Monians to finish at Elie, where my next host, Liz Carnie, collects me.

Liz and her husband Colin, a Highland fishery consultant, have a splendid residence at Earsferry. The Carnies are a CLIMB family. Liz's son Andrew was twenty-eight when he was first diagnosed with the generic metabolic condition Fabry's Disease, which is comparatively rare. He is now forty-four and, with strict medication, is able to live a normal life.

After a great meal I tuck into a comfortable bed. I affix the ear plugs and listen to some other great tracks from Kind of Blue – 'So What', ' Freddie Freeloader Freddie ', 'Blues in Green' etc.

It's been a great day out.

CLIMB parents Liz and Colin Carnie.

DAY 253

9th September – Earlsferry to East Wemyss – 16 miles

The Carnies are a delightful and attentive couple, and we have long discussions. Liz invites me to return one day, and it is with regret that I have to move on.

I strike out for Shell Bay and then swing slowly around the three-mile Largo Bay Beach, calling in the Railway Inn, Lower Largo, for a panini and pint. The most famous person to come out of this place is Robinson Crusoe. A stature marks the thatched cottage where the castaway Alexander Selkirk was born.

There follows a seven-mile slog in the pouring rain through Leven, Methil and Buckhaven to East Wemyss. Not for the first time, I arrive soaked: perspiration is always an added factor. The 'wicking out' label on outdoor clothing in my opinion assures to deceive.

My hosts are Jim and Susan Green, a CLIMB FAMILY. The couple lost their son Murray aged eighteen to the rare genetic metabolic condition Niemann Pick Type C. Their other son, Roy aged thirty-two, lives at home has the same condition. The couple both work tirelessly for the understanding of Niemann Pick, named after the German physicians who isolated it. Susan and Jim, a former head teacher, are both chairpersons of Niemann Pick National General and Research Committees.

They play me several videos explaining the build up of Glycosphingolipids in the nervous system, which causes the condition.

This compassionate couple have made me most welcome.

DAY 254

10th September – East Wemyss to Dalgetty Bay – 17 miles

I find saying goodbye to Jim, Susan and Roy isn't easy. Susan presents me me with an umbrella – just what I need. I will call it Sarah (Gamp) 2. Sarah 1, bought for three quid back in Prestatyn, has long disintegrated. The kindly Jim offers to take my rucksack on to my next B & B.

It is, therefore, another Free day. The weather is fine and I return to the Coastal Path. The scenery is dramatic, almost Mediterranean. On a cliff top I pause at the Dysart Memorial to the hundreds of miners killed or injured in three nearby coalmines between 1915 and 1925.

While having lunch in the Kirkcaldy shopping precinct I'm approached by an elderly gentleman who spots my CLIMB shirt and gives me £10. Later, in a Kingshorn pub, I get the same response – the landlady and customers combine to hand me another £10.

Heavy rain now prevails. A phone call comes in from a Rizi Mohammad for a live interview on Edinburgh's Radio Ramadan tomorrow. (I kid you not – this is not a spoof call.) I struggle to Aberdour to finish up at a dangerous road intersection north of Dalgetty Bay, which is without pedestrian lights.

'Watch it, Col – it's rush hour and raining. I don't want to be spread across the road like a hedgehog, thank you,' warns an anxious Flek.

I take my time to select the correct moves. I am looking for Dale Farm for tenting but, frankly, I don't fancy it. Dripping wet, I plead with a B & B owner Yvonne Barley (01383 417 681), and she grants me a whole cottage plus a food pack.

Flek says she is a peach, and I agree. I'm drenched, and my battered feet are sore and demanding a night inside.

Seventeen miles today: what a relief that Jim transported my rucksack. I ring him to say so. Thanking previous hosts is a custom I have long adopted.

The cottage is spacious and well appointed. I indulge by having a long, hot, decadent bath. The food pack is generous and, well fed, I put my feet up and get the iPod out.

'Got any Oasis?' asks Flek hopefully.

'I'm sorry, mate, you're out of luck again. Besides, they're Manchester City Supporters.'

I opt for Stan Kenton's 'Intermission Riff' and 'Artistry in Rhythm'. His exciting arrangements were not everyone's choice of a big band, but there was always massive support for the innovative 'Stan the Man'. I spared Flek his 'Peanut Vendor'!

For a Classic choice I settle for the majestic Saint-Saens Symphony No.3 ('Organ'). My Wish Track is the Eagles' One of These Nights'.

Martin's promotional artwork.

11th September – Dalgetty Bay – Forth Road Bridge to Edinburgh 9 miles

I make up my bedding. After years of this early morning ritual in the RAF and on fire stations, the practice has become second nature. I drop the keys in a box on the gate, and away I go back over that intersection again to Inverkeithing for a café breakfast.

The road climbs up over Queensferry North, and suddenly I am on to the Forth Road Bridge. There is a strong but warm wind blowing as I take in the breathtaking view.

To my left is the world renowned iconic and over engineered Forth Rail Bridge just half a mile away. The then Prince of Wales opened it in 1890 driving in the last rivet – gold-plated of course. It was not thought, as we say now, 'politically correct' to erect a memorial to the 93 men

Crossing the Forth Road Bridge.

who perished during its construction. One accident logbook contained 26,000 entries!

Down to the left sits Rosyth and its docks. Lines of waterside dwellings stretch away. I slide into Tesco's on the South Qeeensferry side for some lunch.

I must explain that for this project I purchased my Explorer maps at two-thirds cost in bulk from the Backpackers Club. Their secretary warned me that some of them might be out of date, a prediction that is about to ring true.

I get on to what I think is the A90 going into Edinburgh, but after about half a mile I hear a Flek's voice frantically yell out, *'Blimey, Col, this is a bloody motorway! What are you doing?'*

He is so right. The road had only recently been upgraded this side of the bridge with the real A90 forking away to Edinburgh a mile further up.

'You had better get a move on, mate, before the Law arrives', utters an anxious Flek.

I've nearly made it to the A90 exit when from behind me I hear the dreaded words, 'What do you think you're up to?'

It is coming from a police patrol car: they were bound to notice me.

'I'm walking around Great Britain,' I reply weakly.

The copper goes on, 'Well, if you want to finish it then take those steps just over there, go into and though the village at the bottom and join the A90 further on up, which has a cycle track. You can use it to walk into Edinburgh. Got it? Now clear off!'

He laughs and I laugh – don't we all laugh? – and I clear off!

I phone my next host, and Ian Thomson picks me up in the suburbs of the city. Ian and his wife Alison are a CLIMB family. Their daughter Kerry was diagnosed with the generic metabolic condition Leigh's Encephalopathy at three years, and sadly passed away aged twelve in 2003.

This is a busy household and they have plans for me tomorrow.

With the collusion of CLIMB the Thomsons whisk me away in the early morning using taxi driver Stewart, a friend of the theirs, for a meeting at the city's civic offices with the Rt. Hon.George Grubb, the Lord Provost, City of Edinburgh.

Also attending is Nancy Blaik, who from the age of six became blind. She is with her son Daniel*. He has suffered from birth with the rare generic metabolic condition Leighs and Encephalopathy. At thirty-two years he is profoundly disabled, both mentally and physically, and has required special needs most of his life. They are accompanied by three of his carers for the day, Magdalena, Christine and Ariadne.

The Lord Provost receives us for half an hour, offers refreshments and then distributes gifts. An engraved wallet (which I still use) comes my way. There are marvellous views through his parlour windows across this great city. Later our party walks up the Royal Mile ('The largest, longest and finest street for buildings and number of inhabitants, not only in Britain, but in the world,' said Daniel Defoe in 1723) on the way to meal in the castle.

In the civic offices, Edinburh, with the Provost and Nancy Blaik.

The constant stream of visitors is being entertained by a kilted 'Mel Gibson' look-alike covered in blue paint and yelling patriotic rallying cries. For a laugh I get him to shout 'Rangers 1 Hibernian 2' and 'Hearts 3 Celtic 1.'

'So that's your contribution to the Edinburgh Festival is it? Pathetic!' utters Flek.

Daniel is carried to the top restaurant by the special transporter for disabled visitors. He shares it with a gentleman whose wife had brought him all the way from Australia. What commitment! The meal with Daniel becomes fraught with difficulty: the gathering is jolted by the castle's traditional firing of its one o'clock gun,, which makes us all jump.

While the carers do their job, Nancy talks to me constantly about awareness and fund-raising for metabolic conditions. She has devoted much of her life to raising funds for the Charity CHAS (Children Hospices Action Scotland) to build a hospice at Kinross and another Robin Hospice at Balloch. For her services to these causes she was awarded the MBE. She lost her first husband, and with her second husband Jack she struggled for years to maintain care for her son. It has been a privilege for me to meet such a truly inspirational woman.

I say my goodbyes and spend the afternoon around Princes Street shopping and phoning. There seems to be a piper on every street corner. Flek thinks that it is a nice little earner, blowing up what we now know to be a Gortex bag all day! Very visible are the work preparations to bring the city a controversial tram system – which some say may never be finished.

Taxi driver Stewart picks me up. It's finally back to the Thomsons. where I really do have a phone interview with Rizi Mohammed on Radio Ramadan at 11pm! The station only operates through the early hours. It's a sort of reversal to Ramadan.

* Daniel, sadly, has since passed away.

13th September – Musselburgh to North Berwick – 15 miles

Ian runs me to the sea front at Musselburgh on the Firth of Forth. I walk the John Muir Way which extends forty- five miles and honours one of East Lothian's famous sons: born at Dunbar, he became the founder of the USA's National Parks system.

James Braidwood

In Edinburgh I visited the stature of James Braidwood, who founded the first municipal fire brigade in the world in the city in 1824.

Born in the city, he established the principles of fire fighting and building construction, many of which still apply today. He was appointed Master of Fire Engines at the age of 24 years, displaying outstanding heroism at great fires in 1824 (Edinburgh) and later in 1830 (London).

He left Edinburgh to become first chief of the London Fire Engine Establishment, later to become the London Fire Brigade.

He was killed by a falling wall while leading operations at the great Tooley Street fire on 22nd June 1861. The fire burned for two weeks and the estimated cost of the damage at that time was £2 million.

Braidwood is buried at Stoke Newington.

James Braidwood's statue.

I pass through Prestonpans, which saw salt production, then on to Cockenzie/Port Seton power station. For the 'Greens' it's a nightmare – the least carbon dioxide-efficient in the UK.

Here I also see the unacceptable face of Scotland. The Way goes behind some houses where three cars are parked, their doors open and the occupants lying around drunk, tins and bottles all over the place. It's only 10am. One of the inebriated group manages a 'Morning, pal' as I pass by.

Flek comments. 'I like a drink, but not this early. What a sad sight – especially the girls.'

In the main street at Aberlady I meet Alan Aitken carrying a box of plants. He takes a real interest in my long walk, then staggers me when recalling the time in his youth when he cycled around the world.

Flek stutters, 'You're just a beginner at all this long distance stuff, Col. We read about that cyclist bloke in Dundee and now another world beater. The Scots don't just go abroad to build bridges then.'

Alan tells me he regularly visits Chichester, where his best friend has a business. Once again it's a small world.

At Gullane I indulge myself in a superb patisserie, stop to talk to a charming couple Alastair and Catherine who are out for a weekend walk and then pass the rambling Scottish Fire Service training college – all in one road!

In North Berwick I find out that my B & B has been sponsored by the Thomsons of Edinburgh. The landlady, Christine Ray, runs a homely ship, lighting fags continuously. I share a pot of tea in her kitchen; she puffs away and relishes a drop of gin. I hear about her life travelling around the world with her husband, now deceased. Her demeanour is smitten with sadness and longing. She now makes ends meet by permanently housing some local 'socials', together with visitors to the town.

'There's plenty of hot water for a bath,' she shouts up the stairs.

Trouble is, she hasn't said that the taps indicate the opposite. Flek finds this confusion amusing and ventures that 'this walking lark' has scrambled my logic!

14th September – North Berwick to Dunbar – 12 miles

I wander down to the beach to view the sea and sandy bay for a while. A bracing start to the day – must do this more often. It's an interesting coastline. For a start, the single cone-shaped hill Berwick Law juts up incongruously to height of 600ft just behind the town.

The A198 reaches the coast at a tangent in Canty Bay, from where I can look out to the Bass Rock a little over a mile away and, to my right, the ruins of Tantallon Castle, which sits atop a promontory.

Bass Rock holds a huge colony of north Atlantic gannets, the nearest such bird colony to the UK mainland. Forty thousand pairs regularly use the Rock for breeding. The lighthouse was built by Robert Stephenson, grandfather of the author. Viewed together from the elevated main road, these natural and historical landmarks make a stunning combination.

Five miles on, at Tyninghame, I find a village hall-type café buzzing with patrons. The proprietors provide refreshments on the house. Customers chip in with small amounts of cash..

I pick up the John Muir Way again. It skirts an estuary when approaching Dunbar.

Walking into the town, Flek starts sniggering as we pass a non-conformist church. Reading the notice board outside, he ponders, 'Hey Col, I see that the incumbent minister is a Rev Twaddle. I cannot help thinking that when he is delivering his sermons it is only the Almighty who has a clue what he is talking about!'

My next host, Tom Lyons, picks me up. We arrive at Orchard House, a superb bungalow home bustling with friendship and good cooking. He and his wife Lesley are friends of Aliston Thomson: I am indebted to the Edinburgh couple yet again. We have an excellent evening meal in a noisy family atmosphere. Lesley dishes up a superb tray of roast spuds.

As I settle in my bed at these delightful digs, tonight's Concert will include: Dave Brubeck's 'Balcony Rock', Los Sabandenos (a wonderful male choir I heard in Tenerife) singing 'Stefanie' and Tchaikovsky's 'Marche Slave'. My wish track is the haunting Procol Harum 'A Whiter Shade of Pale', one of fewer than thirty single records to have sold ten million copies worldwide.

15th September – Dunbar to Coldingham – 12 miles

The view from Tom and Lesley's home is dominated by the Torness nuclear power Station standing on the coastline just half a mile across the fields. Lesley, with her dog Ruby, walks me down to it. The sea defences are massive. Hundreds of 5- and 13-ton Dolas blocks have been laid at random. They resemble ships anchors. Made of concrete, they dissipate wave energy five times more effectively than any rock of the same weight. A lifeboat is moored nearby. Lesley tells me that some time ago its predecessor slipped its mooring and foundered on the harbour rocks, causing severe damage.

'So it can happen to the best of 'em – what a cock-up!' comments Flek.

I follow the John Muir Way again, crossing the A1 to Cockburnspath and re-crossing it on to the A1107. Along this road I spot dahlias, a favourite of mine, growing under cover next to a cottage, so I knock on the door and ask to photo them. The lady says it has been a bad year for 'showing', but they nevertheless look blooming marvellous to me. So do the onions and leeks in the vegetable patch.

It's a long and boring trudge down to Coldingham. On the outskirts I spot a stature of Snow White against a house and get my camera out. I think of Mavis (*see page 196*). Well it makes a change from garden gnomes! In the village I phone my next host. While waiting for her, I pop into a pub. The time is 4pm. In the bar I find what seems to be an 'afternoon club'. It's a little boisterous, but I notice that many are sitting alone at separate tables. Like chameleons, they stare into space, gradually changing colour: they are quietly getting slammed! I settle for a Coke. Meanwhile one of the imbibers manages to stand up and ostentatiously stuffs a fiver in my hand.

'You can't get a round in with that, Col,' splutters Flek, 'Let's get out of here.'

My next host, Bea Nicholson, has come a long way to collect me from her home at Foulden, a few miles west of Berwick-on-Tweed. She is the mother of Stephen Nicholson, whom I stayed with at Helston in Cornwall back in February. (Her dear mum Mary Kirk – much loved member of the Chichester Jazz Club – was responsible for these host tie-ups, but she had passed away during the year.) Bea and her husband Ray are going to look after me for three days as I pass down the coast.

DAY 260

16th Sepember – Coldingham to Berwick-on-Tweed – 9 miles

It is a significant day as I cross back into England after a hundred days in Scotland.

I start a Free day by using the road for some time and go into Eyemouth to seek out a café, then onto Burnmouth. Shortly I transfer on to the Berwick Path and follow the railway along a dramatic coast. This Edinburgh to Euston main line is very close to the cliffs, and there has been a minor landslide overnight a few yards from edge. Three 'line personnel' are affecting repairs and kindly let me pass, a tight squeeze.

This Path is difficult and uneven, and my progress is further hampered by the state of my second pair of boots. A replacement pair will show up tomorrow, I hope.

Escape to England.

Bea comes out to meet me at the Magdalene golf course. She takes me into the border town of Berwick on Tweed. While she shops I walk around the defensive walls of the town and, boy, have they needed them! This place has come under siege on thirteen occasions. On the way home we stop to get an English border roadsign shot.

The Nicholsons are first class, helping me to plot my course using their computer skills. The day ends with a meal and wine.

Benji

Since leaving the Navy Ray Nicholson has become one of the 3,000 handlers for the dogs and cats charity, Pets as Therapy (PAT). It's estimated that over 100,000 patients a week in hospitals and care homes receive life-enhancing benefit from the service. Ray uses his rescue dog Benji (a Polish Lowland Sheepdog breed) on his visits. I have to say that he's one of the most beautiful dogs I have ever seen, and everybody loves him.

17th September – Berwick-on-Tweed to Goswick
Links Golf Club, Beal – 6 miles

It's a much shorter day. Bea drops me at the city walls and, after joining the A1 for a few miles, I turn left towards the coast, arriving at the Goswick Links Golf Club. It's lovely out here but not exactly quiet. The golfers are exposed to the noise of express trains and the daily screaming Tornadoes from Lossiemouth and Leuchars.

I just have time for a snack she has prepared, and then it's back home with Bea. This caring and efficient lady goes online and secures a B & B for tomorrow just off the road leading to Holy Island, Lindisfarne.

My boots (third pair) – The saga begins: A call to my suppliers reveals that the boots arrived today at the Nicholsons, but because there was no one at home to sign for them they were taken back to a despatch depot. Curses! Ray tells me that he was home at the time of their supposed arrival. I arrange another try for tomorrow.

My Hosts – Bless 'em!
'Mankind is divisible into two great classes: hosts and guests.'
– Max Beerbohm

So I had plotted and planned to complete this journey in approximately 350 days but, there remained a difficult logistical challenge. Where and how was I going to find under-roof accommodation for that length of time? It was going to be necessary to pitch a tent.

The first call from the charity's office at Crewe went out to CLIMB families – the parents, relatives and friends of children directly affected by metabolic disorders.

Some 16,000 families fall into the first category, but only a fraction of them live on my intended coastal route. The final tally brought forty-five stop-overs.

Most gratifying, it meant that I could hear at first hand from the parents about difficulties of caring for children with metabolic conditions. Many of the host parents travelled considerable distances to retrieve me from my route and return me in the morning.

I had many other avenues to follow. An approach to Rotary International produced excellent results: its rallying for hosts is covered elsewhere.

Slowly offers of accommodation started to trickle in, thanks largely to the efforts of the CLIMB staff. This meant that, with the inclusion of occasional B & Bs, it wasn't necessary for me pitch my tent until early April.

Offers came in from many of my contacts in the fire and rescue services of Great Britain, the Chichester Jazz Club and the Old Cicestrians (Chichester High School Old Boys).

Many of YHA premises waived their fees, as did Lee Abbey, St Andrews police station and RAF Kinloss.

The proprietors of camp and caravan sites often let me pitch without payment, sometimes providing the treat of a static caravan. I also received a sympathetic hearing from many commercial accommodation premises as well.

My family sponsored B & B accommodation for me. Youngest son Stewart with partner Christine and her daughters Lauren and Amy came out to Goodwick near Fishguard on my birthday, while daughter Sonya, with grandson Jack and partner Simon, motored all the way to South Wales to treat me in a hotel at Swansea. My oldest daughter Suzanne found me several hosts, and brother Alan and sister-in-law Ann came up to Norfolk arranging a stay with me at a fine B & B near Great Yarmouth. The family worked tirelessly on seeking accommodation sponsors for Walk GB 4 Climb.

Finally I must mention the staff at CLIMB. Lesley Greene, Chris Roberts and Pam Davies kept up the pressure. Many a time I received a mobile call to tell me that a 'room in an inn' had been found.

I have to confess that I had neither the will nor the inclination to face living in a tent for months on end. Outward-bound material I am not, but I take some pride in surviving over forty nights in my Hilliberg tent, brewing up and trying to keep warm, particularly in the wild parts of Scotland. I got to look forward to the late night iPod concerts made possible by the considerable glare of a 'Robert Dyas' headlamp, an invaluable gift from my son Martin.

NOTE: A breakdown of host sources is posted as an Appendix on page 546.

DAY 262

*18th September – Brock Mill Farm at Beal to Holy Island and
return – 8 miles*

Bea makes the long trip to drop me at the B & B at Brock Mill Farm. I leave my rucksack there, and then she runs me a couple of miles to the Lindisfarne causeway. I sadly say goodbye to her: the Nicholson family in Cornwall and the Scottish Borders have served me well. Her mother Mary Kirk would have been so pleased.

It is a Free day. Walking out to Holy Island is about catching the low tide. This gives drivers about five hours to exit. Despite the warnings, vehicle strandings are not unknown. I don't have the luxury of transport and yomp the 5km out to Lindisfarne Castle. A stream of cars pass me continually. I am the only pilgrim (or pillock) on foot!

Lindisfarne.

The name Snook appears several times on the OS map. In these parts it means promontory or point, so I think I am entitled to make one.

Holy Island is not, as I imagined, a seat of learning and devotion. It is like, any other coastal resort, a pocket of commercialism. There is an impressive sculpture of St Cuthbert on the monastery green in the village here, raising his arms towards the heavens. I suspect his gesture is not in exultation but in despair.

The usual tourist haunts of cafés, pubs and gift shops abound. All delivery vans have the exalted words 'Holy Island' stamped on them. The thrust of this little retail world is completed when a resident of the last house before the car park has dug up a selection of his garden produce. He lays it out on the pavement for a final sale to the visitors rushing to their cars to beat the tide. I join them, scurrying along in worn out boots, and find a super café on the mainland.

The boots saga, latest: Back on the mainland I find that my boots *did* arrive but, once again, no signature, no boots. To be fair, the landlady couldn't make a promise that she would on the premises all day.

Flek drives home the point that I left the order for the new pair a little late. However, there were unforeseen import problems and a string of delivery delays were out of my control.

I have entered weather forecast area Tyne.

Day 263
19th September – Brock Mill Farm to Waren Mill Camp Site – 8 miles

My feet are still smarting about the missing boots. The existing pair are 'going home' fast. I will have to arrange with my suppliers an address that can definitely take a delivery.

I make for the A1 and cross it for a series of quieter lanes. It is hot and hard going. I must look pretty scruffy. I've got used to being a man of the road, but I'm not yet quite a tramp. (Mile-post inspectors my Dad used to call them.) It's a shorter day, and in the early afternoon I arrive early at Waren Mill campsite a few miles from Bamburgh Castle.

I have to pitch on wet ground. Leaving the tent to explore the facilities, I suffer a bad attack of cramp. Little do I realise at the time that, thanks to coming good fortune, this is the LAST time I will have to camp out. I visit the site restaurant. It's full of families having a late break. Despite the noise and the 'charming little kiddies' running around my table, I enjoy an excellent, well-presented meal.

I read the *Telegraph*, chat to some visitors, return to my tent and go through the procedures necessary to ensure any chance of a good night's sleep. Perhaps I am going to miss this ritual after all . . .

'I don't think so,' voices a doubting Flek, 'You've done your bit, spending countless nights camping out, making significant savings to the overall costs of the project.'

'Well, thank you, chum – most understanding of you.'

I ring my kit suppliers to arrange yet another suitable host venue to drop off the new boots I should be walking in by now.

DAY 264
20th September – Waren campsite to the Ship Inn,
Newton-by-Sea – 11 miles

On another lovely morning I walk a couple of miles towards the coast. Unexpectedly around a bend in the road the massive edifice of Bamburgh Castle comes into view. Regularly voted into the top three of must-see historical sites in the UK, it's built on an outcrop and dominates the open convoluted coastline of Northumberland. It was clearly visible on my visit to Holy Island yesterday. Extensively restored during the 18th and 19th centuries, much of it is now used for private apartments.

The castle towers over the village, which is so quiet on a Sunday morning. Eating houses haven't yet opened. I wander up the steep approach entrance to the castle and enquire whether there is a visitors' café. The answer is Yes, but, it's seven quid to get in. I retire gracefully and look at my map. Two miles down the road is Seahouses: I'm bound to get some breakfast there.

Seahouses is full of the hustle and bustle of day visitors, made even noisier by a Harley Davidson rally. These glitzy motor bikes are everywhere. After initially satisfying my hunger I sit down in the square and read a broadsheet. My shirt attracts attention, and a few enquiries are answered.

I think an explanation is overdue. I can hear people saying: 'If there's all this interest, why didn't you carry a collecting tin Colin?'

It's a very good question. Well, for a person(s) who collects money in public the problem of its disposal is solved by the larger charities who swamp the project with an accompanying entourage. These administer the collection and organise the regular and correct clearance of monies received. It's because they are well known that they attract the most funds, and so they obviously organise administrative back up.

A lone person operating remotely on behalf of a small charity has the worry and also the weight of mostly small change to contend with: believe me, it presents a dilemma. There were times when I wished I had had a tin in my hand. Larger donations were channelled via the Just Giving Website or by cheque to CLIMB.

I go for an early lunch of fish and chips because they're so good up here.

Fish and chips with Harley Davidson, Seahouses.

What am I going to do about accommodation tonight? For only the second time I enter a tourist information office and book a B & B at the Sportsman five miles up the coast at Newton-by-the-Sea. That settled, I move on through North Sunderland (a long way from its namesake).

I'm experiencing much discomfort, with my worn out boots, and the soles of my feet are throbbing. Added to this is a niggling, stinging pain in the soft tissue under my left small toe which is to plague me for the rest of the journey. I have found that by bending my foot, rather like a horse resting a hind leg, the stinging abates for an hour or so. The sight of this hunchback loner leaning against lamp posts or walls in such a manner must have puzzled many a passing motorist.

'Spect you'll need an op on that when you get back' states Flek, sounding almost concerned.

'Well, it's something to look forward to, my friend. Your anxiety overwhelms me!'

The Sportsman has most friendly staff. The decor of my room, which overlooks the beach, is bijou. I catch up on my blog/log entries and make a few phone calls. I feel very optimistic these days, and hope that my mood is sensed by my blog readers.

A young and beautiful Czech waitress fetches me some tea and cake. Later I see her and a handsome young man prancing down to the chilly sea for a dip. I can hear a cynical Tony Hancock uttering, 'Oh how romantic is that! Don't worry – the freezing water will soon put the mockers on their intentions.'

My musical selection tonight is for the dazzling bop pianist Bud Powell powering his way through 'Un Poco Loco'. Henry Purcell relates the sad tale of Dido and Aeneas. My wish track is the Saint-Saens 'Introduction and Rondo Capriccioso'. Wonderful!

While eating a hearty breakfast, I ask the Czech waitress if anything exciting ever happens here. I'm just making small talk, but it alerts Flek.

'Blimey, Colin, is this a disguised reference to what you saw on the beach yesterday? A little risqué, don't you think?'

'We had a boiler fire here a couple of weeks ago,' she replies. 'The fire brigade turned up.'

'You see Flek, to a reasonable question one gets a rational answer. Happier now?'

Anyway the staff don't seem put out, and they present me with a big cake as I set out to walk several miles of the coastal path. There's a big fishing competition going on, and I question a couple of the entrants.

'It's cod we're after,' says one.

'You seem awfully spread out,' I say, having noted that entrants are casting about half a mile apart.

I'm told that they all meet up later on and decide the winner. It all sounds hit-and-miss, but never question anglers. In my experience they concentrate a lot and say little – a quiet and sullen lot. It's the nature of the sport.

At lunchtime I'm heading for a pub when I see something that should alert 'twitchers' nationwide. On a field wall stands a 2ft high metal modern sculpture.

'It's probably an apprentice piece,' suggests Flek.

'But I wonder if anyone has classified a species name,' I reply.

I ponder for a while and then I came up with, tongue in cheek, Lesser Welded, Whitworth Threaded, Russell Crowe.

Alert all twitchers!

'How does that sound? Now then let me think – it's got to have a habitat classification, be a native of somewhere.'

That's easy,' says Flek. 'It's got to be local because it's bolted to the wall!'

The ornithological field trip completed, I walk on to the Fisherman's Arms up ahead. I get a pint and have just sat down when a spritely old boy and his lady come in and sit at my table.

We started talking. He is Tommy, a Geordie ex-miner who spent thirty seven years down the pit, much of it at Easington, an enormous coalfield. The pit suffered a disaster in 1951 when eighty seven men were killed in an explosion there.

'For year after year we ate dust in cramped conditions,' Tommy explains. 'I went before a claims board but never got any compensation, though. Those bastards never had a clue what we went through.'

Flek, listening intently, whispers 'To be fair, in a way the board were right after all – Tommy has lived on to reach eighty-seven and is still able to drive his car.'

His fancy woman (Tommy's words) Alice is 88 years old. Sitting next to him, she leans over to me and jokes in a delightful Geordie accent, 'He's my toy boy, you know.'

We talk on. Sadly I have to leave him and his tale of a life ravaged by circumstance. Like many elderly folk, he is passing on priceless industrial and social history but is oblivious to the fact.

Warkworth is still a long way off. When I can I keep to the National Cycle Paths, bikers are everywhere, hurtling down the highways without a care for anyone. At Warkwoth, pushed for accommodation, I book into the rather nice Sun Hotel as a treat, but it costs me £60!

My room looks out almost directly onto the walls of a castle which towers above me. I cut the cost by heating up a two course dehydrated meal in my room. No flame is required, only boiling water.

The coastal path hasn't been short of impressive scenery and interest, but once again it's the people who impress most of all.

DAY 266

22nd September – Warkworth to Newbiggin-on-Sea – 15 miles

At breakfast in the hotel I'm amazed that a lady on the next table knows who I am. Her daughter once worked with my daughter Sonya – I can't remember where! Leaving, I pass Warkworth Castle, which stands within an oxbow of the charmingly named Coquet River.

It starts to rain as I amble down to – guess where – the town of Amble! My next hosts, Bob and Monica Mitchell, come out and meet me on the road. They tell me I'm to lunch at a Widdrington pub where they have left payment. They take my rucksack. check me again when I'm en route and are also at Newbiggin-by-the-Sea to meet me.

I give an interview to a local journalist, and have photo shoots, including one of me pushing Dylan, the Mitchells' grandson, along the promenade. The small bay has had an impressive make-over after gaining a multi million European grant.

Dylan, Newbiggin-on-Sea.

The Mitchells are a remarkable family. Their adopted daughter Sarah is the mum of 13-year-old Dylan and twin daughters Anissa and Katrina, aged nine. All have the metabolic condition Coffin Lowry Syndrome, and collectively they have numerous physical and mental disabilities. Bob and Monica now look after them on a permanent basis. Daughter Sarah has another boy, Kai aged five, who has a similar disability.

Despite the difficulties Bob, an ex-colliery electrician, and the ever cheerful Monica are devoted to keeping the children together as a happy family unit. One can only admire their purpose, and it's such a joy to meet them all

Bob takes me on a tour of Ashington, where endless rows of houses built for miners still stand. The streets were never given names, only letters, and the houses were constructed of different coloured bricks to denote the occupants as either 'sinkers' (those who dug out the shafts) or 'pit head' miners.

Due to the Mitchells obvious lack of home accommodation Bob, a thoughtful man, has fixed up a static caravan for me at nearby Sandy Bay. I watch the end-of-season elderly campers enjoying their bingo in the caravan park's entertainment complex, and retire to the 'static', which is large, well appointed but a trifle cold: it's getting late in the season.

'Got any Beatles' enquires Flek.

'I've been expecting another one of your requests, Flek. To tell you the truth, I'm not a great fan. Had I known you were going to turn up I might have brought along 'Norwegian Wood' and 'Eleanor Rigby', but I didn't.'

'Sorry, my friend,' I added. 'We don't seem to have much in common when it comes to music. It's the age gap, you know. When I first got interested in recorded music the Beatles and Elvis weren't even born.

'I now know that the inclusion of the Black Sabbath/Led Zeppelin or The Melvins/Nirvana or even The Sex Pistols/The Stranglers would have added excitement to your journey and might have been a revelation to me, but it's not to be. They will naturally be placed on the Wish List. I'm sorry, mate'.

He understands why I haven't planned his programme, but it doesn't help. Without a further word he takes to his rest.

DAY 267

23rd September – Newbiggin-by-the-Sea to Tynemouth fire station
– 14 miles

The ever-thoughtful Bob arrives to take my rucksack on. The OS Map shows that after getting onto the Blyth Road from the A189 trunk road there's going to be a series of very dicey road crossings.

At first I walk the Sustrains National Cycle Path on a parallel minor road, but, I am going to have to run the gauntlet over two intersections before I escape on the A193 into Blyth. There are no concessions to pedestrians here. It is very dodgy and I have to constantly keep my eyes about me. I'm glad the Law don't turn up!

Finally I get off the trunk road – and who arrives? Yes, it's Bob with Dylan yet again! I'd left some papers in his car. I say a final goodbye to a true friend and his grandson and begin a long urban trudge.

Passing through Blyth and Whitley Bay, I complete the final miles through increasing suburban intensity to arrive at the Tynemouth fire station. I am just in time because it is going to be demolished in a couple of months, to be replaced with a new building on the same site.

Greeted by Trevor Tague, district office, I enjoy a curry with the White Watch. It' a quiet night, but just before sitting down to breakfast they get a 'shout' to assist a passenger in what is now classified as a road traffic 'incident'. Apparently it has now been deemed by the insurance companies that the use of the word 'accident' implies blame!

Settling into the station, Flek suddenly says, 'Day by day you're getting there, Col. Well done – keep it up! I'm always here for counselling, you know.'

It's a kind thought.

24th September – Tynemouth fire station to Newcastle Central – 12 miles

On a sunny morning I stroll down through South Shields. It's an urban pavement journey the whole way on to Wallsend. There are huge public works going on here – the construction of a new road tunnel under the Tyne is under way.

Tucked back in a wasteland cul-de-sac is a refreshment kiosk run by Eric. It's a slack time so he talks to me about the project. His assessment is as professional as you could expect from a frustrated roadside catering operative.

'Is it needed?' I ask.

'No' he says.

Next up is the cost.

'Bloody waste of money' he protests.

'Is it on time? 'I persist.

'Nobody round here seems to know what's going on,'

He is ranting by now.

'Has it affected business?'

I have hit a raw nerve.

'The contractors keep creating diversions.' His face goes red with anger. 'I'm just getting used to a good trade and then they slap up a few bollards and it's curtains for me. '

I finish my coffee and leave. I glance back, the poor bloke looks bored to tears.

There's a maze of works obstructions before I finally veer off to the famous Segedunam Roman Fort. My route then joins the River Tyne towpath, which is busy with ramblers finishing the Hadrians Wall Way, cyclists out on a spin and locals taking a constitutional.

*'Always be prepared for the unusual, '*Flek often prophesies, so he is quite unruffled when two lads appear, each with a large owl perched on an arm. One has an eagle owl called 'Amber' and the other a snowy owl called 'Snowy'. They cost £300 and £150 respectively and are eleven weeks old, the lads tell me.

What amazes Flek is the rate at which these magnificent raptors are devouring dead chicks. The boys' set objective is to open their own falconry, and in this endeavour I can't help but wish them the best of luck.

Amber and Snowy.

Entering Newcastle along the river I'm intrigued by the town's geography. The Tyne has cut out a steep valley across which there are at least six bridges, the first being the Millennium Swing Bridge. I turn uphill into the city and have a light lunch.

My next host, Anita Landells, will come in to pick me up at the bus station. She is the sister of my good friend Daphne Beard of Bognor. We bus it to her home and I meet husband George.

DAY 269
25th Sepember – Rest day – Newcastle

Anita has made an appointment for me to meet the mayor of Newcastle, Councillor David Wood. We catch the bus. I find it fascinating to be in the council chambers of such an illustrious city. It's to be expected that the walls are covered with documents depicting the civic history, yet what really impress me are the striking regalia and symbols of office which adorn the long corridor leading to the lord mayor's parlour.

The mayor tells me that the city is adopting one of the latest Royal Navy destroyers, *HMS Dauntless,* and I am happy to tell him that my father Bill, a chief petty officer, served on an earlier destroyer of the same name in the 1930s. I am also able tell him that I actually saw the Geordie football legend Jackie Milburn performing his magic against Portsmouth at Fratton Park in the Fifties.

With the lord mayor of Newcastle.

He is a genial man and I hope he was as impressed by my remarks as I was by his council chamber.

This is a vibrant and historical place, with superb shopping and marketing parades, and riverside vistas second to none – so many bridges lined up. It also boasts an excellent transport infrastructure; apparently it has a pulsating night life culture as well.

'If only you were still in your twenties, Col,' taunts Flek.

'Listen, you –I'll gladly settle for my fifties!'

I spend the afternoon trolling around the city centre, joining an invasion of university students who are boisterous and half dressed (didn't notice what the men were wearing). I have to say, perhaps a trifle curmudgeonly, that they're spending the taxpayers' grant money without a care in the world, blast em!

An exasperated Flek spouts his perplexing logic again: 'Well, you did tell me that Victor Meldrew is a role model of yours? It's plain that your sympathies are definitely not with the youth of today. You just can't get to grips that they are part of the digital revolution with which you are completely out of touch, you poor old sod.'

He has a point, but I'm not going to tell him so.

Over the evening meal Anita and George tell me that they first met at RAF Rheindahlen in what was then West Germany. This is the base where I spent two years of my RAF service prior to their arrival, another coincidence.

The boots: Apparently my boots will not now arrive for another week, so George is going to lend me his. He thinks that they are a perfect fit. We shall see.

DAY 270

26th September – Newcastle, Gateshead to South Shields – 12 miles

I put George's boots on. They seem to fit OK. Before we leave he ensures that I imbibe the local nectar, the life saving elixir of life for a Geordie, i.e. a glass of Newcastle Brown Ale.

'Wae aye man three bottles of this stuff then it is off to a journey into space!,' he proudly boasts.

I kiss the caring Anita a goodbye and George runs me via some historical sites to the now 'revolutionary' Millennium Tilting Bridge. He explains that due to the Newcastle elders' reluctance to co-finance the project, GATESHEAD has been chiselled on the buttress walls both sides of the Bridge.

'What happened to "We're all in this together"?' ponders Flek

We say goodbye and I walk across this unusual pedestrian bridge, now an iconic link. Unfortunately I am not around to see the daily tilting routine. I immediately rest on the Gateshead side to discard a pair of socks – a fine-tuning exercise necessary in order to embrace George's boots!

Up the hill to my right is the Sage Gateshead Centre, futuristic in design, resembling a giant mollusc and created to be a musical centre of international repute. On a perfect day I take the high-level NCP following the River Tyne through Gateshead and Heburn, Catherine Cookson territory.

Today I continue my 'leisurely' stroll around the land, but in 1936, the year of my birth, a symbolic march began downriver from here at Jarrow, an event which became forever etched in trade union history. Two hundred miners put on the only boots they had and marched down to Westminster to highlight the poverty and plight they were in. Little was done, except they were given £1 each to get the train home.

Apart from the collieries being marked on the OS Map and a few memorials, I saw little structural evidence that the mines ever existed. The whole area has been swallowed up by industrial units and housing schemes.

After many miles of pleasant walking following the Tyne I am back on the coast road at South Shields. My next host is Anthony Marshall, a maths teacher at a local school. He is one of the three pals, the other two being Brian Casson at Middlesborough and Mark Egan, a CLIMB parent, at Herne Bay. The latter has rallied them to help me out.

I meet 'Anth' at the Bamburgh pub, and we sit outside chatting and watching tents being erected as part of the Great North Run. It takes part next weekend and terminates on this long coast road.

Later he takes me to one of the famous local pubs, the Dolly Peel, where I meet his brother Gregg and friends. Subsequently Anth keeps in touch and makes donations – a great bloke!

27th September – South Shields via Sunderland to Seaham B & B – 14 miles

Anth leaves me down on the coast road. He suggests I look out for a couple of local social and engineering attractions along the way. First is the Marsden Grotto, the only restaurant/dining room in Europe which is set in a cave down at the bottom of the cliffs.

Further on down the coast I pass the Souter Lighthouse, the first one in the UK to use AC power. Decommissioned in 1988, it is said to be haunted. Before it was built this coastline was averaging forty four wrecks per mile!

I bypass the colliery village of Seaburn and approach Sunderland. The great surprise to me here is that this city has a lovely long sandy beach at Roker. It's late September and holiday makers are playing football and volleyball on firm sand. The Wearside Way goes past the university and on to the Wearmouth Bridge. I pass over into the shopping centre and get some lunch.

Walking out of the city into the suburbs I approach the Phoenix pub. Passing it on the other side of the road, I am called across by a large group of Geordies standing on the pavement enjoying drinks and a fag. They are attending a christening and are 'wetting the baby's head' with such enthusiasm that many are in a stupor. This inebriated gang make a great fuss of me with drinks and arrange a whip round on the pavement for CLIMB which realises £60. To validate their claim of enforced merriment I asked to see the child at the centre of attention and she was brought out for me to inspect. Such a pretty dress – aaah!

'Your obligation is completed, lads, so carry on boozing!' shouts Flek as we prepare to move off.

I am having a great time, but sadly drag myself away as there is still much staggering to be done before reaching my B & B. Before I left, Alan and Geoff asked to be mentioned on my blog as they make coffins!

Several miles on, at Seaham, I find my Chapel House B & B arranged for me by Lesley Greene at CLIMB. This is a superb but tasteful conversion of an ex-Methodist district church and is run by Gina and Len. I settle in and make up a dehydrated meal of beef noodles followed by chocolate pudding. It's not too bad, and quite filling.

During today's journey I come across more roadside tourist

information lecterns detailing the closing of nearby collieries and the effects on the village manpower which laboured in them. All this has happened within the last fifteen years. Arthur Scargill put his case, but in the end the unions could do little to prevent the passing of the pits that powered the industrial revolution. But I am sure that Arthur knows the proverb 'What goes around, comes around.' Coal mining carries on, but not as we knew it.

Some music is required to finish the day. In the 1920's Louis Armstrong created some outstanding solos with his Hot Five and Hot 7 line-ups. I'm going to listen to him on 'Struttin With Some Barbeque' and 'Melancholy Blues' – also the Modern Jazz Quartet playing 'Softly, As In A Morning Sunrise'.

My Wish Track tonight is the Carpenters' 'Goodbye To Love', mainly because of the exhilerating guitar solo bridge in the middle.

DAY 272
28th September – Seaham to Hartlepool – 11 miles

I take my leave from Gina and Len after a homely stay. My new hosts are Graham and Christine Wylde. They pick me up from Chapel House and I am delighted to hear that Graham is coming with me today. Hooray! someone to walk with.

It's unfortunate that only a dozen or so people were able to join me on stages throughout the year. Although small in number, they all added fillip to my step, and it was so good to have someone new to converse with.

I sense petulance from my permanent confidant.

'You want to remember, mate, that when all your one day wonders have disappeared, who is left to share the burdens of life with you? It's me, that's who it is. I know when I'm not wanted, so there'.

It is pure Flek, said with his usual malice then usually reverting to pathos. I feel obliged to respond to his outburst.

'It's all right Flek, my friend. Your company is very much appreciated It's just a "different face" and all that.'

Graham and I trek nine miles of the Durham Coast Path. He is great company and works for Walkers Crisps. The Wyldes are a CLIMB family, and as we cover the ground he talks about the trials and tribulations of having several genetic condition children.

Their daughters Danielle and Georgia have the metabolic condition Ornithine Transcarbamylase Deficiency. With a strict medication and nutritional regime they are able to live a normal life and go to school. However, such are the uncertainties of this condition that for boys the life expectancy is usually short. Tragically the Wylde's lost their only son Rhys after just three days.

Fortunately their other daughters Bethany and Keira are clear of the disease.

During the day we call into the Easington Colliery 'Officials' Club. The pecking order at the pits means that this club is *not* for coal face miners: they have their own. We have some great banter with the members, who have a card school going – only one man is wearing a cloth cap. The bar lady has the same wear-and-tear look as the men and serves us a pint for £1.50. Graham explains that the miners strike violent picket line scenes in the film 'Billy Elliot' were filmed a couple of streets away.

Christine picks us up and we return to their home at Peterlee. I sit down and have a scrumptious tea with the Wyldes, a happy, loving and noisy family. It's a joyous and uplifting experience. Their youngest, Keira, is a right little madam.

Easington Colliery 'Officials' Club.

DAY 273

29th September – Hartlepool to Middlesborough – 12 miles

All the Wylde kids are going to school. I say good bye to Christine and Graeme drops me off. It's still warm lovely weather. Today is going to comprise three stages. The first road is into Hartlepool city centre, where I get a snack. Lesley Greene of CLIMB rings and we have a general chat about future accommodation and the state of the sponsorship. Basically, after an initial flurry of donations, the total has levelled off at around £18,000.

The second highway takes me to the outskirts of the town, and I get a pub lunch.

The third way opens up on to a plain of past industrial development which stretches beyond the River Tees into Redcar. Although much of it now has been levelled and has had a sensitive change of use put into place (a water nature reserve), the skyline is still dominated by heavy industrial works of all categories.

Oil refineries and storage depots, gas works, steel and chemical plants – they are all here, plus industrial parks. Now add the Hartlepool Nuclear Power Station, the first to be sited near an urban area. There can hardly be more a sustained industrial development area anywhere in the country.

For mostly health and safety reasons, I have resisted using my iPod when on any highway. Today I can proceed unheeded. The through road is strangely quiet, only the occasional lorry or tanker thundering by, so I shove the earplugs in and select the most apt track I can find, viz Chris Rea's 'Road to Hell'.

My compass bearing is already set for me – Middlesbrough's famous Transporter Bridge, which I can see in the far distance.

I call into the Billingham fire station for a drink. Operationally these fire fighters must cover one of the greatest concentrations of major fire risk in the UK. A mile on, and I pay my 50p to cross the Tees on the Transporter Bridge. Already famous for being the only one of its type in the UK, it won more fame when used as a storyline in the TV series Auf Weidersehen Pet. Built in 1911, its suspended gondolier carries cars and pedestrians across the river in 90 seconds. It also provides Britain's only bridge bungee Jump site.

On the other side I enter the first café for a drink. Owner Steve keeps the place open for me and we chat. When learning that I am from West Sussex he tells me he used to be a milkman in Billingshurst.

'What brings you up here?' I ask.

My enquiry triggers an amusing interlude as he relates the story of his first wife, who he says dragged him against his will up here into the 'wilderness'. He slags her off without mercy,

'She cost me a small fortune,' he says, turning puce as he vents his spleen. The ranting has been heard by his second wife, who cleaning up the place and, boy, does she remonstrate with him.

'Was it something I said?' I venture.

We all have a good laugh and he throws me out.

I get on and enter the café in Marks and Sparks, then make some phone calls and prepare my blog. In urban areas carrying a large rucksack and wearing a bandana makes me 'different'. I must look a little out of place but, thank God, I could never seek celebrity status.

'Pull the other one,' argues Flek, 'You would love it if someone asked you for an autograph'

'I'm afraid you're wrong Flek. Now, if I tied a knot in each corner of a handkerchief, placed it on my head and went paddling on the beach with braces and a Fair Isle jumper on then I would be someone. Anyways, if wearing a bandana is good enough for Rafael Nadal, then it is good enough for me!'

My next host is Brian Casson, a friend of Anth (South Shields) and Mark (Herne Bay). He takes me home to Joanne his wife, who is expecting a baby. Over dinner he relates the amusing tale of how he and Joanne got together. One day thinking, he was taking her out on the tiles, she found herself on the Transporter Bridge, where he proposed to her. Their fares must have totalled only a quid. What a Romeo!

DAY 274

30th September – Middlesborough to Skelton – 11 miles

Brian has gone to work, so Joanne sees me off. I wish her luck for the birth of sprog number two. Out of the city I follow the A1085 through Cleveland's industrial heartland, now on the south side of the Tees, and on to Redcar in the pouring rain. I still haven't shaken off the heavy industry, which is all around me. I find a lunch in Tescoe's, where else!

Following the coast road to Marske-by-the-Sea, I have to turn inland. The last two miles into Skelton are quite hazardous. In addition to the rain, I have to put up with a twisting undulating road in heavy traffic with little or no refuge for pedestrians.

With difficulty I make it, getting to the town in a torrential downpour. Once again Sarah (Mk.2) saves me (and Flek) a soaking. I take shelter and ring my next host, Rosemary Light; she is the cousin of my Southern Trails walking friend Ted Powell of Shoreham and lives up the other end of town.

Once again a host opens the front door to a pathetic individual covered in precipitation. I needn't have worried: Rosemary will look after me just fine for the next two days.

Now, then: will my boots arrive tomorrow?

DAY 275

1st October 30 – Skelton to Runswick Bay campsite – 10 miles

As I still only have only shoes to wear I avoid the Cleveland way today and walk the ten miles by road to Runswick Bay. After an hour Rosemary rings to tell that **My boots have arrived!**

En route I come across a striking memorial in the form of a huge pit winding wheel from an iron ore mine. It's now mounted in the middle of a roundabout on the top of a hill. Mightily imposing, it's an industrial heritage commemoration on a mammoth scale!

I have lunch at Loftus and a pint in the Tiger at yet another place called Easington. Later I pass the Old Boulby potash mine, which is now a deep experimental laboratory researching 'dark matter' – whatever that is.

The coastal village of Staithes, where Captain Cook spent some of this formative years working in the local grocery store, is just too far to venture to.

Getting to Runswick Bay, I am just in time to get the bus back to Rosemary's place. At last – there in a box is my third pair of boots. It feels like Christmas. This has been a frustrating tale of a late order, a delay for many weeks awaiting importation, several delivery dates aborted due to administration difficulties (i.e. no one available to sign the docket at delivery addresses) and finally, I have to admit it, bad planning on my part.

I put them on and swing my feet up on to a garden table for Rosemary to take an historic photo. We have a drink to celebrate. I have thought of putting the now discarded pair on ebay, but the postage would surely outweigh the winning bid. Rosemary could grow geraniums in them!

I go to bed promising my tootsies better days ahead.

'You are a first class nutcase, Col,' says Flek, yawning as he turns in.

Does that mean promotion, I wonder!

The third pair of boots arrives at Skelton.

DAY 276

2st October – Runswick Bay to Whitby – 9 miles

Rosemary is going to walk with me today, so it's a threesome that sets off – the two of us plus my boots. With no time to run them in, I am a little apprehensive.

We catch the bus back to Runswick Bay and get on to the beach. Here Jon Hall, a landscape painter, is putting the new local inland rescue boat on canvas. He allows me to sign it on the back. I am tempted to scribble 'J.Constable' but settle for my initials CWS, which have a fame of their own.

Getting off the beach means having to follow a stream into a ravine, then clambering over slippery rocks to ascend two hundred steps to the clifftop. It is worth the effort. Before us is an exhilarating five-mile stroll along the cliffs, the Cleveland Way stretched out before us. There are splendid views overshadowing bays and beaches in early October – a memorable day.

We stop for lunch at the locally well known Twins End Café at Sandend. Rosemary is anxious to catch her bus home on the outskirts of Whitby but, missing one, she settles to walk on with me. We both enjoy tea in the town, and she meets some of her amiable friends. It's time to part: she has been a most caring and knowledgeable friend to me.

I myself have been anxious: it is accommodation news I require. I have brought this up with Lesley Greene earlier and she comes up trumps with bookings at both the Whitby and Robin Hood Bay YHAs. In addition she has been busy contacting the fire brigades along the east coast, and it looks as if I will be stopping at Scarborough and other fire stations.

I negotiate the ninety- nine steps up to the Whitby YHA (next to the haunting Abbey), and then up two floors to my room. The YHA organisation is reported to havie spent a small fortune renovating this building up to at least a three-star Hotel rating.

Flek reads my thoughts: 'Is this the beginning of the end for the traditional hostels that we grew up to cherish?' he asks.

A large party of children is staying at the hostel They, their teaching staff and some parents are from the Minchinhampton Primary School near Stroud in Gloucestershire.

These kids are noisy but well behaved. One of the staff gets to hear what I am up to, announcing it to the children. Suddenly I am besieged: they all want my autograph. All manner of writing surfaces are offered up to take my scribble. Ever realised how difficult it is to write on tiny greaseproof sweet wrappings? Oh, the fame of it all!

And the boots?

They performed without any noticeable discomfort.

Signing Jon Hall's landscape painting.

DAY 277

3st October – Whitby YHA to Boggle Hole YHA at Robin Hood Bay
– 7 miles

I wake up to foul morning. The wind is howling up on the hill here, driving the rain. Because I have a short day, I delay my departure. It pays off, as the weather abates. Crossing the car park I see a coach: the Minchinhampstead children are embarking for their journey home. They are all waving to me, so I go across to say goodbye to them and the interested staff who had befriended me.

Because of the high wind I ignore the coastal path and walk a couple of miles down to High Hawsker. In the Hare and Hounds I meet an Irishman, Michael who likes to chat, and he buys me lunch.

I pick up an old railway line (*God it's heavy!* – old Tommy Cooper joke). The sun comes out, and it's delightful walking along the redundant track in the lee of the old railway embankment. Out at sea several coasters battle against the strong wind, producing huge bow waves. I indulge in some light-hearted banter with three ladies I find sitting on a bench: two of them are from Hurstpierpoint in Sussex.

Robin Hood's Bay is a delightfully quaint place with its main street dropping steeply to the beach. After a short walk along the sand, I face a problem: I have to get across a fast stream, but it's difficult to stand up with my rucksack. A man on the other side throws his walking stick across to assist. Unfortunately the trajectory falls short, and it is in danger of being swept out to sea. I am now forced to wade in and retrieve the aid, returning it to the owner on the other side. It is all a rather pointless (like a scene from Monsieur Hulot's Holiday), but he was only trying to help.

'A potential embarrassment averted, I would say, Col,' lectures Flek, 'Oh and about those autographs yesterday. You said that . . .'

'Yes, yes, Flek' I say, interrupting him. 'Let's get on, shall we? My feet are wet and require some TLC'

I struggle up the stony beach into a lane and find the almost hidden Boggle Hole hostel. The warden waives the fee. In the dining room I meet Neil (from the Whitby hostel yesterday) once again: he is a

Pompey fan and we talk about 'lost' managers. I also make friends with Wendy and Phil, a charming couple who elect to take my rucksack on tomorrow and deliver it to Scarborough fire station. They also donate on Just Giving. Life is full of Samaritans who, amazingly, always turn up when you need them!

'Another action-packed day, eh Flek?'

Too late – he is fast asleep.

DAY 278

4th October – Boggle Hole YHA, Robins Hood Bay to Scarborough fire station – 14 miles

It's wet at first, with a gale force headwind. Thank goodness Wendy and Phil are taking my rucksack on allowing a welcome Free day.

My first stop is at Ravenscar. I visit the National Trust office where, on display boards, the manufacture of alum in this area is explained in great detail. Alum was used in the 16th dentury for fixing dyes in wool. The process involved burning rock for months then mixing the resulting potash with stale urine! The latter was shipped in from London and Newcastle. This went on here for twenty years and must have been the worst occupation in the land.

I catch a friendly café in the village before it closes: they serve me a snack on the house.

The next nine miles are tough going, with ravines, steps and bridges to negotiate over a rough terrain against a strong headwind.

I deserve a snack at the first café in Scarborough and go around the prominent Holms Head passing from north to south beaches.

I have to make a phone call to locate the fire station. Wendy and Phil have delivered my rucksack, and Malcolm Norris, the Watch manager, settles me in. I lie on my bunk just like my operational days and listen to the background of noises within the building – they sound very familiar.

Strangely, despite all my effort today, I have a fitful night of sleep. Perhaps I am sub consciously waiting for a 'shout'.

DAY 279

5th October – Scarborough Fire Station to Reighton Sands Holiday Park
– 11 miles

The duty crew offer me a bacon roll for breakfast. I refuse the sausages as they will stay with me all day. Malcolm kindly offers to take my rucksack on to Reighton, as it's on his way home.

It is a Free day, and I get back on the Cleveland Way and follow a labyrinth of paths, most of which are muddy. I purchase a couple of heavy energy bars (fig/chocolate) and they see me through to lunch.

The Way turns in at Filey Brigg headland, and I arrive in the town. Filey is the smallest of the east coast holiday resorts, and I find it to be the most refined. It is very busy with late holiday day visitors.

'Well Flek, I am going to treat myself,'

Seeing a hotel with an inviting lunch menu, I am finally served an indifferent meal. I have suffered this disappointment before.

'You should have learnt your lesson by now,' insists Flek. 'Stick to grub that you can't go wrong with, Col – you know it makes sense.'

He is right.

On a fine day I march along the firm sand covering the last three miles to the Reighton Holiday Park. Weekenders are pouring out onto the beach.

I arrive at reception to find that my 'fame' has got here before me – Lesley at CLIMB has made sure of that. Not only have the welcoming staff allocated me a six-berth Static with all mod cons, but they have passed around a sponsor form which has resulted in £43 of donations. The lady running the park shop adds another ten pounds.

My new boots are breaking in quite well. I really must take the labels off!

The Static is huge; I stretch out in a double bed and select my Evening Concert: Chris Rea's 'Fool If You Think It's Over', Bill Evans' 'Let's Get Back To The Waltz' and some more of Dag Wiren's 'Serenade for Strings'. My Wish Track is 'Night Birds' by the Eighties group Shakatak.

DAY 280
6th October – Reighton Sands Park to Flamborough – 9 miles

On a short day there will time to relax on the hoof. First a visit to reception is in order, to thank the staff. I walk the coastal path, making my way on to the Flamborough Peninsula, and hike along the top of the Bempton Cliffs, turning inland to the village of the same name. I notice a glass-fronted parish noticeboard at a junction, displaying photos taken between the two world wars. These show the groups of villagers who used to gather at this spot late in the late afternoon to gossip away – a charming record of times past.

An enthusiastic Flek pronounces, 'You know, Col, villages should do this, maybe as a project for the Queen's diamond jubilee – just a thought.'

'What a great suggestion, Flek. It would allow the "national identity" initiative to flourish. Just think, the concept could be expounded in the Vicar of Dibley TV Series. I'm sure their parish committee could set a fine example!'

On the way I pass from north Yorkshire into the East Riding. In the flat fields are countless tractors ploughing in for the next year's yield. Some are spreading you know what on to you know everywhere – phew! It's that time of the year! A line of birds waiting for their turn behind a tractor is a timeless country reminder that the season is changing. What do we need clocks or calendars for?

Lesley has arranged a B & B for me at Rock Cottages, 13 Dog and Duck Square, run by Mrs Geraghty. It is also a café, which will be very handy. I arrive early, so its rucksack off and time for a little relaxation –a two-mile walk out to Flamborough Head!

Along the road I glance through an opening into a camping site to see a smashed up caravan and damaged car. The site owner tells me that a speeding local hoodlum struck the van as it was being towed out on to the road. The youth already has already been convicted of a similar offence, she expands, so it's even more points on his licence. 'Every little helps,' says a well known jingle.

The dramatic coastline at the Head is dominated by a substantial lighthouse. Before it was built there was a wreck on this coast every three months. It's a popular spot for birders. They're looking for pink-footed geese today. It takes all sorts!

There is an interesting structure nearby. It's a chalk tower built in 1674, and it's the oldest (here we go again) complete lighthouse in the country. The 'light' in the old days was achieved by igniting a pile of timber at the top, making it a hell of a chimney fire for the parish firemen!

DAY 281

7th October – Flamborough to Bridlington – 5 miles

Goodness me, my planning for this stage has gone pear-shaped: Bridlington is only five miles away

I cut down to the North Nook IRB station and then continue along the cliffs. Entering suburbs, I reach a cycle path and meet Terry walking his rough collie 'Dino'. I accompany them for a while. He is gentle, lovely man on a late holiday from Barnsley, and is the same age as me – though there the similarity ends.

Flek cannot resist it: 'He has obviously had to work a lot harder for his living than you, Col.'

I move on into the town. In steady rain it is a dour scene, with lots of elderly folk shuffling around aimlessly, having a late, cheap holiday break.

'Well, this is a turn up for the book. It appears you are the youngest OAP here,' calculates a mischievous Flek.

He hasn't finished: 'I've been thinking, Col, we often see students on the telly, jumping for joy over their exam results . They are our next generation of skills and intelligence, but in time they will become the OAPs of the future. It's comforting to know that many might follow their predecessors by contributing, albeit unconsciously, quiet statements of our national identity.

'Such as?' I reply, sensing another of his brain numbing hypotheses. 'What are you getting at, Flek? Spit it out man!'

'Well, just think, in the future there could be old boys shuffling around wearing odd-coloured socks and Fair Isle cardigans. Most will be unaware that their flies are undone and others have blown away convention by pulling their trousers on the wrong way round!'

'Good God, Flek, what is your analogy with academia?' I muse, desperately trying to fathom out his reasoning.

He is adamant and rants on: 'Listen,' he shouts, 'the final academic task for male OAPs will be to monitor their steady decline in sartorial etiquette. They are uniquely qualified to do so — evolution has seen to that.'

Intrigued I press him: 'What about the old girls, then?'

'Ah, that could be a little trickier to explain, Col, but I'll work on it, mate.'

His enthusiasm suddenly wanes. I thought it would.

I have plenty of time to explore the town, or 'Bridders' as it is affectionately known. There is nothing more depressing than an English seaside holiday resort in autumn when it's raining. I know: I was brought up in Bognor Regis.

Things start to look up. Excitement mounts as a minor drama unfolds. Two coppers arrest an East European man, standing next to me in the Boots checkout queue, for skipping his bail. Also I notice that, seeking to rival Vegas for top entertainment, posters are announcing that the council has secured Rolf Harris and Paul Daniels (with Debbie of course) to appear shortly at the Bridlington Spa Theatre.

'Two master magicians of the boards, eh, so who has the audacity to question the resort's leisure strategy,' shouts Flek as we flee from the premises.

I book into a run-of-mill B & B, but do I care? It's cheap, but the full 'English' awaits me at breakfast in the morning.

'You won't get a continental breakfast here. Flek. None of that rubbish,' I confide.

'Well it makes for a very foreign start to the day, Col. I mean, having to face wurst, cheeseboard and hard boiled eggs,' winces Flek.

Now is the time for some entertainment of my own. Out comes my iPod. It's a Dave Brubeck Jazz Goes To College session for me this evening, with his programme of the American Songbook including 'Out of Nowhere', 'I Want To Be Happy', 'Don't Worry About Me' and 'The Song Is You'. Hugh Paddick introduces Round the Horne.

What weather?

'Conversation about the weather is the last refuge of the unimaginative'
— Oscar Wilde

Normally the planning of a journey that takes the best part of a year to complete spells weather trouble. In 2008 this was simply not the case. I made the obvious decision to start in mid-winter from the south coast in order to benefit from a Scottish summer.

There were dire warnings that beginning my GB walk in January could turn out be disastrous, especially if proceeding in an anti-clockwise direction: apparently it's the Devil's way! The legendary long distance walker John Merrill says so in his book *Turn Right at Lands End*. I had a lucky escape, avoiding a rendezvous with Satan by heading off in the opposite direction!

What luck then that, by pure chance, I selected a year when the weather pattern stayed consistently mild. It took me 33 days to get to Land's End. I then sensed that for some inexplicable reason (maybe global warming), a mild weather patterns was going to prevail. I conceded that battling down to Cornwall against raging gales could result in a demoralising start, but I had no choice.

There is a photograph of John Merrill in his book shaking the hand of a local chairman of the council at Sennen Cove in Cornwall: they are standing on the shoreline in several inches of snow. Merrill reports that it was a typical winter scene: I passed the same spot on a sunny winterless day.

As for precipitation, the first soaking I got was at the end of Chesil Beach on the way to Bridport. Others included approaching Swanage, on the road to Holyhead in Anglesey (it hardly rained during the sixty days to get round Wales), from Kinloss to Lossiemouth, on the road from Wick to Lybster, the last six miles into St Andrews, approaching Cromer and from Colchester to Wickam Bishops and that was it!

I sheltered from only two flurries of snow during the whole trip.

On my six-day hike across the northern coast of Scotland (Durness to John o' Groats) in August the sun shone most days, the average temperature being several degrees higher than in Sussex 850 miles to the south.

I took the trouble of bringing gloves but hardly ever put them on!

I wasn't to be embroiled in coastal fog – not even at Aberdeen which is infamous for its sea fog or haar – or bombarded by hailstones, either.

For the first two months frost did present a hazard. I fell over many times trying to keep a footing. Getting back up with a 30lb rucksack still aboard was difficult if not hilarious. Fortunately I avoided embarrassment, as there were seldom any witnesses.

Being constantly exposed to the elements prompted me to do some rudimentary homework on cloud formation before I left, so here goes.

Cumulus: (In laymen's terms, lumps of mashed spud) Fair weather

Stratus: At middle level (balls of cotton wool)

Cirrus: High level mare's tails or mackerel formations – aircraft vapour trails produce Cirrus

Nimbus   Heavy low level – rain (Watch out!)

Over the months I observed a few striking vistas of stratus and cirrus, usually in the evening.

Today's medical advances mean that it may be possible in the future for blind people to gain their sight. Being suddenly confronted by humans and seeing colour for the first time will be a revelation – but they could only but marvel at the sky.

I researched and read up on patron saints for good weather. and there are many of them. All I can say is that they all hitched a ride with me in 2008.

DAY 282
8th October – Bridlington to Hornsea – 13 miles

I go through the suburbs of Bridlington out to the A165. There are temping sandy beaches all the way to Hornsea, but I am always wary of getting bogged down on soft terrain. If it was a Free day, i.e. without the rucksack, I would love to walk the shore, but not today. The road, half a mile inland, always ensures great sea views.

The route today consists mainly of two long, virtually straight roads, the second being five miles in length.

'Don't fret – geometry means that you follow the shortest route, Col.' says Flek making a naive assessment without thinking it through.

'Listen, my clever little friend. I had this dilemma on the roads in Scotland. Ask anyone on foot whether they prefer twists, bends or even corners when walking the roads and the answer will almost certainly be Yes. It's all down to the psychology of the human mind. In lay terms, the boredom factor sets in on the straights, which leads to frustration. I don't know whether this sums it up for you, but it will have to do.'

I get a coffee at a roadside burger bar and have a nice chat with the vender, but oh my, his unit is filthy and unkempt. How he placates any travelling health Inspector I don't know. It gets me thinking that I have never seen any 'hygiene certificates' prominently displayed on any of these refreshment vans. To be fair, most are spick and span.

I encounter pavements during the day, but at times I have to face directly heavy traffic including army columns. 'Stop, step away and wait' is the order of the day in these situations.

At Skipsea the pub is closed, so I find the post office for something to eat. I come across 'Mr Moo's' Ice Cream Farm, a leading brand in these parts – another cottage industry made good. At the tea bar the manager gifts me tea and cake.

'What a cadger you've turned out to be, Colin,' Flek remarks with a jealous overtone.

'I know, it's become a despicable habit. I am quite proficient at it by now, don't you think?

A grudging acceptance followed.

Such a long march follows on to Hornsea and, to cap it all, my next hosts, Arnold and Pat Johnson, live up the other end of town. Just what I needed! I am all-in on arrival, but the Johnsons see to my every need. I can thank Arthur Reynolds of the Chichester Jazz Club for securing their assistance.

DAY 283
9 October – Hornsea to Withernsea fire station – 17 miles

Hosts Arnold Johnson, a retired Methodist minister, and his wife Pat support the charity 'Real Aid', and they have a standard poodle called Tetley, which is a rather apt name for Yorkshire. They are marvellous temporary guardians to a rather dishevelled lodger. I am truly grateful for their interest and care.

Arnold runs me a couple of miles down to Mappleton. Here he points out the effects of erosion along this coastline, a continuous worry.

I shake his hand and start a long tramp down a twisting road, this time to arrive at Roos. J.R.R. Tolkien lived here, and the prime meridian line passes just east of the village. The line is at zero degrees, dividing the eastern and western hemispheres, and longitude is set against it for navigational purposes. In the northern hemisphere it passes through the UK first, and then crosses only seven other nations.

'Got it, Flek? This might turn up on a quiz night.'

'I may be many things, Col, but never an egghead. Anyway,' he pontificates, 'someone once said it's better to remain silent and let people think you're a fool than to speak out and remove all doubt.'

I call in the Roos Arms and purchase an excellent snack/salad. The Landlady tells me the place is haunted. A little girl regularly appears and last night the darts disappeared from the bar.

'Here's a spirit who may want to make a point – get it, Flek?'

'Get what? Oh, I see, it's a pun,' he replies, pretending not to have noticed my crass humour. 'Is that the best you can do? You know, Col, I sometimes think this long hike has put us in a time warp,' he mocks.

During the afternoon, at a gateless opening to a field, miles from anywhere, I come across a dummy slumped in an armchair and fully kitted out in health and safety gear. There seems to be no rhyme or reason for its presence.

'I've got it', says my all knowing companion. 'This bloke was dumped out here to carry out a traffic census (probably two tractors an hour) and the authorities have forgotten to collect him, poor sod.'

It seems a feasible explanation!

What strikes anyone visiting Withernsea for the first time is the White Lighthouse (now disused), situated at a junction within the town! It's now a museum dedicated to the actress Kay Kendall who was born here, as was Kenny Baker the jazz trumpeter.

At Withernsea Fire Station I am met by fire fighter Ricky Drew and then Paul Graves, the station manager, I have rather sore feet, so I'm glad to be here for four days.

When planning this venture I wrote to all the fire brigades with a coastline, asking where they could arrange for stations to host me. Despite my creditable CV the response was disappointing overall.

I'm very happy to say, however, that Lesley Greene at CLIMB has persuaded the Humberside Fire and Rescue Service to open its doors and look after me for the next week.

Forgotten!

DAY 284

10th October – Withernsea fire station to Easington – 8 miles

It's a comfortable stay in the station – almost like being at home. Today is easy, following an eight-mile flat route to Easington in watery sunshine and facing a warm wind. I will be Free for three days.

I keep getting passed by MOD mobile patrols, and soon I come across the reason why. I have arrived at BP's expanding natural gas terminal at Easington. My route takes me through the giant complex.

Reaching thevillage, I enter the Neptune pub for lunch. Ruminating inside are five 'last of the summer wine' types. I become embroiled in intense and amusing banter with this lot. Leo is making the most noise and using an excellent vocabulary of expletives. He purports to dislike the French, Yanks and southerners in that order. He is urged on by the others – and I join in of course. Soon I am verbally bouncing off him like a squash ball.

Firefighter James rescues me, and we return to 'base' via Partrington trying to locate any indication of the arbitrary 0° longitude meridian line. We find an indicator post (well inland) and an insignificant plinth – nothing quite as grand as the pillar at Peacehaven, Sussex, where this invisible line leaves the UK.

I have a walk around the town and then retire for a dehydrated meal. My stomach is getting quite used to them by now!

I have entered the shipping weather forecast area Humber.

DAY 285

11TH October – Easington to Spurn Head and return – 11 miles

'Today I strike out to Spurn Head – a 'must do' target since I plotted the Walk two years ago. This narrow spit of sand three miles long narrows to only fifty yards in places. It resembles a giant tadpole from the air and lies at the entrance to the Humber estuary. It's home to the only full-time RNLI crew in the British Isles: they live at the Head with their families.

The approach road starts with a café and ends with another. On reaching it I have a long conversation with the coxwain of the Humber

Lifeboat, Dave Steenvooden (Dutch father) and his wife Karen, who manages the Caravan Café out here.

The lifeboat has already turned out forty times this year. If you like watching ships, this is the place. Ten thousand ship movements pass through every year, making for the ports of Hull, Goole, Grimsby and Immingham.

The Head is a mecca for birdwatchers because of the continuous presence of native species and the constant migrations of others. I strike up a friendship with a couple of 'twitchers', Geoff (Hull) and Jack (Crosby), who stimulate my interest throughout the afternoon. For the second time recently I am able to watch flocks of goldfinches.

The north shore of the Head is flanked by a superb beach, and the leeside mudflats allow digging for bait. It's a fascinating place, always with something to see.

Firefighter Steve picks me up on the Easington road, and I return to Withernsea a contented man – mission achieved.

The coxwain of the Humber lifeboat, Dave Steenvooden, and his wife, Karen.

The brigade makes sure that I get back down to Easington. I hit the road and, just past the village of Skeffling, come across a frustrated crew of enthusiasts. Their vintage Green Goddess fire appliance engine has just gone 'phutt' on the way to the Welwick Heritage Fair.

I drop into the fair. Everyone has rallied in the sun, as they do in countless villages throughout the country, to raise funds for the church restoration. In an ever increasing secular world, it is still an unflinching trait of ordinary folk to save these monuments of faith. The skyline wouldn't be the same without them.

Everyone is having a great time, and all stalls are well supported. There's a display of classic and vintage fire vehicles – minus a Green Goddess! Fund-raising is also being undertaken by the 'friends' of Martin House children's hospice, who have first hand experience of children with metabolic conditions. I have a long discussion about the hospice movement and make a donation.

One interesting character is promoting an exhibition on 'The Role of the Countryside in War' in a nearby barn. She is dressed up as a yokel, complete with clay pipe. Looking at her begs the question 'Which war?' From her demeanour she is obviously descended from rural stock, but strangely her name doesn't quite fit. Known to everyone as 'Dot', her real name is Dorothy Perkins!

Flek says the obvious: 'M & S use the modelling skills of Twiggy, but some-how I can't see the high street fashion chain that bears her name employing our Dot in that role, can you?'

It's lunchtime, and I call into the Station pub at Patrington.

Flek looks around and utters: 'Blimey, Col. that xenophobic loud-mouth Leo from the Neptune at Easington is sitting over there.'

I go over and tap him on the shoulder.

'Hello, your favourite southerner has turned up,' I utter.

The remark produces a belly laugh, and he buys me a drink. He is sitting with a couple of ex RAF types. One of them, a police dog handler, was in West Germany at the same time as me. Despite his discriminating outbursts, Leo is an interesting bloke. He had a brief career racing motor bikes at the Isle of Man TT Races. We part the best of acquaintances.

Flek surmises, 'I don't suppose his attitude is his fault. I reckon he was probably let down by some bird in Brighton.'

An interesting hypothesis!

I finish at tongue twisting Thorgumbold. Firefighter Steve picks me up again with his brother-in-law. Apparently they are married to twins.

'Any chance of mistaken identity then?' I ask coyly. They look at each other and smile.

It is my last night back at Withernsea.

The original Dorothy Perkins.

13th October – Thorngumbald to Hessle Calvert Lane fire station,
Hull – 12 miles

I am still find it physically difficult to get out of the loaned camper bed and use my tried and trusted manoeurvre.

My chauffer Steve drives me to Thorngumbald. I can't thank him, the Withernsea fire personnel and the Humberside Fire and Rescue Service enough for their assistance to me. The latter haven't finished with me yet.

With my rucksack aboard again, I walk the pavements all the way into Hull. As usual my legs soon warm, the stiffness disappears and I am functional once again.

I pass through Heddon before embarking on the three miles of urban sprawl to the Calvert Street fire station, which is also the service HQ. On the way I pass by the city's huge annual Seven Day Fair.

The kids are coming out of school and Flek anticipates I am going to comment on their clothes.

'So you don't like their shirts hanging out, then.' He provokes.

'Now that you mention it, Flek, there does seem to be some relaxation in the dress code these days. When I was at school, this would not have been tolerated. I mean, we were always a bit untidy going home but it wasn't until we disappeared into the town that we even dared to take our caps off.'

'You had to wear caps to school! What, like Just William does?'

'That's right, we had to watch out for the older boys of the school – prefects they called them – snitching on us for not wearing them. In no time you could tot up enough detentions for a prefects' court appearance and sentence. There were very few acquittals. Most offenders came away with a sore arse after several whacks with the cane delivered by a sombre but enthusiastic master. A last-minute protective atlas in your trousers was soon detected.

'And another thing – our parents insisted that we cleaned our shoes with polish, and that included the underneath as well because my uncle in the Grenadier Guards had to. That's what my mum told me. The next thing these kids will be wearing jeans to school. Where's the discipline, I ask you?'

'You finished?' asks Flek, open-mouthed. 'Stop carping on about what happened in the last century, will you?' he pleads.

Having wound him up, I smile. I'm thinking of my school's old boys who swell with pride that their names are still in the preserved black punishment book.

'Yes, it didn't do us any harm, they say – and it hasn't!'

I settle into the station, and the duty crew kindly offer me some food. For once this busy station has a quiet night.

DAY 288

14th October – Calvert Street Fire Station, Hesle to Barton fire station (via the Humber Bridge) – 5 miles.

I breakfast with the duty crew. It's going to be a short, but (unknown to me) eventful day.

A three-mile stroll brings me to the Humber Bridge. It was completed in 1981, for sixteen years holding a record for the longest single-span suspension bridge in the world: it's still number five in the rankings. There was an almighty row over the delay in its construction, and another row has persisted ever since about an each-way toll in excess of £5. You can imagine my disappointment when I arrive to find it shrouded in mist.

Lesley Green at CLIMB (I am now calling her Mum No. 2) has arranged for me to meet Pam and Royce Parish on the bridge. Pam has long been part of a CLIMB family: her daughter Nicola died aged twenty-five years from the metabolic neurodegenerative Battens Disease.

The three of us walk the bridge. Just discernible above us are the massive suspension cables, but we're going to be denied an all-embracing panorama today. After 2200m we drop down to Barton upon Humber and enter the Sloop pub, where they buy me lunch. The circumstances of Pam's life have lead to a great deal of unhappiness, but it is clear to me that meeting Royce has been a turning point. It is an absolute delight to spend a few hours with them.

I saunter down to the fire station, which I find is shared with the ambulance service. The phone rings and I am told that the chief fire office of Humberside Frank Driffield QSFM is going to cross the Bridge to meet me. I shall be glad of the opportunity to thank him for his staff's assistance. Of all the brigades I contacted, Humberside is one of only three who have really answered the call. On arrival he takes a great interest in my journey.

At mid afternoon I have a radio telephone interview with BBC Radio Humberside, which goes well. The ambulance personnel go about their duties, leaving me on site to make myself at home. I am singing in the shower when I hear a voice through an open window.

'Is that Colin Snook in there?'

I confirm, and the voice goes on, 'When you're cleaned up, open the front door. You'll get a surprise!'

This I do, and standing there is Ray Carey. He and I were on a one-year course at the Fire Service Staff College, Dorking, in 1968 – forty years ago – and haven't seen each other since.

'What on earth are you doing here?' I ask.

'The wife and I were motoring along this morning and she heard your interview on the local radio. You can come and stay with us.'

Pam Parish and Royce, CLIMB parents, on the Humber Bridge.

I explain that I am morally committed to stay at the station for one night at least, and so we compromise. He will take me out for a meal tonight, and I'll proceed to his place tomorrow.

Later we return to his home. I meet his wife Sally and we talk endlessly about old times.

'What an amazing co-incidence, Col. That's the power of local radio, mate,' expounds Flek.

Barton upon Humber is a part-time, i.e. a retained fire station, but ambulance service incumbents (female) use its general office as a control room during the night. so I have to sleep elsewhere. I settle for the gents' toilet floor – I kid you not; there is nowhere else. I thought of 'JC' and his assurance all those years ago that 'hard floors have got a little bit of give in them'. Well, I can now tell him his pronouncement was delusory!

'You've slept in a few places so far, Colin, but now in the ablutions – hardly a convenience!' laughs Flek. He always calls me Colin when in a sarkee mood.

'Watch it, mate, or you'll be off the project,' I warn, but he knows I'm joking.

Ray Carey, past brigade colleague.

In the old days a Teasmade boiling away accompanied by a shrieking alarm signalled the start of the day. Today people use their mobiles, but it wasn't always so scientific. Years ago my mum gave lodgings to a young policeman. He could never wake up for his early morning beat duty, so to 'encourage' him my dad rigged up a fool-proof system by placing a huge alarm clock in a metal plate full of pennies on his pillow. It never worked. His section sergeant recommended an incendiary device!

In contrast my wake-up call this morning is the sound of the automatic flushing men's urinals.

Flek is aroused: 'You can't beat an Armitage Shanks gushing forth to announce another day,' he splutters.

Rain forces me into all-weather gear. I have a Free day to wander the flat Lincolnshire road systems.

My left foot is still playing up. I'm experiencing an intermittent stinging pain in a sinew behind the left small toe. The discomfort is not debilitating, but it's not going to go away.

I follow a round-about route via Goxhill and the remains of Augustinian Thornton Abbey. The magnificent brick gatehouse is 21m in height and is virtually intact from the 14th century – possibly the finest in the country.

I go on to East Halton, where the pub is closed. I make do with a banana and a couple of chocolate bars. The rain has halted and I push on the last 4km to South Killing with a disused airfield on my right and an oil refinery on the left.

Ray picks me up and we do a general interest run around. Following my disappointment of yesterday, he drives me across the Humber Bridge to get an experience of its majestic construction.

After an evening meal I talk to his wife Sally, who has an interesting career as a social researcher. Ray had several posts when leaving the college, culminating in becoming the deputy chief fire officer of Humberside. Unfortunately illness curtailed his career and he had to call it day. Enforced retirement has not abated his interest in all manner of things.

We talk endlessly about our time at Dorking in 1968. The fire service college was situated in Wooten House, the ancestral home and birthplace in 1620 of the diarist John Evelyn, whose family made their money in gun powder. This was manufactured in hamlets along the valley running from Dorking to Guildford. The process was not without hazard: an enormous explosion blew apart one of the sites.

Evelyn chronicled the deaths of Charles 1 and Oliver Cromwell and recorded the Great Plague and Fire of London.

It's been a delightful surprise to be reunited with Ray again.

DAY 290
16th October – South Killiingholme to Cleethorpes (Kirton in Lindsay)
– 13 miles

It's time to say good bye to Ray. He kindly elects to take my rucksack onto Cleethorpes and persuades the train station ticket office to store it for the day. He then meets me en route to confirm the arrangement. What a friend!

This means a Free day, and I'm able to enjoy unhindered hiking in glorious autumn sunshine. I walk on without a care in the world and go through a village with the quaint name of Healing.

'Just the place to get your toe sorted out,' says a flippant Flek.

I eat a ploughman's lunch at a pub on the outskirts of Grimsby. I'm surprised to find that this town, famed for its fishing industry, shares an urban sprawl with the seaside resort of Cleethorpes.

I pass Blundell Park, the home of Grimsby Town Football Club. In the 1946-47 season I remember seeing them play at Fratton Park, Portsmouth. They were in Division One then, the equivalent of today's Premier League. The national fixed wage for all players in the League was twelve quid a week! Grimsby didn't stay long, being relegated the following season.

I retrieve my rucksack from the station and, after a mix up, am finally picked up by my next host, Louise Stone, who has travelled a very long way from Kirton in Lindsay. Rodney and Louise are a CLIMB family who in 2005 lost their daughter Rachael aged thirty-one to the rare genetic metabolic condition Cystinosis.

After breakfast in the Stones' impressive Burton Hall house I chill out until Louise takes me to Lincoln in the afternoon. We visit the old Lincoln Prison, which houses the only intact solitary prison chapel in the world; view one of only four copies of the Magna Carta still in existence; and then tour the magnificent cathedral, followed by refreshments.

How much culture can one take in a day!

Rodney is a potato wholesaler, and later I'm shown around his packing factory. These are the places where spuds are bought in, graded, washed and packed up, and then finally presented to us punters all ready to use on supermarkets shelves. It's very interesting to see at first hand the process we've come to take for granted.

The day culminates with a pub meal with my hosts and a group of their friends.

Finally an extract from today's Blog: 'I would like to thank BOTH readers who answered my recent Blog appeal for telephone chats.'

Louise Stone – trying to be someone else!

DAY 292

18th October – Cleethorpes to Saltfleet – 10 miles

I am reluctant to leave Burton Hall and its colourful autumnal garden. The hospitality of the Stones has been second to none, and they are also making a significant donation to CLIMB in memory of their daughter Rachael.

Louise drives me the twenty-five miles plus (a record distance for this project) to just south of Cleethorpes, and then goes on to deliver my rucksack to tonight's B & B. She reminds me of someone who sang 'The Hills are Alive to the Sound of Music'. I have taken a photo in her lovely garden (*facing page*) to remind me of the likeness.

It is yet another glorious day, the sun now at a low angle. I stride Free of my rucksack into a warm wind, shuffling through fallen leaves on many a pavement. I love this time of year.

Passing piles of sugar beet leaves me in no doubt of which part of the country I am in. It is an absolute delight to be out and about. During the day I am brought to enforced standstills at the Crown & Anchor, the White Horse and an ice cream parlour before arriving at Leslie Cottage, North Somercoates (01507 358734)– run by Mike and Sue Sams. This is a splendidly appointed bungalow, and I am most grateful to the Sams for donating my stay.

The caring Louise has delivered my rucksack.

DAY 293

19th October – North Somercoates to Sutton on Sea – 13 miles

I haul my rucksack on and say goodbye to the attentive Sams family. The bridge at Saltfleet is under repair, so I have to clamber across some sand dunes to proceed. Here I meet a delightful couple, Michael and Kate from Nottingham, with their daughter Sophie, just ten weeks old, Aaah! I hand them my card and they later donate via Just Giving.

I get off the soft dunes and hit the road, which takes me around the Viking North Sea gas terminal and finally on to the seafront at Mablethorpe.

As I approach the town a frightful resonance drifts towards me, the crescendo reaching a roar. I can see the elevated rides of Adventure World, but surely these aren't responsible for this almighty row.

All is revealed as I reach the promenade. A racetrack has been marked out on the beach and trial motorbikes are hurtling around it at a furious pace. This 'whacky races' programme is relentless, as officials rustle up the contestants every ten minutes for the next round. The haste is necessary to beat high tide.

Hundreds have gathered to watch this free show. Many clasp a plastic tray of fish and chips in one hand and a Stella in the other. The hackneyed cliché 'Eee it's champion, having a grand time!' comes to mind.

I turn down into the street of a thousand fruit machines: yes, I think we have the embryo of another Las Vegas here on the windy shores of the north-east coast. Well. maybe!

After a snack I push on down the A52 to Sutton on Sea, where my next host, Graham Houslow (Alford Rotary), collects me.

DAY 294
20th October – Sutton-on-Sea to Skegness – 12 miles

I have had a most comfortable stay with Graham and Paula. Both are involved in local council matters and take a great interest in Walk GB 4 Climb. Graham drops me back at Sutton, where my first task is to get a birthday card off to my youngest son Stewart, who will be forty on the 21st – Trafalgar Day.

I set off on the coast road to Chapel St Leonards. With the road elevated from the flat fields and the sea a few hundred yards away, the ferocious wind blows me all over the place.

Dying for a drink in Chapel, I avoid Wally's Bar, the Maid Marion and Leonardo's Social Club.

'Very wise, Col. Let's face it, you aren't geared up for such sophisticated venues, lowering the tone. These are working class palaces of gratification, and at the moment you're rated below them – just a rambler. Know your place, mate, that's what I say.'

He is pragmatic if nothing else.

With these damning words, I can easily develop an inferiority complex but stoically I march on to the five-star Trafalgar Inn. Nobody takes any notice of the tramp who has just walked in. I feel that this is one in the eye for perceptive Flek.

Approaching Skegness I've never seen such a concentration of caravan sites in one place. To cap it all, the Butlins 'Camp' (the designation we always use in Bognor) has been plonked in the middle of them all. Schedule buses pull up alongside me and disgorge late-season campers who scuttle off to 'reception' and thence to be sucked into a compulsory programme of action-packed activities.

I pass a well known fast food outlet and observe the modern phenomenon of people queuing (in their cars, mind you) to purchase a round of compressed mince laid in a dry roll! How times have changed. Growing up post-war, the only quick meal on offer was cod and chips wrapped up in the *Daily Express*. It you were lucky a gherkin or pickled egg was on offer.

Incidently I don't want anyone to think that this was my staple diet on the Walk. I had many a wholesome meal – my hosts saw to that.

It starts to rain and I have to don all the gear. For many this is a slick action, but not for me. My sense of balance is going, and to compensate I have to lean on something to get the trousers on – in this instance a tree. The embarrassment of incompetence on show to passing traffic is always present.

The local Rotarians have booked me into the Royal Hotel, courtesy of no less than David Platt, their president. It's boots off and crocks on: what luxury! I carry what I think is an appropriate change of clothes for most occasions and slip into them. It's late season and, almost alone in the vast dining room, I enjoy a delicious fish pie followed by apple pie and ice cream, a favourite.

'It's hell out here,' is the phrase I repeat on my Blog later in the evening.

In my en-suite room I flop out and listen to Rachmaninoff's 'Rhapsody on a Theme by Paganini', Stealers Wheel's 'Stuck In The Middle With You' and Artie Shaw's 'Frenesi'. My Wish Tracks are Purcell's haunting 'When I am Laid in Earth' from Dido and Aeneas and George Gershwin's Rhapsody in Blue'.

Rotary International
'Service above Self'

Rotary International of Great Britain is a member of a world movement founded in the USA over a hundred years ago. Its logo is a wheel with twenty four cogs and six spokes, represneting 'civilisation and movement', while its Motto is 'Service Above Self'

There are over 1800 Clubs with 55,000 members throughout GB. Although part of a worldwide movement. the clubs usually follow their own agenda, meeting fortnightly at a regular venue (e.g. a local hotel) for a meal and to discuss their programme of good works. It's estimated that nearly fifty million pounds is raised annually by Rotary International.

Members volunteer their time, talent, professional skills and energy to improve the lives of people in their local communities and others around the world. One of their pursuits is to support charities, and with this in mind I approached a very good friend of mine, David Garforth, past president of the Bognor Regis Club, asking him to seek out accommodation for me during my walk around Great Britain.

David set about the task with great energy, contacting as many of the clubs that fell on my route as he could. I had sought his assistance rather late in the day, but soon invitations came in – to stay mostly in members homes. A few clubs also arranged hotel accommodation for me.

At the final count David's efforts resulted in thirteen members providing twenty seven nights of accommodation, plus bookings in four hotels.

I am very grateful to Dr David Duncan (Kirkcubright Rotary) and Gordon Laird (Girvan Rotary) for arranging for me to attend their meetings. These gatherings exemplified the individual approach that clubs have evolved to deal with the tasks in hand. Handsome donations were made to CLIMB on both occasions.

I have no doubt that if Rotary's work had come to my attention earlier then their involvement would have been greater. Finally I must recognise the liaison work done by the CLIMB Staff in securing Rotary's continuous backing for the Walking GB 4 Climb project.

Just before leaving this splendid establishment I re-enter the dining room and asked a member of staff to fill my water bottle. The supervisor, a middle aged lady, is tending her eastern European waitresses. She recognises me as 'the Walker' and asks which charity I represent. I explain the reasoning behind my journey. She listens intently then explains that she and her first husband lost a baby boy twenty years ago.

'We were told it was something we passed on' she said.

This possibly was the only explanation she ever received.

Using my limited knowledge I explain to her about degenerative disorders. She went on to have two unaffected children with her second husband. It's yet another harrowing tale – one I have heard so many times.

I ask her to take my photo outside and she obliges. We are standing in the grounds of the hotel and suddenly a sparrow hawk crashes into a nearby tree. This kamikaze of raptors is unsuccessful on this occasion. We return to our purpose: her resulting shot is to remain on my Blog for some time.

Rotary four-star at Skegness.

I take to the A52 and stay on it all day, pushing on through miles of flat country roads flanked by fields of leeks, cabbages, cauliflowers and many other crops stretching as far as the eye can see. This is what Lincolnshire is known for – the growing of twenty per cent of the nation's vegetables, and the continuous wind, of course. It seems that every other vehicle on the road is used for agricultural purposes.

At Wainfleet I call into a target golf club cafe for lunch. Where normally an immaculate lawn announces the club house, parked here is a moth-balled English Electric Lightning Jet Fighter.

'A trifle over the top' says Flek, 'Must have got it in a MOD closing down sale. Makes a change from a flower bed!'

Two 'firsts' stand out today: for being the only time on the journey I get a direct hit from above.

'Sposed to be lucky', laughs Flek.

'I'll let you know when the dry cleaning bill comes in' I reply wearily.

Later he spots a house whose exterior is already, in the third week of October, lit up with sparkling Christmas decorations.

My next host needs no introduction. Waiting for me in the Bricklayers Arms, Old Leake, is Ken Marshall, my colleague from the Chichester Jazz Club who now lives near Spalding. His neighbour Tim has run him out to meet me. We have a pint and take the long run back to his home at Weston.

Here I meet Lanka his wife for the first time, and also his sister in law. We all enjoy a spicy meal. Ken is a jazz man through and through and he invites into his studio (conservatory) to hear some classic tracks.

I shall be here for three days, and Ken will be walking with me. He is a spritely 79 and has just finished a cycling tour of the Highlands.

During the evening I call son Stewart, who is having his fortieth birthday party at the Bognor Regis Football Club. Chatting away with him I can hear everyone having a raving time.

22nd October – Weston to Boston and back to Spalding – 13 miles

There is a strong wind and it is cold. These sudden meteorological changes are common here on such an exposed landscape. The locals call the winds 'lazy' because they go through you instead of around.

For logistical reasons Ken and I will reverse this stage and walk direct from his home to Boston. We start by walking the long bank of the River Welland to Fosdyke Bridge.

Field workers are cutting vegetables. Using a power take-off device from a motor unit providing a conveyor belt, they trim the crops then grade them, wrap them in polythene bags and finally box them in a continuous process. It's fast, neat and efficient.

The first of the day's many disappointments, the Ship Inn at Fosdyke Bridge, is closed. We follow five miles of lanes, passing remote kennels and upsetting the dogs. There is nothing more debilitating than the constant barking of dogs. (Sorry, dog lovers!)

At Kirton the first pub doesn't do food. The second pubs lunch hour is promulgated as lasting until 2.30pm, so why is that when we arrive at 2.20pm they won't serve us? Disgusted, we get filled rolls at the baker's across the road. The end scenario shows two old farts sitting on a bench moaning about matters all and sundry. Strangely we both find this emotional release most gratifying: it's like having a fix.

Then Flek joins in and shows some sympathy: 'You both should be demonstrating about the vagaries of life, the lack of social welfare for the elderly. Go on – start yelling "Victor Meldrew rules OK!" '

It's all right for him, but our mouths are full of delicious bacon rolls. The problem is that as our sustenance is consumed, so is our ardour.

In Boston a visit to St Botolph's Church, known as the 'Boston Stump', is obligatory. Spectacular on the outside, it's recognised as the giant of parish churches within the UK. Being the tallest in the land and situated on a wide flat landscape, it can be seen for miles.

Before starting the long road walk back we visit the bus station café for a tea. At 4pm it is closed! Did we moan? Gastronomically the day has been a disaster. (Later waiting at a bus stop we get embroiled in an incident which is described in the 'Got Dun Din I' chapter). It'back to the Marshall's place for a shower, meal and some more jazz classics.

'Got dun, din I?'

'Pride goeth before destruction,   a haughty spirit before a fall.'
— Proverbs 16:18

On Day 296 Ken Marshall and I walk back to Spalding from Boston. He suggests that it made sense for us catch the bus back to his home in Weston from the outskirts of the town.

We find ourselves standing at a bus stop on a busy road. The evening rush hour is just commencing. A 'matey' short in stature and wearing a heavy coat and a cloth cap approaches.. He smiles but moves his head and shoulders, the body talk of a man who is cocksure of himself. With his hands in his pockets he has the outward appearance of a shop steward.

'You haven't seen a bloke arrive here in the last few minutes, have you,' he enquires, 'He is an oppo of mine and we're going to the football match at Holbeach.'

Ken whispers in my ear: 'There'll only be about fifty people and a dog there tonight.'

Matey talks on: 'I went to the match the other night and the bloody lights failed. I know the MD of the club and he gave me a lift home.'

'Haven't you got a bus pass then,' asks Ken, who is in possession of all the concessionary passes going.

Matey does a Del Boy 'He who dares' shrug of the shoulders and, with a half smile of triumph, replies: 'Listen, I've never asked for any favours from anyone in my life, and I am not going to start now!'

Ken persists with his enquiries and says, 'Have you got a car then?'

In a casual manner Matey let on, 'I used to have a Bentley but I lost my licence.'

Ken and I gulp with disbelief. He notices our surprise and shouts as the traffic thunders past.

'When I sold my engineering works I treated myself. I've still got the third best house on the estate over there you know,' he said pointing in some direction.

'Well what happened? How did you lose your licence?' asks Ken.

Anxious to tell all, Matey explains.

'I went to some do and had a few jugs. On the way home I was motoring down a country lane and came across this bird riding a horse which spooked as I went by. I operated the window and she remonstrated with me something rotten so I gave her a mouthful! How was I to know she was an off-duty copper!'

His Oppo has arrived at the bus stop unnoticed, and with a broad smile to us he keeps raising his arm up down continually to indicate that 'Matey' was 'p . . . . . d as a newt' at the time of the encounter. He continues to smile, despite having heard the story on countless occasions.

'Matey' went on,

'She'd obviously called for back-up and I had to blow into a bloody bag; I was over the top, wan I?'

Spoiling for a conclusion. Ken asks again.

'Well, what happened?'

'Got dun, din I?' he exclaims. 'I wasn't having any of that so I got myself a "Brief". Cost me ten grand!'

For the second time Ken and I gulp in disbelief.

In full flight now, Matey' goes on, 'It didn't finish there, either. I had another row with the DVLA. All these years my driving licence had been a neat little booklet and now they wanted to replace it with a piece of plastic, so I had a bloody row with them and all. It didn't do me any good.'

He pauses, but obviously feels the need to offer us assurances as to his present transport arrangements,

'My daughter gives me lifts now, he concludes.

Just then our bus appears and the interview is over. On the way home Ken and I can only but chuckle at Matey's misfortune.

Looking back, this was probably the most spontaneous hilarious incident of the whole year – a 'Dick Emery' Show Special before our very eyes.

DAY 297
23rd October – Weston to Fleet Hargate – 9 miles

Ken has some ankle trouble so he is going to accompany me on his bike for this short stage. First he has to drop his prescription in at Moulton, a daily task for OAPs. We go through Moulton, which turns out to be an interesting village. First up is its windmill, with nine storeys and, at a hundred feet, reckoned to be (here we go again) the tallest in the UK. It is being restored and plans are afoot to add 'sweeps' in the not too distant future. Coffees are ordered in the thriving café.

How often have I bought Gardman products for use in my garden? Surprise, surprise, it has its factory here.

At the end of a close a full size sculpture of a pot bellied pig stands on a concrete plinth. There is no indication of why it should be here!

'Marauding scrappies will have a job getting this pig iron onto the back of their lorry,' chuckles Flek.

The landscape is flat and windy. We scurry along to the town of Holbeach for excellent OAP lunches in the Crown Hotel.

Ken leaves me and cycles home while I claim the remaining miles to Fleet Hargate in the afternoon. I get the 505 bus back to Weston.

'Why do you keep mentioning the bus number, Col?' questions Flek.

'Because, my friend, these numbers represent vital links and are part of the social culture fabric for citizens in rural communities.

'Look around you – who has got on the bus today? There is that young mother struggling with two kids: one is impeccably behaved while the other's screaming could fracture glass. Also getting on is a charming elderly lady who has made a monumental effort to get her invalid husband in his wheelchair aboard – such fortitude! Now observe this old boy boarding: beanie hat, jumble sale clothes, Second World War boots and bottle-top glasses. Notice that he's still got his cycle clips on. He's a cartoonist's dream.'

'Well, I get the point, Col, but you're being a little harsh. He may have left the clips on to stop the draughty Lincolnshire winds getting up his trousers. He's probably missed out in the rush at this time of year to snap up some long-johns at the Charity Shop.'

'That's a very good point you are making, Flek. What a sensitive chap you are! However, I think he has forgotten to take them off since cycling down to the Co-op yesterday. He probably slept with them on and wondered why his feet, starved of the normal circulation, were glowing pink when he got up. Come on – enough of this conjecture. This is our stop. It's time to get off.'

I have a long chat with Lanka and Ken. She is a nurse but has suffered ill health in recent years. Ken's career was with the immigration service. In retirement they ran a nursing home in Littlehampton.

It has been quite an ordinary day really. Although the mileage was low I feel very tired, due to the culmination of past efforts I suppose.

I let the Modern Jazz Quartet's 'Ralph's Blues' and 'Skating in Central Park' hasten my slumbers. My wish track is George Gershwins 'Piano Concerto in F'.

DAY 298

24th October – Fleet Hargate to Sutton Bridge – 8 miles

Lanka patches up Ken's ankle and we get back on the 505 to Fleet. He remonstrates with me for not bringing my bus pass, and he has a point.

We pub lunch it again: I could get used to this.

The east coast is blessed with superb churches and most are much larger than we see in the south. This is due to nineteenth century wealth gained from the land and wool. A good example along the way today is the substantial St Mary Magdalene at Gedney.

The time seems to pass slowly as we two old stalwarts saunter along.

The bus journey back to Weston gets longer every day. Ken is great company and there will more of his escort duties later on in London.

I spend my last evening with the Marshalls and turn in early.

DAY 299

25th October – Sutton Bridge to Kings Lynn – 13 miles

I say goodbye to Lanka. Ken and I board the 505 together for the last time. At Sutton Bridge we strike north up an access road for three miles following the River Neene Outfall Cut and, thankfully, are in the lee of a tree line.

Our way now turns right up a bank and suddenly the vast Wash is in front of us, extending as far as the eye can see. The raised bank is part of the Peter Scott Walk. We now have to endure a fierce and nippy cross-wind and struggle with it for eight miles to our destination. The last three days I have been Free but the rucksack is now on my back again and its resistance to the wind makes the going very unstable. There is nowhere to shelter and rest for lunch; the wind blows on.

Gradually the path veers south east to follow the Great Ouse river into Kings Lynn. It starts to rain as we approach the town and I am heartened to see my next host, Graeme Brown, walking out to meet us.

Graeme drops Ken off at a bus stop. However, it's not my final goodbye to him, but an 'au revoir'. He will pop up again in a few weeks' time at Greenwich.

I will be staying at the Browns, but as CLIMB initially made contact with the Norfolk Fire and Rescue Service, we call into Kings Lynn's large fire station as a matter of courtesy. The on-duty crew make us some tea. The visit is a novelty for the Browns as they have never been in a fire station before: not many of the public have.

Graeme and Wendy Brown are a CLIMB family. Their grandson Lee passed away at two years having developed the degenerative metabolic condition Metachromatic Leukodystrophy..

Wendy prepares a delicious meal and I listen to the harrowing story of Lee's inevitable demise.

Heading for the Wash.

26th October – Kings Lynn to Hunstanton Fire Station – 17 miles

After a comfortable night, Graeme and Wendy set me down en route, taking my rucksack onto the fire station at Hunstanton and meeting me enroute to deliver a key – a great help.

I skirt round the town past the industrial estate and by use of a minor road stay off the main A149 for some time.

It offered to be a nice day but I have just heard the news that Harry Redknapp has deserted Pompey for Spurs, leaving me' distraught on the trail"

'How could he?' I splutter.

Flek offers sympathy: 'There is precious little loyalty left in the world, Col. It's only a game after all.'

I do not respond to his reasoning and carry on disbelieving.

Later I fork right onto a minor access road leading to Sandringham. Just outside the main gate to the house the estate has installed an up- market café and gift shop; it's 'Royal' shortbread here! I meet a lady on the approach road who donates £10 and then joins me in the café for a coffee and a chat.

It was my intension as a gesture of a loyal subject to touch my forelock as I passed the main gate, but I can't find it!

Flek can't resist it: 'Well these problems are bound to arise when you get old. It stands to reason that items are going to be misplaced or fall off after your guarantee runs out!'

'Oh, so very comforting, Flek.'

The map shows me a minor road running parallel to the A149 all the way to Snettisham, where I call into the Queen Vic for a pint. A local lady recognises that I represent a medical charity and confides in me about her battle with cancer. It's good to talk, and I'm learning to listen – an attribute that I sadly lack, according to my family.

I'm passing many a garden with wonderful late-season flower displays. Dahlias abound, and I note that the lovely pink autumn favourite *Nerine bowdenii* are just beginning to show.

I let myself into the retained fire station, and a crew member, Rigil Kent, comes in to see that I am OK. I have enough provisions for a substantial meal and settle down for the night.

I get to thinking how many stations I have slept in over the years. Counting my service in London and West Sussex, out- postings from the Fire Service College, brigades' hospitality during this project and courtesy visits, plus one in Paris, the tally runs to over fifty!

Finally here is one for Trivial Pursuit. Hunstanton is the only seaside resort on the east coast which faces west and where the sun can be seen to set over the sea. Not a lot of people will know that!

Lying on my camp bed in the station I have been struck by a bout of nostalgia. Are you sitting comfortably? I'll begin.

Once upon a time when I was still wearing shorts to school, long before Muffin the Mule, The Flower Pot Men, Magic Roundabout and a host of other new fangled TV hits, we kids only had Children's Hour on steam radio to listen to. A favourite character was Uncle Mac (Derek McCulloch), who used to sign off at 6 o'clock every evening saying 'Goodnight children – everywhere.'

I would like to offer readers the same salutation. After all, we were all kids once!

DAY 301

27TH October – Hunstanton to Burnham Deepdale – 12 miles

Rigil Kent of the Norfolk Fire Brigade sees me off. I go into town for a beans/bacon brekkers and then break out on to the seafront.

In glorious sunshine, and with the vastness of the Wash to my left, I find the Pedders Way and follow it across the golf course. A number of golfers start gesticulating – apparently I am on their territory, having come off the Pedders and stepped inside a boundary hedge. Suitably admonished, I retreat from the hallowed ground and carry on. Why do old men chase a little white ball around the countryside? It has always been a mystery to me.

The Pedders Way eventually crosses the A149 at Thornham. Here I fortify myself with soup in the Lifeboat, then turn left and take the busy road, picking up the Pedders again at Brancaster and wending myself around the back of Burnham Deepdale.

I await my next hosts, Bill (Rotary) and Sandra Barnes, to the sound of Tornadoes making a racket on the coastal bombing range.

They whisk me off inland to Fakenham for a two day stay. This evening I am invited to dinner with other Rotarian friends. Interestingly we get onto stonemasonry and discuss limestone, marble and the problematical clunch which has been widely used in the buildings of East Anglia and along the South Downs.

I have yet to hear what, for me, is the most endearing accent in this country. Remember the singing postman Alan Smethurst's 'Hev you gota loight boy, hev you gota loight.'?

Day 302
28th October – Burnham Deepdale to Stiffkey – 10 miles

We all have our own heroes. Mine is Horatio Nelson, so I am delighted when Sandra Barnes says she will drive me direct this morning to his birthplace at nearby Burnham Thorpe, where his father was the rector. All Saints is an unpretentious church, but displayed inside is an excellent summary of Nelson's life.

Mary Heather, the church warden, tells me that the two huge 'white ensigns' hanging from the rafters were taken off the battleship *HMS Nelson* when she was decommissioned after the Second World War.

In 1936 my father, a petty officer, was a member of her crew, and I was taken on board by my mother when only one month old. Had these same flags been hoisted on that very day? I pondered.

I am on a Free day. Cutting north on a three mile straight brings me back to the Pedders and the Norfolk Coast Way. Passing a birder, I'm told that he has spotted a few pinkfoots flying in.He then adds dryly: 'Even *they* are leaving Iceland' This is a reference to that nation's recent collapse in the European money market.

In the afternoon I end up in Wells–next-the-Sea. Lots of families are about with their children enjoying the half term holiday. I go on a further three miles, watching noisy Brent Geese gliding in to feed on the fields. It's a wonderful mid-autumn scene.

The day ends with a rendezvous at the Red Lion in Stiffkey, and Bill and Sandra take me back to Fakenham.

Bill and Sandra Barnes have entertained friends and Rotarians on two evenings in order that I could explain the CLIMB's work. They are a marvellous couple who have looked after me splendidly – a perfect example of the support Rotary extends to those who seek its help.

There has been a frost during the night, so it's a chilly start to a day which is cloudless. I follow the coastal path and go inland and out at Morston to arrive at Blakeney. With no café in sight, I enter the White Horse Hotel. After hearing my plight the staff surprise me, serving up two huge doorstep bacon sandwiches and coffee – another spontaneous act of generosity at the right time.

I wander down to the quay to find kids 'crabbing', one of those old time pursuits that never cease to fascinate the youngsters.

As I stand watching it, the surreal in me surfaces again. This activity would make a great story in a Nick Park animated film production.

Picture the scene showing excited crabs and their families lining up on the submerged sandy bottom looking up and shouting 'Pick-me'. They are longing for a day out and are vying for the countless hooks breaking the surface. These will haul them aloft to spend a day in a bucket, to have a sort of 'al fresco' party with their continuously arriving friends.

Their day ends as the buckets are emptied and, yelling 'Yippee!', they perform synchronised diving, plunging back down to the submerged sand bar. Some might be lucky again during the next 'half term'. Is there scope here for a computer animated comedy I wonder?

Flek doesn't think so. He rants on about me being carried away with the fairies, but he isn't going to spoil my daydream.

I return to the coast path, but carrying the rucksack over soft sand and shingle is hard going. After three miles I've had enough and get back on the main road. The evenings are drawing in and it is getting dark as I enter Sheringham.

Fire Manager Gary Pegg opens up the station and tells me that his family run a 'chippie' in the town and will provide me with a meal. I walk past the railway station to collect my fish supper. The North Norfolk Railway Steamer has been running an excursion: enthusiasts abound.

I spend the evening preparing my Blogs and phoning family and friends. The station personnel have brought in a bed and I lie back to listen to Rachmaninov's Piano Concerto No.1. My Wish track is Ravel's Piano Concerto in G. It was composed in 1929 after his tour of the United States when he met George Gershwin, and is strongly influenced by jazz.

DAY 304

30th October – Sherringham to Mundesley Fire Station – 10 miles

After an early phone call interview with Southern Counties Radio I set off for Cromer four miles away. It is raining heavily when I arrive, and I am forced to use the first café on the seafront.

What can I say about the deficiencies of the English seaside café? There is no catering expertise about this place whatsoever.

The scenario goes like this: the proprietor is genial, but his badge of office is a Fair Isle jumper, so there is no image of who is running the place; the waitresses haven't any uniforms – clearly not trained, they are performing on instinct; the waiting time to be served is just within the acceptable limits; but then they offer UHT milk (ugh!) and when I request ordinary milk this arrives in a cup, because they haven't any milk jugs; and finally the tea cake is dry and there isn't enough butter.

'You've done an awful lot of complaining here, Col. A regular little Michael Winner, you are. Does all this ineptitude really annoy you?'

'Yes it does, Flek. And do you know what is so sad about it all? It is that the British public come to places like this year in and year out and put up with it. Do you know what's even sadder? Well, I'll tell you. They do it because they don't know any different! We have a lot to learn from our European friends on café service.'

I try to find the proprietor for a few words but he has gone to lunch! Walking through the rain I get a better service in the town, consuming a panini with salad.

There is still another seven miles to go. With no coastal path and little sign that the rain will abate, I take the A149 and branch off on a minor road to Southrepps and then onto Mundesley.

Paul Cosgrove settles me in the station, confirming that Richard Dromey, the district officer, has been made arrangements for me to stay at Martham Fire Station tomorrow. The Norfolk Brigade Stations are coming up trumps.

DAY 305

31st October – Mundesley Fire Station to Martham Fire Station – 12 miles

A couple of miles out I come across a locally famous windmill at Stow Hill. Built in 1825, it was purchased in the 1930s by Douglas McDougal of flour producing fame, who used it as a holiday home. It stands resplendent in the early morning sun.

Touching the coast, I pass the extensive gas distribution station at Bacton. Once again I come under the scrutiny of the Mobile MOD Security bods who constantly tour the surrounding roads in their 4 x 4's.

'A lone individual skulking around wearing a red bandana and carrying a large pack is bound to arouse their suspicions,' supposes Flek.

'They aren't alone, old chap. I have this effect on everyone.'

My words are engulfed by a deafening silence.

A long five-mile minor road brings me to Stalham, where a liver-and-bacon lunch is in order. More back-lane mileage, and suddenly I have stumbled into the Norfolk Broads region. Over the Old Heigham Bridge, I scurry several miles along a busy road to reach the fire station at Martham in the fading light. Watch Manager Mark Johnson greets me. I'm being hosted by the Norfolk Fire Brigade for the third night in a row.

At the end of a fine but nippy day, a nearby pub sorts my hunger out.

I still haven't heard any East Anglian twang yet. No doubt it is still entrenched right out in the sticks – perhaps in places with appealing names like Snoring or even Little Snoring and Trunch, all of which I notice on the OS Map?

1st November – Martham Fire Station to Great Yarmouth – 10 miles

I cook up some porridge for breakfast, using up the syrup flavour this morning, two packets.

'Two packets – a little greedy, aren't we? 'mutters Flek, who has just woken up.

'Napoleon famously said that an army marches on its stomach, Flek. In matters of nutriment, long-distance walkers have to follow the same counsel. I have also taken the precaution of piling up more calories by dunking several chocolate hob knobs in my tea. It is part of my controlled nutritional plan'

'What a load of tosh!'

He is exasperated by my devious reply.

I cut across country towards the coast at Helmsdale for elevenses. At Scratby I enter a holiday area called California. The east coast resorts often fall victim to indifferent weather and low sea temperatures, so to entice the punters holiday site owners have to be a little pretentious up here. Two weeks ago I passed Miami Beach at Skegness!

California is a series of 'pill box'-like holiday cabins set in rows devoid of any landscaping to tone down its bleakness. For interest I amble up a short cul-de-sac which dissects these blocks and leads to the beach. I find a scruffy pub, a run-down amusement arcade and the obligatory 'chippie.' California? It is hardly Malibu!

A little further on I take an access road and enter the Haven Holiday Park to get a cuppa at a booth. Its owner moans about a poor season. Well-wrapped up visitors are making the best of a bargain weekend. Calling into a café at Caister I eagerly scoff an all-day breakfast which sets me back £2.50 – worth every penny.

My brother Alan rings to arrange a rendezvous later today. I choose a place where I have long imagined that, after dark, MI5 agents pass on secrets, MD's just happen to meet their secretaries during the lunch hour and late-night boy racers gather. Where is it? Why it's Tesco's car park of course. I am here for the pleasure of seeing my brother and sister-in-law Ann turn up from Middleton-on-Sea, West Sussex. They are going to treat me to a couple of Rest days in a posh B & B at the village of Acle a few miles inland.

DAY 307

2nd November – Rest day – Great Yarmouth

After a super breakfast at our well-appointed B & B, Alan drives us to Wroxham in the heart of the Norfolk Broads. As we speed along I begin to wonder if my driving ability has diminished since last December: it won't be long before I find out!

It soon dawns on us that if you not mucking about in a boat then after the café stop it's time to move on. However, my brother does purchase a light bulb, though why I should record this I do not know!

We decide to go into Norwich. It's quite a hassle finding a parking spot but, that done, we walk through the charming old town and tour the cathedral. Every one of these individual ancient seats of bishops' thrones has its own timeless history.

Back at Acle the restaurants all seem to be closed, so we settle for the King's Head. At first it doesn't look very promising. We have to push through a group of locals gathered outside having their fags. They are obstructing the entrance – but once inside, what a difference! The bar is bustling with activity and the menu is great. The revelation is an elderly smiling waiter of the 'old school', dressed in the appropriate garb, expounding the service and the servility that I dream about.

I make the point to Flek: 'See what I mean? A person who, seemingly without trying, puts one at ease through the experience he's gathered practising the skills of table service. The same should show up in cafés.'

I hear grunts – he has heard all this before!

We return to our base, having had a long interesting day. It's been a reunion to remember.

DAY 308

3nd November – Great Yarmouth to Lowestoft fire station – 12 miles

Alan drives me into Great Yarmouth. He is going to deliver my rucksack to Lowestoft fire station, and it will be lighter. At last I have off-loaded my camping equipment. I won't need it any more, so he will take it home.

Although all the items were the lightest kit I could purchase, nevertheless there will be a saving in weight of about eight pounds. From now on hoisting the rucksack onto my back will be pure joy!

I wave Ann and Alan goodbye at the harbour car park. The Outer Port here at Great Yarmouth has been constructed parallel to the shore in recent years providing a navigable channel (extension of the River Yare) for a mile and a half. I fork left and proceed down the mainland side past the old docks and warehouses.

Strolling along, I see a touching site coming towards me – one for dog lovers. An elderly gent, Jim, is taking his Chihuahua dog Tiny for a walk. In reality he is pushing Tiny in a customised pink-coloured buggy, because Tiny suffers from a bad back. Altogether now . . . Ahhh!

Jim recognises what I am doing and sympathises, explaining that he has had to look after an invalid daughter for most of her life. She is 28 years old.

Tiny's customised buggy.

Adjacent to the newly constructed harbour mouth I discover to my surprise Gorleston's Edwardian Pavilion. Established over a hundred years ago, it has survived and is a thriving 300-seat theatre with a full programme. The general manager, Kevin Lynch, kindly shows me around. The auditorium on this day is laid out with individual tables and chairs. The decor and ambience reminds me of the BBC series The Good Old Days. Kevin tells me that it was once managed by the parents of Joan and Jackie Collins, and that Bill Pertwee, who is still with us and the last living cast member of Round the Horne, started his career here. He is now best known now as the ARP warden Hodges in Dads Army.

It has all been fascinating, but I have to move on. The view has now changed abruptly from the docklands to a superb four miles of beach with a wide promenade to match.

I pass another Haven Holiday Village. At the entrance I spot a sentry. It is only the first week in November but this unfortunate geezer has been dressed up as Father Christmas – though not fully. I wander over to inspect Sid,, whose festive uniform stretches only to a Ho Ho Ho Hat and an ill-fitting red jacket without the matching trousers.

Flek points out the obvious: 'As a Father Christmas he is half naked. Go on, ask him why he has been short changed?'

Trying not to laugh while expressing deep sympathy, I enquire what's happened. Apparently he drew the short straw in the staff ballot and has retaliated by telling the management that he can't wear a beard because it irritates. He has no idea whether the boots or trousers will ever materialise. He is embarrassed and miserable as sin.

I wish him a Merry Christmas and, in the spirit of the moment, he growls back 'Spherical Appendages'. Weary and fatigued, it takes me a few minutes to fully decipher his good wishes.

The next holiday village along my route is 'Potters', a name that will be resurrected in a few hours' time.

As usual the station manager, this time John Tiffen of the Lowestoft Fire Station, and his crew make me most welcome. Alan has delivered my slimmed-down rucksack.

The time is 11.25pm and the 1st appliance gets a 'shout'. As he pulls the address sheet from the printer, the OIC shouts 'Potters, this could be a big one!' – and it is. It takes the crews of eight appliances to stop the outbreak spreading from the site's laundry, which is destroyed.

There is to be a footnote to this incident. Unbeknown to me. a couple of my Southern Trails walkers, Frank and Daphne Butler, are staying on the site at this time.

Day 309
4th November – Lowestoft Fire Station to Southwold – 13 miles

I grab some breakfast and say a quick goodbye to the off-going Crew who have had a very busy night. Striding out of town along the prom brings me to the A12. I get on to the Suffolk Coast Path and spend most of the day zigzagging along miles of country lanes and byway tracks in perfect, still weather.

The going becomes difficult – busy road traffic over the last two miles. The reduced weight of the rucksack has an amazing effect on my morale. I feel so free. So I waltz into twee Southwold, the quintessential east coast seaside town which has been besieged by second-home owners. George Orwell spent many of his formative years here, living with his parents.

I'm collected by my next host, Barbara Prodger, who motors in from Aldeburgh. She and her husband John are relations of my good friend David Garforth of Rotary, who has arranged so many host families for me. Their splendid house was rescued and refurbished after being the home of a recluse.

Barbara and John Prodger, jazz fans.

Sorting out my maps during the evening in John's study is a delight, thanks to a background soundtrack of Jimmy Giuffre, the jazz sax and clarinet player. The groups he formed featured much interplay and improvisation. His composition 'Train and the River' is a perfect introduction to the famous film Jazz on a Summers Day, shot at the Newport Jazz Festival in 1958. John also shares my interest in the Modern Jazz Quartet.

DAY 310
5th November – Southwold to Aldeburgh – 12 miles

The Prodgers suggest that I leave my rucksack with them: I can pick it up later when reaching Aldeburgh. To avoid problems with ferry availability Barbara drops me off at Walberswick on the south side of the River Blyth.

I have to walk across some marshes. There are defined paths, but it's just as well that a wind pump tower half way across provides an excellent bearing. I reach and skirt the Dunwich Forest and get to Bridge Farm, where I am amazed to find a café which is still open. Pressing on, I rejoin the coastal path. There is no one around.

I go past the famous Minsmere nature and bird reserve and the dome of Sizewell 'B' nuclear power station comes into view. As near as it seems to be, it takes me an age to reach the site of what are two stations, 'A' & 'B' – the seventh and eighth that I have encountered. .

The charming village of Thorpeness is next; here I visit the Brasserie and Emporium. An excellent eating hole, it has been a tradition over the years to cover its walls with past and present journals such as *Picture Post*, *Private Eye*, comics and film posters. The trouble is that once an interest gets a grip it is difficult to leave.

I have been warned by Lesley at CLIMB that this afternoon I will be surprised by someone I know. Intrigued, I cut across some scrub and get onto the prom leading into Aldeburgh. As I enter the town I am ambushed by four elderly gentlemen who suddenly appear from a promenade shelter. These assailants are my old (they are very old) Southern Trails mukkers Brian Coote, Bob Dunn, Ron Lander and David Brand.

I *am* surprised, and my salutation is hardly fitting as I bellow, 'What the hell are you lot doing here?'

'That's nice' says one of them – and Flek concurs.

Brian explains: 'We've spread out today in the hope of cutting you off but decided after an alcoholic break to regroup and nab you here.'

I am, of course, delighted to see them, and they march me to a super hotel on the seafront. They have sacrificed their government 'fuel and light allowance' to billet me in luxury. For them it is self-catering in a house around the corner booked by Deborah, Brian's daughter.

Brian runs me out to the Prodgers to pick up my rucksack. During evening we gather in the hotel's lounge bar for a meal. It's now time to discuss a strategy for tomorrow. Our focus is distracted by a gorgeous Italian receptionist, but none of us can understand why!

Using the pseudonyms Clegg, Foggy, Compo, Smiler and Wesley (disguises, but not necessarily in that order to protect the innocent) we make our plans. I then retire to my luxury suite overlooking the sea and they clear off to imbibe alcoholic nightcaps, argue and probably sleep on the floor.

What a day!

'The Last of the Summer Wine' from West Sussex.

DAY 311

6th November– Aldeburgh to Woodbridge nr Felixstowe – 15 miles

I descend in the lift for a super breakfast, oblivious that my mates are struggling to make themselves toast a few blocks away. The plan is that Brian and Bob will motor to Snape and the rest of us will use Shanks's pony. We take to the road before turning onto the Sailors Way, which cuts through the lovely Black Heath Wood, resplendent in its autumnal colours.

We meet up and all fall into the Crown Inn. This is yet another pub that was once crammed with smugglers. Just how many of these tax dodgers were there in the land? one has to ask. The old boys sit round the blaze in its Inglenook fireplace telling outrageous stories. As they are getting a little dozey, it's prudent to organise 'fire pickets' to remove those whose clothes may start smoking!

They are all getting comfortable – too comfortable. It's all right for them, of course, but I've got a nine-mile slog to Woodbridge this afternoon. I manage to turf them out and we walk down to The Maltings, where Brian has parked his car.

I hoist up my rucksack and go down the line shaking hands. This OAP has got to hit the road, and with great sadness I slip away before anyone realises that it's my 'round'.

It's been great to see these pensioners. I understand that Brian persuaded them all to join him on the pretext that they were all going on a SAGA cruise!

Now for a long, long, never-ending nine-mile trudge down the busy B1069, passing the former USAF base at Bentwaters and on to Woodbridge. From here my next hosts, Paul and Felicity Robinson, take me to their home at Felixstowe.

This is another of Ken Marshall's contacts from his immigration service days: he was posted here for many years.

This evening I'm taken out for a pub meal and then on a tour of this 'container' town. We end up at the ferry dock. It crosses to Harwich but not in the winter, so there will have to be an alternative plan tomorrow. We look down on the container depot, which is ablaze with lights, allowing a twenty four hour turn-around of the massive ships.

I have entered the shipping weather forecast area Thames.

DAY 312

7th November – Martlesham to Felixstowe – 7 miles

Wet with fine periods today is the forecast. Paul runs me back to where he picked me up yesterday. Crossing the A12, I am amazed at the non-stop container lorry traffic en route to Felixstowe.

I arrive back to meet Ken Marshall, and we dine out with a friend Diana. Later she takes us down to the passenger ferry jetty. From here we can view the docks lit up like a city.

DAY 313

8th November – Harwich to Frinton-on-Sea –15 miles

For walkers the problem with Felixstowe is that it is wedged between the Rivers Stour, Orwell and Deban. With the ferry closed, Paul and Felicity opt to transport me to Harwich, an awful long way round. I find out later that they have kindly settled my accommodation bill at a B & B in Frinton, ferrying my rucksack at the same time.

The broken and marshy coastline forces me inland to Great Oakley where I get a lunch in the Maybush.The geography also means that I have to go the long way around the massive areas of nature reserves and through hamlets with delightful names such as Beaumont in Moze and Kirby le Soken, then finally into Frinton-on-Sea.

Frinton has developed a genteel culture since the early 20th century, having an uneasy alliance with those who reside 'beyond the gates'. To explain, a railway line splits the town and social snobbery has apparently long divided those on either side of the only level crossing gates. My B & B is on the 'outside'.

It's only in recent years that the town has adopted fish and chip shops and take-aways. The first pub didn't arrive until 2000. The original developer shunned the idea of a pier – too vulgar!. Amusement arcades and ice cream stalls are banned. Rows of immaculate beach huts epitomise Frinton's social ethic. Consequently it became the butt of musical hall jokes, e.g. 'Harwich for the Continent, Frinton for the Incontinent'!

My jovial landlady settles me in. Looking around, one cannot help but notice the profusion of Doris Day photographs and memorabilia. The actress is her idol, and on a holiday to California she toured the area where Doris lives. She was sitting in a restaurant when the actress walked in, sat down and gave her an impromptu audience. What a thrill for a fan.

I explained that I always had the same expectancy that when I was sitting in a café on Bognor Regis seafront Kim Novak would appear. She never turned up!

Since my visit there has been a controversial end to a bitter row over the manually operated railway crossing gates in Frinton. These were deemed to serve as an essential checkpoint between the town and the rest of the country, befitting a town moulded in aspic. After years of rankle Network Rail turned up in the middle of the night and removed them. The underhanded cads! The provision of automatic gates remotely operated has shaken the local Residents Association to the core. The mayor is quoted as saying, 'The old gates ensured our little enclave kept us away from the madhouse. We wanted to protect our little bit of England.'

As Tony Hancock would have put it, 'Stone me mate, that's ruffled a few feathers with that lot down at the town hall!'

DAY 314
9th November – Frinton-on-Sea to Brightlingsea – 12 miles

I tiptoe out of cosy Frinton and take the prom which runs the three miles to Clacton Pier, pausing at 11.00 (Armistice Sunday). In fine weather it's a nice easy stroll, lots of people out doing the same thing. I join the remembrance service to the fallen on the seafront and follow the parade through the town until I find a café. It serves an indifferent panini: would have been nice to have had some cheese in it!

I have fond memories of family holidays in this town. Mum and Dad avoided Butlins – we'd got our own back at Bognor. My brother Alan and I spent most of our time on the roller skating rink.

From here it's going to be a considerable afternoon's trek to my next hosts. Brightlingsea Creek means another lengthy diversion. It is said that because there are so many rivers, creeks and inlets, Essex has the longest coastline in England.

The arrangements for my stay at Brightlingsea are two-fold. Circumstances conspire, allowing me to be picked up by David Foss-Smith at a church outside the town and taken to his home. There I freshen up and have a superb meal with him and his wife Elizabeth. Her father was a HQ fire officer at Lambeth when I was there: another coincidence! Later I overnight with Alan and Christine Cole. The Coles are friends of Hugh and Daphne Ashton at Chichester.

I have had a map dump here.

DAY 315
10th October –Brightlingsea to Wickham Bishops -Maldon– 13 miles

Alan Cole drops me off at Thorrington on the B1027 Colchester Road and I yomp the five miles to Colchester. It is now raining very hard on the outskirts. Tesco's once again provides a welcome bolt-hole.

The weather sets in and I have a further nine miles to go down the A2082 towards Tiptree, home of the well-known jam factory. I am not looking forward to it.

There are two words beginning with 'P' that describe heavy downpours. In deference to political correctness I shall report that the precipitation today is at times torrential. Surface water together with heavy traffic, no pavement refuge and failing light makes the going very precarious.

With two miles to go I've had enough, and phone an SOS to my next host John Smale, saying that I need assistance. He heeds my call. Soon this 'drowned rat is transformed into a 'happy bunny'. Having been rushed to his home for a soak in the bath, I enjoy a delicious meal prepared by his wife Liz.

John has answered a call from the 'Old Cicestrians' (Chichester High School Old Boys) to put me up. His home is a testament to a successful business career. Liz is a retired GP.

It is a Rest day tomorrow – and after today I deserve it.

DAY 316

11th November – Rest day – Wickam Bishops

John takes me out on a tour of my intended route. First we visit Maldon, which has some of the renowned Thames barges moor at its quay. We stroll out to see the impressive memorial statue of Brythnoth, who was the Earl of Essex. In 991 he saw some invading Vikings on an island in the estuary here at Maldon and, being a 'Mr Nice Guy', he invited them on to the mainland to fight it out. So they came ashore and 'duffed' him and his followers up. It just goes to show what perils you run when trying to 'play cricket' with Johnny Foreigner!

Motoring on, we next visit the remote church of St Peter on the Wall and get a fine view of Bradwell nuclear power station! Also we discover a touching commemorative plaque to the 120 pilots who were lost from the Bradwell Second World War fighter station. Canadian, New Zealand, Australian, Polish and Czech Squadrons flew out of here. Finally we motor down to Burnham on Crouch for lunch at the Queen's Head. The weather is perfect: what a contrast to yesterday.

In the evening I follow the Smales through an exit gate at the bottom of their garden and we all walk down a moonlit lane for a quiet meal at the Green Man. It's a wonderful finish to the day.

DAY 317

12th November – Maldon to Steeple (Canney House Camp) – 8 miles

John motors me into Maldon. I leave the town free of my rucksack and go down a minor road on a south-east course. After two miles I turn off and I walk over to Mundon Hall; a couple of alpacas browse in a front paddock.

Rounding the Hall I discover a church almost completely hidden in trees. The building has been fenced off and a notice board pronounces that it is under the protection of 'The Friends of Friendless Churches', an organisation whose aim is to maintain and protect those churches which have been abandoned.

Walking across a couple of small enclosures I am suddenly presented with an amazing sight. I come to the fence, and in the field are over twenty dead mature oak trees. Their demise is complete, with all bark and growth absent. The trunks have been polished by weathering and they present a unique and spooky spectacle.

The scene is made further intriguing by the presence of a score of alpacas grazing beneath them. These handsome and lovable animals come over to greet me. With their wool showing hues of cream and browns, and with their large, placid brown eyes, I am overwhelmed by their curiosity. I had a similar tender moment with the Welsh Cobbs several months before in Wales.

Strangely it is an enchanting experience and I move on, my karma enriched.

'Get you!' spouts Flek. 'Are we going all soppy now, then?

I am now on St Peters's Way, which wends around the fields and up on a bank above a creek. I clamber over a stile into Maylandsea and Mayland, the latter having an excellent food store which I make good use of. It's just a couple of miles now to Steeple, where John picks me up.

Alpacas grazing under dead oak trees.

John and Liz have to take me a long way back to Steeple. It is the time to say goodbye: the couple's hospitality has been outstanding.

I push east, passing an access road to Stansgate Abbey Farm. Remember Lord Stansgate, later to be known as Anthony Wedgewood Benn and now Tony Benn? I am told that Abbey Farm is a family home.

I take the next lane leading to the Waterside caravan site, following the path along the bank of the River Blackwater. Flocks of Brent geese are flying in, and solitary Little Egrets explore the marsh inlet streams. A Thames barge with its distinctive mast chugs its way downriver. I pass a barrage of ten redundant Thames lighters which have been filled with mud and sand, a cheap bank defence. The silence is broken every so often by gun noise from batteries at Foulness Island.

After a couple of miles I reach the Bradwell waterside marina. My next host, Ian Cundy, who works at the Marina, is here to meet me. He relieves me of the rucksack and I am taken into the office tower. Here I

Ian and Sheena Cundy.

am given tea and make a broadcast on the local Saint FM radio station. I will see Ian later and, now Free, I walk past Bradwell Nuclear Power Station (my ninth), which is now being decommissioned. The site appears deserted. What featureless structures they are. I sit down and in the silence eat the sandwiches that John and Liz have prepared for me.

The path swings around the coastline 90 degrees in a couple of miles and I have returned to the St Peters on the Wall chapel which I visited with John yesterday. The church was built with the remnants of a Roman fort by St Cedd, making it the oldest church in the UK. For many years it was used as a barn by a local farmer before someone recognised its significance. This is a lonely spot, ideal for meditation and devotions.

Nearby is a complex of single- storey buildings that make up the Othona Community. This is an open Christian community whose purpose is to provide, mainly through its two centres in Essex and Dorset, a welcoming and accepting place for patterns of work by people of different faiths. There is nobody on site today.

'Bet it is shut down for the winter,' says Flek, 'It was all right for St Cedd out here in this draughty hole wearing just a hair shirt. The faithful of today want a bit of comfort with their devotions, don't they?'

It is a practical comment from my agnostic friend, but, it would hardly endear him to this community!

A final two-mile straight gets me into Bradwell on Sea and I find the Cundys' home, to be reunited with Ian and meet his wife Sheena and kids Leon and George – plus a springer spaniel .

The Cundys are an interesting couple. Both are part-time musicians, a guitar and vocal duo. Ian has a small recording studio on the ground floor. What is more they are pagans, and they show me photos of their wedding held in a local field and later blessed at St Peter's. These weddings are called 'handfastings', and everyone wears beautiful and elaborate costumes.

I enjoy a meal and then to bed. I snuggle down and reach for the iPod. What shall I play tonight? Dave Brubeck's 'Blue Rondo a la Turk', Bill Withers' 'Ain't No Sunshine' and Erroll Garner's 'Autumn Leaves'. My Wish Track is pure nostalgia from the 1950s: Bill Snyder, a Chicago pianist, playing 'Bewitched' from Rogers and Hart's 'Pal Joey'.

DAY 319
14th November – Bradwell to Burnham on Crouch – 14 miles

I will have to walk back up to the ancient St Peter's Church to continue my journey. Sheena and dog walk a with me for a couple of miles. We part and I now have to tackle ten miles of remote embankment and sea wall, thankfully under a watery sun and against only a light wind.

It is remote out here and I feel very exposed. I am mostly alone, but do meet a few birders who point out a short-eared owl.

It takes most of the afternoon for me to follow the embankment round 90 degrees into the River Crouch. On the way I see a locked metal farm gate which divides the embankment road, and on it is affixed a selection of washed up flotsam. Locals have hung a selection of modern detritus on it, e.g. fishing net, crocks (shoes), children's sand buckets, ball cock marker buoys and single trainers – a right colourful display.

'This is modern art in the raw', says a delighted Flek.

I meet my next host, Lynda George, outside the Crown Inn (I was here yesterday with John), and she introduces me to the deputy mayor of Burnham. We disappear into the pub for tea and biscuits.

Flotsam displayed, River Crouch.

Lynda and I walk along the waterfront to the last moored boat. I meet her partner Peter Hardiman and they take me aboard. I had recognised the type of vessel, but Peter confirms that we are on a 250-ton concrete Mulberry Barge.

These were used on D-Day for constructing the Mulberry Harbour to facilitate the Allied landings. It's 90ft long, and Peter has spent a fortune converting it, with two decks which include a guest cabin. He tells me that these pontoons were moulded in reinforced concrete so that trying to affix fittings is a nightmare.

Lynda tells me that although their location is on the Essex coast, they are able to pick up BBC Southern TV. She had seen an appeal to support Walk GB 4 Climb and had contacted CLIMB to offer hosting.

As it gets dark the barge's lengthy deck lounge-cum-galley is the scene of an event that Lynda has billed as an 'Italian Evening'. A gathering of friends listen to the aims of my Walk, and after consuming an excellent meal they donate £175.

So tonight I sleep afloat. I'm too tired for the iPod Concert, but my Wish Track could have been Josh McRae's 'Messing about on the River'!

Peter and Lynda's Mulberrry Barge.

DAY 320

15th November — Burnham on Crouch to South Woodham Ferriers
— 10 miles

I walk the gangplank and wave goodbye to the lively Peter and Lynda. Against a stiff cool breeze I follow the River Crouch embankment for six miles, arriving at the Ferry Inn, North Fambridge. It has a white shiplack elevation, a tradition around these parts which goes back to boat building.

Outside is a lone smoker. I strike up a conversation and it's not long before he is moaning about the smoking ban law. I feel sorry for him in a detached way.

'Have you every smoked, Flek?'
We've been together for some time and I think the odd prying question is on.
'You name it, I've smoked it.'
His reply is pure bravado of course. Not impressed, I challenge him further.
'Given up, have we? Broken the habit, kicked some cold turkey!'
'Well, I haven't had a drag since we joined up.'
Trying not to sound pious, I encourage him to keep it up. Any more words and I'd be preaching, and that would never do.

I go inside for leek and potato soup. I now have a weathered and dishevelled appearance. I slurp the delicious gruel, but no one in the packed bar seems to regard me as a health & safety hazard. A policy of social, or, if you prefer political, correctness is obviously not pursued in many premises. I am gratified to be accepted without fuss.

I remember an amusing experience I had once had when walking the Thames Path. My friend Brian Higgins and I walked into a pub in Eton, bought our pints and took a pew. An old boy struggled in carrying a load of full shopping bags. After getting his ale he sat down opposite us, politely placed a napkin on the table took his false teeth out (both sets) and laid them before us like trophies.

The management told us that the old boy had ignored all grievance procedures, such as three strikes and you're out, threats of eviction and numerous red cards and just carried on. You can hear his defence counsel arguing that he, and not those residing in that pile across the river, is Windsor and Eton's star tourist attraction!

The density of the traffic on the B1012 over the last four miles is a stark reminder that I am back in the south-east. 'Mum Two' rings from CLIMB with what will probably be the penultimate host situation list.

Susan Wood picks me up at South Woodham Ferrers rail station and we motor to her parents, Geoff and Marie, who are going to put me up. They waste no time is showing me a hot bath and then I am fed. Guess what? It's fish and chips and apple crumble. Luvvly Jubbly!

I mention the 'dead oaks' sighting to Geoff and, being interested in local history, he promises to do some research.

Susan and David Wood are a CLIMB family. Their children Ted (5) and Kitty (3) have the degenerative metabolic condition Medium Chain acy Coa Dehydrogenase Deficiency (MCADD).

DAY 321

16th November – South Woodham Ferrars to Westcliff-on-Sea – 8 miles

Geoff has probably solved the mystery of the 'dead oaks'. In 1953 disastrous flooding occurred along the North Sea coastal counties, which resulted in the deaths of over three hundred inhabitants in Lincolnshire and Essex. The government embarked on a massive programme of drainage to avert any further tragedy. Geoff has traced a local farmer who remembers the area where the oaks were planted being part of the scheme. It's possible that the trees were deprived of their natural water supply and subsequently died. In a way they are still very much alive.

I am forced to head south-west to get over the River Crouch. This I do at Battlebridge, where I find a café in an antiques centre which offers huge eccles cakes. I wash one down with a pot of tea and keep one for later.

I can now tack south-rast towards Westcliff on mainly minor roads. From now on my route is along the outer and then inner conurbations of London. There are plenty of highways but access for pedestrians is going to get difficult. Also, I personally will become more of a curiosity. I now know how Dick Whittington must have felt, and I haven't even got a cat!

It drizzles for two hours today. For those of you who think that I am living the life of O'Reilly out here I am impelled to inform you that I am eating my donated sandwiches huddled in a bus shelter. As the Routemasters stop it is somewhat degrading to once again be gaped at by passengers from the top deck.

I ruminate for a while: I do a lot of that in bus shelters. Looking down, I notice 'strawberry' marks. When my Dad was in his seventies I noticed the same marks on his hands – I thought he had had a fall. He brushed my enquiry aside, saying that's what happens when you get old. Well I have now reached my seventies. *Deja vu!*

Cold and wet, I drift into one of my surreal deliriums imagining that I am embarking on one of those exploration expeditions set up by Colonel Blashford Snell ('Blashers' to his friends). I am forging a way across the open plains of southern Essex, passing through the primitive settlements of Raleigh, Hockley, Hawkwell and Eastwood hoping to discover the long-lost city of 'Sarfend'. I note that the natives have traded in their brace of oxen for 4 x 4's and that the Kraal's of those owning more than five cows can only be entered by pressing metal digits on the their front gates!

I come to, moving on to discover Westcliff-on-Sea instead. At the end of a very long urban street I bang on the door of my next hosts, Victoria and Derek Brown. Victoria is the daughter of Richard Kneller, an ex-committee member of the Cicestrians, by whom I will be hosted shortly.

They extend an enthusiastic welcome to an elderly adventurer. Victoria rises very early each morning, travels into the City of London to deliver and maintain rubber plants and other exotic flora which brighten up the offices of corporate management and think-tanks. Her tall athletic appearance suggests she partakes in sport. She does, and it's cricket: she plays for the Essex Lady's team. Her enthusiasm must run in the genes, because her dad is bowled over with the game!

DAY 322

17th November – Westcliff-on-Sea to Orsettt – 13 miles

Victoria leaves for work at 5.00am. I hear her leave and am overcome with guilt, but I owe it to my legs to lie in until 7.30.

I bid farewell to husband Derek and at the end of the road turn right on to the A13. I don't remember too much about this stage except that it's ten miles of head-down and slog along the pavements accompanied by the incessant noise of traffic. The day finishes with a scary passage along two miles of dual carriageway. I finally escape the hassle at Standord-le-Hope. Once I enter the flow down a main artery into central London there is no hope of any human contact. The presence of a pavement is insignificant. I don't feel safe and the traffic rules OK!

The shopping centre in Stanford is a welcome relief and I find a splendidly appointed fount of refreshment. Now, I have had months of honing my story. Once the café staff of Amy, Cherie and Donna hear it

Richard and Maggie Kneller.

they make me sit down for an afternoon tea. There is no gall on my part. I am always asked a question and I answer it.

Flek is not so complimentary.

'I wouldn't exactly call it scrounging, Col, but you do lay it on a bit thick with the ladies.'

'I'm sorry you take that attitude, Flek. You see most decent and caring folk like to feel that they have helped out, and that is all there is to it. When 'online' they can always check me out on the website.

A relatively comfortable stroll brings me to Orsett Fire Station, where my next host, Richard Kneller, picks me up: he has come a long way. Over the next two days both he and wife Maggie will transport me extensive distances to meet my schedule.

Back at their home I seem to fit in as if part of the furniture. Richard has had an interesting career, and he and family lived in France for a few years. He tunes into the French TV network for their news. I view the pictures with interest but sadly all I can remember of my French at school is singing 'Frere Jaques'.

Flek sighs: 'Your application for the French Foreign Legion would have never stood up to Inspector Clouseau's scrutiny. You're not a francophile, Colin.'

He is perfectly correct, though Jacques Tati did make me laugh in his silent film 'Monsieur Hulot!'

Day 323
18th November – Orsett to Rainham – 10 miles

Maggie runs me the lengthy way to the charming village of Orsett. There follows a nine-mile unremarkable stroll through urban Essex via the areas of Grays, between West Thurrock, South Ockendon Averley and into Rainham.

I am able to keep off the trunk roads and complete ninety per cent of the journey on a series of minor ones. Luckily one of them crosses the M25 half a mile from junction 30. I am now on the Metropolitan Inner Circle and proceed to Rainham railway station without a problem.

Maggie comes even further to collect me. She has a sat-nav device in the car. Being a Luddite, I have never had the pleasure of listening to some anonymous female instructing a driver where to proceed. Despite all the adverse publicity about these devices I am delighted, if not surprised, that we are directed to Danebury Vale, our destination, and do not finish up in a field, scrapyard or even a cemetery – the ultimate dead-end!

'Bit of an anti-climax really,' complains Flek. 'I was hoping for something exciting to happen today, like being directed into a ploughed field or a sewage works, requiring a tractor to pull us out. What a let down!'

Getting back early allows me to make umpteen phone calls about arrangements for the final month of the Project. Despite struggling through the TV news from France, I spend another splendid evening with the Knellers, reminiscing about all manner of things.

DAY 324

19th November – Rainham to Woolwich Pier – 10 miles

It is a reluctant goodbye to the Kneller's. Maggie is running me to Rainham, which is a long way off, so we have an early start.

There are no minor roads today. I have to follow the A13(T) and, goodness me, heavy traffic is really beginning to funnel its way into the East End of London. There are walkways, but it's impossible not to be inhibited by the constant vehicle movements, particularly at junctions where there are no recognised ways to cross.

'Where on earth does it all go to,' puzzles Flek.

'Let me try and explain, my friend. The City has a great number of measures to absorb traffic, but it also has a way to constrict it called the congestion charge, brought in by that nice mayor of London, Ken Livingstone. There is a sort of analogy here with the Scottish midge. The traffic flows unrestricted like the midges in calm weather. Now 'whistle' up a little breeze and the little beggars disappear to where no one knows. Ken's little scam is the 'charge' which performs the same trick.

'I'm sure you've grasped my analysis. Flek. Now – there's a good chap – let me concentrate on the threats to our wellbeing until we reach Woolwich.'

After passing the Ford motorworks at Dagenham, I reach a major junction and turn left heading for the Woolwich Ferry and walk straight on towards the customs house at the head of King George V Dock. From here I am able to look down the runway of London City Airport.

At North Woolwich I take the pedestrian subway under the Thames.

I have an arrangement with Ken Marshall to meet him at the Great Harry pub on the other side. We have a drink and catch the train to Westcombe Park Station.

Ken's daughter Natasha and her husband James will be our hosts for the next two days in Charlton. In the evening I am taken to a vibrant local pub for a meal. So ends another pretty hectic day

DAY 325
20th November – Woolwich Pier Greenwich – Cutty Sark to Tower Bridge – 8 miles

In fine weather this is going to be an easy Free day. Ken and I stroll from the flat in Charlton through the grounds of the National Maritime Museum. We stop for coffee at Costa in Waterstones, then walk past the Cutty Sark to take the pedestrian subway under the Thames to the Isle of Dogs.

This part of the Thames waterfront has changed beyond recognition during the last three decades. Wandering on wide promenades, we pass mile after mile of high rise flats and apartments with the occasional commercial premises breaking up the skyline. Alleyways split up the route, which makes the going a little more interesting. What strikes us is the relative peaceful environment which prevails and the fact that, albeit it is a weekday, there is no one around. Not once over the next two days do we even see anybody at a window.

At Canary Wharf we face dire warnings posted up to warn the walking public of the penalties imposed if straying off what is the Thames Path (North Side) and into the Canary complex. No doubt this is a consequence of the terrorist outrage of a few years back. Because of this and continuing improvement works we have to run the gauntlet of a road underpass to get back on to the Thames Path.

Our lunch stop is at the Prospect of Whitby, reputedly the oldest riverside tavern site in the UK. Although it's a famous pub, our timing meant that there are few customers about.Runners continue to pass us in large numbers and it would appear that those so inclined, mostly 'young things', are leaving the air conditioning of their offices to partake in a sponsored jog during the lunch hour.

'They are just showing off their leotards – posing – that's what they are doing,' spouts Flek. 'My Grandad told me that when he left the army after the war he used his local church hall as a gym for two nights a week. The only gear he had to train in was his second best vest, baggy black shorts and pumps (plimsolls) made in India which he bought in Woollies. The only bloke owning a tracksuit was the instructor.'

'Flek, you are displaying a prejudice completely out of proportion to the event, ' I challenge. Sulking he rests on his comments.

As we approach Tower Bridge, the memorial to all civilians who died in the Blitz comes into view. It is simplicity itself. portraying the outline of a dove cut out of a dark background.

Finally we walk around the St Katherine Docks with its posh shops and swanky moored yachts. A brisk walk takes us up to Cannon Street for the train back to Charlton.

It has been a marvellous, leisurely day with Ken, who is great and often amusing company – what a change from my normal daily routine. I look forward to the return journey tomorrow.

Day 326
21th November – Tower Bridge to Greenwich to Charlton – 8 miles

Ken and I repeat our walk down to Greenwich Pier and catch a Thames Clipper to Tower Bridge. These splendid 200-passenger hydrofoil river buses are a star transport feature, and soon we are speeding up the river. With regular 'bus stops', a small fleet of these pick up over seven thousand passengers a day.

After drinks at the Tower Embankment we have our photo taken. The shot shows the oldest swingers in town. Crossing the famous bridge our task is to return down the river via the Thames Path (South). We find ourselves in the Jamaica Road area and rove through the narrow streets which must have been such a hive of activity in its Dockland days. This iconic area is now a labyrinth of small business cafés, restaurants, art galleries and the odd boutique – they have revolutionised the area.

We rejoin the Thames Path and grab a drink in the Mayflower Pub at Rotherhithe.

Another one of those coincidences which have been such a feature throughout the year crops up. In the residential Rotherhithe Street I notice a terraced house with balloons attached. In the small front garden stands a lectern displaying some information. I cross the road to read it.

The text announces an appeal for funds. The occupiers of the house are collecting donations for some neighbours who have already lost a child to the degenerative metabolic condition Battens Disease, or to give it its full name Neuronal Ceriod Lipofuscinoses. They have another child so afflicted whom they wish to take to China for stem cell treatment.

I knock on the door and a young lady answers. She is Michelle Thorp and, together with her parents Peter and Violet, she regularly raises funds for 'causes' – she recently completed a sponsored parachute jump. I explain to the Thorps the coincidence of my purpose and their charity activity. They make us very welcome.

Tower Bridge – my last.

Ken spots a small well stocked bar in the lounge. We are offered tipples. I can truly say that we left refreshed both in inspirational and alcoholic high spirits. The Thorps are the epitome of a public spirited family.

The Blacksmith Arms provides us with a super Thai lunch. I re-discover an ancient mulberry tree planted by the Tsar of Russian in Peyps Park and we visit the City Farm at Surrey Docks for a cuppa. The latter had also been a refreshment stop for a 50 strong Southern Trails group walking the Thames Path a few years back.

We finish our visits of the day in the Bell and Dog pub in Depford for a drink and a chat with some interesting locals and its Scottish landlord.

It is quite a stroll from here back to James and Natasha Passmore's flat in Charlton, but it is not every day one can saunter past the Cutty Sark (it's devastating fire yet to come) and Greenwich Maritime Heritage Park area plus the grandeur of the Royal Naval College buildings. Today's heritage trail has been unbeatable.

DAY 327
22th November – Charlton to Gravesend – 10 miles

The dire Met Office predictions do not materialise. I rise to a crisp sunny morning, and it's going to stay like this. Ken and I are on the move, this time in opposite directions. Ken is off to home at Weston, Spalding, but he is not finished with me yet. My bet is he will turn up again at Deal next week.

I am to go the other way into deepest Kent. We both say goodbye to his daughter Natasha and hubby James, their hosting of us having been ace in providing an endearing family atmosphere.

I am sporting long-johns to counteract today's 'brass'monkey' temperatures. Although I am relatively near to the end of my journey, the geography dictates that I shall be heading in the wrong direction until I get to Margate. I pass the Valley football ground: Charlton F.C. will get beaten 5-2 here later in the day, so it's just well I'm through in the morning. When Charlton won the FA Cup in 1947 their ground the

Old Valley held 75,000 spectators, the East Bank being the largest single standing area in English football. Those were the days!

I turn on to the A20 (the old Roman Watling Street) and arrive at Welling, where I get a hearty cowboys' breakfast. It's a lively café and the family staff are welcoming, offering me a second coffee. A swarthy old boy sits inside the door and he looks on approvingly. Obviously the 'godfather' of the place, he watches every move.

At Dartford I enter another interesting pub. The Royal Victoria and Bull is an old coaching inn with ancient tiled floor around a central square bar with lantern light directly above. A pint of Stella sees me on my way and I am joined for a while by a kitted-out day walker whose name escapes me – though I do remember that he was a dustman from Newham!

I cut up through Northfleet and get to my £28.00 'basic' B & B. A knock on the door produces a mid Asian proprietor whose first move is to get out his cashbox. The place has been extensively renovated and made fit for purpose, although I do notice an 'improvement notice' (a do-it-or-else document) from the fire authority pinned to the notice-board. Most landlords would hide this away in the deepest filing cabinet, but here it is defiantly on show.

He takes my money and, without a smile, hands me my breakfast, which comprises a cardboard carton holding a packet of corn flakes, some UHT milk and biscuits . . . and that's it! I get a flashback to similar 'service 'at the Travelodge, St Clears, back in March.

The room is stark. Some pictures and a bedside lamp would be nice. However this cell is warm and relatively comfortable. I 'cook' a dehydrated meal, make some coffee and settle on the bed to watch Match of the Day, witnessing a wonder goal from Pompey's Glen Johnson.

I include Henry Purcell, Dizzy Gillespie, Beethoven and Oscar Peterson in my late night Concert. The Wish Track is the haunting Valse Triste by Sibelius.

DAY 328

23th November – Gravesend to Strood fire station – 6 miles

It takes me two minutes to gobble up the breakfast generously 'donated' by Mr Sanghera. I step out to find that snow has fallen overnight, although it is thawing already. This is only my fourth sighting (including a snow field on top of Ben Nevis) of the white stuff on the entire trip. Conversely Gravesend has several times held the UK's record temperature, the last being 33.1°C. A joker at the time called it 'Death Valley by the Thames', but not today.

I quickly find a café for breakfast (I'm starving) and ring Lesley at CLIMB for an update. She mentions that she was born here, her father holding down a job locally.

It turns out to be a very unpleasant six miles in freezing rain. I pass through Denton, which is the fictional location for TV's Touch of Frost. The name is apt, considering today's weather.

I also pass close by to Gads Hill Place, the home of Charles Dickens (another Pompey boy). Strood fire station is a most welcome sight, and Station Manager Liam Hudson and his duty crew look after me. A photographer and reporter from the *Kent Messenger* arrive to prepare a write up for the next edition, so I get a mug-shot with the Red Watch and later buy provisions locally. I am panicking a little, fearing that I have lost photos from my Sony Ericson, and will have to seek out some help in the Medway towns tomorrow.

DAY 329

24th November – Strood Fire Station to Medway Fire Station, Chatham – 4 miles

White Watch feed me after a quiet night, but they get a 'shout' after breakfast.

My call to Lesley confirms that I shall have to tread water for the next couple of days to get my schedule right. She is working very hard to firm up all my accommodation needs for the final three weeks.

It is cold and wet as I set out on the shortest stage – just four miles to the Medway fire station. I cross the Medway Bridge,and remember doing this with a Southern Trails group when we were walking the North Downs Way a few years back. I get into the Chatham shopping precinct and find a phone shop. To my almighty relief the assistant, who I bet hasn't started shaving yet, fixes the fault on the camera in seconds.

Flek has to get a quip in: 'You see, Col, the lad is still developing his brain cells – yours started to diminish years ago. It's just another example of youth having to come to the rescue of the elderly. You were lucky he was kind, friendly, and helpful. Much of the youth of today regard OAPs as troglodytes. Do you remember 'The Troggs'? What a group of 'wild things' they were!'

Well, I suppose I asked for it by dragging him along. Why does he have to so confrontational?

As I pass the Odeon Cinema Flek chirps up again.

'It's a pity we haven't caught a movie on our travels, Col.'

'To tell you the truth, Flek, I have been too knackered on my rest days. We used to call such an outing "going to the flicks" you know.'

'How come? ' he enquires.

'Well the early film cameras were, by today's standards, crude devices, their shutters constantly flickering – hence the nickname "flicks". The cameras would break down regularly.

'There were usually hoots of derision from the packed auditorium, followed by cheers when the overhead projection beams came on again. Everyone looked up to view smoke from a hundred fags billowing through the shaft of light now impinging on to the screen. It's a miracle that our lungs survived. Nobody had heard of health and safety then. (They have now!) That horror gone, we have now got another – the excruciating soundtrack. particularly during the adverts. Are you any the wiser?'

'That's really cool, Col, and endorses what we were told at school.'

'What was that, then?'

'That youth should always listen to the Old Fogies of today because they are passing on history, rather like a tribal elder or Inuit grandmother.'

Is he being too perceptive? I wonder!

I walk on up the hill and book in at the Medway fire station. I get the usual welcome and questions on what the hell I am doing. Sadly, during the last thirty years three fire fighters from this station have lost their lives on operational duties.

In the evening I wander down to a pub a few doors away and get an adequate meal.

25th November – Rest day at Medway fire station

Lesley has programmed this 'break' in my progress in order to get my schedule back in sync. Although officially she has created a Rest day, I have decided to walk down the A2 to the other Rainham in Kent and back again to keep my legs ticking over. When developed into an efficient machine, you have to undergo rigorous maintenance!

'Oh get him,' is Flek's initial reaction, but he softens. 'Well, you got up Ben Nevis on a Rest day, Col – bully for you, mate.'

He is being unusually complimentary as we get near to the close. I expect he is looking for a good reference on his CV.

On this jaunt my sometimes surreal outlook on life surfaces regularly, I suppose it a way of escaping detail.

It's appropriate that what comes into my mind today is one of the most prophetic utterances in recent years, which came in the film The Life of Brian, when John Cleese uttered those immortal words 'So what have the Romans ever done for us?' Well, here I am on one of their legacies, Watling Street, which is possibly the most important 'straight' road they constructed in Britannia. Here we are two millennia later and it's still the shortest distance across Kent between two points. The only legions using it these days are gas guzzlers!

A rather strange tower looms up at Rainham. In a Tesco's car park a huge golf ball stands on top of a giant tee. the whole creation being about forty foot high!

Flek comes up with a summary: 'I suppose it's not that unusual. After all, the well-heeled of old used their wealth to upstage their land-owning neighbours with unusual structures. They were called follies, you know'

'Your knowledge astounds me. I suppose it comes from reading all those Readers Digests *when you're down at doctor's getting yet another 'sickee' note!*

I enter the supermarket, buy a *Telegraph* and read it from end to end over a couple of coffees, then have a light lunch. People who are not savvy to long-distance walking would find it odd that its participants would regard an eight-mile amble as having a day off. But I can't help it: by now my legs are in overdrive. Any loafing cannot be sanctioned.

I return to the the station early enough to hear a dialogue directed at the Duty Crew from a visiting female representing the Fire Service Charity, as it is now known. During my Service I had rendered much time and assistance to this worthy body but, oddly, having been retired for two decades I have forgotten that its benefits are still open to me should I ever wish to take advantage of them.

I ask the lady a question on fund-holding and she informs me that the charity has assets running to several million. A week ago Natasha stated that the Terrance Higgins Trust, for whom she is employed, has a roughly similar budget. It is a sobering thought that CLIMB services its commitments with an income of less than a million a year!

After discussions with Lesley, I have sorted out my last eighteen-day schedule. The Duty Watch offers me a meal and later I relax watching football on TV with them.

DAY 331
26th November – Medway fire station to Sittingbourne – 10 miles

Leaving the station, my route couldn't be easier – straight down the Roman road (A2) to Sittingbourne. Richard Kneller would be pleased to hear that I have lunch in the Long Hop Pub.

Idling way the time in Sittingbourne, waiting for my hosts Huw and Cheryl Yardley (friends of my next host Mark Egan) to return from work, I wander into W.H. Smith on the High Street. I am pleased to find that someone has written an authoritative account of the 'Dambusters raid'. I am even more pleased that the 'someone' is Max Arthur, a schoolboy friend of my brother Alan. Max has become a notable war historian over the years.

Huw and Cheryl return home, and soon I am being made comfortable in another home and have super meal.

Due to the renovation of the house, the first floor lavvy has got an old fashioned fireplace within it. Just think, locked in here one could sit for many an hour with the daily newspaper, flushing out the day's Sudoko and stoking the fire in utter contentment with an inner peace!

A nice couple, and it has been a most pleasant stay.

DAY 332

27h November – Sittingbourne to Faversham – 9 miles

It's time for me to get away from the A2 and its traffic to get some peace. I seek out the Swale Heritage Trail, turning north. It leads me into traditional Kent countryside.

Gradually the two O's become apparent, i.e. orchards and oast houses surrounded by windbreaks of poplars and pollarded trees. I get a coffee at the Ship by the creek at Conyer.

Pressing on for several miles, I enter Faversham and, for logistical reasons, catch the train to Herne Bay. Arriving early, I have to wait a long time for my next host, Mark Eagan.

Mark works at the Houses of Parliament and is late because of a broken down train at Victoria. In the circumstances, when he arrives we settle for a take-away and, wheeling his bike (the local railway station is a long way from his place), he escorts me home for a meal and to meet his kids, son Sean (6) and daughter Louisa (9). They are playful, inquisitive and delightful. Being with them is a pleasure.

DAY 333

28th November – Faversham to Herne Bay – 12 miles

The weather forecast tells me it's not going to much of a day. As it's the weekend, Mark runs me back to Faversham in order to complete the twelve-mile hike back to Herne Bay.

On a Free day I set off out of the town across the Graveney Marshes to reach Whitstable Bay and follow the coast to Seasalter. The rain is persistent and although Sarah (Gamp) is doing her best, I am getting wet.

I escape into the Blue Anchor at Seasalter and linger quite a while setting up a small office in a corner. I order and devour egg, ham and chips, send off a couple of blogs and make some phone calls.

Flek pipes us with some encouraging words: 'You're a busy man these days, Col, getting on top of the paper work. Well done! But it's still raining and you still have six miles to go, so let's pop along shall we, old chap!'

I think to myself: 'I wonder what he's after?'

Goodness me, it's getting very murky, but my spirits are lifted by the pub names that I am passing – The Absent Riflemen, the Rose in Bloom and the Two Brewers to mention just three.

As I pass the Duke of Cumberland in Whitstable I hear some jazz, so enter. A trad band is blazing away in a corner of a large bar. I get a pint and in the interval approach the trumpet player,: he may know my brother, and he does. Alan has being offering up a similar foot-tapping programme, mostly around London, for the last fifty years.

Down the road I pick up the promenade which runs for several miles into Herne Bay.

Mark cooks me up a delicious meal. Young Sean insists on showing me all of his pocket money. He lays is out on kitchen table and it amounts to over fifty quid!

'I have never had that much pocket money in all my life,' I tell him. His eyes open wide with astonishment. For a moment he believes me.

Mark Egan, Louisa and Sean, my last CLIMB family.

Meanwhile his sister Louisa has had her waist-length hair washed and it is now being combed by her father. I am having a privileged view into their family life.

This family bliss belies the fact that the Egan's are a CLIMB family. Mark lost his son Sam at the age of nine months with Leigh's Disease, which is a rare metabolic disorder. Daughter Louisa is a 'carrier' and her future is uncertain. I have nothing but admiration for Mark, who with neighbourly help has been holding down his job down commuting to Parliament every day whilst struggling to keep his family together.

On a personal level, Mark has also arranged four other hosts for me on my way round – a wonderful help. I sleep soundly in a loving home.

29TH November – Herne Bay to Margate – 15 miles

I have to say goodbye to these smashing kids, and Mark kindly takes my rucksack onto Margate fire station. I shall be seeing this gentle man again in the future, I am sure.

It's another dull and wet day. I walk the sea wall to Reculver. This coastline saw the trials of Barnes Wallis 'bouncing bomb' prior to its use in the Dambusters raid in May 1943.

At Birchington I eat up my prepared sandwiches, get a cup of tea and then take the road into Margate.

I book into my last fire station hosting of the trip. I'm asked to chip in with the crew, and we sit down to a huge Indian take-away. One of the crew mentions he was born at Rustington. When I enquired where, his reply just had to be Zachery Merton maternity hospital, and it was. My daughter Sonya was born there in 1965, and so it seems was the half of West Sussex. Yet another coincidence!

The station has a 'shout' at 2am, but I sleep through it!

Flek can't resist a reprimand: 'You mean to say that you wouldn't have caught the appliance? It's a capital offence, isn't it?'

I hold my head in shame.

Strange things do happen when a' shout' comes in during the early hours. I remember once at Lambeth fire station several of the duty crew had to stop a colleague, who was still technically asleep, from getting out of a first floor window after an alert (bells in those days) had gone down. My Red Watch colleagues could not afford to lose him, because apart from his operational duties he had a pivotal role in the annual pantomime that our 'governor' (officer in charge) George Hunt produced every year. The Watch performed for the children of brigade members.

The memory sets me preening.

'I once played Robin Hood, and also Jack (in the Beanstalk). How about that, Flek?'

'Did you have to wear a box in your tights?' he replies.

Trust him to stoop to the unsavoury basics. I'm not going to tell him that the device was unnecessary!

DAY 335

30th November – Margate to Sandwich – 12 miles

I say farewell to my last fire station. This will be a significant day. First I have to get out of Margate, which frankly has seen better days. There is a stiff and bitter easterly wind to face but I console myself that within a few miles the compass will swing ninety degrees to head south again for the last time.

There doesn't seem to be a recognised south-east point of GB. After reaching the fortifications at Hackendown Point I pass the North Foreland Lighthouse, which for my purposes is the spot.

I have now bagged all four corners of the UK – Lands End, Cape Wrath (via the Kyle of Durness), John o Groats (Duncansby Head) and today North Foreland.

Now onward, ever onward, along the Thanet Coastal Path. I take coffee in the Old Curiosity Shop Café at Broadstairs (Dickens influence is everywhere here), and then reach Ramsgate to get a pint in the interesting Belle Vue pub.

North Foreland, Kent – the last GB corner.

A short distance later I come across the replica Viking Ship *Hugin*, which sailed from Denmark in 1949 with an amateur crew. It was a gift to celebrate the landing 1500 years ago of Hengist and Horsa to deliver a daughter for marriage.

On the last mile of today's journey I walk the road that dissects the giant Pfizer pharmaceutical factory at Sandwich. I get a stiff neck viewing the sheer size, height and number of the building units!

My next hosts are Jennifer Kaduruwane and her partner Horia, who pick me up in Sandwich and drive me to their apartment home in Deal, my base for the next two days

Jennifer is the sister of my primary school friend Sonia Whitaker who I stayed with way back in January at Ivybridge. Horia is from Rumania, and later after dinner he portrays what it was like to live under the repressive president Nicolae Ceausescu. It must be one of the oldest questions of civilisation: how is it that a population allows a megalomaniac to take hold of a nation?

DAY 336
1st December – Sandwich to Deal – 10 miles

In fine weather, on an oh so easy Free day, I go out of the town through a rather nice private estate. To get onto the coastline's White Cliffs Country Walk I first take the Stour Valley Walk, passing the Open golf links course venue of Royal St George's. The last Open winner here was Ben Curtis of the USA in 2003.

On the coastal track I follow five miles of shingle bank Sea defences require constant maintenance and here is no exception. A giant 'dozer' is swinging its bucket in a contorted manner, like a stag beetle posing with its out-of-proportion single claw.

Just before Deal I pass another exclusive golf club – The Royal Cinque Ports.

'Exclusive, isn't it. I bet you have to know someone to gain membership? Fleck conjectures, and goes on, 'The subs must be astronomical – and all for knocking a little white ball around the countryside.

'I've seen some of the best players around. like Terry Wogan, Bruce Forsyth and Jimmy Tarbuck on the telly,' he relates proudly, trying to impress me.

'I don't expect you will understand what I am about to say,' I reply, 'but I'll say it all the same. Just stick to what you know, got it? It's painfully obvious that you aren't into sport, particularly golf.'

He displays his usual mischievous demeanour.

I reach Deal seafront by midday. The pier is the third one built and was constructed in 1957, being extensively renovated in 1997. It has a nice café at the end so I add another 600m to my day's walking tally and get myself some refreshment and peace. I am eventually driven out by the screaming kids.

Flek is on a charge: 'I suppose if you have uncontrollable children then the end of the pier is the obvious place to take them for a day out'. He's right this time.

I have another pleasant social evening with my hosts Jennifer and Horia.

DAY 337
2nd December – Deal to Dover – 10 miles

My invaluable friend Ken Marshall has turned up again from Lincolnshire, this time with another of his old buddies, Keith Gawn – my next host. With them are four friends, including Ivor Powell who I stayed with at Barry in March. They have all come over by bus from Dover. I meet them in the town and the elderly little band moves off.

The path is now both the Saxon Shore Way and the White Cliffs (of Dover) Country Trail: the party presses on steadily nattering on like old boys do. At Kingsdown a short diversion brings an extended lunch hour at the Hope pub.

Returning to the cliffs, it isn't long before the port of Dover is laid out before us. Looking down at the continuous stream of traffic (mostly lorries at this time of the year), is absorbing. The port is the busiest ferry crossing in Europe, if not the world: ferry boats queue up to berth.

We move on through the town to Keith's. He prepares an evening meal for us all in an 'interesting' rambling Victorian house. Keith, a widower, turns out to be the only Pompey FC supporter living in Dover. We talk endlessly about the club's modest successes over the seasons.

I retire to bed glad escape his noisy cat, Tom.

3rd December – Dover to Folkestone – 8 miles

Oh, if only I had planned a rest day! Ken, Keith and Ivor are up early and are off to France for a day's walkabout. A chance to give WALK GB 4 CLIMB an international theme has sadly been missed!

From the town I negotiate Dover's western heights. I use the A20 underpass to get up onto the Shakespeare Cliff. Memories come flooding back of the Southern Trails North Downs Way Walk in 2001. It was a summer walk and hot. Not today – a bitter wind prevails.

I spend some time at the Battle of Britain Memorial site at Capel le Ferne. There is much more on display than on my previous visit. The names of five hundred pilots who didn't make it are now scrupulously displayed on an impressive black marble memorial wall. A Spitfire and Hurricane are on display.

I take a steep descent into Folkestone, and half way up the opposite hill I am met by Stephen Allyn and others of Folkestone Rotary Club. After photos they march me to meet their president, Gordon Elliot, who presents me with a cheque for £150. I'm booked into the Quality Hotel, a perfect example of how Rotarians make a difference. I slum it up in a posh hotel, but the weather forecast for tomorrow morning is awful!

I have now entered the shipping weather forecast area Dover.

Rotary supports me again.

4th December – Folkstone to New Romney – 14 miles

I wake up to atrocious weather. The TV has reported heavy snow up north. This weather front upholds my meteorological decision to start the Walk from the south during the winter months. Everybody seems to be getting it today.

I step out of the hotel into a howling wind and driving rain, both head-on.

Flek starts to protest: 'You're not taking me out in this! It's so cold, wet and windy here, we'll take a battering. Are you mad?'

'If I have to rough it, Flek old chap, then so can you,' is my reply, which must sound as bitter as the wind.

With eleven miles to go the weather might yet relent. An Alan Sherman-like verse from his hilarious 1963 classic 'Hello Muddah, Hello Fadduh' sums up the effect of sudden weather change – like so. Readers should sing this, not just read it. Note: if you've forgotten the tune, Sherman sang it to Poncheilli's 'Dance of the Hours':

> *Just a minute it's stopped raining,*
> *And the stair rods they are failing.*
> *What a turn-up, its getting better –*
> *Folks at home, kindly disregard this letter.*

After a few miles the downpour has suddenly ceased. I arrive at the Hythe terminus of the famous narrow gauge railway. What a story here! Built by a Melbourne millionaire in 1928, it's fourteen miles long, runs to schedule (taking children to school) and has over fifty permanent staff.

I begin a long walk out on to the Dungeness peninsula. At New Romney I have been sponsored for a night's accommodation by a CLIMB family at the Broadacre Hotel.

After I book in, CLIMB family parents Andrew and Fran Fryer-Kelsey arrive and over a drink talk about their children. Both Ezre (10) and Amelia (3) have the degenerative metabolic condition Alexander's Disease. At present the future for them is unsure.

After a stormy start I am once again snuggled down into the bed of another hotel. God, I am being spoilt!

As I get out my iPod, Flek stirs

'Got any Rap?' he spouts.

I have been expecting this request for some time. I try to respond in a conciliatory tone.

'Flek, my mostly loyal friend, I might be old-fashioned but I can quote Bob Marley who said, "The one thing about music – when it hits you feel no pain".

'Well, that was his experience, but I wonder if he'd ever listened to Bartok, Philip Glass or Ornette Colman he might have just have winced a little. The great thing about music is that there's something for everyone, although I have to confess that any appealing qualities' Vanilla Ice' might expound have escaped me.'

'Fair enough,' he says disconsolately.

I feel I have let him down and turn in early somewhat uneasy.

DAY 340

5th December – New Romney via Dungeness peninsula to Old Romney – 11 miles

I leave the comfort of the hotel and take the long road out towards the Dungeness headland. I get back onto the coastal road and a chap working outside a property recognises me from a Radio Kent broadcast. He's a local lifeboat man and we have a chat about our very separate interests.

After another three miles I reach the lively Pilot pub. Four of the 'belles' behind the bar, all in Father Christmas hats, bicker about who is going to serve me my lunch donated by the manageress. Well, perhaps my memory is a little befuddled regarding their exact emotions. Let's put it this way: I found myself on the end of some early festive spirit.

The nuclear power station (my eleventh) is beginning to dominate the headland. My idea of skirting around the back of it to pick up a minor road is ditched – too much shingle to negotiate. I tramp on to find another pub, the Britannia, and in it find some of the new-found friends I made an hour earlier in the Pilot One of them is from Hayling Island, not far from my home, and the other from Chiswick, where I lived for a number of years

The brewers Shepherd Neame are advertising their successful prime Kentish ale 'Spitfire' on placards. One hanging over the bar proclaims that this ale is 'Downed all over Kent, just like the Luftwaffe!'

This headland is a unique spot, being one of the largest expanses of shingle in the world. It also has SSSI status. Apart from the power station it has two lighthouses, three pubs, scores of timber cottages, chalets, huts and upturned boats spread out randomly over this vast shingle beach. To cap it all, it's served by the world's smallest permanent narrow gauge public railway, running the fourteen miles from Hythe to Dymchurch and Romney. Also here is Prospect Cottage, home of the late Derek Jarman, the critically acclaimed, but controversial, film director, whose sculptured garden still attracts interest.

I backtrack to the Dungerness road and walk three miles into Lydd, where Steve Aldridge, a local Rotarian, picks me up.

We motor to the Rose and Crown in the small village of Old Romney, which will host me for the night. I eat a large meat pie with trimmings, but have to listen to cocky youths who are all trying to impress. Thankfully they are 'influenced' by an experienced landlord and leave. Left in the bar is a trio of locals – a banker, a channel tunneller and a Laura Ashley delivery driver who, like thousands of such ad hoc 'panels' in bars throughout the land, are trying to sort out the nation's ills.

Memories of nearby Lydd Airport come back to me. In the late Fifties I travelled down here with a large group of uniformed Lambeth fire personnel. We piled into a Silver Cities Airways Douglas Dakota, then flew to Le Touquet. The purpose of this trip was to take on the Paris Sapeurs Pompiers (the city's military fire brigade) at volleyball. They thrashed us, of course – our intelligence unit failed to tell us that they were the champions of France. The Sapeurs made sure that we had a good time 'on the tiles', though. The morning we left they rustled up a thirty-egg omelette washed down with Calvados. It was just what we needed after a boozy night out. I just thought I would bring it up!

DAY 341

6th December – Old Romney to Rye – 9 miles

Seven days to go. John Barber of the local Rotary takes me to Lydd. On a wonderfully sunny early winter's day I make my way along the Gap Road which dissects the marshes and coastal firing ranges.

Three miles out a car stops and a CLIMB family jumps out. They are Bert and Carol Rolfe with their son Lee from Ashford in Kent. Lee wasn't diagnosed with the degenerative metabolic condition Metachomatic Leukodystrophy until his early twenties.

They have got to hear on the Walk GB 4 Climb grapevine that I will be tramping this road today, and by taking it in turns to shunt the car they walk with me to Camber Sands. Their appearance is a wonderful surprise at a time when I need to be reminded of my purpose.

By the very nature of his condition, Lee is a boisterous and noisy young man. The holiday season is well past, but we find that the 'Café Grot' is still open and settle down in a corner for a cuppa and chat. Their story is familiar, although their troubles started earlier when Lee had a nasty motor cycle accident.

The Rolfes have such a cheerful disposition. As on so many occasions during my wanderings, I find that the strength and fortitude shown by these parents is truly humbling – they have often brought a tear to my eye. It is easy for me to talk in glowing terms, but their daily task of 'getting on with it' is daunting.

Saying goodbye to the Rolfes is a wrench, but of course I have to move on. On the outskirts of Camber I am met by another party. It's my next host Noel Varley, who has brought his friends Ian and Elaine Draper and Derek Baynton. Nattering away, we soon gobble up the last few miles into Rye and proceed to Noel's home. In a delightfully comfortable lounge his wife Kathy organises one of our national culinary high points, an English pot of tea and a superb homemade cake. Their son Scott joins us.

Flek makes a salient point: 'It's at times like this, Col, that the strains of 'Jerusalem' should ring out from the outdated Decca radiogramme in the corner. It's obligatory at the Women's Institute.'

It's a patriotic touch, but said more in hope than expectancy.

This evening the town's Christmas lights will be turned on. We all trundle down to join a packed crowd and watch a heavy horse pull 'the man of the moment' up the High Street. Some dignitary utters an unintelligible speech into the tannoy, pulls the switch and the town lights up. Watching the kids' faces reflecting both the palette of the colours and their excitement is a delight. Rockets lift off and boom out.

These annual celebrations are perhaps routine, but when witnessed in an ancient town setting such as Rye, an early Cinque Port, the occasion is magical.

We retire to Rye's famous Mermaid Inn to quaff ale, later returning to the Varleys' abode for a superb evening meal.

Any more days like this and I am not coming home! I have been asked on numerous occasions what was my favourite place during my travels. I know that it's almost home ground, but if fate decreed where I should finally discard my rucksack for the last time then it might be here.

Tilling

The middle-Eighties TV series Mapp and Lucia was based on a series of books written by E.F. Benson, who lived in Rye. They depict the upper-middle class of Tilling (based on Rye), who indulge in gross snobbery, their life awash with gossip, gentle intrigue and humorous incidents.

Benson lived at Lamb House in the town, and (as Mallards) it was the home of his Miss Mapp in the stories. Its garden room was later damaged by enemy bombing during the Second World War.

The TV series starred Prunella Scales, Geraldine McEwan and Dennis Lill. The part of Georgie was played brilliantly by Nigel Hawthorne.

Five of us stride out into a hard frost. It's a glorious morning as I accompany the appropriately named Noel, wife Kathy, son Scott and Derek Baynton along the Royal Military Canal path past Camber Castle, whose ramparts are catching the early rays of the sun

At Winchelsea Beach village I say a fond farewell to the Varley family. What hosts – I shall never forget them. Derek elects to walk with me on to Hastings. There are still beach cafés open, and we find one. Here elevenses consist of a huge mince pie with a pyramid of vanilla ice cream.

Flek is scathing.

'This is outrageous and gluttonous!' he protests.

Ignoring him, we tuck in like kids.

He rants on: 'Your resistance is weak, mate. I've noted for some time that your discipline has steadily declined on matters of ingestion. Telling people that you're only burning off the calories will no longer wash.,'

He really is on principled crusade.

'Back in the real world,' he warns, 'you'll have a hell of a job weaning yourself off these practices.'

'I perfectly agree with you, my friend,' I reply with overt arrogance, 'but do you know what? I don't care a jot, because after 338 days on the hoof I deserve it.'

This should sweep his views under the carpet, I hope.

At the end of the two-mile sea wall we meet the Pett IRB crew clearing up after an exercise. The female members look very fetching in their Mae Wests. From here we take the Fairlight Road, which presents three consecutive steep hills.

'I thought that I'd finished with all this huffing and puffing,' I say.

Derek nods and manages a sympathetic smile.

Finally we tumble down the urban two miles to reach Hastings Old Town seafront. Derek treats me to a fish and chip lunch. An interesting character, he ran a well known restaurant in Rye for many years until family problems forced him to quit. We have some great banter along the way and I appreciate his company very much.

At the end of the prom we say goodbye and, facing a setting sun, I traipse along the coast five miles into Bexhill. It's dark on my arrival and I wait outside the De la Warr Pavilion, often described as a 'modernist icon for the contemporary arts', for my next host, Peter Day. He and his wife Jan occupy a splendid apartment along the seafront. They are the sixth and final hosts contact made by my good Old Cicestrian friend Doug Murgatroyd. What a pal he has been!

DAY 343

8th December – Bexhill to Eastbourne – 13 miles

I have received wonderful hospitality from Peter and Jan, a most congenial couple. We talked a lot, Peter recalling his long association with Doug. They expressed a great interest in what I was doing, and I leave their company a contented man.

I drop into the Star Inn at Normans Bay. It's quiet and I'm able to talk to the landlord, David, who is an Italian. His wife Hannah has just presented him with a daughter, Tilly.

Previously called the Star of Bethlehem, the pub is steeped in local history. Not far from here, at Sidley Green, the last great battle in Sussex between smugglers and excisemen took place in 1828. It was a brutal affair with several fatalities. Many of the smugglers were sentenced to hanging, later commuted to transportation. Despite this smuggling continued to be regarded in a romantic light. It was said that smugglers were, ' brave souls who went about their work under great adversity'.

Continuing around Pevensey Bay I can see a string of Martello Towers. Unfortunately they hadn't been constructed in 1066 when we needed them!

It's lunchtime, and I enter the Bay Hotel. I order a drink and stand at the bar, my thoughts engrossed by my forthcoming reception on returning home.

Flek interrupts: 'Your comedy hero Kenneth Williams might have described your long awaited appearance thus – "Sitting in the back of an open Lincoln gliding through a storm of ticker tape, or, being held shoulder high with laurels, or, even on horseback ahead of a returning Roman Legion – no, you can stop laughing at me Duckie; now stop mucking about! When you're a star you have to think of these eventualities.'

So deep in thought am I that I pick up another bloke's beer by mistake. He accepts the error graciously, but had this been a Hollywood John Wayne western I would have gone out straight out through the window!

My next hosts, Grant and Kara Eager, have walked out from Eastbourne Pier to meet me with young son Miller. Their hospitality comes via Grant's relative Karol Eager of Shoreham on Sea – one my Southern Trails walkers. He drives us to the fire station and we meet the on-duty crew. Following a station 'cuppa' we return to their home to face the clutter of Miller's toys.

Grant has involved himself in the administration of volleyball, and knows the personalities of the game I remember from my involvement in the early days.

I have sent my Blog which concludes, 'I Hope you are all now on the countdown 4 . . . 3 . . . 2. . . . 1 . . .

DAY 344
9th December – Eastbourne to Bishopstone – 13 miles

Grant runs me to Eastbourne Pier. Many south coast resorts are sun-traps, and Eastbourne is no exception. The one-mile walk along the prom allows my limbs to warm up before I tackle the steep ascent up and over Beachy Head.

At the top the Beachy Head Hotel café is closed! I press on into a cold north-westerly. Ahead lies the panoramic vista to Belle Tout and beyond.

The first few miles are, thankfully, a gradual descent, first bringing me to the Belle Toute Lightouse This famous landmark gathered national prominence when it was jacked-up and run inland on rails to remove it from the eroding cliff edge. Partly financed by the infamous Sussex MP John 'Mad Jack' Fuller in 1828, it has had a chequered history and is at present a B & B. The BBC's adaptation of Fay Weldon's Loves and Lives of a She Devil was filmed here.

Shortly I am at the Birling Gap café. I get a snack-type lunch. There are few people about.

I now have to tackle Went Hill Brow, Baily's Hill, Flagstaff Point, Brass Point, Rough Brow, Short Brow and Haven Brow, which are collectively the Seven Sisters. Having walked them many times, I think there may be eight or even nine siblings!

Needless to say, the afternoon undulations take their toll and I am mighty relieved to be descending towards the unique Cuckmere River with its oxbow bends. What a gem of a walk, but I don't suppose I have seen more than a dozen walkers all day.

Tired, I ignore the Vanguard Way, following the coast. Crossing the Exceat bridge I follow the A259 and await at the prescribed location for my next host, Jean Parks, to pick me up. I am very glad, as she lives at the top of a long hill at Bishopstone.

I have known Les and Jean Parks for fifty years. On joining Lambeth (headquarters) fire station in 1958, Les was a fellow crew member on Red Watch, and a member of the volleyball party to Paris previously described. I must also add that he did stirring work painting the stage scenery for our Lambeth pantomimes.

When my eldest daughter Suzanne came along the Parks agreed to be her honorary godparents. Her christening took place at Christ Church on Turnham Green at Chiswick.

We spend time catching up on decades of news. It's an absolute delight to see them again, and it's lucky that they live on my route home.

DAY 345
10 December – Bishopstone to Brighton – 13 miles

It's goodbye to Les. Jean runs me back down to the A259. I hurry into Newhaven as I have a rendezvous. At the swing bridge I spot three old boys who turn out to be walking mates – Doug Cheal (he secured my accommodation in the 'nick', St Andrews), David Martin and Pete Edwards. Looking at them I feel like the 'receiver of wrecks'!

After greetings (no hugging – we leave that to the French) we set off up the hill and are soon on the coast path to Peacehaven. We stop to admire the Greenwich Meridian Line memorial monument. I passed its other GB entry point near Withensea in October.

I'm pursued by a reporter/photographer from the Brighton *Argus*. Following an interview and photo shot we seek out some half-way refreshment. As we amble on, the banter proliferates, with disguised insults reminiscent of Hilaire Belloc's *The Four Men*.

Witherspoons at Brighton Marina delivers a well earned lunch. Later, approaching the Palace Pier at Brighton, we're just in time to witness the evening spectacle when scores of thousands of starlings gather to carry out their roosting ritual. Splitting into huge groups, they perform dazzling formation displays and then most of them drop like stones onto the pier. Roosting starlings are one of the great sights of the natural world, but many strollers on the prom seemed oblivious of what is going on in the air above them.

The rest of the birds prefer Brighton's most infamous location a mile away – the pile of steel girders out to sea which was once the West Pier. The pier featured prominently in Richard Attenborough's 1963 film Oh! What A Lovely War. Isolated steelwork is now all that remains after a major fire and the ravages of the sea.

The Last of the Summer Wine, Brighton.

I say a fond farewell to the motley crew who have escorted me to a city with a disparate cultural history, – 'London by the Sea with a touch of Regency elegance.' My companions, former Ovaltinies, tail off to be reunited with their slippers and pills.

Flek sums them up: ' Just think, Col, you've had to walk all this way to find your right audience. Admit it, although a tad cantankerous, they were great company.'

He is dead right.

My next host, an old Southern Trails walker David Hunt, now picks me up. In the evening I am entertained to a meal at a local pub, getting a chance to explain the work of CLIMB to a group of his friends

DAY 346

THE PENULTIMATE DAY

11th December – Brighton to Littlehampton – 15 miles

David gets me back to Palace Pier. Interest is beginning to gather. Parked up is an East Sussex fire appliance. The crew jump out, and the OIC presents me with a donation and good wishes. They drive off.

My old Southern Trails friend Brian Higgins turns up to accompany me, along with a lovely lady, Sue Fawcett – the grandmother of a CLIMB family. Her granddaughter Yasmeen, aged 13 years, suffers from what must be one of the most distressing metabolic conditions of all, Progeria. It's characterised by the appearance of premature ageing and is extremely rare: the chances of it occurring have been put at 1 per 8 million births, and an early termination of life can be expected. I am awestruck by her story.

It's a sunny Brighton as we move off. Later, at Hove, other friends Clive and Marion Botting and David Brand join us. Responding to numerous questions I spend time trying to condense my Walk GB 4 CLIMB experience into a digestible summary, something I am going to have to do many times in the future.

Leaving the promenade, we plod on along the A259 coast road. Sally Jordan and Karol Eager are among others who join the welcoming party.

We all pause outside the Marlipins pub in Shoreham High Street. I am met by Tina Biss, whose daughter Kirsty has the degenerative metabolic condition Cystinosis. She is joined by her mother-in-law Ann Woods, and I am given a cheque for £250. My next host, Brian Coote, arrives to take my rucksack back to his place at Worthing.

Our party moves on via Shoreham Beach. Walking toward us are some more Southern Trails stalwarts, Frank and Daphne Butler with Mary Sims. It's all too much for Daphne, and I have to administer a big cuddle – aaah!

At Worthing Pier a small crowd has gathered, and we all sit down in its café for afternoon tea.

Moving off, everybody gradually splits away leaving me to forge on alone. The best way for me to get to Littlehampton is to walk along the beach. The tide is out, so I go for it. By now darkness has fallen and I pick my way round the groynes with just enough street light from the shore. It's amazing how much activity there is in the gloom. Men are digging bait, and courting couples are out for a 'walk'.

What puzzles me are two multi-coloured lights dancing around the beach. I get up close and all is revealed. A woman has bought her dogs some battery-operated lighting collars for Christmas, a heart-warming yuletide story for animal lovers.

I reach the promenade at Littlehampton and walk up the shingle. Brian Coote is waiting patiently to whisk me back to Worthing for the night. His wife, the caring Beryl, is so pleased to see me.

Later I receive a splendid letter from Councillor Garry Peltzer Dunn, the mayor of Brighton, accompanied by a set of cufflinks emblazoned with the city insignia.

Dressed Christmas lobster at Shoreham.

THE LAST STAGE

12 December – Littlehampton to Bognor Regis – 8 miles

Brian drops me back in Littlehampton. I cross the bridge over the River Arun and follow a long muddy path to Clymping car park. I am met by my son Stewart, his partner Christine with daughters Lauren and Amy, and my grandson Jack. We have a chat while the kids play and climb on the concrete sea defences.

There's a cold wind blowing hard, and it's overcast, but fortunately the rain holds off. We stumble along the coastal stony paths with the sea roaring in. The kids love the freedom of running and climbing. I almost come unstuck on an icy puddle – a fractured hip a few miles out, how unfortunate would that have been?

At Middleton we turn down a twitten (Sussex dialect word for alley) to meet up with my brother Alan and sister-in-law Ann, and then return to the promenade. One of my fire service colleagues, Peter Clamp, arrives from nowhere with best wishes and suddenly my other grandchildren, Lewis and Lauren, are running towards me, followed by my daughters Suzanne and Sonya with son-in-law Rob and my other son, Martin.

The family walk me in on the last day. [Mike Parry]

The proprietor of the nearby Beachcroft Hotel has kindly offered me a shower facility and refreshments for my family. I get a call from Steve Hannigan, executive director of CLIMB at Crewe, expressing their congratulations.

Making sure I am all 'shipshape and Bristol fashion', I take the kids by the hand and we string out across a line to parade the last 800 yards, followed by the adults carrying banners made by Stewart, to the bandstand I left all of 347 days ago.

A crowd of family and well-wishers has gathered as I break the tape to the sound of my brother's jazz ensemble. I find myself happily enduring seemingly endless hand-shaking and back-slapping. The mayor of Arun District Council, Councillor Ashvin Patel, adds his congratulations, while Chris Owen-Roberts represents the CLIMB Office at Crewe.

I'm pulled to one side to give interviews to Sean Killick of BBC South TV and another reporter from Southern TV. To my astonishment Jonathan Pearce, the exuberant BBC 'Match of the Day' football commentator, introduces himself. Unsolicited, he has travelled down to meet me. He tells me of his involvement in fund-raising following the death of a neice with a metabolic condition, and as a result he has come along to add his best wishes. It's a nice gesture.

Everyone wanders off along the prom to the Royal Norfolk Hotel for the proper reception which Lesley Greene (Mum 2) from the CLIMB office has been busily organising.

Jonathan Pearce adds his congratulations. [Stewart Snook]

A Touching Reception

'Be resolved and the thing is done.'
— Chinese proverb

Because of media Interviews I am the last to arrive at the official reception. The Royal Norfolk Hotel's lounge is teeming with recognisable faces. I have tried to tidy myself up for the event, but subsequent photographs clearly show that I failed.

After the 'feast' the meeting is called to order by Lesley Greene. Paul Roper, a trustee of CLIMB and the father of a deceased metabolic son, speaks in emotional terms about the work and tasks of CLIMB. On behalf of the charity, he thanks me for my efforts. Mayor Ashvin Patel thanks me likewise on behalf of the local community. I am presented with a super trophy and various documents, including a framed map and a typed-up complete 347 days' schedule, which will come in handy later. I am passed a letter from Boris Johnson the mayor of London – fancy that!

In reply I thank my family for standing by me and working tirelessly on my behalf while I was away. Their efforts were outstanding. Next my gratitude is extended to the countless individuals – and in particular the host families – who smoothed my path in so many thoughtful ways during my long trek.

The Youth Hostel Association were so helpful, too, and as an ex-fire officer I acknowledge the assistance of the Lancashire, Cumbria, Highland & Islands, Tyne and Wear, Lincolnshire Humberside, Norfolk, Suffolk and Kent fire and rescue services. Many commercial premises waived their fees. Stay-overs provided at Lee Abbey, RAF Kinloss and the police station at St Andrews also warrant a mention.

Finally I thank the Royal Air Force, who scrambled a helicopter out from Lossiemouth to check on my welfare, which was awfully nice of them!

I am able to hand over a 'giant' cheque for £22,297.94 to Paul Roper representing CLIMB. This splendid sum was raised by scores of supporters, either direct to the charity's HQ or via the 'Just Giving' website. This sum will shortly rise significantly to over £30,000 due to continuous fiscal support.

I am delighted to acknowledge the input of certain individuals whose loyalty to me was outstanding, three of whom are present here today. I request that they come forward.

First I feel I must heap thanks onto my old friend David Garforth of Rotary GB, Bognor Regis branch, whose untiring efforts produced so many host families. Never was Rotary's motto 'Service above Self' so evident.

Next up for my praise is Doug Murgatroyd of the Old Cicestrians (Chichester High School Old Boys), who alerted so many of his relations and ex-military service colleagues to give me a bed for the night.

536

The third stalwart is Ken Marshall, a former Chichester Jazz Club member, whose career in the immigration service means that he has many former colleagues who still live in coastal ports – ideal locations for hosting me.

I also mention Ray Pratt, exChichester Jazz Club (who found me hosts and involved Fred Dineage of Southern Television) and Mark Egan from Herne Bay,

With Lesley Greene (Mum 2) at the reception.

father of a deceased metabolic son, who rallied so many of his friends for me.

Finally I have very special words for the CLIMB back-up Team led by Lesley Greene (who became my Mum No. 2). These include Pam Davies (who waved me off from Bognor a year before on behalf of CLIMB), Chris Owen-Roberts and Steve Hannigan, chief executive of the charity, and his office staff back in Crewe.

The noisy reception continues, but finally it is time to leave. Alone, I walk the two miles to my dear friends John and Hilda Alderton with whom I shall stay for the night.

'Walk GB 4 CLIMB' may have been completed, but my ambitions are not satisfied just yet.

Later that evening I invite the Aldertons and friends Lynn and John Mercy from Kent to dine with me and Jane Taylor in the Spur at Slindon.

Presenting the cheque to Paul Roper of CLIMB.

Drawing to a Close
13th December – in Chichester

My dear friends John and Hilda Alderton look after me again as they have always done. I feel a need to walk into Chichester, a town which has played so much a part in my life. Unfortunately my plans for a second triumphal finish are scuppered by some atrocious weather.

John runs me to Chichester, and I meet my family at Eastgate Square. I'm still humping my rucksack, and we all walk up East Street in the rain to the Market Cross, the epicentre of this ancient town Huddled under its protection is a small party of friends, including Harry Fletcher who has come up from Portsmouth. The mayor, Councillor David Siggs, is here, too.

At the mayor's invitation we retire to his parlour in the Assembly Rooms for refreshments and a chat. This is an honour, and although my grandchildren will not, of course, realise the significance of the occasion, they revel in the plush surroundings of this intimate room and enjoy its cold drinks

Later I take the family to a well known restaurant in South Street, but sadly I am once again let down by poor service. It's an embarrassing episode for me, and a brings an unfortunate ending to what should be a joyous occasion. This is just the sort of unprofessionalism that I have beefed about throughout my journey.

I have been invited by Hugh and Daphne Ashton to the locally famous 'street party' in Tregarth Road, Chichester, where they have their home. The Ashtons have been part of my life for many years: Hugh is chairman of the Chichester Jazz Club, of which I'm a founder member. Readers will remember that he made the long journey to South Wales to walk with me at St David's.

This event is a twice-a-year 'indoor' happening at which all the neighbours of this small cul-de-sac get together in different homes on rotation. I enjoy it very much, and Hugh and Daphne invited me to stay over.

Goodbye, Friend!

Suddenly a dark cloud descends: it was going to happen. Flek has gone. Where there was camaraderie, now there is silence. My critical friend, mentor, counsellor and chum in adversity has slipped away. It's devastating.

I am reminded of the last poignant farewell in Hilaire Belloc's *The Four Men,* when the character 'Myself' releases his three adversaries 'Gizzlebeard,' 'The Sailor' and 'The Poet' from his companionship: 'Then they all three turned about and went rapidly and with purpose up the village street. I watched them, straining my sad eyes, but in a moment the mist received them and they had disappeared'

Au revoir my good friend!

The Final Push

'Up, lad: when the Journey's over
There'll be time enough to sleep'
A.E. Houseman: *The Shropshire Lad*

14th December – Chichester to Westergate and Home – 5 miles

I have my very last breakfast away, persuade Hugh and Daphne to pose for a photo shot and then move off for the very last time.

I get on the A27 and am astonished that in my absence the highways department have erected a massive over engineered footbridge over this trunk road at Tangmere. I can't help thinking, *Have they done this for me?*

From here I can pick up a footpath to the slip road to Westergate, my home village. I first pass my house and go the couple of hundred yards on to the Aldingbourne Sports Club. Despite a circular distributed of my impending arrival there is little response from local residents. The disappointment is offset by seeing my next door neighbour Sue Black and her daughter Julia, a few local well-wishers with a total of £50 in donations, and the chairman of the parish council.

The real surprise is seeing Norman Baker (now sadly deceased), a coach driver for Westrings Coaches. He regularly drove Southern Trailers on their trips. I remember him saying to me before I left that he would donate collections from his passengers to CLIMB while I was away. True to his word, he hands me an envelope containing £730. I am overwhelmed that a significant donation like this comes in on the very last stride of my 4,000-mile hike. Norman by nature helped people: he was a wonderful man.

Norman Baker's 'last stride donation'.

With my son Stewart I walk back the short distance to my house and get into the six-foot bath. I have been dreaming about this moment for a year! He opens a bottle of wine and we chat on while I have a well earned soak.

THAT'S IT, FOLKS!

Do you remember Spike Milligan side-stepping off the stage and asking his audience: 'What do I do now? What do I do now? What do I do now?'

That's exactly what I ask myself: What on earth am I going to do with myself now – apart, that is, from promoting this book.

One thing is for sure: I shall cherish these memories of 2008 for the rest of my life.

APPENDICES

UNFORGETTABLE PLACES

It is inevitable that on my return I should be asked what I thought were 'the unforgettable places' encountered during my long journey. I have little hesitation in selecting the following which have left such an indelible mark on my memory.

Early morning cross of the River Dart on the lower ferry at Kingswear

This spot is a tourist's dream. For a start, nearby stands a terminus of the Dartmouth Steam Railway which runs to Paignton. A short walk brings me down under an arch to the slip jetty, where I board the ferry. On a lovely sunny morning, but in the shadow of the buildings pressing down to the quay, I accompany scores of children in pristine uniforms going to school on the Dartmouth side.

The journey takes only a few minutes to Dartmouth's riverside embankment, but there's time to admire the course of the river up to the Royal Naval College and the rows of houses which rise steeply opposite, above the town. The view of these can best be described as representing the ascending shelves of miniatures often seen in a china shop window display. The whole scene at this time in the morning is magical.

This is the route of the South West Coastal Path. Coming ashore I walk on to Blackstone Point then further to Stoke Flemming and Blackpool sands.

The route from Mawnan Smith down the Helford Passage

Having left Melanie Williams' splendid B & B in the village of Mawnan Smith I stroll down a long gentle slope for a couple of miles through a hushed wooded area to emerge on the Helford River bank.

The sun is rising and the mist along the River is just beginning to burn off. I cross the small beach at the foot of Trebah, one of the finest gardens in Cornwall. The walk goes on to the ferry at the Helford Passage. The ferry isn't running, but the Jig Rowing Club ferries me across as part of their training routine – an unforgettable start to a long day's coastal hike.

The mountains of Sutherland – Assynt – Wester Ross in Scotland

These are quite spectacular remote mountains. They often stand on their own, as if they have been sculpted and set down at random. The isolated sandstone peaks of Foinhaven, Arkle, Stac Pollaidh and – perhaps the most well know of them all – Suilven are good examples. A tourist postcard shows the latter during the winter looking spectacular under a dusting of snow.

Confined to the main roads I only have a fleeting glance of these peaks. I'm not here to conquer any of them, but observing Sutherland's mountains I have blissful memories of their summits turning pink in the setting sun on summer evenings. As a mountain range they are something else.

The Spey Viaduct

On Day 233, following a splendid breakfast in Garston Hotel, I find myself on the Spey railway viaduct. Completed in 1885 to carry the Great North Line between Portsoy and Elgin, it has a central Bow Spring structure of 380ft and approach spans of 3 x 107ft on each side. When closed in 1968 by Beeching, it was deemed to be too costly to salvage and was saved to become part of the Speyside Way Path.

The River Spey spates very quickly due to its wide catchment area in the mountains. With a twisting course, it is the fastest in Scotland and a prime salmon river.

I arrive the day after an inch of rain has fallen. What makes it special for me is that on a warm afternoon I am alone looking down at a river which couldn't get to Spey Bay downstream in the Moray Firth fast enough. The backdrop for this dramatic scene is provided by small islands of rocks and stones covered with wild flowers, mostly the pink perennial Rosebay willowherb (Fireweed). The river's hydraulic release into Spey Bay is a half a mile away, but there is still a chance for several anglers present to make a catch.

The only noise comes from the rushing water itself. I find the experience both calming and exhilarating.

SOUTHERN TRAILS

Fortunately there always seems to be a quotation handy to make a case, so – not to disappoint – here goes: 'Today's preparation determines tomorrow's achievement' (*Anon.*)

Of course I wasn't to know that the following programme would turn out to be preparation for WALK GB 4 CLIMB – 2008. In fact these itineraries testify that I had been in training for years. .

In my early forties I started leisure walking for real. Good friends of mine, John and Daphne Beard, introduced me to the South Downs Way Walk organised every June by the West Sussex Council and stewarded by the local and well known walker and journalist Paddy Welsh.

Having tramped the South Downs for many years, I decided to organise my own walking outfit, and in 1995 I put together 'Southern Trails', which until 2007 programmed more than fifty major walks and many minor ones. The walks, usually attracting fifty participants, took place in the south-east of England and not only covered established routes but some others I mapped out to offer diversity.

They were, as one punter put it, 'Delightful strolls, of dubious mileage and had a loose organisation that usually came off!'

I would like to pay tribute to my dear friend, the late Bill Bloy. He and I carried out full reconnoitres of these walks, spending countless days covering several thousand miles during a twelve-year period – on one occasion clocking up a 28-mile day. We chatted about this and that, becoming regular pub imbibers, and had the occasional row. Utter bliss!

Our annual programmes included:

1995	WEST SUSSEX BORDER PATH	Emsworth to Southwick (10 days)
1996	SUSSEX BORDER PATH	Emsworth to Rye (11)
1997	MID-SUSSEX LINK	East Grinstead/Southwick (3)
	SUSSEX BORDER PATH	Rye to Emsworth 11
	ACROSS THE WEALD	(Hilaire Belloc walk) Robertsbridge/ South Harting (9)
1998	HIDDEN SUSSEX	Lodsworth to Lancing (3)
	NORTH DOWNS WAY	Farnham/Dover, via Canterbury (11)
	ACROSS THE WEALD	Robertsbridge/South Harting (9)
	AUTUMN TINTS	Surrey Hills/Leith Hill Tower (2)

1999	THE NEW FOREST	Lyndhurst/Brockenhurst/Burley (3)
	NORTH DOWNS WAY	Dover/Farnham via Folkstone (11)
	SUSSEX DIAMOND WAY	Midhurst to Heathfield (6)
	THE SOLENT WAY	Christchurch to Emsworth (7)
	ASHDOWN FOREST	(2 days)
2000	ISLE OF WIGHT COAST PATH (7 days)	
	MERIDIAN LINE MEANDER	East Grinstead/Peacehaven (3)
	THREE SUSSEX WINDMILLS	EastWittering/Halnaker/ Barnham (?)
	AUTUMN TINTS	Surrey Hills/Leith Hill Tower (2)
2001	THE SOLENT WAY	Christchurch to Emsworth (7)
	NORTH DOWNS WAY	Dover/Farnham via Folkstone (11)
	FIVE SUSSEX WINDMILLS	Nutley/Chailey/Keymer/ Jack & Jill (3)
	AUTUMN TINTS	Blackdown/Hindhead/ (Devils Punchbowl) (2)
2002	THE THAMES PATH	Kemble to Pangbourne (8)
	SUSSEX BORDER PATH	Rye to Exceat (4)
	ACROSS THE WEALD	Robertsbridge to South Harting (9) (Hilaire Belloc centenary walk)
	AUTUMN TINTS	Blackdown/Hindhead (2)
2003	THE THAMES PATH	Pangbourne to Thames Barrier (9)
	PILGRIMS TRAIL	Winchester to Portsmouth (3)
	WALK FOR DIANA	London's Royal Parks (1)
	PORTLAND ISLAND	Tolpuddle/Corfe/Lulworth (3)
	AUTUMN TINTS	HangersWay/Selbourne/QE Country Park (3)
2004	I.O.W. 'VECTIS	(8 days)
	WALK FOR DIANA	London's Royal Parks (1)
	ST SWITHUNS WAY	Farnham to Winchester (3)
	MALVERN HILLS	SymondsYat/Monmouth 3
	AUTUMN TINTS	HangersWay/Selbourne/QE (2)
2005	THE GREENSANDS WAY	Haslemere to Limpsfield Chart (5)
	THE MENS	Petworth (1)
	STANDSTED FOREST	Rowlands Castle (1)
	COTSWOLD WAY	Chipping Campden to Painswick (6)
2006	COTSWOLD WAY	Painswick to Bath (6)

	EDEN VALLEY WALK	Hever Castle (2)
	THE GREENSANDS WAY	Limpsfield Chart to Ham (5)
2007	SOUTH DOWNS WAY	Winchester to Washington (4) (Alternative Route)
	SOUTH DOWNS WAY	Washington to Eastbourne (5) (Alternative Route)
	SUSSEX OUSE VALLEY	Lower Beeding to Newick (3)
	SUSSEX OUSE VALLEY	Newick to Seaford Bay (3)

Over the years there were also one-day Spring get-togethers at Goodwood, Small Dole, Petworth Park, Midhurst, Stanmer Park, Highdown, Slindon, Chichester Canal and Whiteways Lodge, Houghton.

PRESENTED TO THEIR WORSHIPS THE MAYOR

LYME REGIS	Councillor Sally Holman with Jane Whittington
PENZANCE	Councillor Richard Clark
ST JUST	Councillor Monty Nichols
ST JUST (2007)	Councillor Sylvia Smith
ST IVES	Councillor Bill Fry
FORT WILLIAM	Provost Allan Henderson
EDINBURGH	Provost George Grub
NEWCASTLE	Councillor David Wood
BURNHAM ON SEA	Deputy Mayor
LONDON	Boris Johnson *
BRIGHTON	Councillor Gary Peltzer *
BOGNOR REGIS	Councillor Ashvin Patel
CHICHESTER	Councillor David Siggs

* Correspondence only

HOST ACCOMMODATION

This information is included not only for any interest it might attract but as a possible guide to anyone who is seriously thinking of a long expedition requiring accommodation.

Clearly evident is the role that host families played in supporting me up to the hilt with a bed, meals, washing my clothes, transport and, in some cases, logistical support. I was often received like a long-lost son in the evening and turned out next morning – as Captain Mainwaring might have put it – 'fighting fit and operationally sound'.

I must heap praise on the tireless efforts of the CLIMB support staff, led by Lesley Greene, who did their best to ensure that I was tucked up in a warm bed as often as possible.

The Roll of Honour reads thus:

CLIMB Registered Families   33 Nights
CLIMB Families Relations and Friends   16
Friends (Mine)   15
Friends of Friends   12
Relations (Mine)   16
Rotary International   31
Youth Hostel Association (most donated)   12
Other hostels, Private, Bunkhouses, Bothies   14
Camping & Caravan Sites   44
Rough Camping   5
B & B   29
B & B/Hotels (donated)   12
Fire Stations   27
Fire Brigade friends   5
Old Cicestrians (Chichester High School Old Boys)   19
Chichester Jazz Clubs Members   30
South West Coastal Path Members   5
Southern Trails members, friends and relations   15
Mayors   3
Lee Abbey, RAF Kinloss, St Andrews Police Station   4

TOTAL 347

BRIDGES
Notable bridges crossed during WALK GB 4 CLIMB 2008

ITCHIN
LYMINGTON (former Toll Bridge)
WHITE BRIDGE (Budleigh Salterton)
SHALDON - (Teignmouth)
LOOE
SEVERN (M48)
CLEDDAU (Pembroke)
BARMOUTH (Toll Bridge)
PORTHMADOG (Ffestiniog Rail Bridge)
MENAI
QUEENS FERRY (Shotton)
GLENNFINNAN VIADUCT (Rail Bridge) *
KYLESKU (Highlands)
DORNOCH FIRTH BRIDGE
KESSOCK (Inverness)
TAY
SPEY
FORTH
GATESHEAD (Inverter)
WEARMOUTH (Sunderland)
MIDDLESBOROUGH (Transporter)
HUMBER
ORWELL
TOWER (London)

* I camped at the foot of this viaduct and have included it because of its recent connection with several Harry Potter films.

RIVERS
Notable rivers crossed

HAMBLE
BEAULIEU
DART
FOWEY
HELFORD
CAMEL
SEVERN
TAFF
MERSEY (by rail link tunnel)
SPEY
TAY
TEES
TYNE
HUMBER
ORWELL
THAMES
MEDWAY
OUSE
ADUR
ARUN

FERRIES
Ferry transportation necessary during Walk GB 4 CLIMB 2008

ITCHENOR	Chichester Harbour
GOSPORT	Portsmouth Harbour
HAMBLE	Hamble River
HYTHE	Southampton Water
SANDBANKS	Poole Harbour
SOUTH SANDS	Salcombe
DARTMOUTH	River Dart
GIG ROWER CLUB	River Helford
FOWEY	River Fowey
ST MAWS	Falmouth Harbour

CREMYLL	Plymouth
ROCK	Camel Estuary
FORT WILLIAM	Loch Linnhe
DURNESS	Kyle of Durness
NIGG	Cromarty Firth

I missed out on:

TOPSHAM	Exe Estuary – Closed winter months but ferryman obliged.
HELFORD	Closed winter months. Gig Club crew rowed me across.
MERSEY	Liverpool (suspended for technical problems).
FELIXSTOWE	Closed in winter months.
WOOLWICH	There is a pedestrian tunnel under the Thames.

NUCLEAR POWER STATIONS

Almost without exception nuclear power stations have been built on coastlines because of technical and logistical requirements. I have included them in my statistics as they presented formidable landmarks on my journey around GB.

HINCKLEY POINT – Somerset
WYLFA – Anglesey
HEYSHAM – Lancashire
SELLAFIELD (Reprocessing) – Cumberland
WINDSCALE (Decommissioned) – Cumberland
DOUNREAY (Decommissioned) – Caithness
TORNESS – East Lothian
HARTLEPOOL – County Durham
SIZEWELL – Suffolk
BRADWELL (Decommissioned) – Essex
DUNGENESS – Kent

REGIONAL DELICACIES

Through sheer hunger I was often forced to sample regional culinary delights. I would particularly like to mention a couple of delightful Scottish experiences.

It's a tale of two opposites, the first being the famous Scottish host's coy enquiry of visitors: 'You'd have had yur tea then?'

An alternative outcome is actually sitting down to a Scottish high tea – a gastronomic endurance test. It can start with a continuous tea and toast with butter, plus mixed sandwiches followed by a main course of steak pie, fish or bacon and eggs; there follows a mixture of scones, crumpets and fancy cakes. The teapot has to be heavy, unwieldy and continually topped up. You will definitely need a sufficient supply of napkins. A Scottish host made me sit one out, a Billy Bunter dream!

Devon cream teas (Not too many)
Cornish pasties (Hard going)
Welsh tea cakes (Like little rubber flanges)
Cawl (Welsh soup – OK without lamb)
Laverbread (Richard Burton described it as 'Welsh caviar'.
        Did he, now?)
Mushy peas (Take with a pickled onion and you can belch for
        England!)
Haggis (The jury is out)
Arbroath smokie (Two-faced haddock with no guts)
Fish & chips (On their own, please)
Black pudding (As long as you close your eyes)
English breakfast (Quick start or the full monty)
Shortbread (Enough around to repair Hadrian's Wall)
Dundee cake (Messy for dunking)

ACKNOWLEDGEMENTS

I have a great many people to thank for the successful outcome of my WALK GB 4 CLIMB adventure.

The first accolades go to Jemma Neave, without whose IT expertise this book would not have been published, and my partner Karol Eager, whose support and devotion to its production has been incalculable. My dear friends Hilda and John Alderton did a great job in deciphering my blogs when I returned.

My sincere thanks to photographer Mike Parry from the Chichester Jazz Club, who sorted and processed my snaps taken on the journey Surfing the net I came across Geo Parkin of Brighton who produced the eye-catching front cover illustration. Hove Prontaprint graphic design ensured the necessary reference map. Also I'm grateful to Pauline Misselbrook regis ctv for some vital printing.

My daughters Suzanne, Sonya with Simon Hill, and son Stewart pulled off many grand fund-raising feats, while son Martin chipped in with a vital piece of kit.

David Garforth of Bognor Regis Rotary worked endlessly to awaken the organisation's coastal branches around GB. Also Doug Murgatroyd (Old Cicestrians) and Ken Marshall (Chichester Jazz Club) pulled in their friends and relations to provide a bed on many a night. Mark Egan of a CLIMB family and his many chums really got involved.

Great credit goes to Ray Pratt of Chichester Jazz Club, who roped in his vintage vehicle pals for hosting. He also linked me to Fred Dineage for Southern TV coverage.

My appreciation goes to Andrew Smith, manager of the Arun Leisure Centre, Bognor Regis, for giving me the run of its training facilities

I have many happy memories of staying with countless hosts, including several dozen CLIMB families, i.e. those having children stricken with metabolic conditions.

My gratitude is heaped on so many people providing transport to get me to and from my route each day, not the least Jane Taylor who helped enormously during my initial training period and also to launch the first few days. Thanks also to the Grafham families for their continual support.

I would like to mention my brother Alan and great friend Malcolm Oliver for loading my iPod with music and comedy which kept me entertained throughout the trip. I'm also indebted to my sister-in-law Ann for arranging a break in Great Yarmouth.

Scores of commercial premises plus YHAs waived their charges and many fire stations opened their doors to welcome me, as did St Andrew's Police Station (non custodial), Lee Abbey and RAF Kinloss on the Moray Firth.

Alan Stiling of the Backpackers Club and Liz Wallis of the South West Coastal Path Association were of considerable assistance when planning my route.

Last, but not least, my admiration goes out to CLIMB, its executive director Steve Hannigan and his staff, particularly Pam Davies and Chris Owen Roberts. However I must reserve my very special thanks to the charity's development manager Lesley Greene, who diligently toiled on my behalf like a second 'mum', sending supplies, schedules and, with purpose, always 'bargaining' for digs. She and her husband Peter had personally been under the metabolic shadow for so long.

Fund-raising targets are always difficult to achieve if a charity is comparatively unknown. My sincere thanks to the scores of individuals who donated either direct to CLIMB or via the 'Just Giving' website, including a mysterious significant sum from Bulgaria! I mention Janet Tester's Southern Trails coffee mornings to represent the many ad hoc fund-raising events. I was staggered by the substantial donation presented to me on the very last stride of my Walk by Norman Baker, a regular Southern Trails coach driver from Westrings Travel Ltd.

Following my return I received many further significant donations. They emanated from Bognor Regis, Chichester and Midhurst Rotary functions, the Masonic Lodge at the Pallant Suite, Chichester, and the local radio station Spirit FM. The proceeds from two golden wedding celebrations from couples Gooch and Cheal were magnificent gifts.

All this added up to a grand total of £30,000 being achieved. For all this support my every step of the way was worth it! I and the charity CLIMB remain for ever grateful to you all.

Colin Snook
WALK GB 4 CLIMB – 2008